€50
118.
Varra

The Use and Status of Language in Brunei Darussalam

Noor Azam Haji-Othman
James McLellan · David Deterding
Editors

The Use and Status of Language in Brunei Darussalam

A Kingdom of Unexpected Linguistic Diversity

Springer

Editors
Noor Azam Haji-Othman
University of Brunei Darussalam
Gadong
Brunei Darussalam

David Deterding
University of Brunei Darussalam
Gadong
Brunei Darussalam

James McLellan
University of Brunei Darussalam
Gadong
Brunei Darussalam

ISBN 978-981-10-0851-1   ISBN 978-981-10-0853-5 (eBook)
DOI 10.1007/978-981-10-0853-5

Library of Congress Control Number: 2016938652

© Springer Science+Business Media Singapore 2016
This work is subject to copyright. All rights are reserved by the Publisher, whether the whole or part of the material is concerned, specifically the rights of translation, reprinting, reuse of illustrations, recitation, broadcasting, reproduction on microfilms or in any other physical way, and transmission or information storage and retrieval, electronic adaptation, computer software, or by similar or dissimilar methodology now known or hereafter developed.
The use of general descriptive names, registered names, trademarks, service marks, etc. in this publication does not imply, even in the absence of a specific statement, that such names are exempt from the relevant protective laws and regulations and therefore free for general use.
The publisher, the authors and the editors are safe to assume that the advice and information in this book are believed to be true and accurate at the date of publication. Neither the publisher nor the authors or the editors give a warranty, express or implied, with respect to the material contained herein or for any errors or omissions that may have been made.

Printed on acid-free paper

This Springer imprint is published by Springer Nature
The registered company is Springer Science+Business Media Singapore Pte Ltd.

Preface

Brunei Darussalam is a small country, but it exhibits substantial linguistic diversity: Brunei Malay is generally the lingua franca, Standard Malay is taught in schools, different groups speak a range of other indigenous languages such as Kedayan, Dusun, Tutong and Iban as well as various dialects of Chinese, and English is also widely spoken especially by the well-educated. Description of the ways that these languages are used in Brunei therefore provides a fascinating snapshot of the kind of multilingual diversity that tends to occur in Southeast Asia.

This book offers insights into various facets of the linguistic diversity of Brunei, including the status of minority languages in the country, the language of shop-signs, the pronunciation of Brunei English and Brunei Mandarin, the acquisition of Malay, attitudes of university students towards non-native teachers, language choice among foreign workers, code-switching in the courtroom, the adoption of Malay compliment strategies by young people, the lexical choices and discourse of online texts, the English and the Malay of newspaper articles, literature in Brunei, and language in education in both secular and religious schools. All of these represent new studies, most of them based on the substantial analysis of fresh data.

The book should be of crucial importance to students and scholars in Brunei, but it will also be of considerable relevance to everyone interested in language usage and linguistic diversity throughout the world, as it provides a diverse collation and in-depth analysis of material occurring in a country with some fascinating patterns of language usage. We hope that a wide range of students, scholars and researchers as well as general readers will appreciate this rich collection of fresh material.

February 2016

Noor Azam Haji-Othman
James McLellan
David Deterding

Contents

1 Introduction 1
  Noor Azam Haji-Othman, James McLellan and David Deterding

Part I Language Status

2 The Language Situation in Brunei Darussalam 9
  James McLellan, Noor Azam Haji-Othman and David Deterding

3 The State of Indigenous Languages in Brunei 17
  Noor Azam Haji-Othman and Siti Ajeerah Najib

4 The Language of Shop Signs in a Modern Shopping
  Centre in Brunei 29
  Susilawati Japri

Part II Pronunciation and Grammar

5 The Role of Fast Speech in Misunderstandings
  in Brunei English 41
  Ishamina Athirah

6 A Comparison of the Vowels of Brunei Mandarin
  and Beijing Mandarin 57
  Shufang Xu

7 Comprehension of Aspect Markers by Brunei
  Malay L1 Learners 75
  Aznah Suhaimi and Noor Azam Haji-Othman

Part III Language Choice

8 The Attitudes of University Students Towards Their Native
  and Non-native English Speaking Lecturers in Brunei 97
  Debbie G.E. Ho

9   Patterns of Language Choice and Use in Interactions Among Foreign Workers in Brunei Darussalam: A Preliminary Study 125
    Fatimah Chuchu and James McLellan

10 Courtroom Discourse: A Case Study of the Linguistic Strategies in Brunei Courtrooms 135
    Hjh Masmahirah Hj Mohd Tali

Part IV   Discourse

11 Politeness Strategies of Bruneian Malay Youths in Compliment Speech Acts 167
    Kamsiah Abdullah

12 The Discourse of Online Texts in Brunei: Extending Bruneian English 187
    Alistair Wood

13 Identity Representation in Press Releases of a Brunei-Based Banking Institution 201
    Mayyer Ling

14 Similar Story, Different Angles? A Comparative Study of 'Hard News' Texts in the Malay and English Print Media in Brunei Darussalam 211
    Sharifah Nurul Huda Alkaff, James McLellan and Fatimah Chuchu

Part V   Literature and Language in Education

15 Contemporary English and Malay Literature in Brunei: A Comparison 241
    Kathrina Mohd Daud, Grace V.S. Chin and Maslin Jukim

16 Bilingual Education Revisited: The Role of Ugama Schools in the Spread of Bilingualism 253
    Noor Azam Haji-Othman

17 Changing Patterns of Education in Brunei: How Past Plans Have Shaped Future Trends 267
    Gary M. Jones

Index 279

Editors and Contributors

About the Editors

Noor Azam Haji-Othman is Associate Professor of English language and linguistics, and teaches Communication and Media studies in UBD. His research interests include the interactions between the languages in Brunei and bilingualism in relation to/ as a result of state policy on language, education and society.

James McLellan is Senior Lecturer of English language and linguistics at Universiti Brunei Darussalam. He previously taught at secondary and tertiary levels in the UK, France, Malaysia, Australia and Aotearoa (New Zealand). His research interests include Malay-English language alternation, Southeast Asian Englishes, Borneo indigenous language maintenance, and language policy and planning in education.

David Deterding is Professor at Universiti Brunei Darussalam, where he teaches phonetics, Malay-English translation, forensic linguistics and research methods. His research concerns acoustic measurement, phonetic description of English, Malay and Chinese, and description of varieties of English in Southeast Asia, including those of Brunei, Singapore, China and Hong Kong.

Contributors

Sharifah Nurul Huda Alkaff is Senior Lecturer at the Faculty of Arts & Social Sciences, Universiti Brunei Darussalam (UBD). She is currently doing research on media and discourse. She is Principal Investigator of a UBD-funded research project that investigates media texts in Malay and English in Malaysia and Brunei.

Aznah Suhaimi is English Language and Linguistics Lecturer at the Faculty of Arts and Social Sciences, UBD. Her research and teaching activities are in the areas of L1 acquisition and psycholinguistics. She is currently working on the temporal system of Brunei Malay as part of her doctoral study at Cambridge University.

Grace V.S. Chin is affiliated to Universiti Brunei Darussalam and has published journal articles and book chapters that examine the intersections between postcolonial and Southeast Asian literature, with an emphasis on gender in contemporary societies and diasporas. She is co-editing a forthcoming book publication by Springer, titled Women in Postcolonial Southeast Asian Literature: Gender, Identity and Nation.

Fatimah Chuchu is Senior Lecturer at Universiti Brunei Darussalam, where she teaches sociolinguistics, language and communication, translation, language and politics, and dialectology in the Malay language programme. She has published on *Bahasa Dalam* (the Palace Language), Malay speech etiquette, and code-switching.

Debbie G.E. Ho is Senior Lecturer at Universiti Brunei Darussalam, where she teaches discourse analysis, language in society, analyzing talk and systemic functional grammar. Her research interests include the use of functional grammar in language classrooms and exploring language use in society, particularly those in the Asian and Southeast Asian regions.

Ishamina Athirah is a Ph.D. student at Universiti Brunei Darussalam. Her research is on the intelligibility of Brunei English in international communication, focusing on misunderstandings arising out of pronunciation, grammar and code-mixing. She has recently published a paper on the role of grammar in misunderstandings in *Journal of English as a Lingua Franca*.

Gary M. Jones is Associate Professor at Universiti Brunei Darussalam, where he is Director of the Institute of Asian Studies. His teaching is on bilingualism, language planning and language acquisition, and his research focuses on language in education and language planning, especially in Brunei Darussalam.

Kamsiah Abdullah is Associate Professor at Universiti Brunei Darussalam, where she teaches pragmatics, sociolinguistics, psycholinguistics and language education in the Malay language and linguistics programme. Her research focuses on Malay language studies, Malay language education and the role of Malay in Singapore and Brunei.

Kathrina Mohd Daud is Lecturer at Universiti Brunei Darussalam. She holds a Ph.D. in Creative Writing from the University of Manchester, and has previously held fellowships at the Oxford Center for Islamic Studies and the University of Washington. Her research explores global Islamic fiction, popular romance and Bruneian literature.

Maslin Jukim is Lecturer at Universiti Brunei Darussalam where he teaches folklore, oral literature, and classical Malay literature on the Malay literature programme. His recent research includes collecting oral histories in Brunei, especially concerning the period of the Japanese occupation during the Second World War.

Hjh Masmahirah Hj Mohd Tali graduated in 2013 from Universiti Brunei Darussalam with a Bachelor of Arts in English Language and Linguistics. Her research interests transpired during her discovery year in Malaysia, where she learnt Language and the Law.

Mayyer Ling is an aspiring academic who is currently working as Research Assistant at Universiti Brunei Darussalam. She received her BA from UBD and MA from Essex University. Her research interests lie in the area of applied linguistics, ranging from English for specific purposes, professional communication, and intercultural communication.

Siti Ajeerah Najib was formerly Lecturer at UNISSA and YIU before she joined the Legislative Council of Brunei as a Public Relations Officer. Her research interests include language endangerment and language use which she explored during her BA in UBD and MA in University of East Anglia, UK.

Susilawati Japri has taught primary and adult English for about 12 years. She has a diploma in primary education and a Bachelor's degree in English Language and Linguistics from Universiti Brunei Darussalam. She is involved in the Brunei-US English Language Fellow programme, teaching English at Suan Sunandha Rajabhat University, Thailand.

Alistair Wood is Senior Lecturer at the Faculty of Arts and Social Sciences, Universiti Brunei Darussalam. He has taught ESP and applied linguistics in a number of countries, mostly in Central Europe and SE Asia. His main research interests include scientific English, ESP, online discourse and Bruneian English.

Shufang Xu is a Ph.D. student at University of Brunei Darussalam. Her research focuses on acoustic investigation on the pronunciation of Mandarin, code-switching between Mandarin and English and lenition in connected speech, with a particular attention to the Mandarin spoken outside mainland China.

Chapter 1
Introduction

Noor Azam Haji-Othman, James McLellan and David Deterding

1.1 Rationale for This Volume

There is an advertising slogan that is widely seen in Brunei, promoting the country as 'A Kingdom of Unexpected Treasures', and the subtitle of this book, 'A Kingdom of Unexpected Linguistic Diversity', makes a direct allusion to this slogan. We suggest that, just as there is an abundance of dense jungle in the country that represents a hugely important treasure trove of flora and fauna, at the same time the kingdom is home to a fascinating range of languages and patterns of linguistic usage that are equally worthy of detailed scrutiny. Furthermore, we firmly believe that celebrating and preserving linguistic diversity in a place such as Brunei is as important as maintaining the forests, for just as trees provide oxygen for us to breathe, linguistic diversity supplies the vital cultural energy that enables human communities to thrive.

The topic of this volume is the current state of language usage in Brunei Darussalam, including Malay, English, Chinese and other minority languages in social interactions, education, the courtroom, the media, on the web, and in literature. It is inspired by and envisioned as a follow-up to Martin et al. (1996), the first book-length volume which attempted to present a sociolinguistic profile of Brunei Darussalam. 20 years later, much has changed, and we, the editors and contributors, perceive the need for an updated volume with wider coverage, something that will be of considerable value not just to students and researchers in applied linguistics, but also to sociolinguists, educationalists, and language policy makers and planners, as well as those interested in multilingualism and World Englishes.

Noor Azam Haji-Othman (✉) · J. McLellan · D. Deterding
FASS/UBD, Universiti Brunei Darussalam, Jalan Tungku Link,
Gadong BE1410, Brunei Darussalam
e-mail: azam.othman@ubd.edu.bn

J. McLellan
e-mail: james.mclellan@ubd.edu.bn

© Springer Science+Business Media Singapore 2016
Noor Azam Haji-Othman et al. (eds.), *The Use and Status of Language in Brunei Darussalam*, DOI 10.1007/978-981-10-0853-5_1

The earlier volume had separate sections on Malay, English, and the other languages of Brunei. The present volume follows a different organising principle, thematic rather than language-based. In line with the ways in which the country has developed and changed, fresh avenues for research are developed in many of the chapters, as fields such as language acquisition, literature, the linguistic landscape, and online language use are covered. Several of the chapters are co-authored by Bruneians and non-Bruneians, and overall there is a greater contribution by Bruneian scholars compared to the 1996 volume.

Brunei is known for consistency, stability and maintenance of its core traditions and practices: hence we aim to build on, rather than replace, the knowledge and insights contained in Martin et al. (1996).

Some chapters focus on pronunciation, specifically the intelligibility of Brunei English when spoken to speakers from elsewhere and the vowels of Brunei Mandarin, while others look at the grammar and discourse of Malay, the use of language on-line, the language of shop signs, the status of Dusun, and English and Malay literature in Brunei. There is therefore a diverse range of material, all of which is fresh, written especially for this volume, and based on current research. We believe that this collection of chapters on language usage in Brunei Darussalam will constitute essential material for researchers and students in Brunei and elsewhere for many years to come.

There is a wealth of books on language in Singapore, including monographs describing pronunciation, grammar and discourse, as well as edited collections of research, and these have become essential reading for students of World Englishes. But there is no reason why investigation of language usage in Brunei should not inspire equal enthusiasm around the world, particularly as there is just as much diversity that can be investigated even though the country is so small, with less than one tenth the population of Singapore. In providing wide-ranging research materials on language usage in Brunei Darussalam, we hope that the current volume will fill this niche perfectly and become an exceptionally valuable resource for researchers and scholars around the world.

1.2 Overview of Chapters

The sixteen chapters in this book are divided into five sections:

- Language Status
- Pronunciation and Grammar
- Language Choice
- Discourse
- Language and Literature in Education

Here, we offer a brief overview of all the chapters in these five sections.

1.2.1 Section 1: Language Status

Section I includes three chapters, all of which highlight the multilinguality that is evident in Brunei. Chapter 2, by the three co-editors, describes the language situation in Brunei, and serves both as essential background and as a taster for the more detailed and narrowly-focused chapters that follow.

Chapter 3 reports on the state of the languages of Brunei's ethnic minority groups. Noor Azam and Siti Ajeerah first provide an overview of the ongoing language shift towards Brunei Malay, and the consequent level of endangerment of the languages of Brunei's six other *puak jati* (indigenous ethnic groups) aside from Brunei Malay. Their model highlights the centrality of what they refer to as 'pan-Bruneian Malay' as distinct from the Brunei Malay which is the first language of the Brunei Malay community who were the original inhabitants of Brunei's *Kampung Ayer* (the Water Village). In addition, they discuss the results of a study into language use in the Dusun community.

In Chap. 4, Susilawati Japri uses Linguistic Landscape methodology to present an analysis of multilingual language use in shop signs in a commercial complex located near Brunei's international airport. Issues of the status of the languages occurring in signs are central here, as Brunei has laws which prescribe that the name of the business in *Jawi* (Arabic-based) script should be at the top and twice the size of the name in *Rumi* (Roman) script or in English, but not all shops adhere to these guidelines.

1.2.2 Section 2: Pronunciation and Grammar

Chapter 5, by Ishamina Athirah, is concerned with the role of fast speech as a factor causing misunderstandings in spoken communication between Bruneians and non-Bruneians. She demonstrates how, in many instances, intelligibility is compromised as a consequence of conversation participants speaking too quickly.

In Chap. 6, Shufang Xu provides a comparative investigation of vowels in the speech of Bruneian speakers of Mandarin Chinese with the speech of standard Mandarin speakers in Beijing. This study is a welcome addition to the still small inventory of research into language use among Chinese Bruneians.

Aznah Suhaimi and Noor Azam's Chap. 7 is on the developing comprehension of aspect markers by children acquiring Brunei Malay as their first language. This offers a counterbalance to the predominance of research into first language acquisition of English, and it highlights the role played by aspectual markers in Malay, as distinct from the inflectional morphemes which mark tense and aspect in English.

1.2.3 Section 3: Language Choice

Clearly language choice is a central research topic in any multilingual society. In Brunei the choices involve not just languages but varieties within languages, especially Brunei Malay or Standard Malay.

How do Bruneians feel about Standard British, US English, and Brunei English? In Chap. 8, Debbie Ho investigates student perceptions and preferences concerning the English accents of their lecturers, and her findings show how these attitudes have shifted to a certain extent over the past 20 years.

In Chap. 9, Fatimah Chuchu and James McLellan present preliminary findings on a previously unresearched topic, the patterns of language use among foreign workers in different sectors in Brunei. As foreigners currently make up about one-third of the total workforce in the country, this is clearly an important topic. The chapter presents findings from a survey and from interviews with workers and their employers in the construction industry, in retail trades including catering, and in spa therapy centres.

Another under-researched area is the focus of Chap. 10, contributed by Hjh Masmahirah Hj Mohd Tali: language use in the Brunei civil law courts. Officially the law courts constitute a domain where the use of English is expected, but her study of language choice in courtroom interactions reveals instances of bilingual Malay-English negotiation by participants, including judges and magistrates, lawyers, witnesses and defendants. The complex relationship between language and power is foregrounded in this formal interactional setting.

1.2.4 Section 4: Discourse

Chapter 11, the first chapter in the section on discourse, is by Kamsiah Abdullah, who investigates the discourse-pragmatic features of compliment responses by Bruneians. She adapts the conceptual framework of politeness theory and maxims of politeness and applies these to examples collected from interactions between young Bruneians. Compliment responses are classified in terms of their frequency of occurrence, thereby enabling comparison between the strategies used by Bruneians when responding to compliments and those reported elsewhere by other researchers using the politeness theory framework.

In Chap. 12, Alistair Wood provides an overview of recent research into language use, including code-switching, in Brunei's vibrant social media. Research into language use in social media is a major growth area worldwide, and this chapter includes data from text messaging (sms), Facebook, Whatsapp, Twitter and an interactive online gaming forum. His analysis suggests that the social media discourse of Bruneians is distinct from both face-to-face conversation and from written communication, and that, just like their counterparts elsewhere, young

Bruneians are adept at innovative linguistic usage, including coining new words when these are appropriate.

Mayyer Ling's Chap. 13 is yet another ground-breaking study, investigating the discourse of media releases from a Brunei bank. Using corpus-based methods, she discusses global-related and national-related lexis as well as the use of names and titles to mark solidarity in order to investigate the way that the bank addresses its target audience through its media releases.

Media discourse is also the focus of Chap. 14, co-authored by Sharifah Nurul Huda Alkaff, James McLellan and Fatimah Chuchu. They offer a comparative corpus-based study of 'hard news' texts in the Brunei Malay- and English-language print media, *Media Permata* and the Borneo Bulletin respectively. Their findings challenge the a priori assumption that Malay texts are longer and more complex than those in English, and they show that Malay news reports may sometimes be more graphic and sensational. The textual analysis is complemented by findings derived from interviews with some of the reporters and editors who are the text producers for the two newspapers.

1.2.5 Section 5: Literature and Language in Education

In Chap. 15, Grace Chin, Kathrina Daud and Maslin Jukim offer a comparison between contemporary Brunei literature in Malay and English. Their study outlines both the opportunities and the constraints experienced by those working in the domain of creative literature in Brunei, and they observe a growing divergence between official mainstream literature written in Malay and literature in English which is more of a response to global trends. Their chapter also discusses ways in which the languages come together in literature, for example in the use of *bahasa rojak* (code-mixed Malay and English) in literary works.

Noor Azam in Chap. 16 opens up another new research area of central importance, by comparing mainstream government schools with Islamic religious schools (*Ugama* schools) in terms of language use and medium of education policy and practice. He suggests that the predominant use of Malay in the religious educational domain counterbalances the bias towards English which is evident in mainstream schools in Brunei, especially under the current policy which uses English as a medium of instruction for some subjects from pre-school onwards.

Recent developments in language policy in education are also the topic of the final chapter, Chap. 17, contributed by Gary Jones. He makes a direct comparison between the early 1990s and the present, and his overview of the development of education policy is grounded in an analysis of the changing economic climate, both in Southeast Asia and globally. Discourses of economic diversification and the employability of school leavers and graduates impact on the current language policy in education, and will continue to do so.

1.3 Significance of This Collection

We believe that the research presented here is not just important for students and scholars interested in language usage in Brunei, but that it also has substantial relevance beyond the narrow confines of this small country. In a small but highly connected multilingual polity that is located in a dynamic region of immense geopolitical significance, Brunei exemplifies the complex interplay of local and global discourses.

There are also considerable implications from the material in this book for policy makers and planners, both locally and abroad. For example, the contributions on education provide a timely reflection on the current state of language usage in Brunei schools, the analysis of detailed transcripts from magistrates courts provides plenty of food for thought about effective language usage in the legal system, and the chapter on local literature suggests that more effort and resources might be allocated to stimulating the development of creative writing in the country. In addition, we note that many of the minority languages of Brunei, such as Tutong and Dusun, are under serious threat of extinction, and we believe that additional resources could be allocated to efforts to preserve them. Brunei is keen to encourage tourists to visit its pristine forests while at the same time appreciating its rich culture; but if we lose some of the varied heritage that is preserved and handed down from generation to generation by means of this linguistic diversity, a vitally important cultural component will disappear forever.

We hope that readers will agree that this volume achieves its objectives of providing up-to-date information on current research on the state of language in Brunei, and that it also opens up new avenues for further collaborative and comparative research between scholars based in Brunei and those working elsewhere; and we further hope that the chapters in this book contribute to an understanding and celebration of language variation in the country, enabling it to continue to be a kingdom that exhibits abundant linguistic diversity, though maybe, as a result of our contribution, this diversity will no longer be quite so surprising to readers around the world.

Reference

Martin, P. W., Ożóg, C., & Poedjosoedarmo, G. (Eds.). (1996). *Language use and language change in Brunei Darussalam*. Athens, OH: Ohio University Center for International Studies.

Part I
Language Status

Chapter 2
The Language Situation in Brunei Darussalam

James McLellan, Noor Azam Haji-Othman and David Deterding

2.1 Introduction

This chapter aims to provide an introduction to Brunei Darussalam for readers, giving essential background information for the other chapters in this volume and also offering a valuable overview of language issues in the country.

Negara Brunei Darussalam (henceforth Brunei) is a small Malay Islamic sultanate on the northern coast of the island of Borneo. Apart from the South China Sea to the north, it is entirely surrounded by the East Malaysian state of Sarawak. It is divided into two parts, with the rural district of Temburong separated from the three other districts by the Malaysian district of Limbang. The capital, Bandar Seri Begawan (often referred to as BSB), is located in the smallest district, Brunei-Muara, and most of the rest of the population live in towns along the coast, especially Kuala Belait and Seria in Belait District and Tutong in Tutong District (see Fig. 2.1).

Brunei has a population of about 429,000 (World Population Review 2015), the majority of whom are Malays, though there are also a substantial number of minority groups such as the Kedayan, Dusun and Murut (Lun Bawang), and also about 40,000 Chinese. In addition, there are many expatriate workers from the Philippines, Indonesia, Malaysia, Thailand and Bangladesh, as well as from more distant places such as the UK, USA, and Australia.

Brunei is ruled by a Sultan. His Majesty Sultan Haji Hassanal Bolkiah, the 29th Sultan, has reigned since 1968, and the national philosophy and ideology is called *Melayu Islam Beraja* (MIB, 'Malay Islamic Monarchy') which incorporates the

---

J. McLellan (✉) · Noor Azam Haji-Othman · D. Deterding
FASS/UBD, Universiti Brunei Darussalam, Jalan Tungku Link,
Gadong BE1410, Brunei Darussalam
e-mail: james.mclellan@ubd.edu.bn

Noor Azam Haji-Othman
e-mail: azam.othman@ubd.edu.bn

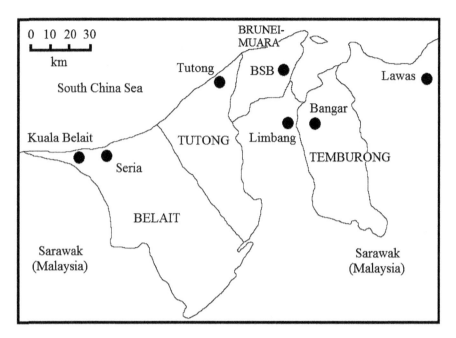

Fig. 2.1 Map of Brunei, showing the four districts and main towns

three core elements central to the identity of Bruneians: the Malay language and culture, respect for the Islamic religion, and loyalty towards His Majesty the Sultan.

Formerly the centre of a large maritime empire, Brunei became a British protectorate in 1888. The previous Sultan, Omar Ali Saifuddin III, oversaw the drafting of a constitution, signed in 1959 (Hussainmiya 1995), which eventually led to the restoration of full independence in 1984, when Brunei became a member of the United Nations, the Commonwealth of Nations, the Association of South East Asian Nations (ASEAN), and the Organisation of the Islamic Conference (now known as the Organisation of Islamic Cooperation).

Oil and natural gas exports have been the major exports and the main source of Brunei's development and wealth since the mid-20th century. Earnings from these primary products have brought about rapid improvements in the infrastructure of Brunei and the standard of living of its residents, and the development of these industries has contributed to Brunei's global connectedness as well as to an influx of foreign labour.

In this chapter, we offer an overview of the language situation in Brunei. We include a brief look at the history of language usage in Brunei, a description of the range of languages that are spoken, an overview of the domains of usage of Brunei Malay, Standard Malay and English, and a discussion of the status of some of the threatened minority languages. In addition, we consider the education system, including the history of separate English and Malay streams, the rationale for the adoption of the *Dwibahasa* ('Two Language') system in 1985, and the introduction of SPN21 (*Sistem Pendidikan Negara Abad Ke-21*, 'National Education System for the 21st Century') in 2009.

2.2 History of Language Use

As noted above, *Melayu* (Malay) is one of the three core elements of Bruneian identity, referring to both Malay ethnicity and the Malay language. Traditionally, the majority of the Bruneian people spoke Brunei Malay, a conservative variety of Malay that is substantially different from Standard Malay, which is the official language of the country and the lingua franca of Malaysia (Clynes and Deterding 2011). Officially, seven subgroups of indigenous people are recognised in Brunei, each with their own distinctive language: Brunei Malay, Kedayan, Dusun, Bisaya, Tutong, Belait and Murut. In addition, there are a number of Iban people, especially in the enclave of Temburong, who are not recognised as natives of Brunei. They constitute the largest group in neighbouring Sarawak (Asmah 1983, p. 483; Coluzzi 2011), and most of the Iban people in Brunei migrated into the country from elsewhere in Borneo in the past century.

The use of English in Brunei gradually expanded during the period of the British protectorate from 1888 to 1984 (Gunn 1997; Hussainmiya 2005), especially after the introduction of the bilingual system of education in 1985 (Jones 1996; see also Chap. 16, by Noor Azam, and Chap. 17, by Gary Jones, in this volume). Brunei Malay remains the most widely occurring lingua franca, but English is frequently spoken, especially among the educated elite (Ożóg 1996), and there is substantial code-switching even in the most formal of contexts (McLellan 2010). Some of the minority languages are now no longer used, and others are threatened with extinction, something we will discuss further in the next section.

2.3 Range of Languages Spoken

Martin and Poedjosoedarmo (1996) provide an overview of the languages spoken in Brunei, and the situation is similar today. Brunei Malay (Clynes 2014) is spoken by about two thirds of the population, many of whom traditionally lived in *Kampung Air*, the Water Village that is at the heart of the capital of Brunei. Brunei Malay is closely related to Kedayan (Soderberg 2014), the language of the land-dwellers who traditionally planted rice and tended orchards, whilst the Brunei Malays were seafarers and fisherfolk. Nothofer (1991) reports that the level of lexical cognates between Brunei Malay and Kedayan is 94 %, while that between Brunei Malay and Standard Malay is 84 %.

Of the other Austronesian minority languages, Dusun and Bisaya are similar, some people describing them as varieties of the same language (Nothofer 1991), and Belait and Tutong are also closely related (Martin and Poedjosoedarmo 1996).

The other language recognised as an indigenous language of Brunei, Murut, is mostly spoken in the Temburong District. It is also known as Lun Bawang, and it is a major indigenous language in Lawas District in neighbouring Sarawak (Martin 1996). Lun Bawang is also closely related to the Kelabit language that is spoken by people living in Bario in the mountains south of Brunei and close to the border of Kalimantan, the Indonesian part of Borneo.

Iban is spoken by a few thousand people especially in Temburong, but also in Tutong and Belait districts. It is quite closely related to Malay (Asmah 1983, p. 483; Nothofer 1991, pp. 157–158), and serves as a lingua franca in rural upriver areas of the Belait, Tutong and Temburong Rivers where Iban people live alongside other ethnic groups.

The Chinese residents of Brunei traditionally spoke a range of dialects, including Hokkien, Cantonese and Hakka, but most of the young people now speak Mandarin, as well as Malay and English, and nowadays they may have only a limited knowledge of their heritage languages (Dunseath 1996).

There are a large number of foreign workers from the Philippines, so Tagalog is also heard. Many are domestic helpers (*amahs*), but there are also about 200 teachers from the Philippines in Brunei schools, many of them teaching English. Some foreign workers come from Bangladesh, southern India, Pakistan and Thailand, so Bangla, Tamil, Urdu and Thai are also spoken.

English is widely spoken, both by educated Bruneians and also by the large expatriate community of teachers, university lecturers, and professionals working in the industry. In the past, there have been generous scholarships for Bruneians to study abroad, both as undergraduates and for postgraduate degrees, in the UK, the USA, Australia and New Zealand, so many well-educated Bruneians have an excellent command of English.

Finally, there is a small community of Penan people, the traditional forest people of Borneo, also considered as non-Brunei indigenous people. They are based in a longhouse in the village of Sukang on the Belait River (Martin and Sercombe 1996; Sercombe 2007) and number less than 50.

2.4 Domains of Use of Malay and English

The domains of use of Standard Malay and Brunei Malay may be described using the concept of diglossia (Ferguson 1959): Standard Malay is the H(igh) variety, as it is used in formal contexts such as government speeches, newspapers, and television broadcasts; Brunei Malay is the L(ow) variety, as it occurs in informal situations, in conversations in the home, family and friendship domains. In fact, although everyone learns Standard Malay in school and all can understand it, almost nobody uses it on a regular basis.

All educated people become proficient in English, as it is the medium of education for most subjects from the primary school onwards. However, many people who do not do well at school may end up with just a rudimentary knowledge of

English. For educated people, especially students and academics at *Universiti Brunei Darussalam* (UBD), the main university in the country, the English spoken is developing its own distinct identity as it is spoken competently and fluently but at the same time contributes to world-wide trends in the global evolution of English (Deterding 2014).

Ożóg (1996, p. 159) observes that, for Bruneians, English is the language of knowledge, but Malay is the language of the soul. In fact it is very common for most well-educated Bruneians to code-switch regularly between English and Malay (McLellan 2005, 2010; McLellan and Noor Azam 2012).

2.5 Minority Languages in Brunei

Of the seven indigenous language which are officially designated 'dialects' or varieties of Malay, Brunei Malay is dominant, whilst all the others are threatened to a greater or lesser extent (Noor Azam and Siti Ajeerah, this volume, Chap. 3), partly because they are squeezed out by the domination of Malay and English (Noor Azam 2012). Belait is almost completely extinct, and Tutong is also threatened, though there are now university classes offered in the language by UBD in an effort to preserve it.

Dusun and Bisaya are also severely threatened. Of the minority languages, Kedayan has the largest number of speakers, but extensive intermarriage and the high level of similarity between Kedayan and Brunei Malay has resulted in Kedayan also being under threat.

Coluzzi (2011) reports that Murut is in a healthier state, partly because it receives some support from across the border in Malaysia. And he similarly reports that the survival of Iban is more assured, again because of the large number of Iban speakers in Sarawak, where there is some institutional support for the language, including radio programmes and some newspapers.

2.6 The Education System of Brunei

The Bilingual Education System was introduced in 1985 (Jones 1996), with Malay-medium education for the first three years of primary school, and then a shift to English-medium education for most subjects from the fourth year of primary school onwards. One problem with this system was that children started to learn vocabulary for subjects in Malay and then had to relearn the same vocabulary in English in the fourth year of primary school. In 2009, a new system of education was introduced, called *Sistem Pendidikan Negara Abad ke-21* (SPN21, 'National System of Education for the 21st century'), and from then on mathematics and science have been taught in English from the start of primary school (Jones 2012). This eliminates the sudden switch in medium for these two subjects, though it remains to be seen if the new system helps improve the overall performance of Brunei children.

The national university, *Universiti Brunei Darussalam* (UBD), was established in 1985 as a bilingual institution, with some programmes in English and others in Malay, and some such as History in a mixture of English and Malay. Although a few programmes such as Malay Language and Malay Literature continue to be taught in Malay-medium, the overwhelming majority of programmes are now English-medium. Originally, programmes in Islamic Studies were mainly in Malay, though Arabic was also offered as a subject and sometimes courses were taught in Arabic. However, in 2007 the *Institut Pengajian Islam Sultan Haji Omar Ali Saifuddin* (IPISHOAS) at UBD separated to become *Universiti Islam Sultan Sharif Ali* (UNISSA), Brunei's second national university. There is also a university dedicated to training Islamic teachers, *Kolej Universiti Perguruan Ugama Seri Begawan* (KUPU-SB), from which about 230 students obtain a degree or diploma each year.

There has recently been considerable expansion and development in technical and vocational education. This is driven by concerns over the employability of school leavers, by the need to replace foreign skilled workers with skilled and qualified Bruneians, and by a desire on the part of educational planners to supplant traditional notions of the superiority of so-called academic over technical subjects and qualifications. The *Institut Teknologi Brunei* (ITB) offers English-medium degree-level programmes in fields such as Computer Science and Electrical and Electronic Engineering; other secondary and tertiary-level technical and vocational providers are under the collective Institute of Brunei Technical Education and use both English and Malay as mediums of education.

2.7 Language Use in Schools and Society

There is a substantial linguistic divide in Brunei, between those who attend good schools and become proficient in English and those who go to less fashionable schools and only develop a rudimentary knowledge of English (Deterding and Salbrina 2013, p. 19). In fact, Wood et al. (2011) have shown that pupils in a good secondary school in the capital have a reasonable command of English in year 3 and then they improve by year 5, while similar students in a rural school in Temburong District have much poorer English in year 3 and show little or no improvement at all by year 5. A popular perception, yet to be fully supported or challenged by research, is that the private schools, including Chinese schools, mission schools and international schools, achieve better results in both English Language and English-medium subjects than most government schools.

Although well-educated Bruneians are all proficient in English, Brunei Malay continues to be the language of choice in society, often exhibiting substantial code-switching with English. And even on the UBD campus, Brunei Malay is generally the lingua franca among students and also among most local staff, even though nearly all students and staff are highly competent in English.

References

Asmah Haji Omar. (1983). *The Malay peoples of Malaysia and their languages.* Kuala Lumpur: Dewan Bahasa dan Pustaka.
Clynes, A. (2014). Brunei Malay: An overview. In P. Sercombe, M. Boutin & A. Clynes (Eds.), *Advances in research on linguistic and cultural practices in Borneo* (pp. 153–200). Phillips, ME: Borneo Research Council.
Clynes, A., & Deterding, D. (2011). Standard malay (Brunei). *Journal of the International Phonetics Association, 41*(2), 259–268.
Coluzzi, P. (2011). Endangered languages in Borneo: A survey among the Iban and Murut (Lun Bawang) in Temburong Brunei. *Oceanic Linguistics, 49*(1), 119–143.
Deterding, D. (2014). The evolution of Brunei English: How it is contributing to the development of English in the world. In S. Buschfeld, T. Hoffmann, M. Huber & A. Kautzsch (Eds.), *The evolution of Englishes. The dynamic model and beyond* (pp. 420–433). Amsterdam: John Benjamins.
Deterding, D., & Salbrina, S. (2013). *Brunei English: A new variety in a multilingual society.* Dordrecht: Springer.
Dunseath, K. (1996). Aspects of language maintenance and language shift among the chinese community in Brunei. In P. W. Martin, C. Ożóg & G. Poedjosoedarmo (Eds.), *Language use and language change in Brunei Darussalam* (pp. 280–301). Athens, OH: Ohio University Center for International Studies.
Ferguson, C. (1959). Diglossia. *Word, 15,* 325–340.
Gunn, G. C. (1997). *Language, power, and ideology in Brunei Darussalam.* Athens, OH: Ohio University Center for International Studies.
Hussainmiya, B. A. (1995). *Sultan Omar Ali Saifuddin III and Britain: The making of Brunei Darussalam.* Kuala Lumpur: Oxford University Press.
Hussainmiya, B. A. (2005). *Brunei: Revival of 1906.* Bandar Seri Begawan: Brunei Press.
Jones, G. M. (1996). The Bilingual education policy in Brunei Darussalam. In P. W. Martin, C. Ożóg & G. Poedjosoedarmo (Eds.), *Language use and language change in Brunei Darussalam* (pp. 123–132). Athens, OH: Ohio University Center for International Studies.
Jones, G. M. (2012). Language planning in its historical context in Brunei Darussalam. In E. Low & Azirah Hashim (Eds.), *English in Southeast Asia: Features, policy and language use* (pp. 175–187). Amsterdam: John Benjamins.
Martin, P. W. (1996). A comparative ethnolinguistic survey of the Murut (Lun Bawang) with special reference to Brunei. In P. W. Martin, C. Ożóg & G. Poedjosoedarmo (Eds.), *Language use and language change in Brunei Darussalam* (pp. 268–279). Athens, OH: Ohio University Center for International Studies.
Martin, P. W., & Poedjosoedarmo, G. (1996). Introduction: An overview of the language situation in Brunei Darussalam. In P. W. Martin, C. Ożóg & G. Poedjosoedarmo (Eds.), *Language use and language change in Brunei Darussalam* (pp. 1–23). Athens, OH: Ohio University Center for International Studies.
Martin, P. W., & Sercombe, P. (1996). The Penan of Brunei: Patterns of linguistic interaction. In P. W. Martin, C. Ożóg & G. Poedjosoedarmo (Eds.), *Language use and language change in Brunei Darussalam* (pp. 302–311). Athens, OH: Ohio University Center for International Studies.
Martin, P. W., Ożóg, C., & Poedjosoedarmo, G. (Eds.). (1996). *Language use and language change in Brunei Darussalam.* Athens, OH: Ohio University Center for International Studies.

McLellan, J. (2005). Malay-English language alternation in two Brunei Darussalam online discussion forums. Unpublished PhD thesis, Curtin University of Technology.

McLellan, J. (2010). Mixed codes or varieties of English? In A. Kirkpatrick (Ed.), *The Routledge handbook of world Englishes* (pp. 425–441). London/New York: Routledge.

McLellan, J., & Noor Azam Haji-Othman. (2012). Features of the Brunei Darussalam variety of English. In E.-L. Low & Azirah Hashim (Eds.), *Englishes in South East Asia: Features, policy and language in use* (pp. 75–90). Amsterdam: John Benjamins.

Noor Azam Haji-Othman. (2012). Is it always English? 'Duelling aunties' in Brunei Darussalam. In V. Rapatahana & P. Bunce (Eds.), *English language as hydra: Its impact on non-English language cultures* (pp. 175–190). Clevedon: Multilingual Matters.

Nothofer, B. (1991). The languages of Brunei Darussalam. In H. Steinhauer (Ed.), *Papers in Austronesian Linguistics* (pp. 151–176). Pacific Linguistics A-81. Canberra: Australian National University.

Ożóg, A. C. K. (1996). The unplanned use of English: The case of Brunei Darussalam. In P. W. Martin, C. Ożóg & Gloria Poedjosoedarmo (Eds.), *Language use and language change in Brunei Darussalam* (pp. 156–172). Athens, OH: Ohio University Center for International Studies.

Sercombe, P. (2007). Small worlds: The language ecology of the Penan in Borneo. In A. Creese, P. W. Martin & N. H. Hornberger (Eds.), *Encyclopedia of language and education: Ecology of language* (pp. 183–193). Amsterdam: Kluwer.

Soderberg, C. D. (2014). Kedayan. *Journal of the International Phonetic Association, 44*, 201–205.

Wood, A., Henry, A., Malai Ayla Surya Malai Hj Abdullah, & Clynes, A. (2011). English in Brunei: "She speaks excellent English"—"No he doesn't". In L. J. Zhang, R. Rubdy & L. Alsagoff (Eds.), *Asian Englishes: Changing perspectives in a globalized world* (pp. 52–66). Singapore: Pearson.

World Population Review. (2015). Brunei population. Retrieved October 31, 2015, from http://worldpopulationreview.com/countries/brunei-population.

Chapter 3
The State of Indigenous Languages in Brunei

Noor Azam Haji-Othman and Siti Ajeerah Najib

3.1 Introduction

According to Nothofer (1991), the Austronesian languages and dialects spoken in Brunei are Belait, Bisaya, Dusun, Brunei Malay, Kampung Ayer Malay, Kedayan, Standard Malay, Murut, Tutong, Mukah, Iban and Penan. Nothofer grouped Brunei Malay, Kampung Ayer Malay, Kedayan and Standard Malay together as the 'Malay group', and labelled the remaining codes 'Non-Malay'. Following the treatment of these languages by Martin and Poedjosoedarmo (1996, p. 13), the latter group can be further divided into three groups: the Dusunic languages consisting of Dusun and Bisaya; the Murutic group which just includes Murut (or Lun Bawang); and the North Sarawak group that consists of Belait and Tutong. Dusun, the subject of the case study presented in this chapter, and Bisaya are 'mutually intelligible dialects' (Nothofer 1991, p. 155) despite the fact that they are listed as separate ethnic groups in the Brunei Constitution. All of these languages have undergone language shift, with some languages faring better than others.

Language shift in Brunei has rarely been discussed purely on a linguistic basis, but it has often been described within a cultural framework by researchers over the last few years. Leach (1950) was one of the earliest to record sociolinguistic change by saying the 'ethnic population have become Malay'. Brown (1960, p. 4) then spoke of the 'merging of lesser ethnic groups with the greater', while Maxwell (1980) refers to the shifts as 'semantic reclassification'. Martin (1990, p. 130; 2002) suggests a causal link between 'cultural and linguistic redefinition' and the contact and movement of previously rural populations with the coastal culture, which at the same time broke down the social network support for ethnic language and culture maintenance—a process which Jones (1994) refers to as 'assimilation into the

---

Noor Azam Haji-Othman (✉) · Siti Ajeerah Najib
FASS/UBD, Universiti Brunei Darussalam, Jalan Tungku Link,
Gadong BE1410, Brunei Darussalam
e-mail: azam.othman@ubd.edu.bn

coastal culture'. Braighlinn (1992, p. 19) calls the same phenomenon of change a 'convergence on a dominant Malay culture'. In relation to this process of cultural shift, Gunn (1997, p. 6) argues that the linguistic impact from explicit as well as implicit pressure for more use of Malay in Brunei has been a visible shift away from ethnic languages to the Malay language through Islamicization and Malayicization. These processes, sometimes called 'nation-building' or 'Bruneization' (Noor Azam 2005), involve a shift in both language and identity as a result of voluntary acquiescence on the part of the ethnic groups themselves.

Researchers have also made observations about the specific linguistic impact experienced by the ethnic groups. The study by Martin (1996b) of the Belait community found that their identity has become gradually submerged by their use of a new language, Brunei Malay, and the importance of this code in the Bruneian speech community as a whole (Sercombe 2002). A case in point made by E.M. Kershaw (1994) is that the language shift among the Dusun community was a 'progressive demise' and that the current speakers are 'terminal heirs' of their language and culture. In this regard, Sercombe comments that 'parents have unwittingly aided in the progressive demise of Dusun by encouraging their children to use Malay as a route to academic and material success' (Sercombe 2002, p. 13), and he further notes that younger Murut speakers are also making more and more use of Brunei Malay. According to McLellan and Jones (2015, p. 20), Kedayan is also endangered because of its high shared percentage of cognates with Brunei Malay, and they furthermore confirm the endangered status of Belait, 'with almost no younger speakers' (Clynes 2005). Although Tutong, Dusun and Bisaya have younger speakers, they are generally similarly considered at risk of extinction, by both their communities of speakers and by researchers (McLellan and Jones 2015, p. 20).

On this shift away from indigenous languages to Malay, Sercombe states the following:

> Much of the literature reporting on language situations in Borneo suggests a general linguistic levelling process taking place throughout coastal areas of Borneo towards the superordinate code of an area, more often than not Malay, whereby the roles of indigenous minority languages are being usurped for the following main reasons: [i] demographic factors comprising a tendency to migrate towards urban coastal areas where there are greater opportunities for wage employments and access to facilities, such as education and health care as well as a wide variety of material goods; and where language and ethnic identity may be less closely intertwined; [ii] Malay is the medium of education in Malaysia and Indonesia; as well as being the national language in each of these countries and that of Brunei; [iii] Malay also has the status associated with the ruling elites of these countries; and [iv] Malay has acted as a trade language and lingua franca among peoples from different linguistic groups throughout the Malay archipelago for over half a millennium.
>
> (Sercombe 2002, p. 14)

3.2 Language and Dialect Shift

Noor Azam's (2005) study of the indigenous languages of Brunei identified a definite shift among Bruneians, particularly evident among the minority ethnic population, thus confirming earlier findings by Martin (1990, 1996b) and Sercombe (2002). Significantly Noor Azam has also found evidence that among the Malay-speaking communities identified by Nothofer (1991), the Brunei Malay and the Kedayan people, their languages are moving away from their traditional characteristics (as also observed with Kedayan by McLellan and Jones 2015). But at the same time, so are the languages of the traditionally non Malay-speaking communities.

Figure 3.1 shows both dialect shift and language shift occurring at the same time, and the most significant outcome of these processes is the convergence toward a pan-Brunei Malay. The term 'pan-Brunei Malay' is suggested here to highlight its supra-ethnic qualities in terms of its dissociation from any particular ethnic group, including the Brunei Malays, and it refers to the form of Malay that most Bruneian young people are now making their own and speaking as their first language all over the country. It may be described as a variant of Brunei Malay that contains elements of Standard Malay, and also some elements of English, with minor variations in terms of lexis depending on the speakers' location.

3.2.1 Cultural Implications

Of course, language shift cannot happen without cultural implications. R. Kershaw (1998) notes that linguistic and cultural differences between the existing Muslim groups are becoming progressively eroded among the younger cohorts. This is in combination with growing national consciousness in the country. In this regard, Kershaw observes what seems to be happening is not the rise of a new term but an incipient shift of *Melayu Brunei* from its role as synonym for the ethnic Brunei Malays into an aggregative term to include all indigenous Bruneian Muslims. In a deeper sense, R. Kershaw (1998) argues, the use of this new term can mean that officials who are mostly from the Brunei Malay ethnic group have come to perceive

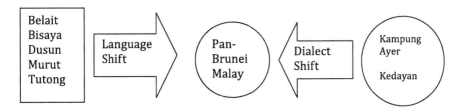

Fig. 3.1 Language and dialect shift

a need to play down their ancestral primacy in the stratified population of Brunei, by consciously severing the old, exclusive link between the *Melayu Brunei* terminology and the society of *Kampung Ayer* (lit. 'Water Village'—the traditional settlement area of Bruneians on the Brunei River). Noor Azam (2005) further extends Kershaw's re-conceptualisation of *Melayu Brunei* to include all indigenous Bruneians, not just Muslims, in his use of the term 'Pan-Bruneian', and he suggests that, with all the language shift and cultural shift that he observed taking place among the various ethnic groups, the degree of cultural diversity in Brunei is being significantly reduced too.

3.2.2 The Ethno-Vitality Rating

What emerges from the study of Noor Azam (2005), following that of Martin (1995), is a linguistic hierarchy in which the Malay language overrides the other ethnic languages in Brunei. This ranking is attributed to various factors such as positive and negative images that a language has, the available number of speakers, and the support the language receives. All of the languages have significant symbolic value in expressing ethnic identity, but because of negative stereotypical notions associated with the minority ethnic languages, their status is perceived to be low. On the other hand, Malay enjoys association with the elite and powerful, and it is also seen to have wider national and international currency than the ethnic languages, perpetuated by its academic value and its historical value as a regional lingua franca. Noor Azam (2005) also found evidence which shows that the working policies of government institutions do not generally reflect the linguistic diversity of Brunei, nor do they see any need to do so. Although Malay has more support in terms of its use in the country and linguistic diversity may not be encouraged, English is widely used and plays a huge role in many areas such as education. In fact, because of the status that English has nationally and internationally, the current generation is observed to be adopting it as their lingua franca and thus making it more difficult for other indigenous languages to survive in contemporary Brunei.

Specifically within the scope of the seven indigenous groups and languages in Brunei, the implication is that the younger generation, regardless of their inherited or self-identified ethnicity, are becoming 'monolingual' speakers of Brunei Malay only, suggesting a reduction of the linguistic diversity in Brunei. In fact, some speakers of indigenous languages are abandoning their heritage language altogether, and the younger generations of all of these communities are brought up speaking Malay as a first language. The maintenance of these languages, it seems, is not an important priority for them.

On the other hand, while this is true in general, it is significant to note the study of Murut in Temburong by Coluzzi (2010) which found evidence that the language

Table 3.1 Vitality rating of languages of Brunei (on a scale of 0–6: higher figures indicate greater vitality) (adapted from Martin 1995a)

Language/dialect	EV rating	New prediction
Brunei Malay	6.0	6.0
Kedayan	3.0	2.0
Tutong	2.5	2.5
Belait	0.5	0.1
Dusun	2.0	2.0
Bisaya	3.0	2.0
Murut	3.5	2.0

appeared to be widely used in the area. Indeed, only 5.9 % of the Murut respondents in the study claimed they could not understand the language. Coluzzi's survey showed that 77.4 % of the younger respondents (15–30 years old) claim to use Murut as their first language, indicating that the language has not been affected or replaced by Malay in personal settings such as the family domain.

A feature article in the Brunei Times by Yap et al. (2015) provides a platform for Bruneian young people to express their views on the subject. For instance, Muhd Azim (age 23), a university student, acknowledges the slow disappearance of indigenous languages and its potential consequences on culture, and Azizi Hj Abd Rahim (age 24) suggests that the Bruneian identity would fade with the loss of these languages.

Despite genuine concern among Bruneians, such as that highlighted by the Brunei Times report, and despite recent efforts by Universiti Brunei Darussalam's Language Centre to offer popular classes in Dusun and Tutong (from 2011) and Iban (from 2013), there is no doubt that the natural process of language shift is on-going in Brunei, and there is little that can be done to slow it down.

The vitality rating by Martin (1995a, b, c, 1996a, b) in Table 3.1 shows his assessment of the effect of the culmination of all the factors described above up till 1995.

Martin's vitality rating takes into account the inter-generational rate of transmission of each language/dialect, the media and institutional support the language enjoys, and the geographical concentration of speakers, although he admits that these ratings are impressionistic. These vitality rates remain the same when compared with rates drawn by Coluzzi (2010), based on works of others such as Martin (1995a, b, c, 1996a, b), Sercombe (1997) and Rabinah (1994). A more realistic and current EV rating of these languages is presented above in the 'New Prediction' column based on Noor Azam's (2005) re-assessment of all those factors.

To provide further evidence about these issues, especially in view of Martin's admission of the ratings being impressionistic, a cross-generation test was conducted to investigate active and passive knowledge among speakers from one of the minority communities, the Dusun. The results are predictable, but the significance of this test is that it can provide another objective measure to consider in the EV rating, and thereby lead to a more informed evaluation.

3.3 A Dusun Case Study: Kampung Bukit Udal

Kampung Bukit Udal was chosen due to the fact that it is a Dusun-speaking village, and most of the residents identify as Dusun and still observe Dusun cultural practices and celebrations. It has a population of about 1000, of whom about 35 % are Muslims (projected from figures stated in Johno 2009). The Dusun language is still used in the village today although it is increasingly influenced by Malay. Traditional events such as Adau Gayoh (the Dusun harvest day) are still celebrated annually, and Dusun weddings and funerals are still practiced by the people in the village, so within this close-knit community there is still a strong group-identification as Dusun.

3.3.1 The Active and Passive Knowledge Tests

In the context of this study, the active and passive knowledge tests examine speaking and listening skills respectively. Active knowledge is associated with speaking and writing, and it involves retrieval of forms of words, whereas passive knowledge is associated with the reading and listening skills, which involve the retrieval of the meanings of words (Stewart 2012, p. 53). The two tests were conducted so comparison and measurement of both types of knowledge can be made for all the age groups involved in this study.

3.3.2 The Active Knowledge Test

For the Active Knowledge Test, participants were asked to talk in Dusun about the following question in a span of one minute:

> Apakah yang kamu buat kelmarin, dari semasa kamu bangun sehingga kamu tidor?
> ('What did you do yesterday, from the time you woke up until you went to sleep?')

The question was asked casually in Dusun. The one minute duration was to let participants answer the question spontaneously. The aim of the test was to determine how naturally the participants can use the Dusun language.

3.3.3 The Passive Knowledge Test

For Passive Knowledge Test, participants were asked to listen to a Dusun recording of the story of a farmer with an ape and a bird called 'Ncariak', during the harvesting month of padi (see the Appendix).

After the participants listened to the recording, they were asked, in Brunei Malay, the following questions:

1. What was the story about?
   (a) a fisherman,
   (b) the padi, or
   (c) the orchard.
2. What were the names of the animals in the story?
3. What was the food that the animals were waiting to ripen?
4. Which animal knew earlier when the padi ripened?
5. Which animal went home before the padi ripened?
6. Why did the bird's wings make the cracking sound when it flew?

3.3.4 Participants

A total of 20 participants were tested. Five individuals were tested from each of the following age groups: 15–30 years old, 31–45 years old, 46–60 years old and 61+ years old. They were randomly chosen, so their level of proficiency in the Dusun language and also their occupations varied.

3.3.5 Methodology

Participants were asked a few background questions including their language preference and their highest level of education. After these background questions, they were given a brief explanation on the two tests without revealing which specific linguistic aspects were being investigated.

3.3.6 Results

The average percentage of scores for each age group are shown in Table 3.2.

Table 3.2 shows that the average percentage of both knowledge increases with age. The youngest age group (15–30) obtained the lowest scores for both active and passive knowledge, 11 and 36.7 % respectively. In comparison, the oldest age group (61+) achieved the highest scores, 89 % for active knowledge and 90 % for passive knowledge.

Table 3.2 also shows that the average passive knowledge for all age groups is higher than their average active knowledge. This is not a surprising finding, reflecting what was reported by Hajilou et al. (2012, p. 1), 'passive vocabulary was

Table 3.2 Average percentage of active and passive knowledge per age group

Age group	Avg. active knowledge (%)	Avg. passive knowledge (%)
15–30	11	36.7
31–45	58	85
46–60	63	86.7
61+	89	90

always larger than active vocabulary at all levels'. However, in fact, when comparing the active and passive knowledge for each age group, there is no significant difference between the two kinds of knowledge except for the 46–60 age group (t = 2.704, df = 8, p = 0.027).

3.3.7 Discussion

It is no surprise that the Active and Passive knowledge test found the older Dusun speakers performing better than the younger ones. The significance of this test is that it is a systematic and objective means of testing and confirming the existence of ongoing language shift. Even though the sample size is small, it is doubtful if a bigger sample size would result in substantially different findings.

The youngest age group of this research obtained an average percentage of 11 % for the active knowledge test and 36.7 % for the passive knowledge test. On the other hand, the oldest age group obtained 89 and 90 % for the same tests. This shows that there are huge differences in both speaking and listening skills between the young generation and the old generation, although again this is no big surprise. However, it confirms that the younger population of Dusun speakers are using the language significantly less than the older generation.

3.4 Conclusion

In the bigger picture, this case study can serve as an indication of what the other indigenous languages (Belait, Bisaya, Kedayan, Murut, Tutong, and also Iban and Penan) are facing. It is safe to assume that the active and passive knowledge of the younger generation of each ethnic group would be significantly lower than those of their elders. But if the active and passive knowledge test were conducted across all the indigenous languages, then we would have a more objective means for comparison. In addition, it would be valuable to investigate inter-generational transmission, media and institutional support, distribution and concentration of speakers, stereotypes and status, academic value, and historical value.

Within the context of the seven indigenous languages in Brunei, it can be argued that what was once a linguistically diverse population is now steadily morphing into a homogeneous and 'monolingual' Malay speech community. Spurred by the nature of the relationship between the dominant Malay and the threatened ethnic languages, as a result of a lack of effort at maintenance, or even the inclination to maintain them, the minority ethnic languages are fast disappearing.

There is clearly an inter-generational switch from indigenous languages to Malay within ethnic minority families, the final line of defense for their languages in the country. What is emerging, as a result, is a new generation of Bruneians who all speak Malay and can rightly claim it to be their mother tongue, regardless of their ethnic affiliation. It has been suggested that there is a process of convergence on a 'pan-Bruneian Malay' code, and concurrently a 'pan-Bruneian identity', attributable to an increase in interethnic mixed marriages, and the detachment from, if not indifference to, traditional ethnic perceptions or identities among the population. Certainly there is an apparent absence of strong resistance to the forces of language shift, but then there have never been explicit bans of ethnic languages in Brunei. In other words, Bruneian indigenous groups tend not to protest as they have nothing to protest against.

Appendix. Story Used in the Passive Knowledge Test

Carita Jalama Baparai na Sanginan Gabuk na Ligawau Ncariak
Atih aroh lah carita laid gulu, aroh sanginan jalama ngiang rarau untuk o baparai. Mpak anoh aroh saginan gabok ngitong unuh naal jalama baparai onoh, mpak onoh pun aroh saginan ligawou ncariak tanulud andih sadu mok sawat ulu gabok, ewooh nukop mok raan kayu. Ligawau ncariak ati pun tarus nuwot mok gabok onoh alan mu ngitong no gabok? Gabok pun njawab, ikow ngitong no jalama ngiang na nagad kayu alan jati mapong, mahie nayoh alan jati mapong la o. Kajun ncariak, koo baal o gabok, samo-samo todo makan lah o sudah bua parai mancak.

Babulan bulan tad ano, bua parai mbuloh ngurai, andih buai lagih kan mancak. Salalom ngintai bua parai mancak, gabok nuli ngakap keluarga mok kampung, ewoh ngara mok ligawou ncariak, adong kamuan ngara diso kalau buah parai mancak la o samo-samo makan. Ara gabok lagi, kalau ligawou ncariak makan tangalan andi ngara diso, alad ligawou ncariak alan o mutol. Ara ligawou ncariak adong susah ganawou gabok, kan kah todo samo-samo macam seganak. Ara ligawou ncariak lagi, moncoi kow muli malawat yapa ina mu. Salalom ganawoh ligawou ncariak, lagih moncoi kalau gabok muli ni kampung o, andih ni yodo pagahauh makan bua parai.

Samasa gabok nuli ni kampong o, bua parai pun sudah mancak, sanang ganaow ligawou ncariak makan bua parai, lagih pun gabok angop lagih nikot. Ewoh ngibat kawan-kawan makan samo-samo bua parai saboi nahie. Andih buai tad anoh gabok pun nikot lapas malawat ina yapa o. Gabok pun muot mok ligawou ncariak, sudah kah bua parai mancak ncariak? Kajun ligawou ncariak andih lagi gabok, kakal mata. Gabok taraso andih mancoi ganawou o. Eyoh pun ngitong tagalan mok parai, salalom ganawoh gabok baal-baal o kuji tih suat tipu. Utang ncariak no kajun gabok! Alan ku nipu-nipu alad o no bila indo batamu la o, ara o bua parai andih lagi mancak, tapi sudah nahie nakan o.

Gabok pun ngium ligawou ncariak saboi malap, turih o ligawou ncariak nalap nakom gabok, unoh lagih gabok pun nipu alad ligawou ncariak saboi mpugol. Sabab anoh nayoh katab alad ligawou ncariak karuput-karuput bila eyoh tamulod saboi adau atie.

Translation (English):
The Story of a Farmer With an Ape and a Bird Called Ncariak
This is an old story. There was a farmer who was clearing and chopping wood for him to make a padi field. The farmer's action caught the attention of an ape and at the same time there was a bird called ncariak flying and perching at the branches of wood not far from the ape. The bird asked the ape, 'What are you looking at, ape?' The ape replied, 'Look at that farmer, clearing and logging timber where we are staying, our home is ruined'. The bird then said to the ape, 'Let it be, ape! When his padi ripens we will eat it together'.

Several months later, the padi began to blossom and soon it would ripen. While waiting for the padi to ripen, the ape wanted to visit his family in the village. So he reminded the bird not to forget to tell him when the padi ripened so they could eat it together. The ape also said that if the bird ate the padi all by itself and did not tell the ape, the ape would break its wings. To reassure the ape, the bird then said nice words so that the ape would feel at ease, 'Aren't we like brothers?' and he added, 'It's better for you to visit your parents in the village.' Secretly, the bird felt that it was better for the ape to go back to its village so that they would not fight for the padi when it ripened.

While the ape went to visit his family in the village, the padi began to ripen. The bird happily ate the padi as the ape was still visiting its family. Since the ape was still away, the bird then brought its friends to eat the padi until they finished eating all of it. Several days later, the ape returned from its visit. It then asked the bird, 'Has the padi ripened?' The bird answered that the padi had not ripened and was still raw. The ape felt uneasy and went to see for itself if the padi was really raw. As the ape reached the padi field, the ape felt very disappointed because the bird had already cheated and eaten all of the ripened padi.

The ape then went to search for the bird and finally found and captured it. The ape then broke the bird's wings even when the bird asked for forgiveness for its wrongdoing. However, the ape did not care and did not feel sorry anymore. In the end, that is why, even today, when the bird flies, the wings make the cracking sound.

References

Braighlinn, G. (1992). *Ideological innovation under monarchy: Aspects of legitimation activity in contemporary Brunei*. Amsterdam: VU Press.
Brown, D. E. (1960). *Brunei: The structure and history of a Bornean Malay sultanate*. Bandar Seri Begawan: Brunei Museum.
Clynes, A. (2005). Belait. In K. A. Adelaar & N. Himmelmann (Eds.), *The Austronesian languages of Asia and Madagascar* (pp. 429–455). London: Routledge Press.
Coluzzi, P. (2010). Endangered languages in Borneo: A survey among the Iban and Murut (Lun Bawang) in Temburong, Brunei. *Oceanic Linguistics, 49*(1), 119–143.
Gunn, G. C. (1997). *Language, power and ideology in Brunei Darussalam*. Athens, OH: Ohio University Center for International Studies.
Hajilou, Y., Yazdani, H., & Shorkpour, N. (2012). The relationship between Iranian EFL learners' creativity and their lexical reception and production knowledge. *English Language Teaching, 5*(3), 131–146.
Johno, P. (2009). Ketua Kampong Bukit Udal: Biodata. Retrieved October 18, 2013, from http://kampong-bukit-udal.blogspot.com.
Jones, G. (1994). *A study of bilingualism and implications for language policy planning for Negara Brunei Darussalam*. PhD thesis. University of Aberystwyth.
Kershaw, E. M. (1994). Final shifts: Some why's and how's of Brunei Dusun convergence on Malay. In P. W. Martin (Ed.), *Shifting patterns of language use in Borneo* (pp. 179–194). Williamsburg, VA: Borneo Research Council.
Kershaw, R. (1998). Marginality then and now: Shifting patterns of minority status in Brunei Darussalam. *Internationales Asienforum, 29*(1–2), 83–106.
Leach, E. R. (1950). *Social science research in Sarawak*. London: HMSO.
Martin, P. W. (1990). The pattern of language communication in Brunei Darussalam and its pedagogic implications. In V. Bickley (Ed.), *Language use and language teaching and the curriculum* (pp. 175–185). Hong Kong: Institute of Language. in Education.
Martin, P. W. (1995a). Whither the indigenous languages of Brunei Darussalam? *Oceanic Linguistics, 34*, 44–60.
Martin, P. W. (1995b). *Ethnic and linguistic interaction in urban Borneo*. Paper presented at the first conference of EUROSEAS 'Keys to South–East Asia,' Leiden, June 29–July 1, 1995.
Martin, P. W. (1995c). Some views on the language ecology of Brunei Darussalam. In V. T. King & A. V. M. Horton (Eds.), *From buckfast to Borneo: Essays presented to Father Robert Nicholl on the 85th anniversary of his birth* (pp. 236–251). Hull: Centre for South-East Asian Studies, University of Hull.
Martin, P. W., & Poedjosoedarmo, G. (1996). Introduction: An overview of the language situation in Brunei Darussalam. In P. W. Martin, C. Ozog & G. Poedjosoedarmo (Eds.), *Language use and language change in Brunei Darussalam* (pp. 1–26). Athens: Ohio University Press.
Martin, P. W. (1996a). Brunei Malay and Bahasa Melayu: A sociolinguistic perspective. In P. W. Martin, C. Ozóg & G. R. Poedjosoedarmo (Eds.), *Language use and language change in Brunei Darussalam* (pp. 27–36). Athens, OH: Ohio University Center for International Studies.
Martin, P. W. (1996b). Social change and language shift among the Belait. In P. W. Martin, Conrad Ozóg & G. R. Poedjosoedarmo (Eds.), *Language use and language change in Brunei Darussalam* (pp. 253–267). Athens, OH: Ohio University Center for International Studies.
Martin, P. W. (2002). One language, one race, one nation? The changing language ecology of Brunei Darussalam. In M. K. David (Ed.), *Methodological and analytical issues in language maintenance and language shift studies* (pp. 175–193). Frankfurt am Main: Peter Lang.
Maxwell, A. R. (1980). *Urang darat: An ethnographic study of the Kadayan of Labu Valley, Brunei*. PhD thesis, Yale University.

McLellan, J., & Jones, G. (2015). Maintaining and revitalising the indigenous endangered languages of Borneo: Comparing 'top-down' and community-based policy initiatives and strategies. In C. Mari Jones (Ed.), *Policy and planning for endangered languages* (pp. 18–30). Cambridge: Cambridge University Press.

Noor Azam Haji-Othman. (2005). *Changes in the linguistic diversity of Negara Brunei Darussalam*. PhD thesis, University of Leicester, UK.

Nothofer, B. (1991). The languages of Brunei Darussalam. In H. Steinhauer (Ed.), *Papers in pacific linguistics A-81* (pp. 151–176). Canberra: Australian National University.

Rabinah Uja. (1994). *Language maintenance and shift in the Iban community in the Seria-Belait area*. Unpublished BA (Education) project paper. Brunei: Universiti Brunei Darussalam.

Sercombe, P. (1997). *Emic and etic perceptions of linguistic and cultural change among the Penan in Brunei*. Paper presented at the seventh meeting of the Southeast Asian Linguistics Society, University of Illinois, May 9–11.

Sercombe, P. (2002). Language maintenance and shift: A review of theoretical and regional issues with special reference to Borneo. In M. K. David (Ed.), *Methodological and analytical issues in language maintenance and shift studies* (pp. 1–19). Berlin: Peter Lang.

Stewart, J. (2012). Multiple-choice test of active vocabulary knowledge. *Vocabulary Learning and Instruction*, *1*(1), 53–59.

Yap, A., Billah Hasan & Analisa Amu. 2015. Preserving our local dialects. *Brunei Times*, Tuesday, 23 June 2015, B2–B4.

Chapter 4
The Language of Shop Signs in a Modern Shopping Centre in Brunei

Susilawati Japri

4.1 Introduction

Landry and Bourhis (1997, p. 25) define linguistic landscape (henceforth LL) as follows:

> The language of public road signs, advertising billboards, street names, place names, commercial shop signs, and public signs on government buildings combines to form the linguistic landscape of a given territory, region, or urban agglomeration.

The inaugural works on LL noted that public spaces offer fresh and interesting ideas about language usage that are often not in line with formal policies. The sites are also places where new words are continuously invented in a fusion of local and global usage that is constantly interacting with the target audience.

Researchers on LL do not perceive these phenomena as a coincidence. Instead there is:

> a goal to understand the system, the messages it delivers or could deliver, about societies, people, the economy, policy, class, identities, multilingualism, multimodalities, forms of representations and additional phenomena.
>
> (Shohamy and Gorter 2009, pp. 2–3)

Sociolinguistic research on LL is an area of study that can be explored more in Brunei Darussalam. This chapter looks at some shop signs in a modern shopping centre in the capital of Brunei, Bandar Seri Begawan (henceforth BSB), and it analyses the role and meaning of these signs.

Susilawati Japri (✉)
No. 2 Simpang 66 Jalan Mulaut Kilanas,
Kg Kilanas BF2520, Brunei Darussalam
e-mail: suzie.japri@gmail.com

© Springer Science+Business Media Singapore 2016
Noor Azam Haji-Othman et al. (eds.), *The Use and Status of Language in Brunei Darussalam*, DOI 10.1007/978-981-10-0853-5_4

4.2 LL in Brunei

The current study builds on the work on LL by Coluzzi (2012), which analysed signs along Jalan Sultan, one of the main streets in BSB, with lots of old-fashioned traditional shops. This site was chosen because of the high density of shops and businesses with a significant number of public buildings and signs. The study involved 102 units of analysis, and the data was collected by means of photographs, using the same methodology as Cenoz and Gorter (2006) for their linguistic landscape research in Italy. Coluzzi reported that there were 21 signs in Standard Malay only, 17 monolingual in English, and 64 that were multilingual, and he further noted that 19 signs included Chinese characters. He concluded that, apart from Chinese, minority languages have no visibility in Brunei. Meanwhile, English carries both informational and symbolic functions while retaining its aura of prestige as an international language.

The current study investigates the LL in some modern buildings in BSB, so it complements the work of Coluzzi that investigated signs in a street that mostly had traditional shops.

4.3 Official Language Policy in Brunei

Malay can be written in Jawi, which is derived from the Arabic script and has been modified in order to represent the sounds of Malay, as well as in Roman script, which we will here call Rumi. See for example Fig. 4.1, which includes the same message in the two different scripts.

Fig. 4.1 Road-side sign in BSB saying 'Prioritise the Malay language' in both Jawi and Rumi

The government promotes the use of Jawi, and official regulations state:

> In compliance with the speech delivered by His Majesty Haji Hassanal Bolkiah, Sultan of Brunei, it is hereby declared that all Ministries and Departments should observe and enforce the use of the Jawi script in addition to the Roman script on signs on Government buildings and on private businesses, including name signs, letterheads, notice boards, posters, advertisements, banners, names and street signs and so forth. The Jawi script must be twice as big as the Roman script and should be placed on top.
> (DBP 2009, p. 19. Translated from the Malay by Coluzzi 2012, p. 6)

This regulation only discusses the use of Jawi and Rumi on the signs for all government and private buildings. It is not clear if English is allowed or not, or if Chinese might be allowed. However, a leaflet issued by the Jabatan Bandaran Bandar Seri Begawan ('Municipal Office, BSB') states

> Apart from Jawi and Rumi, it is forbidden on signboards to add any foreign scripts or logos that have no link with the business. (my translation)

While this seems to forbid Chinese script, one might argue that Chinese characters are allowed if they are linked with the business.

4.4 The Study

The current research looks at the linguistic landscape in three buildings in the Times Square Area (TSA) in BSB, a modern shopping development near Brunei's airport. The methodology is similar to that used in the study of Jalan Sultan by Coluzzi (2012).

Times Square was originally the name of the first building on the site, but locals have adopted the name to refer to the whole commercial area. So TSA will refer to the area, while Times Square Building will refer to one actual building.

In October 2013, photographs were taken of 133 commercial signs in TSA: Times Square Building (45), Citis Square (36) and The Airport Mall (52). The entrance to each of these commercial buildings is shown in Fig. 4.2, in which it can be seen that the name in Jawi script occurs in all cases. In this respect, all the main

Fig. 4.2 Times Square Building, Citis Square (Medan Citis) and The Airport Mall

entrances to the three buildings comply with official guidelines, except that for Citis Square, the Jawi is at the side rather than at the top.

The linguistic objects that mark public spaces can be viewed from many different angles (Ben-Rafael 2009, p. 40), but this study will just focus on the language of shop signs in TSA. In addition to analysis of the photographs of the shop signs, mention will be made to some informal interviews with some of the owners of the shops.

4.5 Findings and Analysis

In the TSA data, there was no use of Chinese script on any of the shop signs, only Jawi, Rumi and English. These shops therefore contrast with the more traditional shops in the study by Coluzzi (2012).

According to the official regulations, the shops in TSA might be expected to have one common style adopted on their boards that is Jawi-Rumi-English, where Jawi is placed on the top followed by Rumi then English, as illustrated in Fig. 4.3.

However, this is not actually the most common style, as 55 of the shops do not include any Jawi, while 26 have Jawi together with Rumi or English but not both. The full results are:

- 52 (39 %) have Jawi, followed by Rumi, followed by English (e.g. Fig. 4.3) though in some cases the Jawi is to the side (e.g. Fig. 4.4)
- 54 (41 %) just put the name of their shop on the sign, with no Jawi (e.g. Figs. 4.5 and 4.6)
- 26 (19 %) have the name of the shop (either English or Rumi) alongside the Jawi version (e.g. Fig. 4.7)
- Just one unit (1 %) has the name in both Rumi and English with no Jawi script.

From this it may be concluded that there is no consensus in the employment of scripts in the area, and furthermore that the requirement to use Jawi script is not always followed. This may be due to the fact that there is no single agency responsible for coordinating internal language planning activities, so lack of monitoring from the authorities may be a factor. In this context, according to government directives, the Ministry of Education, Dewan Bahasa dan Pustaka Brunei ('Language and Literature Bureau of Brunei') and Radio Television Brunei

Fig. 4.3 Sample of the expected structure in signs in TSA: Jawi, Rumi, English

Fig. 4.4 Signboard with Jawi, together with Rumi, followed by English

Fig. 4.5 Signboard with only the name of the shop with no Jawi

(RTB) are the main agencies that carry out activities in the sphere of language planning (Coluzzi 2011). These three agencies mostly use Standard Malay and English, though one of RTB's radio stations, Pilihan Network, broadcasts some programmes in Chinese and Gurkhali. Meanwhile, Dewan Bahasa dan Pustaka Brunei has published a few basic grammars and dictionaries for Brunei Malay, Kedayan, Tutong and Belait (Coluzzi 2011, p. 4).

Fig. 4.6 Signboard with only the name of the shop and no Jawi

Fig. 4.7 Signboard with Jawi and English but no Rumi

4.6 English in Signs

Although Malay is the official language in Brunei, English is recognised as important by all sectors of the population, and in fact it is ranked as more important than Malay in certain domains (Ożóg 1996, pp. 156–159). Currently, in Brunei there are about 260 expatriate teachers employed by CfBT, mostly from the UK, New Zealand and Australia (Deterding and Salbrina 2013, p. 18) and this contributes to the promotion of English in the country. Furthermore, the influence of the internet, globalisation, and English-dominant education enhances the status of

English among Bruneians due to its association with prestige in certain domains (Noor Azam 2009).

Though some signs in TSA only put the name in Jawi and Rumi with no English, more than half of the signs do have English on them. This may partly be influenced by the fact that the area is located near the international airport. Kallen (2009, p. 271) notes the danger of language barriers if one wants to attract international tourists. Therefore, being only a few minutes away from the country's international airport, in the interviews some vendors in TSA stated that they used English in their signs in the hope of attracting tourists that come to Brunei.

It may be concluded that many shop owners use English to present their business in an attractive and prestigious manner and thereby attract customers from various walks of life or backgrounds, both locals and visitors. In this context, English is seen as a marketing tool, adding prestige to a shop, and it also accommodates the needs of tourists visiting the country.

4.7 Brunei Malay in Signs

There is one commercial sign in TSA that uses Brunei Malay: *Qidiaku* (see Fig. 4.8).

This name originates from the Brunei Malay word *kadiaku* which is a local variant of the first person pronoun *aku* (DBP 2011, p. 5). Oi (2013) reports that it is a 21st century edutainment centre designed by educational specialists to give children experience of creative learning with high quality activities and programmes.

Clynes (2014) notes that Brunei Malay is spoken as a mother tongue by about two-thirds of the population, and by others as a second language. Ożóg (1996) states that it is used in all walks of life, even in government offices. It will be interesting to see whether the use of Brunei Malay becomes more common in modern shopping centres such as TSA in the future.

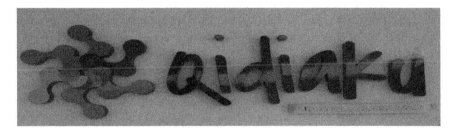

Fig. 4.8 Shop sign in TSA incorporating Brunei Malay

4.8 Lexis in the Signs

Borrowing of English words into Malay, usually with some respelling, is common in Brunei, and there are many examples in the TSA data. Some of the words borrowed from English with some respelling are *Butik* (boutique), *Galeri* (gallery), *Kafe* (café), *Restoran* (restaurant), and *Tekstil* (textile). In the first three of these, the Malay word sounds similar to the English equivalent, but in *Restoran* the final /t/ is omitted, and in *Tekstil* the final vowel is /i/ rather than /aɪ/ as in the English word.

Use of initialisms is also widespread in Brunei (Deterding and Salbrina 2013, p. 100), and it is common in the signs in TSA. In some cases, it is possible to determine the original words, e.g. PHB (Pure Healthy Beauty) and SCR (Singapore Chicken Rice), but in other cases the original words remain a mystery, e.g. OKKY Jewellery, U.R.S. & Inc, and F.A.E. Sports Sdn Bhd.

4.9 Conclusion

This study has focused on the LL of the Times Square Area, thereby offering insights about the shop signs found in a modern shopping complex in Brunei. The results show that there is some inconsistency in utilising the Jawi and Rumi scripts on the signboards, and not all of the establishments comply with the regulations set by the Prime Minister's office. Indeed, 55 units (42 %) do not include Jawi, despite the official regulations that Jawi be included on all signs, and this is higher than the proportion (about 35 %) with no Jawi reported by Coluzzi (2012) along Jalan Sultan. One possible explanation for this is that the latter are more visible as they occur along a busy public road, while the current study investigates shop signs inside shopping centres, so they would not be visible from outside. It would be valuable to investigate further why so many shop signs in TSA omit Jawi: Are the shopkeepers unaware of the regulations? Or have they made a conscious decision for some reason to omit Jawi, perhaps because they feel it is incompatible with the modern image of their outlets? In-depth additional research such as this might be addressed by future studies.

In one other aspect, many of the signs in TSA deviate from the official guidelines to a certain extent, as even when Jawi is shown, it is sometimes not twice as large as the other scripts and it often does not appear above them (see, for example, Figs. 4.3 and 4.4). One possibility here is that is not really feasible to show all scripts one above the other in a long shop-sign above the entrance to an establishment, so some shopkeepers have chosen instead to show the scripts side-by-side. The exact size and juxtaposition of the different scripts is beyond the scope of the current study, but it would be an interesting avenue to pursue in future research.

Even though not all shops adhere to the official guidelines, the Jawi-Rumi-English pattern is common in the TSA data, and it is suggested that many of the signs use English both for prestige and to accommodate foreign visitors to Brunei. However, there are no traces of Chinese in any of the signs, and in this respect the results contrast with the study of Jalan Sultan by Coluzzi (2012), in which over 18 % of signs were noted to include Chinese, often in order to maintain the traditional Chinese name of an outlet, and this was generally accompanied by a translation into Rumi and also Jawi. One reason for this may be that the TSA establishments include few traditional shops like those along Jalan Sultan.

In one other respect, the current study confirms the findings by of Coluzzi (2012): there is no evidence anywhere of the minority Austronesian languages of Brunei, such as Dusun, and as Coluzzi remarks, these minority languages have no visibility at all in the linguistic landscape of Brunei. Indeed, as he notes elsewhere (Coluzzi 2011), they are under serious threat of extinction.

The one exception to the dominance of Jawi, Rumi and English is the occurrence of *Qidiaku* in the current study, suggesting the possible emergence of Brunei Malay in public signage. It will be interesting to see whether this use of Brunei Malay becomes more common in the future.

References

Ben-Rafael, E. (2009). A sociological approach to the study of linguistic landscape. In E. Shohamy & D. Gorter (Eds.), *Linguistic landscape: Expanding the scenery* (pp. 40–54). Abingdon: Routledge.

Cenoz, J., & Gorter, D. (2006). Linguistic landscape and minority languages. *International Journal of Multilingualism, 3*, 67–80.

Clynes, A. (2014). Brunei Malay: An overview. In P. Sercombe, M. Boutin & A. Clynes (Eds.), *Advances in research on linguistic and cultural practices in Borneo* (pp. 153–200). Phillips, ME: Borneo Research Council.

Coluzzi, P. (2011). Majority and minority language planning in Brunei Darussalam. *Language Problems and Language Planning, 35*(3), 222–240.

Coluzzi, P. (2012). The linguistic landscape of Brunei Darussalam: Minority language and the threshold of literacy. *Southeast Asia: A Multidisciplinary Journal, 12*, 1–16.

Deterding, D., & Salbrina, S. (2013). *Brunei English: A new variety in a multilingual society*. Dordrecht, Netherlands: Springer.

DBP. (2009). *Utamakanlah Bahasa Melayu*. BSB: Dewan Bahasa dan Pustaka Brunei.

DBP. (2011). *Daftar leksikal 7: Dialek Brunei Darussalam*. BSB: Dewan Bahasa dan Pustaka Brunei.

Kallen, J. (2009). Tourism and representation in the Irish linguistic landscape. In E. Shohamy & D. Gorter (Eds.), *Linguistic landscape: Expanding the scenery* (pp. 270–283). Abingdon: Routledge.

Landry, R., & Bourhis, R. Y. (1997). Linguistic landscape and ethnolinguistic vitality: An empirical study. *Journal of Language and Social Psychology, 16*(1), 23–49.

Noor Azam Haji-Othman (2009). *The changing linguistic profile of Brunei: Notes for language education*. Plenary paper at International Conference on the Teaching and Learning of English in Asia 3 (TLEiA3), Bandar Seri Begawan, 19–20 November 2009.

Oi, R. (2013). Qidiaku: educational playground for kids. *The Brunei Times*. Retrieved November 11, 2013, from http://www.bt.com.bn/happenings/2013/11/10/qidiaku-educational-playground-kids

Ożóg, C. (1996). The unplanned use of English: The case of Brunei Darussalam. In P. W. Martin, C. Ożóg & G. Poedjosoedarmo (Eds.), *Language use and language change in Brunei Darussalam* (pp. 156–172). Ohio: Ohio University Center for International Studies.

Shohamy, E., & Gorter, D. (2009). Introduction. In E. Shohamy & D. Gorter (Eds.), *Linguistic landscape: Expanding the scenery* (pp. 1–10). Abingdon: Routledge.

Part II
Pronunciation and Grammar

Chapter 5
The Role of Fast Speech in Misunderstandings in Brunei English

Ishamina Athirah

5.1 Introduction

Over the last two decades, there have been a growing number of studies on Brunei English. Early research provided basic descriptions of its features, such as the description by Mossop (1996) of phonological features and the analysis by Cane (1996) of syntactic features. More recently, Deterding and Salbrina (2013) have explored Brunei English in a wider scope, including a detailed analysis of the phonology, and they report that there is a tendency to use [t] and [d] for the voiceless and voiced TH sounds, to reduce consonant clusters in final position, to realise the FACE and GOAT vowels as monophthongs, to use a full vowel rather than [ə] in unstressed syllables, and to adopt spelling pronunciation such as having [ɒ] in the first syllable of *company*. They also show that some Brunei speakers do not differentiate between long and short vowels, and that about half of young Bruneians have a rhotic accent.

In terms of syntax and discourse, some features of Brunei English have been claimed as typical of English as a Lingua Franca (ELF), such as pluralising uncountable nouns like *furnitures* and *stuffs*, the omission or addition of articles, the use of a preposition between some verbs and their objects, the intermittent absence of the -s suffix on third person present tense verbs, and the fronting of topics (Deterding and Salbrina 2013, p. 70).

However, there has been little research on how intelligible Brunei English is in international communication. Deterding and Salbrina (2013, p. 122) briefly note that, according to the suggestions of Jenkins (2000), some features of pronunciation may cause misunderstandings, such as the lack of distinction in vowel length and the uncertain placement of the intonational nucleus. They also suggest that

---

Ishamina Athirah (✉)
Baitul Athirah, Spg 490, Kg Beribi, Jln Gadong,
Bandar Seri Begawan BE1118, Brunei Darussalam
e-mail: ishamina.athirah@gmail.com

non-standard syntactic features, such as pluralising uncountable nouns and topic fronting, are unlikely to be problematic, but their suggestions about intelligibility need to be investigated.

In his study of misunderstandings in ELF spoken in Southeast Asia, Deterding (2013) found that one of the most common causes of loss of intelligibility is when participants speak fast and at times not very loudly. The current study investigates misunderstandings in Brunei English in ELF communication that may be caused by the fast speaking rate of some of the speakers. Feedback obtained from non-Bruneian participants is used to identify tokens in which intelligibility in Brunei English conversational speech is impaired by the Bruneians speaking rapidly.

5.2 English as a Lingua Franca (ELF)

Jenkins (2009, p. 143) defines ELF as 'English as it is used as a contact language among speakers of different first languages'. According to this, which is in agreement with the definition of Seidlhofer (2011, p. 7), native speakers of English may be included when they are talking to speakers whose first language is not English.

Actually, the concept of a native speaker is rather hard to define (Davies 2003). When dealing with Bruneian speakers of English, classifying them as native or non-native speakers can be problematic, as some Bruneians grow up speaking the language at home although they also regularly speak Malay (Deterding and Salbrina 2013). If English is the first language they learn, should they be classified as native speakers? This study investigates Bruneian speakers talking in English to people from elsewhere without worrying about whether they are native speakers or not.

5.3 The Lingua Franca Core (LFC)

Jenkins (2000) suggests that not all features of English are important for intelligibility, and she proposes a Lingua Franca Core (LFC) of essential pronunciation features that are necessary for ensuring mutual intelligibility in ELF communication. The core features include all the consonants of English except dental fricatives, a contrast between long and short vowels, the avoidance of consonant deletion in word-initial clusters and only certain deletions permissible in word-medial and final position, and the placement of nuclear (tonic) stress (Jenkins 2009, p. 147). Features that are regarded as non-core include the dental fricatives, small shifts in vowel quality, lexical stress, rhythm and intonational tone, because they are not important for intelligibility.

In their corpus of ASEAN speech, Deterding and Kirkpatrick (2006) found examples of pronunciation features that led to misunderstandings, including omission of [r] in *three*, the use of [n] at the end of *holes*, initial [ʃ] in *sauce*, and the occurrence of [t] in *us*, all of which would be core features in the LFC. However, other features shared by speakers from the various countries did not result in a break-down in communication. Some phonological features found among many new varieties of English which do not seem to cause a problem include the use of [t] for voiceless TH, reduction of final consonant clusters, and the use of syllable-based rhythm; and some grammatical and discourse features include the absence of past tense marking, regularisation of the count/non-count distinction on nouns, use of the invariant *is it* tag, and topic fronting (Kirkpatrick and Deterding 2011).

5.4 Intelligibility

In defining the concept of 'intelligibility', Smith and Nelson (1985, p. 333) note that understanding is not just speaker- or listener-oriented but is an interactional process between both interlocutors. Smith (1992, p. 76) posits three levels of understanding: 'intelligibility' which refers to word or utterance recognition; 'comprehensibility' which represents knowing the meaning of the word or utterance; and 'interpretability' which concerns understanding the intended meaning behind the word or utterance. However, Nelson (2011, p. 37) and Deterding (2013, p. 10) point out the difficulty in using the concept of interpretability, as it is often hard first to be sure of the intended message behind an utterance and second to determine if it is understood or not.

Kaur (2010, p. 195) differentiates between a 'misunderstanding', which occurs when the listener interprets a word or utterance with a meaning that is not intended by the speaker, and a 'non-understanding', when the listener is unable to make sense of a word or utterance. However, Deterding (2013, p. 13) argues that in reality it is difficult to classify instances based on these two terms, as listeners may make a guess about the meaning of words or utterances but not be certain. The current study similarly does not try to differentiate between misunderstandings and non-understandings.

In her study of ELF communication in an academic setting, Mauranen (2006, p. 135) found that misunderstandings rarely occur and that there is a tendency for the speakers to prevent misunderstandings by rephrasing their utterances and by providing additional explanations. We should however note that there is a possibility that some misunderstandings that occur in her data were not identified because the analysis was based on instances of misunderstanding that were signalled by the interlocutors.

5.5 Data

The corpus used in this study consists of ten audio recordings collected over a period of 6 months in late 2013 and early 2014. Each recording involves two speakers, a Bruneian and a non-Bruneian, and we are concerned with how well the latter understands the former. A total of seventeen participants took part in the study and they are identified by their gender (F or M) followed by a two-letter code representing their country of origin. Details of the participants are listed in Table 5.1. Sixteen of the participants were students at Universiti Brunei Darussalam (UBD) and one was a visiting researcher at the university. All participants listed English as either their second or foreign language. They were asked to rate their fluency and proficiency in English which showed a range from 'very good' to 'fair'. These participants were selected because they were able to come back and meet the researcher to help identify areas of misunderstandings and also to clarify speech that was unclear to the researcher.

In each recording, the Bruneian speaker was being interviewed by the non-Bruneian participant. The researcher prepared a set of questions for the non-Bruneian participants. However, this only served as a guide to help give some ideas to the non-Bruneians, as many of them were able to come up with their own questions spontaneously and did not use the questions prepared by the researcher. A total of 3 h and 39 min of data was collected, with each recording lasting an average of about 22 min.

Table 5.1 Speakers

Speaker	Sex	Country	Age	L1	Occupation
FBr1	F	Brunei	33	Malay	Undergraduate student
FBr2	F	Brunei	31	Malay	Undergraduate student
FBr3	F	Brunei	24	Malay	Undergraduate student
FBr4	F	Brunei	19	Malay	Undergraduate student
FBr5	F	Brunei	19	Malay	Undergraduate student
MBr1	M	Brunei	24	Malay	Masters student
MBr2	M	Brunei	26	Malay	Masters student
MBr3	M	Brunei	30	Malay	Undergraduate student
FCh1	F	China	28	Cantonese	PhD student
FCh2	F	China	21	Cantonese	Exchange student
FCh3	F	China	21	Mandarin	Exchange student
FCh4	F	China	19	Mandarin	Exchange student
FMd	F	Maldives	32	Dhivehi	Masters student
FOm	F	Oman	33	Arabic	Masters student
FVn	F	Vietnam	28	Vietnamese	Masters student
MFr	M	France	30	French	Visiting researcher
MKo	M	Korea	23	Korean	Exchange student

5 The Role of Fast Speech in Misunderstandings in Brunei English

Table 5.2 Recordings

Code	Participant 1	Participant 2	Duration (min:s)
Br + Ch1	MBr2	FCh1	20:48
Br + Ch2	FBr3	FCh2	22:46
Br + Ch3	FBr4	FCh3	20:56
Br + Ch4	FBr5	FCh4	20:27
Br + Fr	MBr3	MFr	22:28
Br + Ko	MBr3	MKo	21:04
Br + Md1	FBr1	FMd	21:45
Br + Md2	MBr1	FMd	21:31
Br + Om	MBr1	FOm	22:29
Br + Vn	FBr2	FVn	25:12
			Total: 3:39:26

The recordings are listed in Table 5.2. The identifying code for each recording is labelled with a two-letter code representing the speakers' countries of origin, the first country listed being the country of the interviewee and the second being that of the interviewer. Three participants took part in two separate recordings: MBr1 in Br + Om and Br + Md2; FMd in Br + Md1 and Br + Md2; and MBr3 in Br + Ko and Br + Fr.

5.6 Methodology

Data collection was conducted in a quiet room at UBD, using a Handy H4n recorder to record the conversations which were saved in WAV format. The recordings were then transcribed by the researcher following the conventions adopted in VOICE (2007). Where there are unclear and uncertain words and phrases, the researcher met up with the participants to ask for clarification. As noted by Deterding (2013, p. 25), it is essential to be able to obtain feedback from participants because it allows one to correct transcription of speech that is not clear, and it also enables the researcher to identify instances of misunderstanding that are not signalled in the recordings. In fact, the majority of instances of misunderstandings in ELF communication such as this do not result in any obvious communication breakdown, as speakers have a tendency to adopt a 'let-it-pass' strategy in the hope that failure to understand a few words will not matter in the long run (Firth 1996).

The primary aim of the study is to identify instances of misunderstanding in Brunei English, so the researcher relied substantially on feedback from the non-Bruneian participants. In obtaining feedback from them, instances were selected in which misunderstandings may have occurred. This was done by selecting short extracts from the recordings and asking the non-Bruneians to listen to them and transcribe what they heard.

Following Deterding (2013), misunderstood words and phrases are identified as 'tokens'. A total number of 152 tokens of misunderstanding are identified from the corpus. These tokens are numbered 1 to 152, but only those that involve fast speech (based on what the non-Bruneians said) are discussed in this paper. From their feedback, the non-Bruneians indicated that fast speech was a factor in causing a problem in 26 of the tokens (17 %). As such, it represents one of the most frequent factors that seem to interfere with the intelligibility of the Bruneian speech.

5.7 Data Analysis

The 26 tokens in which fast speaking rate was reported by the non-Bruneians to have been a factor in causing words or phrases to be misunderstood are listed in Table 5.3. In the 'Heard as' column, '?' is used to indicate tokens for which the

Table 5.3 Misunderstandings involving fast speech

Token	Speaker	Listener	Word(s) said	Heard as
13	MBr2	FCh1	leisure	?
21	FBr1	FMd	education area	educationary
37	FBr2	FVn	further	final
41	FBr2	FVn	cooperating	?
45	FBr2	FVn	although	look
50	FBr2	FVn	accommodation	conditions
59	FBr3	FCh2	major	?
62	FBr3	FCh2	i don't know i	?
63	FBr3	FCh2	hopefully	probably
74	FBr3	FCh2	experience	many
75	FBr3	FCh2	studied	said
79	FBr4	FCh3	intimidated	stimulated
90	FBr4	FCh3	fun	quite
92	FBr4	FCh3	national day	?
97	FBr5	FCh4	forgot	don't know
98	FBr5	FCh4	so i'm	some
100	FBr5	FCh4	ridden	in
106	MBr3	MKo	both of	but if
112	MBr3	MKo	accommodation	?
114	MBr3	MKo	comment	can
125	MBr3	MFr	d y (= discovery year)	d 1
129	MBr3	MFr	what do you call that	mahkota
135	MBr3	MFr	i've taught	after
136	MBr3	MFr	five	four
138	MBr3	MFr	food technology	? technology
144	MBr3	MFr	furthering my study	foreign master

non-Bruneians were unable to make a guess about the word(s). Nine tokens occur in the speech of MBr3 and five in the speech of FBr3, while the other twelve tokens occur in the speech of five of the other speakers. Of all the Bruneian participants, only MBr1 did not give rise to any misunderstandings as a result of fast speech (though there are some tokens of misunderstanding in the two recordings in which he participated that arose from other features of his speech). Moreover, there is only one token each from the recordings of FBr1 and MBr2. It is therefore clear that not all Bruneians regularly cause problems by speaking fast.

In many of the tokens that are listed in Table 5.3, other features such as lexis and syntax may also have an impact on intelligibility, and in many cases, these were probably the main factors that caused the problem. In fact, Pitzl et al. (2008) suggest that determining the precise cause of a misunderstanding is often difficult and that multiple factors are regularly implicated. These issues are discussed in the sections below. First, however, let us consider fast speech.

5.8 Fast Speech

Abercrombie (1967, p. 96) notes that 'speed of speaking ... is best measured by rate of syllabic succession', so this study focuses on measurement of the speaking rate using syllables per seconds. Roach (1998, p. 153) reports that speaking rate in English varies between 3.3 and 5.9 syllables per second, while Fletcher (2010, p. 571) claims that speech rate can range from 5.2 to 5.9 syllables per second. However, Deterding (2013, p. 81) argues that these rates represent English in the inner circle (where English is used as the first language), and it may be different for interactions in ELF. He therefore suggests that we should adopt the midpoint of the range from Roach, which is 4.6 syllables per second, and this rate is used as a benchmark in this study. We may also note that avoiding vowel reduction may result in a slower speaking rate, so for Brunei speech, we may expect a lower figure than that suggested by Fletcher (2010).

Stretches of speech excluding pauses surrounding the tokens are identified. The duration of these stretches of speech and the calculation of speaking rate are presented in Table 5.4. Out of the 26 tokens, 12 tokens are classified as fast speech being the main reason behind the misunderstanding. These tokens are 21, 50, 62, 90, 97, 98, 112, 114, 129, 135, 136 and 138. All of these tokens except Token 136 have a speaking rate above the benchmark of 4.6 syllables per second. The other 14 tokens are classified as mainly involving other features of speech that play a bigger role in the misunderstanding, and they are analysed separately in subsequent sections.

There are 23 tokens with a speaking rate above the benchmark of 4.6 syllables per second, and only three tokens (Tokens 21, 74 and 136) that are in line with it. The token with the fastest speaking rate of 10.4 syllables per second is Token 129, because it represents a fixed phrase. The phrase *what do you call that* has five syllables and it is spoken rather fast. In his feedback, the listener MFr guessed it to

Table 5.4 Duration (s) and speaking rate (syllables per second)

Tok.	Spk.	Words	Syl.	Dur.	Spk.rate
13	MBr2	time do to any **leisure**	7	1.06	6.62
21	FBr1	**education area** for ten years	9	1.93	4.66
37	FBr2	the chance to **further** your	6	1.07	5.61
41	FBr2	as a **cooperating** teacher	9	1.48	6.08
45	FBr2	**although** it's a small country but	8	1.51	5.30
50	FBr2	there's **accommodation** also there	9	1.54	5.84
59	FBr3	a **major** in linguistics	7	1.15	6.09
62	FBr3	**i don't know i**	4	0.48	8.33
63	FBr3	**hopefully** it will	5	0.66	7.58
74	FBr3	**experience** different things	6	1.30	4.62
75	FBr3	i **studied** there right	6	1.05	5.71
79	FBr4	i feel **intimidated** so i started	11	1.51	7.29
90	FBr4	well actually it's **fun** it's	7	1.38	5.07
92	FBr4	choir **national day** it's	6	1.01	6.93
97	FBr5	i **forgot** what she drew	6	0.87	6.90
98	FBr5	**so i'm** just saying	5	0.74	6.76
100	FBr5	i've never **ridden** a motorcycle before	12	1.83	6.56
106	MBr3	**both of** my parents	5	0.92	5.43
112	MBr3	**accommodation** and the meals	8	1.08	7.41
114	MBr3	i **comment** one of the	6	0.95	6.32
125	MBr3	before my **d y**	5	0.75	6.67
129	MBr3	**what do you call that**	5	0.48	10.40
135	MBr3	**i've taught** in primary school so	8	1.05	7.62
136	MBr3	i have **five** siblings	5	1.10	4.55
138	MBr3	she has a degree in **food technology**	11	1.47	7.49
144	MBr3	**furthering my study** here	7	1.00	7.00

be *mahkota*, which has only three syllables. (This is a Malay word which means 'crown' in English. We may note that MFr is fluent in Malay.) However, MBr3 utters all five words without omitting any consonant or vowel sound, though perhaps the /l/ at the end of *call* is omitted as a result of L-vocalisation. We can therefore conclude that the listener finds this utterance difficult to understand just because the speaker MBr3 is speaking rather fast.

The second fastest is Token 62 with a speaking rate of 8.33 syllables per second. The utterance *i don't know i* is hard for the listener FCh2 to decipher because the speaker FBr3 is speaking fast. Furthermore, she does not pronounce the initial consonant [d] in *don't*, and this is most likely a major contributing factor to the misunderstanding.

The third fastest with a speaking rate of 7.58 syllables per second is Token 63. Although this token has a fast speaking rate, it is suggested that the elision of the medial consonant [f] in *hopefully* may have been the biggest problem here. In both these tokens, we can say that the fast speaking rate led to the omission of consonants.

Several other tokens of fast speech are found to have elided consonant and vowel sounds that caused misunderstanding such as in Tokens 21, 112, 135 and 136. Of course, the elision of sounds is likely to have occurred partly because of the fast speaking rate.

Tokens 21, 74 and 136 have a speaking rate of 4.66, 4.62 and 4.55 syllables per second respectively, which is in line with the benchmark rate. Even though the listeners identified fast speech as a problem, the real issue may actually have been something else about the pronunciation. Segmental features that may have contributed to the problem are discussed in the next section.

5.9 Pronunciation of Segments

In this section, the analysis of segments is discussed in subsections based on the classification of the probable cause of the misunderstanding. These subsections include analyses of consonant reduction, TH sounds, vowels, and syllables.

5.9.1 Consonant Reduction

Simpson (2013, p. 158) notes that the phonetic patterns and shapes in conversational speech tend to be reduced compared to citation forms. Reduced consonants and vowels also have a shorter duration than in words that are spoken in citation form. He states that the most common form of reduction is elision, which occurs when a vowel or consonant in citation form is no longer present in conversational speech.

There are a number of tokens in this data in which a consonant sound is omitted. The following sounds are omitted: medial [f] sound in *hopefully* (Token 63), medial [d] in *studied* (Token 75), initial [d] in *day* (Token 92), and final [t] in *taught* (Token 135).

Simpson (2013, p. 159) also notes that elision is the most extreme form of lenition, or weakening, where lenition refers to 'a range of consonantal reduction patterns in which some aspect of the articulation or the voicing of a consonant in the spontaneous speech form appears weaker than it is in its corresponding citation form'. In Token 59, the medial affricate [dʒ] in *major* is reduced to the fricative [ʒ]. In Token 136, MBr3 does not pronounce the final [v] in *five*, but uses a glottal stop instead, pronouncing the word as [fʌʔ]. This illustrates an example of another form of lenition called debuccalization, where there is a loss of the oral component of an obstruent, thus leaving behind just the glottal component (Simpson 2013, p. 160).

5.9.2 TH Sounds

Previous studies have found that the TH sounds in Brunei English are commonly realised as the plosives [t] and [d] rather than the dental fricatives [θ] and [ð] respectively (Mossop 1996; Salbrina 2010; Deterding and Salbrina 2013), and Deterding (2013, p. 34) notes that this is also salient in Singapore and Malaysia. Jenkins (2009, p. 147) excludes the dental fricatives from the LFC, arguing that substitution of these sounds does not result in loss of intelligibility in ELF communication (Jenkins 2000, p. 137), but the current study suggests that the pronunciation of TH sounds may be a factor in a few tokens.

Four tokens in this corpus of fast speech are identified with pronunciation of a TH sound as the probable main cause of misunderstanding. In *further* (Token 37), *although* (Token 45) and *furthering* (Token 144), the medial voiced TH is realised as [d], and in *both* (Token 106), final TH is realised as [d]. The analysis therefore indicates that use of [d] for TH in medial and final position can sometimes cause misunderstandings. Deterding and Salbrina (2013, p. 121) propose that [t] for initial voiceless TH and [d] for initial voiced TH in Brunei English may not be problematic for international intelligibility; and there are no tokens in the fast speech analysed here that contradict their suggestion.

5.9.3 Vowels

Early studies of the vowels of Brunei English suggested that long vowels tend to be shortened and that some vowels with diphthongal quality are realised as monophthongs (Mossop 1996), and later studies have confirmed this (Salbrina 2006, 2010; Deterding and Salbrina 2013). These tendencies are also found in this study of fast speech, and it is suggested that they can cause misunderstandings.

The shortening of long vowels is found in two tokens. In Token 45, FBr2 pronounces *although* [ʌldɒ] with the short vowel [ʌ] in the first syllable rather than with [ɔː] which is expected in the standard RP pronunciation [ɔːlðəʊ] (Wells 2008, p. 24), and in Token 138, MBr3 uses the short vowel [ʊ] in *food* for the long GOOSE vowel.

Other tokens illustrate the use of monophthong vowels for sounds that are diphthongs in standard RP English. In Tokens 41, 45, and 63, the Bruneian speakers use the short vowel [ɒ] for the GOAT vowel that is pronounced with the diphthong [əʊ] in RP. This occurs in the first syllable of *cooperating* in Token 41, in the second syllable of *although* in Token 45, and in the first syllable of *hopefully* in Token 63. In *education area* of Token 21, the speaker FBr1 has [ɪ] in the second syllable of *area* rather than the expected diphthong [ɪə] for the NEAR vowel (Wells 2008, p. 41) thus pronouncing the phrase as [ɪdʊkeʃənerɪ]. In Token 136, the vowel in *five* is realised as [ʌ] rather than the expected diphthong [aɪ] for the PRICE vowel. For Token 98, FCh4 heard *some* instead of *so i'm* because FBr5 has the long monophthong vowel [ɑː] rather than the expected diphthong [aɪ] in *i'm* because she is speaking fast.

In Token 13 of *leisure*, there seem to be a number of factors that contribute to the misunderstanding. The speaker, MBr2, pronounces the first syllable with the long vowel [iː] following the General American pronunciation [liːʒər] (Wells 2008, p. 458). In fact, the listener FCh1 is not familiar with this pronunciation and is only familiar with the alternative RP pronunciation [leʒə] (Wells 2008, p. 458). She further claimed that MBr2 was speaking very fast, and indeed the speaking rate of the phrase *time to do any leisure* is 6.62 syllables per second, which is higher than the suggested benchmark rate of 4.6 syllables per second. Therefore, although fast speech may play a role in the misunderstanding, it seems that the difference in pronunciation is more important here and that the problem also lies with the listener who is not familiar with American pronunciation.

Although shortening of long vowels may be expected for fast speech, in most of these cases there is a change in quality as well, for example with [ʊ] in *food* and [ɒ] in *hopefully*.

5.9.4 Syllables

In two tokens, fast speech resulted in a loss of syllables. For example, in Token 112, the third syllable in *accommodation* seems to be elided. It is, however, noted that this syllable contains a sonorant consonant, the nasal [m], and therefore syllabicity may be carried by this consonant. Furthermore, this is an unstressed syllable and it has been noted that vowels in unstressed syllables are most likely to be elided (Simpson 2013, p. 158). Therefore, although it seems that the speaker MBr3 has missed out a syllable, it may have just been an extreme case of a syllable being unstressed.

In Token 41, *cooperating* is pronounced [kɒpretɪŋ] with three rather than the five expected syllables [kəʊˈɒpəreɪtɪŋ] (Wells 2008, p. 184), so FBr2 merges the first two syllables and drops the vowel [ə] in the third syllable.

5.10 Lexis

In his analysis of 183 tokens of misunderstanding, Deterding (2013, p. 92) found that lexical usage is quite a common problem. In his data, there are 17 tokens of words and 8 tokens of phrases that the listeners are not familiar with, where shifted meaning occurs, and where words have more than one meaning and the listener understands the wrong one. This study identifies five tokens involving fixed phrases or words that the listeners subsequently stated they did not know but which they also claimed involve fast speech.

Extract 1 shows Token 41 where FBr2 uses the phrase *cooperating teacher*, a phrase which FVn is not familiar with. In her feedback, FVn subsequently told the researcher that she knew the word *cooperating*, but did not understand it when it was used in this phrase. (In the extracts, the misunderstood words are shown in bold font and underlined. In this transcription, the use of uppercase letters in *upper* indicates unexpected emphasis.)

Extract 1 Br + Vn: Token 41
Context: FBr2 is talking about her role as a helping teacher.

> FBr2: but ah as a **cooperating teacher** to help the main teacher? but i am ah an english teacher for ah lower secondary UPPER secondary

In Token 79, shown in Extract 2, FCh3 subsequently explained in her feedback that she did not know the word *intimidated* and therefore guessed a word that she is familiar with: *stimulated*. (In this transcription, '(.)' is used to indicate a pause in the speech.)

Extract 2 Br + Ch3: Token 79
Context: FBr4 is talking about how she started reading English books.

> FBr4: i was in secondary school like i saw my friends reading like english books i feel **intimidated** so i started to read english books but the young teens (.) young teens for the books for young teenagers

Extract 3 shows Token 100, in which FBr5 uses the word *ridden*, and afterwards FCh4 told the researcher that she was not familiar with this past participle form of *ride*. (In this transcription, '<1> … </1>' indicates overlapping speech.)

Extract 3 Br + Ch4: Token 100
Context: FBr5 is telling FCh4 that she had never experienced riding a motorcycle.

> FCh4: he just took me home using his motorcycle <1> ah yeah </1>
> FBr5: <1> ah motorcycle i've never been </1> you know i've never **ridden** a motorcycle before or ever (.) you know sat on it

In Token 125, shown in Extract 4, MBr3 uses the initialism *d y*, referring to Discovery Year, which is a student exchange programme or internship programme for third-year students at UBD. Being a visiting researcher from France, the listener MFr was not familiar with the structure of the academic programmes at UBD. (In this transcription, '<spel> … </spel>' is used to show individual letters that are spelt out, and the question mark '?' which occurs at the end indicates rising intonation.)

5 The Role of Fast Speech in Misunderstandings in Brunei English   53

Extract 4 Br + Fr: Token 125
Context: MBr3 is telling MFr that he is going to study in the United States for a year.

>   MBr3:   ah this is my second year before my <spel> **d y** </spel> i will be going to (.) michigan?

In Token 138, shown in Extract 5, MBr3 uses the phrase *food technology* which the listener MFr is not familiar with. (In this transcription, '<tsk>' indicates an alveolar click that probably indicates some frustration in being unable to think of the term.)

Extract 5 Br + Fr: Token 138
Context: MBr3 is telling MFr about his sister's academic qualifications.

>   MBr3:   erm she has a degree in (.) <tsk> what you call that she has a degree in **food technology**

Uttering these unfamiliar words and phrases suggests that sometimes the Bruneian speakers fail to accommodate to the needs of the listeners. Therefore, although pronunciation and fast speech may have contributed to the misunderstandings, lexical usage can also sometimes cause loss of intelligibility.

There are many other tokens in this study with unfamiliar words and phrases, but only the five shown above involve unfamiliar expressions which the listeners claimed were spoken fast.

5.11 Syntax

In his study, Deterding (2013) reports only a few tokens of misunderstanding caused by grammatical issues, such as omitted verbs and unusual word order, while other unusual grammatical features are not problematic.

In the current study, only one of the fast speech tokens is found to have non-standard grammatical features which may or may not have played a part in the misunderstanding. In token 114, shown in Extract 6, MBr3 describes a past action but does not use the past tense of the verb *comment* by adding the –ed suffix, an omission that is common in Brunei English (Deterding and Salbrina 2013, p. 59).

Extract 6 Br + Ko: Token 114
Context: MBr3 is talking about pictures he had seen on social media.

>   MBr3: i think i **comment** one of the
>   MKo: ah
>   MBr3: erm i think one of the f- pictures?

Furthermore, *comment* is an intransitive verb, so the preposition *on* is expected if there is an object. In this token, the speaker includes an object *one of the pictures* but does not use a preposition after *comment*. It is not clear whether this non-standard usage of the word in terms of tense, and also the absence of a preposition, play a role in the misunderstanding, as the listener MKo only explained that he could not understand it because MBr3 was speaking fast.

5.12 Miscellaneous

In token 74, shown in Extract 7, the listener, FCh2, hears *many* instead of *experience*. However, it is perhaps the overlapping speech that is the problem here. Liddicoat (2011, p. 123) points out that having more than one person speaking at a time can cause an interactional problem. In this case, the overlap shows FCh2 providing backchannels to agree with FBr3 while the latter is still talking.

Extract 7 Br + Ch2: Token 74
Context: FBr3 is talking about travelling by ferry.

> FBr3: yeah it's good to: go erm boat riding or other than just go on airplanes (that) like you get to
> FCh2: <1> mm mm mm </1>
> FBr3: <1> **experience** different </1> things yeah

This token is included in fast speech because the listener, FCh2, claimed that she misheard this token because FBr3 was speaking fast, even if overlapping speech may have been the bigger problem here. The speaking rate of the utterance is 5.38 syllables per second, which is just a little faster than the benchmark rate.

5.13 Conclusion

Altogether, 26 tokens of misunderstandings have been identified as involving fast speech, but the pronunciation of vowels and consonants seems to be a factor in many instances. In some cases, the reduction of vowels and consonants may arise as a result of the fast speaking rate. In addition, lexical choice, syntax, and overlapping speech are implicated in seven tokens. However, in twelve of the tokens, speaking rate is either the only or the probable main cause of the misunderstanding.

It seems that fast speaking rate is found in the speech of seven out of the total of eight Bruneian speakers. In Deterding's (2013) study, many of the tokens involving fast speaking rate are from one speaker who was from Indonesia. Perhaps there may be a pattern here involving native Malay speakers with a fast speaking rate, though this suggestion should be treated with caution. In fact, Yuan et al. (2006) show that there is a correlation between a speaker's native language and their speaking rate in English, giving the example of Japanese speakers having a slower speaking rate in English which may be influenced by their culture of politeness. It is possible that Bruneian speakers are accustomed to speaking fast and some non-Bruneian participants may not habitually speak so fast when speaking in English.

Furthermore, as English is a second language for most Bruneians, and as current university undergraduates have been exposed to English as a medium of education since the fourth year of primary school (Jones 2007), we may assume that their level of proficiency in English is higher than those who speak English as a foreign language. Brunei English speakers should therefore be aware that when speaking to others whose English proficiency may not be as high as theirs, they should speak clearly, avoid speaking fast, and avoid using words and phrases that are uncommon or have special local meanings.

References

Abercrombie, D. (1967). *Elements of general phonetics*. Edinburgh: Edinburgh University Press.
Cane, G. (1996). Syntactic simplification and creativity in spoken Brunei English. In P. W. Martin, C. Ożóg & G. Poedjosoedarmo (Eds.), *Language use & language change in Brunei Darussalam* (pp. 209–222). Athens, Ohio: Ohio University Center for International Studies.
Davies, A. (2003). *The native speaker: Myth and reality*. Clevedon, UK: Multilingual Matters.
Deterding, D. (2013). *Misunderstandings in English as a lingua franca: An analysis of ELF interactions in South-East Asia*. Berlin: De Gruyter.
Deterding, D., & Kirkpatrick, A. (2006). Emerging South-East Asian Englishes and intelligibility. *World Englishes, 25*, 381–409.
Deterding, D., & Salbrina, S. (2013). *Brunei English: A new variety in a multilingual society*. Dordrecht: Springer.
Firth, A. (1996). The discursive accomplishment of normality: On 'lingua franca' English and conversational analysis. *Journal of Pragmatics, 26*, 237–259.
Fletcher, J. (2010). The prosody of speech: Timing and rhythm. In W. J. Hardcastle, J. Laver & F. E. Gibbon (Eds.), *The handbook of phonetic sciences* (2nd ed., pp. 523–602). Oxford: Wiley-Blackwell.
Jenkins, J. (2000). *The phonology of English as an international language*. Oxford: Oxford University Press.
Jenkins, J. (2009). *World Englishes: A resource book for students* (2nd ed.). London: Routledge.
Jones, G. (2007). 20 years of bilingual education: Then and now. In D. Prescott (Ed.), *English in Southeast Asia: Varieties, literacies and literatures* (pp. 246–258). Newcastle: Cambridge Scholars Publishing.
Kaur, J. (2010). Achieving mutual understanding in World Englishes. *World Englishes, 29*(2), 192–208.
Kirkpatrick, A., & Deterding, D. (2011). World Englishes. In J. Simpson (Ed.), *The Routledge handbook of applied linguistics* (pp. 373–387). London: Routledge.
Liddicoat, A. (2011). *An introduction to conversation analysis* (2nd ed.). London: Continuum.
Mauranen, A. (2006). Signaling and preventing misunderstandings in English as lingua franca communication. *International Journal of Sociology of Language, 177*, 123–150.
Mossop, J. (1996). Some phonological features of Brunei English. In P. W. Martin, C. Ożóg & G. Poedjosoedarmo (Eds.), *Language use & language change in Brunei Darussalam* (pp. 189–208). Athens, Ohio: Ohio University Center for International Studies.
Nelson, C. L. (2011). *Intelligibility in World Englishes: Theory and application*. New York and London: Routledge.
Pitzl, M.-L., Breiteneder, A., & Klimpfinger, T. (2008). A world of words: Processes of lexical innovation in VOICE. *Vienna English Working Papers, 12*(2), 50–71.
Roach, P. (1998). Myth 18: Some languages are spoken more quickly than others. In L. Bauer & P. Trudgill (Eds.), *Language myths* (pp. 150–158). London: Penguin.

Salbrina, S. (2006). The vowels of Brunei English: An acoustic investigation. *English World-Wide, 27*, 247–264.
Salbrina, S. (2010). The sounds of Brunei English—14 years on. *South East Asia: A Multidisciplinary Journal, 10*, 39–56.
Seidlhofer, B. (2011). *Understanding English as a lingua franca*. Oxford: Oxford University Press.
Simpson, A. (2013). Spontaneous speech. In M. J. Jones & R.-A. Knight (Eds.), *The Bloomsbury companion to phonetics* (pp. 155–169). London: Bloomsbury.
Smith, L. E. (1992). Spread of English and issues of intelligibility. In B. B. Kachru (Ed.), *The other tongue: English across cultures* (2nd ed., pp. 75–88). Urbana and Chicago: University of Illinois Press.
Smith, L. E., & Nelson, C. L. (1985). International intelligibility of English: Directions and resources. *World Englishes, 4*(3), 371–380.
VOICE (The Vienna-Oxford International Corpus of English) (2007). Transcription Conventions (Version 2.1): Mark-up conventions. Retrieved December 2, 2014, from https://www.univie.ac.at/voice/documents/VOICE_mark-up_conventions_v2-1.pdf
Wells, J. C. (2008). *Longman pronunciation dictionary* (3rd ed.). Edinburgh: Pearson Education Limited.
Yuan, J., Libermann, M., & Cieri, C. (2006). Towards an integrated understanding of speaking rate in conversation. In: *Interspeech 2006—ICSLP, ninth international conference on spoken language processing*, Pittsburgh, Pennsylvania.

Chapter 6
A Comparison of the Vowels of Brunei Mandarin and Beijing Mandarin

Shufang Xu

6.1 Introduction

Standard Chinese is a variety of Mandarin and its pronunciation is based on the Beijing dialect (Duanmu 2007). In China, it is Standard Mandarin that is generally codified in grammatical descriptions, dictionaries, and manuals of usage. Like any other language, Mandarin has many varieties, such as Taiwan Mandarin, Singapore Mandarin and Brunei Mandarin.

In Brunei, the Chinese form the largest minority group, accounting for approximately 11 % of the total population (Gallop 2006, p. 140). As part of a vast Chinese diaspora that originated mainly from the southern part of China, they speak different dialects such as Hokkien, Hakka and Cantonese. Though most Chinese Bruneians are able to speak their heritage dialects, Mandarin is actually used as the main medium of communication among the different Chinese groups because their dialects are mutually unintelligible. In addition, because Mandarin is taught in local Chinese schools and programmes in Mandarin are broadcast on the national radio station, there has been a substantial increase in the number of Mandarin speakers among young people in recent years (Dunseath 1996, p. 295). This kind of Mandarin is referred to as Brunei Mandarin, and just like Singapore Mandarin and Taiwan Mandarin, it has common features with other varieties of Mandarin as well as some unique characteristics.

Nowadays, Brunei Mandarin is gradually developing a distinctive identity. For example: there is /t/ lenition in the 3rd person pronoun, so *tā* is pronounced as [ha] in connected speech (Xu 2014); the neutral tone is less frequent than in Standard Mandarin (Deterding and Xu 2015); rhotacisation (*r*-suffixation) is absent; and the post-alveolar sibilants are merged with the alveolar ones. When looking at the

---

S. Xu (✉)
Melbourne, Australia
e-mail: fennyxu210@gmail.com

vowel system, there is also the possibility that there are fewer vowel distinctions than in Standard Mandarin.

When inspecting the vowel space, a vowel merger is a common phenomenon across languages. A merger is a phonological process in which a distinction between two or more phonological categories is absent (Lin 2007). Vowel shifts and mergers in varieties of English have been widely documented, such as the THOUGHT-NORTH merger in British English (Wells 1982, p. 145), the FOOT-GOOSE merger in Scottish Standard English (Maguire et al. 2013), and the LOT-THOUGHT merger in North American English (Wells 1982, p. 131). However, not much work on vowel mergers has investigated varieties of Mandarin. Indeed, description of the acoustic properties of Brunei Mandarin is generally scarce.

In this chapter, the acoustic characteristics of monophthongs and diphthongs in Brunei Mandarin will be compared with those of Standard Mandarin by investigating the acoustic distribution of the vowels, including a possible merger of /i/ and /y/.

6.2 Previous Studies on Vowel Distinctions

Vowel quality is principally determined by the frequencies of the first and second formants (F1 and F2) (Johnson 2012, p. 142; Ladefoged and Disner 2012, p. 38). Generally, open vowels have high F1 while close vowels have low F1, and front vowels have high F2 while back vowels have low F2 (Johnson 2012, p. 144). However, Ladefoged and Johnson (2011, p. 196) acknowledge that the correlation between F2 and the degree of backness is not as good as that between F1 and vowel openness.

Traditionally, vowels are plotted in a quadrilateral to represent their acoustic quality. Nowadays, there are an increasing number of studies that use the F1/F2 plane to show vowel distributions. For instance, Jacewicz et al. (2007) plot three regional varieties of American English using the F1/F2 plane, Mayr and Davies (2011) show Welsh, and Shi et al. (2015) investigate Cantonese and Mandarin. Generally, if vowels are at different locations in the F1/F2 chart, they can be assumed to be auditorily distinct. Researchers can plot the vowels in different ways. Some plot the averaged values of F1 and F2 (e.g. Huang et al. 2011; Nance 2011), while others use scatter plots showing all the vowels of each speaker (e.g. Escudero et al. 2009; Mayr and Davies 2011).

Therefore, vowel charts provide an excellent way of comparing different dialects of a language (Ladefoged and Disner 2012, p. 44). A F1/F2 plane can show vowel shifts and mergers and also the trajectory of diphthongs, so it is an effective tool to describe the quality of vowels.

6.2.1 The Vowels of Mandarin

Table 6.1 summarises the vowel inventory of Standard Mandarin, excluding the retroflex vowel [ɚ].

In the literature about Standard Mandarin, it is generally agreed that there are three close vowel phonemes /i, y, u/, one mid vowel phoneme /ə/, and one open vowel phoneme /a/ (Howie 1976; Duanmu 2007; Lin 2007), so Table 6.1 shows allophones rather than phonemes. Here, we will analyse the basic allophones [i, y, u] of the three close vowels /i, y, u/. [i] is a close unrounded vowel, while [u] and [y] are close rounded vowels. [i, y, u] can occur in syllable-final position in CV syllables, and [i, u] can also serve as the second part of closing diphthongs.

In Table 6.1, the mid vowels [e, ə, ɤ, o] are allophones of /ə/. Except for [ə] which only occurs before a nasal final, all these allophones of /ə/ can occur in syllable-final position in Standard Mandarin. For example, [e] can be in syllable-final position preceded by the glides [j] or [ɥ], [o] can be in syllable-final position preceded by [w], and [ɤ] can be in syllable final position in a CV syllable (Lin 2007, p. 76).

The open vowel phoneme /a/ has two different phonetic realisations: [ɑ] and [a]. [ɑ] can be in syllable-final position while [a] is usually followed by a nasal coda, [n] or [ŋ] (Duanmu 2007, p. 67).

In addition, in Standard Mandarin there are two apical vowels which can be shown as [z] and [ʐ] and which can occur in syllable-final positions (Chao 1968; Duanmu 2007). [z] only occurs after the alveolar consonants /ts, tsʰ, s/, and [ʐ] only occurs after the post-alveolar consonants /tʂ, tʂʰ, ʂ, ʐ/. Therefore, [z] and [ʐ] can be considered as allophones of the same phoneme in complementary distribution. In the Pinyin romanisation system, these apical vowels share the same symbol with the close front vowel [i]. For example, *mì* ('dense') and *shì* ('is/are') actually do not have the same vowel, as the former has the close front vowel [i], while the latter has the apical vowel [ʐ]. The use of 'i' in both *mì* and *shì* is therefore an orthographic convenience and does not suggest [i] and [ʐ] are necessarily allophones of the same phoneme.

These apical vowels (sometimes called syllabic consonants) have various transcriptions in the literature. For example, Wiese (1997) uses a similar transcription as Duanmu's but he adds a diacritic [ˌ] under [z] and [ʐ] to highlight the fact that they

Table 6.1 The vowel inventory of Standard Mandarin (adopted from Duanmu 2007)

		Front		Central	Back	
		Unrounded	Rounded		Unrounded	Rounded
Monophthongs	Close	i	y			u
	Mid	e		ə	ɤ	o
	Open	a			ɑ	
Diphthongs		Front		Back		
	Close	ai, əi		au, əu		

are syllabic, and he called them syllabic fricatives. Howie (1976) and Shi et al. (2015) use two non-IPA symbols [ɿ] and [ʅ] to represent [z̩] and [ʐ̩], while Zee and Lee (2001) transcribe them as [ɹ̩] and [ɻ̩] and Lin (2007) uses [ɹ̩] for both apical vowels. Lee-Kim (2014) proposes that they can best be analysed as approximants [ɹ̩] and [ɻ̩]. To avoid confusion, in this chapter, the symbols [z̩] and [ʐ̩] will be used even when other researchers have adopted alternative symbols.

Finally, Standard Mandarin has one retroflex vowel [ɚ] (Howie 1976; Chen 1999; Duanmu 2007; Lin 2007). This is sometimes called a rhotacised vowel (Lee and Zee 2003). It can occur in two environments: in words without a suffix such as *èr* [ɚ] ('number two'), and as a suffix to replace the coda of the syllable it attaches to, such as *gāner* [kaɚ] ('dried food') (Duanmu 2007, p. 40). However, Brunei Mandarin generally does not have *r*-suffixation.

The number of diphthongs in Standard Mandarin is not certain, and their transcriptions vary among researchers. Duanmu (2007) lists four diphthongs: [əi], [əu], [ai] and [au] and suggests no triphthongs. Although Lin (2007) agrees that Standard Mandarin has four diphthongs, she adopts different transcriptions: [ei], [ou], [ai] and [ɑu], and she maintains a skeptical attitude towards the existence of triphthongs. Wiese (1997, p. 226) uses more detailed transcriptions for nine diphthongs [a̯i, e̯i, a̯u, o̯u, i̯a, i̯e, u̯a, u̯ɤ, y̯e] and points out that the last five actually contain glides and might not be diphthongs in a real sense. On the other hand, Lee and Zee (2003) suggest that Standard Mandarin has 11 diphthongs ([ai], [au], [ou], [ei], [uo], [ye], [ie], [ia], [ua], [uə], [iu]) and four triphthongs ([iau], [uai], [uei] and [iou]). This study will just deal with the four basic diphthongs listed by Duanmu (2007).

6.2.2 Vowel Space in Mandarin

Vowel distributions of Mandarin in the F1/F2 plane were reported as early as 1976, but further research on vowel features is limited. Howie (1976, pp. 63–64) investigated seven monophthongs [i, u, y, z̩, ʐ̩, ɤ, a] in CV syllables (p. 65) by plotting their average formant frequencies, and he reported that [i, y, ʐ̩] are relatively close to each other, and [z̩] and [ʐ̩] are far apart from each other, indicating that [ʐ̩] is more front and [z̩] is more back. In addition, [ɤ] is directly below [z̩], indicating it is a back unrounded vowel. However, the data in Howie (1976) was from the recording of just one speaker, and it is not ideal to describe a vowel system based on a single speaker. In addition, the frequencies of vowel formants were estimated from traditional paper spectrograms in the 1970s, which might not be as accurate as the computer speech analysis software used nowadays.

Zee and Lee (2001) provide a spectral analysis of nine vowels: [i, u, y, z̩, z̩ₒ, ɤ, a, ə, ɚ] in CV syllables of Beijing Mandarin based on the speech data of 20 speakers (10 males and 10 females). They report that, in the scatter plots for male speakers, [ə] is close to the high vowels and the syllabic approximants [z̩, z̩ₒ]. In addition, [z̩], [ʐ̩], [ɤ] and [ɚ] have substantial overlap, while [i] and [y] partially overlap with each other. For female speakers, [z], [ʐ] and [ɚ] also have substantial overlap but there is no overlap with [ɤ], while [i] and [y] are largely distinct.

Shi et al. (2015) recorded 60 Cantonese speakers and 20 Beijing Mandarin speakers reading isolated Chinese characters. In their study, a scatter plot of seven Mandarin vowels [i, u, y, z, ʐ, ɤ, ɑ] is compared with seven long vowels in Cantonese. The overlapped ellipses in Mandarin show that [z] and [ʐ] are partly merged with each other. However, it is unclear if this is a merger in a real sense because no further measurements were carried out, and the dialect background of the Beijing language speakers is also uncertain.

6.2.3 Vowel Mergers in Mandarin

For vowel mergers, it has briefly been reported that in Taiwan Mandarin, the high front rounded vowel [y] is absent and is usually replaced by its unrounded counterpart [i] (Lin 2007). Duanmu (2007) also mentions the absence of [y] in Taiwan Mandarin, stating that it is replaced by [i]. However, these accounts of vowel mergers in Taiwan Mandarin are only impressionistic because they are not supported by any experimental data. Although some degree of vowel overlap occurs in Beijing Mandarin in the F1/F2 chart, the vowels are not actually merged when F3 or phonotactics are taken into account (Zee and Lee 2001).

6.3 Data

In this section, the subjects and the recording materials of the current study are described.

6.3.1 Subjects

40 tertiary students in Brunei and Beijing were recruited for this study, 10 females and 10 males in each country. At the time of the study, except for one male student who did not want to reveal his age (BM5 in Table 6.2), the other Brunei speakers had a mean age of 21 years, ranging from 19 to 23 years, while the Beijing speakers had a mean age of 24 years, ranging from 20 to 30 years. The 20 Brunei speakers were all undergraduate students. 12 were from Universiti Brunei Darussalam (UBD), seven were from Institut Teknologi Brunei (ITB), and one was from Kolej IGS Brunei Darussalam (IGS), a private tertiary institution in Brunei. The 20 Beijing students were all from Beijing Language and Culture University (BLCU). Of the 10 male students in Beijing, five were undergraduate students, and the other five were postgraduate students. All the female Beijing students were

Table 6.2 Brunei speakers

Speaker	District	Age	First language	Other dialects
BF1	Belait	23	English	Mandarin, Hakka
BF2	Brunei-Muara	23	Hokkien	Mandarin
BF3	Belait	22	Mandarin	Cantonese, Hakka
BF4	Brunei-Muara	20	Hokkien	Mandarin
BF5	Belait	21	Mandarin	None
BF6	Belait	22	Mandarin	Hakka
BF7	Belait	21	English, Mandarin, Malay	Mandarin, Hakka
BF8	Brunei-Muara	21	Cantonese	Mandarin, Hokkien
BF9	Belait	20	Mandarin	Cantonese, Hokkien
BF10	Belait	20	Mandarin	Hokkien, Cantonese, Hakka
BM1	Belait	22	Mandarin	Cantonese, Hakka
BM2	Belait	19	Mandarin	Hakka
BM3	Brunei-Muara	21	Mandarin	Hokkien, Cantonese, Hakka
BM4	Brunei-Muara	20	Mandarin	Cantonese, Hakka
BM5	Brunei-Muara	–	Cantonese	Hokkien
BM6	Tutong	19	Mandarin	Hokkien
BM7	Brunei-Muara	21	Mandarin	None
BM8	Brunei-Muara	20	Mandarin	None
BM9	Brunei-Muara	20	Mandarin	Cantonese
BM10	Brunei-Muara	23	Cantonese	Mandarin

postgraduate students. Two speakers were from Beijing, while the 18 others were from various provinces (see Table 6.3).

Due to the competing linguistic forces in Brunei society, including Standard Malay, Brunei Malay, English, Mandarin and other Chinese dialects (Dunseath 1996, p. 285), though most Chinese Bruneians are able to speak fluent Mandarin, many are not good at reading and writing Chinese. Furthermore, even though most of those enrolled in Chinese schools have reasonable proficiency in Mandarin, it is not comparable to that of the participants from China in terms of character recognition, reading and writing. For the Brunei speakers, the ability to read simple Chinese characters and reasonable fluency in oral Chinese were requirements for inclusion in this study. Many potential participants were excluded because they could not read Chinese even though they might be able to hold a fluent conversation in Mandarin.

The Beijing speakers had no problems reading Chinese characters. The first languages of all the 20 speakers belong to the Mandarin family except for the two students from Zhejiang and one from Anhui who all speak the varieties of the Wu dialect. All the Beijing students claimed to speak Standard Mandarin most of the

Table 6.3 Beijing speakers

Speaker	Province	Age	First language	Other dialects
CF1	Henan	27	Henan dialect	Mandarin
CF2	Shandong	26	Shandong dialect	Mandarin
CF3	Beijing	26	Mandarin	None
CF4	Shandong	25	Mandarin	Jinan dialect
CF5	Inner Mongolia	24	Mandarin	None
CF6	Shandong	30	Shandong dialect	Mandarin
CF7	Inner Mongolia	25	Northwest dialect	Mandarin
CF8	Hunan	25	Southwest dialect	Mandarin
CF9	Liaoning	28	Northeast dialect	Mandarin
CF10	Hebei	26	Northern dialect	Mandarin
CM1	Zhejiang	20	Wu dialect	Mandarin
CM2	Shandong	21	Shandong dialect	Mandarin
CM3	Guizhou	26	Guiyang dialect	Mandarin
CM4	Jilin	28	Northeast dialect	Mandarin
CM5	Henan	25	Henan dialect	Mandarin
CM6	Heilongjiang	30	Northeast dialect	Mandarin
CM7	Anhui	22	Wuhu dialect	Mandarin
CM8	Heilongjiang	26	Northeast dialect	Mandarin, Tibetan
CM9	Zhejiang	20	Dongyang dialect	Mandarin
CM10	Beijing	21	Hebei dialect	Mandarin

time, even though their first languages vary. In this study, we will label the Brunei females, Brunei males, Beijing females and Beijing males as BNF, BNM, CNF and CNM respectively.

6.3.2 Recordings

Recordings were conducted in a quiet office at the various institutes using a high-quality microphone positioned a few inches from the mouth of the speakers. They read a passage called The East Wind and the Sun (the EWS text—see the Appendix), and the recording was directly onto a Sony laptop computer at a sampling frequency of 44,100 Hz.

This chapter will describe nine monophthongs and four diphthongs of Mandarin, using the transcription of Duanmu (2007): [i, y, u, e, o, ɤ, a, z, ʐ] and [əi, əu, ai, au]. All the vowels that were measured are in open syllables because the CV (consonant + vowel) structure is the most common syllable structure in Mandarin. Though the CVN (consonant + vowel + nasal) structure also occurs, the final nasal results in a nasalised vowel which can sometimes disturb the formants of the

Table 6.4 Monophthongs in open syllables

Vowels	Syllables in EWS (in Pinyin)
[i]	nǐ, jǐ, dì, lǐ, lì, bǐ
[y]	nǚ, yú
[u]	fú, fú, fú, fú, bù, bù
[e]	yě
[o]	shuō, pò, shuō, tuō, tuō, suǒ
[ɤ]	hé, hé, rè
[ɑ]	dà, mā, mā, tā, bǎ, dà, tā, tā, bǎ, lā, fǎ, tā, bǎ
[z̩]	zì, sì, sì
[ʐ̩]	shì, shí, shì, zhǐ, shì, shǐ, shì, shì

preceding vowels, making measurements difficult (Zee and Lee 2001; Johnson 2012).

Although there is a long-standing debate whether the apical vowels are vowels or not, they are included in this study because, on the one hand, they have clear formants and vowel-like articulation, and on the other hand, it is a common approach in the literature of Mandarin to include apical vowels in the F1/F2 plane to view their distribution.

As mentioned earlier, the retroflex vowel [ɚ] can only occur in the syllable *er* (e.g. 二, 'two') in Standard Mandarin or as an *r*-suffix in Beijing Mandarin. It is not considered here as the retroflex vowel does not occur in Brunei Mandarin, and *èr* ('two') is pronounced as [ɤ].

All the vowels under investigation occur in the EWS passage, though the number of tokens for each is not the same. Table 6.4 shows the monophthongs that were measured. Note that in Table 6.4, though some forms of Pinyin are identical, they are not necessarily the same morphemes. For example, the first token of *shì* and the second token of *shì* that both include the apical vowel [ʐ̩] are different. The first *shì* is 事 (as in *běnshì*, 'skill'), while the second *shì* is 是 (as in *yúshì*, 'therefore').

For the monophthongs, there are 48 tokens for each speaker. However, when reading the passage, some speakers mispronounced one or two words. For example, *běnshì* [bənʂʐ̩] ('skill') was mispronounced by CM2 as [bənliŋ]. Furthermore, some Beijing speakers exhibited vowel reduction for syllables with the neutral tone, resulting in a few vowels having no visible formants in the spectrograms. For example, *yīfú* [jifu] ('clothes') was sometimes pronounced as [jifØ] in which [fØ] has a neutral tone and [Ø] represents the absence of a vowel. Nevertheless, at least 44 tokens were measured for each speaker.

Table 6.5 shows the four diphthongs that were investigated. There are eight tokens for each speaker, two for each diphthong. Although there are some other words with these four diphthongs in the EWS text, such as *zài* [tsai] ('in') and *dōu* [təu] ('all'), they were excluded because they are function words which are sometimes substantially reduced.

Table 6.5 Diphthongs in open syllables

Vowels	Syllables in EWS (in Pinyin)
[əi]	*méi, lèi*
[əu]	*kŏu, hòu*
[ai]	*kāi, lái*
[au]	*dào, lăo*

6.4 Methodology

Four different analyses were conducted: plots of the first two formants; Euclidean distance between the locations of *nǐ* [ni] ('you') and *nǚ* [ny] ('female') on the F1/F2 plane; comparison of the third formant of [i] and [y]; and trajectory length for the diphthongs. Each of these will be discussed in turn.

6.4.1 Vowel Plots

The frequency of the first two formants (F1 and F2) of the monophthongs was obtained using Praat (Boersma and Weenink 2014) at the midpoint of each vowel using a formant tracker overlaid on spectrograms. For the diphthongs, the F1 and F2 near the start point and the end point were measured.

In order to show the distribution of vowels, scatter plots with ellipses were generated in R using the phonR package (McCloy 2013). First, visual comparison of the plots is made between the female data, BNF and CNF. Second, visual comparison of the plots is made between the male data, BNM and CNM.

Using an arrow has been a traditional method to represent the phonetic quality of the onset and offset of diphthongs (Ladefoged and Johnson 2011, p. 90). In this study, the average frequencies of the F1 and F2 of the start and end of the diphthongs are plotted in the F1/F2 plane, with an arrow pointing from the onset to the offset. It is unfortunate that this averaging of results for diphthongs fails to show individual variation. However, showing the trajectories of all the tokens would result in too complex a plot to allow easy interpretation.

6.4.2 Euclidean Distance

For each speaker, the minimal pair *nǐ* [ni] ('you') and *nǚ* [ny] ('female') in the EWS text is compared. The distance between [i] and [y] in the F1/F2 plane was measured by calculating the Euclidean distance on an auditory Bark scale. The Bark scale is used to ensure that distances on the F1 axis are auditorily equivalent to distances on the F2 axis (Heeringa 2004).

6.4.3 F3 Measurement

Though the F1/F2 plot provides a detailed representation of vowel quality, F3 is also important in determining qualities such as retroflexion and rounding (Flemming 2002). For rounded vowels such as [y], when the lips are protruded, the front cavity lengthens, yielding a lower F2 and F3. Since F3 lowering has been shown useful in distinguishing [i] and [y] in French (Schwartz et al. 1993), this study also measures F3 to provide additional evidence about potential vowel mergers in Brunei Mandarin. As with the measurement of F1 and F2, the formant tracker in Praat was used to obtain the frequency of F3 at the mid-point of the tokens of [i] and [y] shown in Table 6.4.

6.4.4 Trajectory Length

For the diphthongs, the arrows represent the trajectory involved in the diphthongs, and the distance between the onset and the offset of a diphthong represent the distance of movement in the F1/F2 plane. The length of the trajectory of each diphthong was calculated and a comparison is made between the results for the Brunei speakers and the Beijing speakers.

6.5 Results

First, the results for the monophthongs will be presented and then there will be a discussion of the diphthongs.

6.5.1 Monophthongs

Scatter plots for the two groups of speakers are shown in Figs. 6.1, 6.2, 6.3 and 6.4. Ellipses enclose 68 % of the tokens of each vowel (McCloy 2013).

Figure 6.1 shows the vowel distributions of BNF. Nearly all the ellipses are clearly separated from each other except two pairs of highly overlapped close vowels: [i]/[y] and [z]/[ʐ]. To be precise, [i] and [y] almost completely overlap, while [z] and [ʐ] overlap substantially.

In contrast, in Fig. 6.2, the vowels of CNF show less overlap between [i]/[y] and also between [z]/[ʐ], though there is some. However, for CNF, all the vowels except [e] and [ɑ] show some degree of overlap with other vowels.

Figures 6.3 and 6.4 show the vowels of BNM and CNM respectively. Just as with BNF, the vowels in Fig. 6.3 are all clearly separated except [i]/[y] and [z]/[ʐ],

Fig. 6.1 Scatter plot for BNF

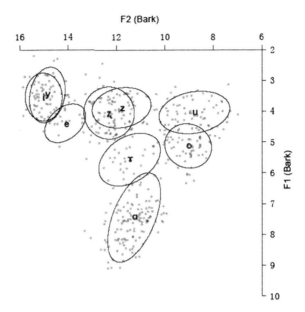

Fig. 6.2 Scatter plot for CNF

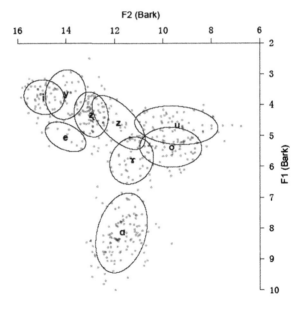

which show a high degree of overlap. Compared with BNM, each of the vowels of CNM in Fig. 6.4 is spread over a range of values in the F1/F2 plane, represented by expanded ellipses and greater overlaps, particularly for [u]/[o], but there is less overlap for [i]/[y] and for [z]/[ʐ].

Fig. 6.3 Scatter plot for BNM

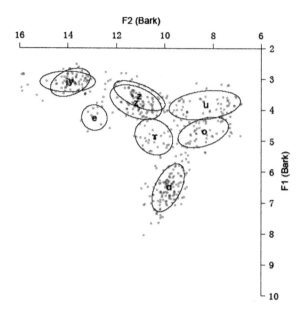

Fig. 6.4 Scatter plot for CNM

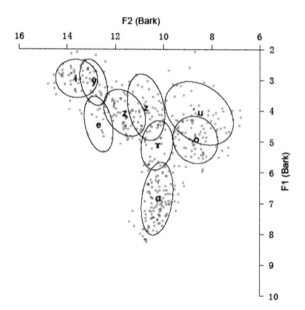

The visual comparison of the scatter plots indicates that Brunei speakers have two vowel mergers: [i]/[y] and [z]/[ʐ]. For the latter, it is well established that [z] occurs after alveolar consonants such as /s/ and /ts/ while [ʐ] occurs after post-alveolar consonants such as /ʂ/ and /tʂ/, so [z] and [ʐ] can be regarded as allophones of the same vowel phoneme. The lack of a distinction between [z] and

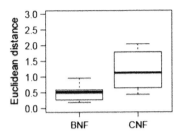 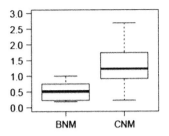

Fig. 6.5 Euclidean distance between [i] and [y]

Table 6.6 Mean F3 values for [i] and [y] (standard deviation is in brackets)

Group	[i] (Hz)	[y] (Hz)	t	p
BNF	3410 (233)	3226 (399)	1.95	0.063
BNM	3061 (291)	2898 (283)	2.21	0.034
CNF	3309 (239)	2834 (187)	9.15	<0.00001
CNM	2904 (244)	2342 (143)	12.49	<0.00001

[ʐ] therefore represents a merge between the alveolar and post-alveolar consonants in Brunei Mandarin. Consonant mergers are beyond the scope of this study, so this merger will not be considered further here, and the focus will be on the [i]/[y] merger.

Figure 6.5 shows the distribution of Euclidean distances on the Bark scale F1/F2 plot between [i] and [y] for the four groups of speaker.

It can be seen that the distance between [i] and [y] for the Brunei speakers tends to be much smaller than for the Beijing speakers, confirming that [i] and [y] in Brunei Mandarin tend to be merged, while they are differentiated in Standard Mandarin. For the female speakers, the mean distance for the BNF speakers is 0.49 Bark, while for the CNF speakers it is significantly greater at 1.18 Bark ($t = 3.40$, $df = 38$, $p = 0.006$). For the male speakers, the mean distance of the BNM speakers is 0.52 Bark, while for the CNM speakers it is significantly larger at 1.32 Bark ($t = 3.42$, $df = 38$, $p = 0.005$).

The average F3 values for [i] and [y] for the four groups of speakers are shown in Table 6.6, in which independent sample t-tests compare the F3 of [i] and [y] of each group.

No significant difference is found between the F3 of [i] and [y] for BNF, while the difference for BNM is marginally significant, suggesting that the BNM speakers may maintain a small distinction between [i] and [y]. However, the difference between [i] and [y] for CNF and CNM is highly significant, confirming that [i] and [y] occupy a distinct phonetic space in the Standard Mandarin of speakers in Beijing.

6.5.2 Diphthongs

Figures 6.6, 6.7, 6.8 and 6.9 display the four diphthongs in the F1/F2 plane for the two groups of speakers. As seen in the figures, Mandarin has two sets of diphthongs. [əi] and [ai] move towards a close front quality, while [əu] and [au] move towards a close back quality. The plots confirm that the speakers make a clear distinction between these four diphthongs.

Comparison of Figs. 6.6 and 6.7 indicates that there are considerable differences in trajectory length for [ai] and [au] between BNF and CNF. To be precise, the trajectory of [ai] and [au] in BNF is longer than that of [ai] and [au] in CNF, indicating a greater movement in these two diphthongs. In addition, the trajectory of [əu] in BNF is a little shorter than that of [əu] in CNF. Indeed, its length is substantially less than that of the other diphthongs, and it appears to be a monophthong instead, so it might be better represented as the monophthong [o].

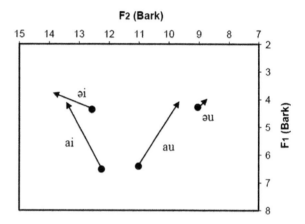

Fig. 6.6 The diphthongs of BNF

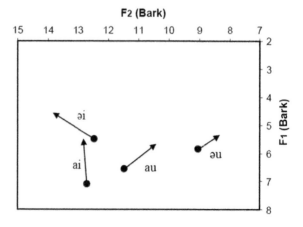

Fig. 6.7 The diphthongs of CNF

Fig. 6.8 The diphthongs of BNM

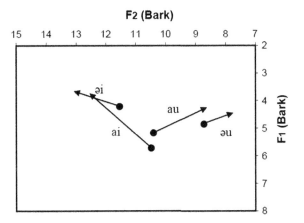

Fig. 6.9 The diphthongs of CNM

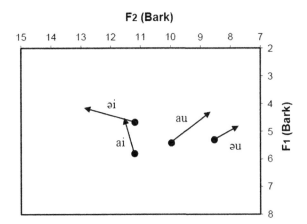

In addition, [əi] is closer in BNF than CNF, and [əu] is also closer in BNF than CNF. Both these diphthongs in CNF have consistently higher F1 frequencies, so these diphthongs of BNF have a more close quality than those of CNF.

Figures 6.8 and 6.9 display the four diphthongs in the F1/F2 plane for the two groups of male speakers. Inspection of these two figures indicates that, for the male speakers, only [ai] differs noticeably between the two varieties. Precisely, [ai] has a larger trajectory length and is more front in BNM, while any differences in trajectory length are minimal for [əi], [au] and [əu] between BNM and CNM. (The *t*-tests are presented in Table 6.7 below.) In addition, the onsets of [ai] and [au] are more central in BNM than in CNM.

Table 6.7 shows the mean length of trajectories of the four diphthongs for the four groups of speakers including an independent-samples *t*-test to compare each of the four diphthongs between Brunei speakers and Beijing speakers.

[əi] and [əu] are most similar, showing no significant differences between Brunei speakers and Beijing speakers. For both females and males, there are substantial

Table 6.7 Mean length of trajectories (standard deviation is in brackets)

		BN (Bark)	CN (Bark)	t	p
[əi]	Female	1.51 (0.53)	1.79 (0.46)	−1.24	0.231
	Male	1.67 (0.46)	1.84 (0.43)	−0.87	0.398
[ai]	Female	2.77 (0.95)	1.59 (0.64)	3.27	0.005
	Male	2.79 (0.51)	1.30 (0.41)	7.17	<0.0001
[əu]	Female	0.89 (0.55)	1.06 (0.68)	−0.60	0.556
	Male	1.25 (0.62)	1.24 (0.62)	0.04	0.968
[au]	Female	2.62 (1.02)	1.54 (0.47)	3.05	0.009
	Male	2.09 (0.57)	1.78 (0.67)	1.15	0.264

differences for [ai], confirming the visual observations in the vowel plots. The difference between BNM and CNM is highly significant ($t = 7.17$, $df = 38$, $p < 0.0001$), while the difference between BNF and CNF is not so great but is still statistically highly significant ($t = 3.27$, $df = 38$, $p = 0.005$). In addition, the trajectory length of [au] between BNF and CNF is also significantly different ($t = 3.05$, $df = 38$, $p = 0.009$), but no difference is found between BNM and CNM. All these differences confirm that there is more movement involved in the diphthongs [ai] and [au] in Brunei Mandarin.

6.6 Discussion and Conclusion

This study provides a first systematic acoustic account of the vowel system in Brunei Mandarin. For the monophthongs, Brunei speakers make a clear distinction between all the vowels except for [i]/[y] and [z]/[ʐ]. As with Taiwan Mandarin, this study indicates that the lack of distinction between [i] and [y] may be an important feature of Brunei Mandarin.

It is not clear why there is greater spectral overlap between the other monophthongs in the Beijing data than in the Brunei data, but it is possibly due to the wide distributions of speakers' first languages even though they speak Standard Mandarin most of the time. On the other hand, we should also note that, being more fluent than the Brunei speakers, the Beijing speakers were speaking faster. As a result, they might have a greater amount of coarticulation, so the vowels may have been affected by the preceding and following consonants, resulting in a wider range of values for the formants of their monophthongs.

With respect to the diphthongs, it was found that [ai] in Brunei Mandarin is characterised by a longer trajectory length, indicating greater movement from onset to offset. Although the trajectory of [əi] and [əu] is not different between Brunei Mandarin and Standard Mandarin, the quality of both [əi] and [əu] is actually much closer among females in Brunei. In addition, the trajectory of [əu] in Brunei females is short and it might best be characterised as a monophthong [o], though we should note that there is no statistical difference from the Beijing data. The greater trajectory length for [ai] may have arisen because the Brunei speakers were speaking more slowly, allowing for a more careful enunciation of their vowels. However, the closer quality of [əi] and [əu] in the Brunei data may reflect a distinct quality for these vowels.

The directionality of [i]/[y] merger is not represented in the scatter plots or from the Euclidean distance, so it remains unclear whether [i] is pronounced as [y] or vice versa. Besides, it is uncertain what causes this vowel merger to occur. Moreover, as only tertiary students were involved in this study, it is not certain whether the acoustic features identified are applicable to other groups of Brunei speakers, and it is also unclear whether the merger is a sound change in progress, or whether greater exposure to Standard Mandarin might one day lead to a separation of these vowels in Brunei. Further studies should probe these questions by including different age groups and a wider range of speakers in Brunei.

Appendix: The East Wind and the Sun (EWS) Text

东风和太阳

一天中午，白云听见东风和太阳在那儿你争我吵，都说自己的本事大。这时，从森林的草地里来了一个老公公，一个妈妈和她的女儿，还有一个小王子，全身都穿着破旧的衣服。于是，白云说，只要谁能让这四个人把衣服脱下，就算谁的本事大。然后，东风就张开口，使劲儿地吹。但是，它刮得越用力，他们四个就把衣服拉得更紧。最后，东风累了，也没什么办法了。一会儿，轮到太阳了，他们一看见阳光，热得快快把衣服脱了下来。所以，东风不得不同意，还是太阳比较强。

References

Boersma, P., & Weenink, D. (2014). Praat: Doing phonetics by computer. (Version 5.3.80). Retrieved July 10, 2014, from http://www.fon.hum.uva.nl/praat

Chao, Y.-R. (1968). *A grammar of spoken Chinese*. Berkeley, CA: University of California Press.

Chen, P. (1999). *Modern Chinese: History and sociolinguistics*. Cambridge: Cambridge University Press.

Deterding, D., & Xu, S. (2015). Acoustic investigation of neutral tone in Brunei Mandarin. In *Proceedings of the 18th International Congress of Phonetic Sciences, ICPhS XVIII*, Glasgow, 10–14 August 2015.

Duanmu, S. (2007). *The phonology of Standard Chinese* (2nd ed.). Oxford: Oxford University Press.

Dunseath, K. (1996). Aspects of language maintenance and language shift among the Chinese community in Brunei. In PW. Martin (Ed.), *Language use & language change in Brunei Darussalam*, Conrad Ożóg, and Gloria Poedjosoedarmo (pp. 280–301). Athens, OH: Ohio University Center for International Studies.

Escudero, P., Boersma, P., Rauber, A. S., & Bion, R. A. H. (2009). A cross-dialect acoustic description of vowels: Brazilian and European Portuguese. *Journal of the Acoustical Society of America, 126*(3), 1379–1393.

Flemming, E. (2002). *Auditory representations in phonology*. New York: Routledge.

Gallop, C. H. (2006). Brunei Darussalam: Language situation. In B. Keith (Ed.) *Encyclopedia of language and linguistics*, 2nd edn (Vol 1, pp. 140). Boston, MA: Elsevier.

Heeringa, W. J. (2004). *Measuring dialect pronunciation differences using Levenshtein distance*. Doctoral dissertation, University Library Groningen.

Howie, J. M. (1976). *Acoustical studies of Mandarin vowels and tones*. Cambridge: Cambridge University Press.

Huang, T., Chang, Y.-C., & Hsieh, F.-F. (2011). An acoustic analysis of central vowels in Malaysian Hokkien. In *Proceedings of the 17th International Congress of Phonetic Sciences, ICPhS XVII*, Hong Kong, 17–21 August 2011, pp. 914–917.

Jacewicz, E., Fox, R. A., & Salmons, J. (2007). Vowel space areas across dialects and gender. In *Proceedings of the 16th International Congress of Phonetic Sciences, ICPhS XVI*, Saarbrücken, 6–10 August 2007, pp. 1465–1468.

Johnson, K. (2012). *Acoustic and auditory phonetics* (3rd ed.). Oxford: Wiley-Blackwell.

Ladefoged, P., & Johnson, K. (2011). *A course in phonetics* (6th ed.). Boston, MA: Wadsworth.

Ladefoged, P., & Disner, S. F. (2012). *Vowels and consonants* (3rd ed.). Malden, MA: Wiley-Blackwell.

Lee-Kim, S.-I. (2014). Revisiting Mandarin 'apical vowels': An articulatory and acoustic study. *Journal of the International Phonetic Association, 44*(3), 261–282.

Lee, W.-S., & Zee, E. (2003). Standard Chinese (Beijing). *Journal of the International Phonetic Association, 33*(1), 109–112.

Lin, Y.-H. (2007). *The sounds of Chinese*. Cambridge: Cambridge University Press.

Maguire, W., Clark, L., & Watson, K. (2013). Introduction: what are mergers and can they be reversed? *English Language and Linguistics, 17*(2), 229–239.

Mayr, R., & Davies, H. (2011). A cross-dialect acoustic study of the monophthongs and diphthongs of Welsh. *Journal of the International Phonetic Association, 44*(1), 1–25.

McCloy, D. (2013). PhonR: R tools for phoneticians and phonologists. R package version 1.0.0. Retrived July 1, 2014, from https://github.com/drammock/phonR.

Nance, C. (2011). High back vowels in Scottish Gaelic. In *Proceedings of the 17th International Congress of Phonetic Sciences, ICPhS XVII*, Hong Kong, 17–21 August 2011, pp. 1446–1449.

Schwartz, J.-L., Beautemps, D., Abry, C., & Escudier, P. (1993). Inter-individual and cross-linguistic strategies for the production of the [i] vs. [y] contrast. *Journal of Phonetics, 21*, 411–425.

Shi, F., Peng, G., & Liu, Y. (2015). Vowel distribution in isolated and continuous speech: The case of Cantonese and Mandarin. In W. S.-Y. Wang & C. Sun (Eds.), *The Oxford handbook of Chinese linguistics*, (pp. 459–473). New York: Oxford University Press.

Wells, J. C. (1982). *Accents of English*. Cambridge: Cambridge University Press.

Wiese, R. (1997). Underspecification and the description of Chinese vowels. In J. Wang & N. Smith (Eds.), *Studies in Chinese phonology* (pp. 219–249). Berlin: Mouton de Gruyter.

Xu, S. (2014). Acoustic investigation of /t^h/ lenition in Brunei Mandarin. In *Proceedings of INTERSPEECH, 15th Annual Conference of the International Speech Communication Association*, Singapore, pp. 14–18 September 2014, 1974–1977.

Zee, E., & Lee, W.-S. (2001). *An acoustical analysis of the vowels in Beijing Mandarin* (pp. 643–646). Aalborg, Denmark: Proceedings of INTERSPEECH.

Chapter 7
Comprehension of Aspect Markers by Brunei Malay L1 Learners

Aznah Suhaimi and Noor Azam Haji-Othman

7.1 Introduction

The study of aspect markers in Brunei Malay is a relatively new area. Much of the previous research on aspect markers has been on other varieties of Malay (notably Asmah 2000; Grangé 2010, 2011). Descriptions of aspect markers in most scholarly books, for obvious reasons, have also dealt with Standard Malay—akin to the official language of Brunei Darussalam but quite unlike the spoken vernacular of its people which is what this study will be investigating.

Aspect markers may be described using various terms. Asmah (2000) talks about 'aspect verbs' in Standard Malay which she explains are used to describe various stages in the processes of action: action-in-waiting (*belum, akan*), progressive action (*sedang, tengah*), non-progressive action (*masih*), action done (*telah, sudah*) and action experienced (*pernah*). Grangé (2011) on the other hand, describes a wider range of what he terms 'preverbal aspect markers' in Indonesian: *sudah, telah, sedang, tengah, lagi, semakin, terus, masih, tetap, pernah, sempat, belum, akan* and *bakal*.

For the purpose of our study, we identified five aspect markers we believe are commonly used in Brunei Malay namely *sudah, baru, tangah, lakat, masih*. Our primary aim is to determine how these markers are understood by children learning Brunei Malay as a first language.

Aznah Suhaimi (✉) · Noor Azam Haji-Othman
FASS/UBD, Universiti Brunei Darussalam, Jalan Tungku Link,
Gadong BE1410, Brunei Darussalam
e-mail: aznah.suhaimi@ubd.edu.bn

Noor Azam Haji-Othman
e-mail: azam.othman@ubd.edu.bn

© Springer Science+Business Media Singapore 2016
Noor Azam Haji-Othman et al. (eds.), *The Use and Status of Language in Brunei Darussalam*, DOI 10.1007/978-981-10-0853-5_7

7.2 Grammatical Aspect Versus Lexical Aspect

We are working under the premise that there are two types of aspect, namely, *grammatical aspect* (sometimes referred to as *viewpoint aspect*) and *lexical aspect* (also called *situation type* or *aktionsart*). Smith (1997) explains that sentences convey these two kinds of aspectual information which are independent of each other but interact with each other to provide aspectual meaning.

Grammatical aspect or *viewpoint aspect* (Soh and Nomoto 2009; Smith 1997), as the name implies, refers to the different temporal views that can be taken with reference to the internal temporal constituency of a particular situation (Comrie 1998). It puts the focus of our attention on all or part of a situation giving it a temporal perspective (Smith 1997). In discussing grammatical aspect, we need to distinguish between *perfective aspect* and *imperfective aspect*. A basic distinction is that perfective aspect views the situation from outside, paying no particular attention to the internal structure of the situation, whereas imperfective aspect views the situation internally, allowing us to look at it backwards towards the beginning of the situation or look forward to the end of the situation and even allowing for the situation to be viewed as one that lasts through all time without an ending.

Grammatical aspect is expressed by means of morphological marking specific to that particular language and also by the use of adverbials and specific particles (Comrie 1998). With a language like Brunei Malay, which does not have a grammaticalised system for marking aspect the way, say, English does, grammatical aspect is instead conveyed using linguistic devices like aspect markers. We explain the use of aspect markers further in the next section.

Lexical aspect is the inherent temporal characteristic of verbs and predicates. It is encoded in the semantics of a language (Saeed 2009) such as whether a verb or verb phrase describes an action with inherent duration like *talk* or *sleep* or is punctual like *recognise* or *notice*. Temporal characteristics also include whether a verb has both duration and culmination like *build a house* or *paint a picture*. These inherent temporal qualities of verbs have been found to influence the acquisition of tense and aspect (Bardovi-Harlig and Reynolds 1995).

Using Vendler's (1957) framework, verbs can be categorised into four lexical aspectual classes: *statives*, *activities*, *accomplishments* and *achievements* (see Table 7.1). These four lexical aspectual classes are differentiated from each other by three semantic features, namely *punctility*, *telicity* and *dynamism*. A verb is *punctual* if it has the property of occurring at a single point or is thought of as instantaneous (e.g. *begin to sing*) and this condition is contrasted with verbs with *duration* (e.g. *sing*). *Telic* verbs are those verbs that have an end point (e.g. *sing a song*), in contrast with verbs that do not have an end point (atelic verbs e.g. *sing songs*). Finally, *dynamic* verbs (e.g. *play, read* and *talk*) are contrasted from verbs

Table 7.1 Semantic features of aspectual categories

Features	Lexical-aspectual categories			
	Statives	Activities	Accomplishments	Achievements
Punctual	–	–	–	+
Telic	–	–	+	+
Dynamic	–	+	+	+

Source Bardovi-Harlig and Reynolds (1995, p. 109)

which are stative, which is the condition of being non-dynamic (e.g. *seem, know* and *be*) (Smith 1997).

These semantic features allow us to distinguish between the four lexical aspectual classes mentioned above. The main division falls between stative and non-stative (or dynamic) verbs (activities, accomplishments and achievements). From Table 7.1, we can see that stative verbs are non-dynamic (persist over time without changing), atelic (no end point) and non-punctual. Examples of stative verbs include *have, want, know, believe* and *be*. Likewise, activity verbs are also atelic (because they have no specific end point like *I studied all week*) and non-punctual but are dynamic and have inherent duration because they involve a time span such as *sleep, swim, run* and *walk*. Verbs that are accomplishments are non-punctual (like activity verbs because they also have inherent duration) but are telic (because they have a set terminal point) and are also dynamic (Vendler 1957). *Build a house* is an accomplishment verb because it has both duration and an endpoint which is the completion of the house. Other accomplishment verbs include *make (a chair), run (to school)* and *walk (a mile)*. Achievements are different from other dynamic verbs because they are punctual in that they capture the start or end of an action and can be reduced to a point as in *reach (the summit), the game ended* and *win the race*. Achievement and accomplishment verbs can be classified together as telic verbs and are the most event-like verbs and are often known as events (Bardovi-Harlig and Reynolds 1995; Kawamura 1994).

We now provide examples of each lexical aspect using Brunei Malay. For the purpose of clarification (and especially for those readers with knowledge of Standard Malay), we would like to point out that the spelling of some words used in our examples is substantially different from the spelling of their Standard Malay equivalents. As Brunei Malay is essentially a spoken form, it does not have a standardised spelling convention. The orthographic form of the Brunei Malay words in our study therefore reflects how they would normally be pronounced by a typical Brunei Malay speaker, from the authors' perspective. (Other Brunei Malay speakers might of course have a different way of spelling some of these words.)

(1) a. Activity:
   Bini-bini   atu **bajalan** kaki.
   Female-REDUP that ba-walk   foot.
   'The girl is walking (on foot)'

   b. Accomplishment:
   Ambuk   atu **mangambil** buah dari balakang rumah kami.
   Monkey   that maN-take   fruit from behind   house us.
   'The monkey took some fruit from our backyard'

   c. Achievement:
   Kalapa   atu **gugur** dari puhunnya.
   Coconut   that fall   from tree-ENC
   'The coconut fell from the tree'

   d. Stative:
   Aku **suka** makan nasi ayam.
   I   like   eat   rice chicken
   'I like to eat chicken rice'

7.3 The Functions of Aspect Markers in Brunei Malay

In this section we describe the five aspect markers we identified in Brunei Malay: the perfective markers *sudah* and *baru* and the imperfective markers *tangah, masih* and *lakat*.

7.3.1 Perfective Aspect Markers

Two aspect markers used to denote perfective aspect in Brunei Malay are *sudah* and *baru*. These perfective aspect markers have slight nuances in how they are used and the meaning each conveys. We describe their functions in the following subsections. Most of our examples are adapted from Grangé (2010).

(i) Sudah
The most frequently used aspect marker in Brunei Malay is the perfective aspect marker *sudah*. According to Gonda (1973 as cited in Van Minde and Tjia 2002) *sudah* originates from the Sanskrit word *suddha* which means acquired or completed. In Brunei Malay, *sudah* still has the core meaning of being complete and done and can be used with all four situation types (achievements, accomplishments, activities and statives).

Svalberg and Fatimah (1998) explain that *sudah* is translatable to a perfect form or the adverb *already* in English as in (2):

(2) Ia **sudah makan**
    S/he PRF eat
    'S/he already ate' / 'She has eaten'

7 Comprehension of Aspect Markers by Brunei Malay L1 Learners   79

When used with a telic verb, it gives a resultative meaning as examples (3) and (4) show with an achievement verb and an accomplishment verb respectively:

(3) Achievement:

Syah **sudah sampai** ka puncak.
Syah PRF reach to summit
'Syah already reached the summit'/ 'Syah has reached the summit'

(4) Accomplishment:

Syah **sudah mambuat** rumah.
Syah PRF maN-make house
'Syah already built a house' / 'Syah has built a house'

With activity verbs, *sudah* can denote completion and can also be used to describe an activity that has just begun or has already begun. In (5a), it can either mean that the swimming has already reached the stage of completion or it can mean that Amyr has begun swimming. Likewise, in (5b), *sudah* describes that the water is already boiling but what is essential here is the fact that the gradual process of boiling has reached its completion. In (5c) depending on the context, *sudah* can be used to describe that Aysya has worked (and has now gone home) or that she has started to work (and is now in her office). The former use of *sudah* conveys a perfect of result while the latter provides an ingressive reading.

(5) Activity:

a. Amyr **sudah baranang**.
   Amyr PRF ba-swim
   'Amyr finished swimming' or 'Amyr already swam' / 'Amyr has started swimming'

b. Aing dalam kitil atu **sudah mandidih**.
   Water in kettle that PRF maN-boil
   'The water in the kettle is boiling' (process complete)

c. Aysya **sudah bakaraja**.
   Aysya PRF ba-work.
   'Aysya has finished working' / 'Aysya has started work'

When the perfective marker *sudah* is used with certain statives (including posture verbs), an inceptive reading may be achieved as illustrated in (6a) or it may describe a state of completion as in (6b).

(6) a. Stative (Inceptive reading):

Rumbungan pangantin laki-laki **sudah duduk** di bilik tamu.
Entourage bridegroom male-REDUP PRF sit in room guest
'The bridgeroom's entourage has sat down in the living room'

b. Stative (Completion):

Kalamarin pukul 5 atu, aku **sudah bangun**.
Yesterday time 5 that, I PRF rise
'Yesterday I was already awake at 5 o' clock'

In example (6a), an inceptive reading is achieved as *sudah* marks the beginning of the stative posture verb of 'sitting down'. In example (6b), the person who is speaking is indicating that his or her rising from bed had reached its completion at 5 am.

The aspect marker *sudah* can also be used predicatively, usually in yes/no questions to indicate that an action has been completed as in (7) below which is a conversation between two interlocutors:

(7) A: **Sudah** kau **malawat** Babu Kamsiah di hospital?
    PRF you maN-visit Aunty Kamsiah at hospital?
    'Have you visited Aunty Kamsiah at the hospital?'
    B: **Sudah**.
    PRF.
    'I have (visited her)'

(ii) Baru

The perfective marker *baru* functions similarly to the perfect in English as it is used to denote an action or event that has just occurred. In addition, it can describe a recent event the way the simple past does in English. Translations into English for temporal situations described using *baru* will normally have the adverb *just* for added emphasis of their recentness. *Baru* can be used with activities, accomplishments, achievements and statives:

(8) a. Activity:
Syah **baru babiskal**.
Syah PRF ba-bicycle
'Syah has just cycled' / 'Syah just cycled'

b. Accomplishment:
Urang atu **baru manyambalih** kambing atu.
Person that PRF maN-slaughter goat that
'That man has just slaughtered the goat' / 'That man just slaughtered the goat'

c. Achievement:
Aku **baru tajumpa** jam ku samula.
I PRF ta-find watch my again
'I have just found my watch' / 'I just found my watch'.

d. Stative:
Ia **baru ingat** yang ia minjam duit bulan lapas.
S/he PRF remember that s/he borrow money month past
'S/he has just remembered that s/he borrowed money last month' / 'S/he just remembered that s/he borrowed money last month'

As can be seen from examples (8), *baru* can be used to indicate a recent action, a recent event and a recent state.

7.3.2 Imperfective Aspect Markers

(i) Tangah
Like the English progressive, the aspect verb *tangah* is typically used with activity verbs and accomplishment verbs.

(9) Activity:

    Ia **tangah mandangar** lagu.
    S/he IMPF maN-listen music
    'S/he is listening to some music'

(10) Accomplishment:

    Ia **tangah bajalan** ka sakulah.
    S/he IMPF ba-walk to school
    'S/he is walking to school'

When *tangah* is combined with achievement verbs that describe changes of state very quickly (or instantaneous events), the sentence is ungrammatical as (11a) shows with the Malay verb *kanal* ('recognise'). However, as Smith (1997) points out, some achievement verbs allow or require preliminary stages and it is these types of verbs that can be used with *tangah* as shown in (11b–d) below:

(11) a. Achievement:

    *Mizah **tangah kanal** urang atu.
    Mizah IMPF recognise person that
    *'Mizah is recognising that person'

    b. Achievement (affected object):
    Ia **tangah mamacahkan** cawan atu.
    S/he IMPF maN-break-CAUS cup that
    'S/he is breaking a cup' (i.e. in the act of doing so)

    c. Achievement (consumed object):
    Ular atu **tangah manalan** ayam
    Snake that IMPF maN-swallow chicken
    'The snake is swallowing a chicken'

    d. Achievement (affected object):
    Ahli sakti atu **tangah mangilangkan** arnab.
    Magician that IMPF maN-disappear-CAUS rabbit
    'The magician is making the rabbit disappear'

To explain further, it seems that Malay speakers conceptualise these achievements as requiring 'preliminaries' thereby allowing an imperfective marker such as *tangah* to be used with instantaneous events. In other words, when Malay speakers use *tangah* with certain achievement verbs, attention is being focused on the external stages of the situations (i.e. *marked* imperfective viewpoints) so for examples (11b–d) above, the viewpoints are that the scenes/events are unfolding in front of the speaker.

With stative verbs, *tangah* does not seem to combine with those that describe mental states so (12a) is ungrammatical but seems to work well with personal property predicates as well as posture verbs.

(12) a. Mental state:
*Anis **tangah tau** yang jawapan atu salah.
Anis IMPF know that answer that wrong
'*Anis is knowing that the answer is wrong'

b. Personal property predicate:
Nini **tangah sanang (h)ati**.
Grandma IMPF at-ease heart
'Grandma is being happy' / 'Grandma is happy (right now)'

c. Posture verb:
Laila **tangah malimpang** di lantai.
Laila IMPF maN-lie at floor
'Laila is lying on the floor'

(ii) Lakat

Lakat is another Brunei Malay aspect marker used to convey imperfectivity for situations/actions that have not completely ended or changed and are still on-going up to a particular time (usually the time of utterance). When translated into English, sentences in Brunei Malay with *lakat* usually have the adverb *still*. With activity verbs and accomplishment verbs, *lakat* describes the continuation of an action or situation (13a–b).

(13) a. Activity:
Rania **lakat balari**.
Rania IMPF ba-run
'Rania is still running'

b. Accomplishment:
Aidan **lakat manyuci** karitanya.
Aidan IMPF maN-wash car-POSS
'Aidan is still washing his car'

Lakat does not combine well with achievement verbs since sentences with *lakat* and achievement verb constellations are ill-formed in Malay or sound odd, at best (13a–b).

(13) Achievement:

a. *Ia **lakat sampai** ke puncak.
S/he IMPF reach to summit
*'S/he is still reaching the summit'

b. ?Ia **lakat malantak** paku (sakali).
S/he IMPF maN-hammer nail (once)
?'S/he is still hammering on the nail (once)'

Interestingly, *lakat* can be used with achievement verbs that describe abilities which remain true up to the time of utterance as in the ability to *find* (14a) or the ability to *recognise* (14b). This can be seen from the use of the modal *can* in the English translations:

(14) Achievement:
    a. Ia **lakat** lagi **tacari** tampat atu
        S/he IMPF still ta-find place that
        'S/he can still find the place'

    b. Ia **lakat** lagi **kanal** jirannya atu.
        S/he IMPF still recognise neighbour-POSS that
        'S/he can still recognise her/his neighbour'

When used with stative verbs, the aspect marker *lakat* describes a state that remains unchanged as (15) shows:

(15) Stative:
    Ia **lakat** baranggah.
    S/he IMPF ba-squat
    'S/he is still squatting'

(iii) Masih

According to Sneddon et al. (2010) in Indonesian *masih* is used to describe an action that is still occurring. In Brunei Malay, the aspect verb *masih* functions in the same way as *lakat* and all the sentences above with *lakat* can be replaced with *masih* without any notable change of meaning. The only difference between *masih* and *lakat* is that *masih* is also available in Standard Malay whereas *lakat* is unique to Brunei Malay.

7.4 The Aspect Hypothesis

The aspect hypothesis is based on a theory of lexical or inherent aspect. According to the aspect hypothesis, there is a relationship between verb morphology and lexical aspect as studies have shown that children acquiring an L1 are strongly influenced by the lexical aspect of the verb to which the morphology is attached (Shirai and Kurono 1998). To provide an example from the acquisition of English, learners tend to initially mark achievement verbs with the past tense inflection and rarely do they mark stative verbs (Bardovi-Harlig 2000; Shirai and Kurono 1998). As a further example, studies have also found that children learning their L1 generally restrict the use of progressive inflection to stative verbs. These observed tendencies have been called the aspect hypothesis and its four separate predictions are as follows (Bardovi-Harlig 2000, p. 227; Shirai and Kurono 1998, p. 248; Andersen and Shirai 1996, p. 533):

1. Children first use (perfective) past marking on achievements and accomplishments, eventually extending its use to activities and statives.

2. In languages that encode the perfective/imperfective distinction, imperfective past appears later than the past, and imperfect past marking begins with statives, extending next to activities, then to accomplishments, and finally to achievements.
3. In languages that have progressive aspect, progressive marking begins with activities, then extends to accomplishments and/or achievements.
4. Progressive markings are not incorrectly overextended to statives.

To put it simply, the aspect hypothesis predicts strong associations between perfective inflections with telic verbs (achievements and accomplishments) and imperfective inflections with durative verbs (activities and statives, followed by accomplishments and achievements) during the early stages of L1 child acquisition.

Although the aspect hypothesis has been tested out with many languages, it has never been tested with Brunei Malay. Therefore, it will be interesting to find out whether its predictions can be applied to our data. The aspect hypothesis is usually described in relation to inflectional morphology and its interaction with lexical aspect. We will however extend its claims to aspect markers.

Additionally, as our study involves examining the comprehension of aspect markers, we therefore modify the claims and make the following predictions for Brunei Malay:

(a) Perfective markers will be comprehended easily/preferred with accomplishments and achievements.
(b) Imperfective markers will be comprehended easily/preferred with activities and statives.

7.5 Participants

Our participants were 108 children (54 females; 54 males). There were three age groups (5 years, 4 years, 3 years), with an equal number of 36 children in each group. The participants were from *Sekolah Seri Mulia Sarjana* in Brunei. The average age of the children was 5;7 years (age range from 5;0 to 5;11 years), 4;9 years (age range from 4;0 to 4;11 years) and 3;7 years (age range from 3;0 to 3;11 years). Participants were selected by their teachers in terms of their ability to speak Malay during class interaction. A simple questionnaire was then given to parents whose children had been selected to confirm that the language they spoke at home was indeed Brunei Malay as we were only interested in children who spoke it as a first language. We divided the 36 children in each group into two equal groups of 18 and called them group A and group B.

7.6 Materials

7.6.1 Story Sets

The children in our study were shown 16 story sets. Each set contained two stories: one depicting a perfective situation, and another depicting its imperfective counterpart as shown in Fig. 7.1a, b respectively:

Following Li's (1990) line of reasoning, the temporal contour to represent viewpoint aspect can only be 'captured' using two pictures so each 'story' was created using two pictures. The perfective story always shows the completion or the end of a given situation while the imperfective story tries to show a situation as one that is ongoing. For each set, there was always one identical picture shared by the perfective situation and the imperfective situation (e.g. the left picture in Fig. 7.1a and the right picture in Fig. 7.1b are identical).

The four lexical aspects of activity, accomplishment, achievement and stative were represented four times in the 16 story sets (4 lexical aspects × 4 = 16 story sets).

The story set had a border that was either green or red. If the perfective situation had a green border, the imperfective story would have a red border and vice-versa. The reason for this colour-coding will be made clear in Sect. 7.8.

Fig. 7.1 a A story depicting a perfective situation using the verb *makan* ('eat'). **b** A story depicting an imperfective situation using the verb *makan* ('eat')

7.6.2 Target Sentences

To match the 16 story sets, there were 16 target sentences containing verbs from either one of the four lexical aspect classes, corresponding to the lexical aspect depicted in the story.

For example, if a story set was meant to depict a lexical aspect class categorised as an activity (like Fig. 7.1a, b above), the sentence that the participants heard when the story set was shown would contain an activity verb. In the case of Fig. 7.1a, b, the sentence was 'Ali *makan* ikan' (lit. Ali eat fish) which involves the activity verb *makan* ('eat').

In addition, the target sentence would be combined with either a perfective aspect marker (*sudah* or *baru*) or an imperfective marker (*tangah, lakat* or *masih*) during the experiment, so for instance, the participant would either hear: 'Ali *sudah* (a perfective marker) makan ikan' or 'Ali *masih* (an imperfective marker) makan ikan'. The perfective markers tested were *sudah* and *baru* while the imperfective markers were *tangah, lakat* and *masih*. There was an equal number of lexical aspect versus aspect marker combinations.

As mentioned earlier, the participants were divided into two groups. The presentation of target sentences was different for children from group A and those from group B. If a child from group A received a test item that was combined with a perfective aspect marker, a child from group B would receive the same test item with an imperfective aspect marker, and vice-versa.

7.7 Task

The participants were required to match the target sentence they heard to one of the stories they were shown in any given story set. In other words, we wanted to determine their understanding of the aspect markers they heard—whether they would combine the sentence containing a particular aspect marker with a story showing the completion or end of a situation (i.e. perfective aspect) or a story showing the continuation of a situation (i.e. imperfective aspect). We also wanted to examine whether children's comprehension of aspect markers was affected by the lexical aspectual classes of the verbs being marked. Finally, we wanted to test the claims of the aspect hypothesis with L1 Brunei Malay.

7.8 Procedure

Before we began the experiment, we made sure our participant was comfortable. We made use of a stuffed animal who we introduced as Nonnie to aid our interaction with the child. We appealed to a child's nature of wanting to act grown-up by explaining that Nonnie was a little baby who did not understand things and therefore needed to observe a bigger and more grown-up person (i.e. the child). Once the child was at ease, we showed them two cards, one green and one red and asked the child to tell us what colour each card was. This was to make sure that the participant did not suffer from colour-blindness and knew the correct colours as this was crucial for participating in our experiment.

We then proceeded to explain that we were going to show the child several stories. We explained that like any other story they were familiar with, the one we were going to show them began from the far-left picture and that they were to look at the left picture first before moving on to the second one. We further explained that one story was called *cerita hijau* ('the green story') while the other was called *cerita merah* ('the red story'). Throughout our instruction, we kept alluding to the story sets as *cerita* ('stories')—this was our way of ensuring that the pictures were viewed together, as a sequence of events, and not in isolation so that the child could hopefully view the temporal sequence depicted. We explained that the child had to listen to our target sentences carefully and to match the sentence they heard with the correct story. As the stories were bordered green or red, we explained that the child should do this by choosing between 'the green story' or 'the red story' and describing their choice as such. We also explained that the child's answer would help Nonnie understand which stories were being described by the experimenter.

The experiment began by showing the story sets one after the other. The child would then hear something equivalent to the following, in Brunei Malay:

Ali (sudah/masih) eat fish. Which story is 'Ali (sudah/masih) eat fish'? The 'green story' or the 'red story'?

If a child did not respond when the target sentence was initially read out to them, we would repeat our utterances above. Once the child had made their choice, the response was recorded. We would then move on to the next test item.

7.9 The Comprehension of Brunei Malay Aspect Markers

This section looks at the comprehension of aspect markers by our participants by investigating the interaction between grammatical aspect (perfectivity vs. imperfectivity) and lexical aspect (activities, accomplishments, achievements and statives). We take participants to be unequivocal in their response if the frequency of their choice was 85 % and over. When responses fall below this value, we look at the preferred reading of the majority and discuss this.

7.9.1 The Comprehension of sudah as an Aspect Marker

We will first look at the results with *sudah*. As explained earlier, *sudah* can have several interpretations when combined with different lexical aspects. However, the most common interpretation of *sudah* is one of completion.

From Fig. 7.2, *sudah* is understood as a perfective marker with all lexical aspects, except with statives. Telic verbs (accomplishments and achievements) have the highest frequency match with perfective situations, at above 85 % for all age groups, with the exception of achievements in the 3 year old group at 83.3 %. With activities, although the 4 year old only matched the use of activities with *sudah* with perfective situations at 75 % frequency (both the 3 year olds and 5 year olds matched them with perfective situations at 91.7 % frequency), the preferred reading for all age groups is nevertheless perfective aspect.

The interesting case involves the marking of statives with *sudah*: although participants are less unequivocal in their choice of aspect, this combination seems to be mostly understood as indicating imperfective aspect. It should be explained at this point that statives in our experiment were depicted as showing the coming about of some state, i.e. an inchoative reading in the perfective story whilst the imperfective option showed a state having gone on for some duration. Therefore, *sudah* with statives seem to be understood as a continuous or ongoing state.

7.9.2 The Comprehension of baru as an Aspect Marker

In Fig. 7.3, *baru* as an aspect marker is only clearly understood as a perfective marker by all ages with achievements. Surprisingly, this perfective interpretation decreases with age—83.3 % frequency with the 3 year olds, 79.2 % with the 4 year

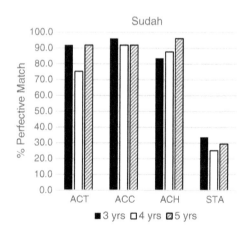

Fig. 7.2 Participants' comprehension of *sudah* as a function of lexical aspect

Fig. 7.3 Participants' comprehension of *baru* as a function of lexical aspect

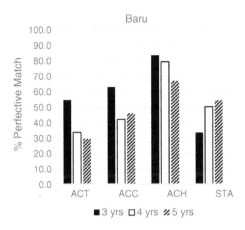

olds and 66.7 % with the 5 year olds. No clear pattern seems to emerge with the other lexical aspects.

We can however see a kind of age-effect with the way *baru* is understood in combination with activities and accomplishments. The two older groups both prefer the imperfective interpretation when *baru* is used with activities and accomplishments. Only the 3 year olds prefer an imperfective reading for these lexical aspect classes. Perhaps children are still unclear as to how *baru* should be understood because of its dual function of describing either (i) a completed event (the perfective meaning of *baru*) or (ii) a situation that has culminated but has continued relevance as it is still ongoing (the perfect meaning of *baru*). This latter meaning of *baru* is similar to the perfect in English as described by Comrie (1998).

7.9.3 The Comprehension of **tangah** as an Aspect Marker

We will now discuss the comprehension of imperfective aspect markers, turning first to the comprehension of *tangah*, as shown in Fig. 7.4. Two patterns occur at all ages: (1) durative verbs (i.e. activities and statives) obtain a higher frequency match with imperfective situations and (2) although the preference differs by only by a small margin, children seem to prefer the imperfective reading when *tangah* is combined with achievements. No real pattern can be seen with accomplishments.

7.9.4 The Comprehension of **masih** *and* **lakat** *as Aspect Markers*

As *masih* and *lakat* function the same way, we will look at their results together. For both aspect markers, as seen in Fig. 7.5, the occurrence with activities have the

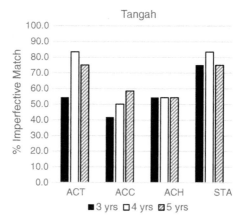

Fig. 7.4 Participants' comprehension of *tangah* as a function of lexical aspect

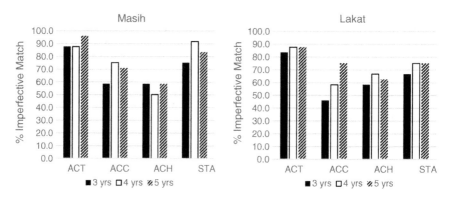

Fig. 7.5 Participants' comprehension of *masih* and *lakat* as a function of lexical aspect

highest frequency match with imperfective situations (all at above 85 % frequency). This is followed by their combination with statives (matched at 75 % frequency and above with *masih* and at 65 % frequency and above with *lakat*).

There is also a slight preference for an imperfective reading with achievements across all age groups, with the exception of the 4 year olds with the aspect marker *masih* as they are divided in their aspectual comprehension (50 % match with both imperfective and perfective situations).

Finally, with accomplishments, *masih* is clearly understood as a marker of imperfective aspect by the two older groups (75 % and 70.8 % frequency for the 4 year olds and the 5 year olds respectively). With *lakat,* only the 5 year olds seem to show a clear understanding of its function as an imperfective marker (at 75 % frequency).

7.10 Testing the Aspect Hypothesis

In this section, we evaluate the predictions of our modified version of the aspect hypothesis. We repeat our predictions here for ease of reference:

(a) Perfective markers will be comprehended easily/preferred with accomplishments and achievements.
(b) Imperfective markers will be comprehended easily/preferred with activities and statives.

From Table 7.2, we can see that the perfective marker *sudah* is marked at high frequency rates with perfective situations when the target sentences contain the telic verbs of achievement and accomplishment. Similarly, with the perfective marker *baru*, the highest frequency match with situations depicting perfective aspect is with achievements across all age groups. Therefore, it would seem that the predictions of the aspect hypothesis for perfective markers are borne out in our child L1 Brunei Malay data.

With regards to the imperfective markers, when *tangah* is given, participants comprehend it as conveying perfective aspect when combined with verbs with the

Table 7.2 Distribution of participants' perfective/imperfective choice by aspect marker

			3 years		4 years		5 years	
			PRF	IMPF	PRF	IMPF	PRF	IMPF
Perfective markers	Sudah	ACT	**91.7**	8.3	**75**	25	**91.7**	8.3
		ACC	**95.8**	4.2	**91.7**	8.3	**91.7**	8.3
		ACH	**83.3**	16.7	**87.5**	12.5	**95.8**	4.2
		STA	33.3	66.7	25	75	29.2	70.8
	Baru	ACT	**54.2**	45.8	33.3	66.7	29.2	70.8
		ACC	**62.5**	37.5	**41.7**	58.3	**45.8**	54.2
		ACH	**83.3**	16.7	**79.2**	20.8	**66.7**	33.3
		STA	33.3	66.7	**50**	50	**54.2**	45.8
Imperfective markers	Tangah	ACT	45.8	**54.2**	16.7	**83.3**	25	**75**
		ACC	58.3	**41.7**	50	50	41.7	**58.3**
		ACH	45.8	**54.2**	45.8	**54.2**	45.8	**54.2**
		STA	25	**75**	16.7	**83.3**	25	**75**
	Masih	ACT	12.5	**87.5**	12.5	**87.5**	4.2	**95.8**
		ACC	41.7	**58.3**	25	**75**	29.2	**70.8**
		ACH	41.7	**58.3**	50	50	41.7	**58.3**
		STA	25	**75**	8.3	**91.7**	16.7	**83.3**
	Lakat	ACT	16.7	**83.3**	12.5	**87.5**	12.5	**87.5**
		ACC	54.2	**45.8**	41.7	**58.3**	25	**75**
		ACH	41.7	**58.3**	33.3	**66.7**	37.5	**62.5**
		STA	33.3	**66.7**	25	**75**	25	**75**

inherent semantic feature of durativity i.e. statives and activities. With achievements and accomplishments, the results are inconclusive because the participants are rather divided in their responses.

As for the aspect markers *masih* and *lakat*, a similar pattern emerges: both markers are matched at the highest frequencies with activities, followed by statives.

The fact that all three imperfective markers are comprehended easily as describing imperfective situations when it comes to activities and statives could possibly serve as evidence to support the aspect hypothesis.

7.11 Conclusion

This chapter has presented findings of our comprehension experiment with children acquiring Brunei Malay as an L1. Our experiment aimed to determine how aspect markers in Brunei Malay are understood by its L1 learners. As a theoretical framework, we employed the two-tier classification of aspect, namely grammatical aspect and lexical aspect. In addition, we wanted to test the claims made by the aspect hypothesis whose claims have never been tested with Brunei Malay. We present a summary of our findings here.

7.11.1 *Sudah*

Sudah is understood as a perfective marker by all age groups and with all lexical aspectual classes, with the exception of statives. The result with statives points to the fact that *sudah* with statives may be better understood as describing a state that has already begun, is still ongoing and has gone on for some duration (the imperfective reading). The alternative (perfective) reading of a state that has come about or has ended seems to be rejected by all our participants.

7.11.2 *Baru*

The results with *baru* does not really provide a clear picture as to how this aspect marker is comprehended by L1 children. We believe that this may stem from the dual function of this aspect marker, that is, as a marker for a completed situation or for marking situations that have already begun but continue up to the present moment. In sum, *baru* is only matched with perfective situations across all age groups when combined with achievements.

7.11.3 Tangah

Participants seem to understand *tangah* as a marker of imperfective aspect most easily with statives, and then followed by activities. The result is divided with accomplishments and achievements as the difference between the perfective and imperfective do not differ significantly.

7.11.4 Masih/Lakat

Similar to the results with *tangah*, with the imperfective markers *masih* and *lakat*, there is a clear tendency for participants to choose imperfective aspect when presented with activities and statives. If we compare the results between these two imperfective markers, *masih* seems to be comprehended more easily than *lakat* as conveying imperfective aspect. We believe that two things could be the cause of this. Firstly, as a general observation of Brunei Malay, it seems to be the case that *lakat* is slowly being replaced by *masih* in most contexts. This is not surprising since they have been shown to function the same way. Secondly, *masih* may perhaps have more pragmatic value as it can be understood by speakers of other varieties of Malay like Malaysian Malay (Asmah 2000) or Jakarta Malay (Mintz 2002).

7.11.5 Support for the Aspect Hypothesis

We sought out to test the claims of the aspect hypothesis using our comprehension data. Our main aim for doing this was because the theory has been extensively tested with other languages. Therefore, determining whether or not it can be applied to children acquiring Brunei Malay as an L1 would be interesting. The results with both perfective and imperfective markers in Brunei Malay, namely *sudah, baru, tangah, masih* and *lakat*, seem to match the predictions made by the aspect hypothesis. Specifically, Brunei Malay perfective markers combine well (or are understood to combine well, at least) with telic verbs. In addition, with Brunei Malay imperfective markers, the preferred reading of imperfective aspect (which would be the only reading obtained by adult speakers) is obtained with durative verbs. Therefore, our data would seem to support the aspect hypothesis.

References

Andersen, R. W., & Shirai, Y. (1996). The primacy of aspect in first and second language acquisition: The Pidgin-Creole connection. In W. C. Ritchie & T. K. Bhatia (Eds.), *Handbook of second language acquisition* (pp. 527–570). New York: Academic Press.

Asmah Haji Omar. (2000). *Malay perception of time in Malay*. Kuala Lumpur: Akademi Pengajian Melayu Universiti Malaya.

Bardovi-Harlig, K. (2000). *Tense and aspect in second language acquisition: Form, meaning, and use*. Oxford: Blackwell.

Bardovi-Harlig, K., & Reynolds, D. W. (1995). The role of lexical aspect in the acquisition of tense and aspect. *TESOL Quarterly, 29*(1), 107–129.

Comrie, B. (1998). *Aspect*. Cambridge: Cambridge University Press.

Gonda, J. (1973). *Sanskrit in Indonesia*. New Delhi: International Academy of Indian Culture.

Grangé, P. (2010). Aspect and modality in Indonesian: The case of sudah, telah, pernah, sempat. *Wacana: Journal of the Humanities of Indonesia, 12*(2), 243–268.

Grangé, P. (2011). Aspect in Indonesian: Free markers versus affixed or clitic markers. In *Proceedings of the International Workshop on TAM and Evidentiality in Indonesian Languages*, 43–63.

Kawamura, M. (1994). Vendler classes and reinterpretation. *Kansas Working Papers in Linguistics, 19*(1), 53–88.

Li, P. (1990). *Aspect and aktionsart in child Mandarin*. Unpublished doctoral dissertation. Max-Planck Institute for Psycholinguistics, Nijmegen, The Netherlands.

Mintz, M. W. (2002). *An Indonesian & Malay grammar for students* (2nd ed.). Perth: Indonesian/Malay Texts and Resources.

Saeed, J. I. (2009). *Semantics* (3rd ed.). Oxford: Wiley-Blackwell.

Shirai, Y., & Kurono, A. (1998). The acquisition of tense-aspect marking in Japanese as a second language. *Language Learning, 48*(2), 245–279.

Smith, C. S. (1997). *The parameter of aspect* (2nd ed.). Dordrecht: Kluwer Academic Publisher.

Sneddon, J. N., Adelaar, A., Djenar, D. N., & Ewing, M. C. (2010). *Indonesian: A comprehensive grammar* (2nd ed.). London: Routledge.

Soh, H. L., & Nomoto, H. (2009). Progressive aspect, the verbal prefix meN-, and stative sentences in Malay. *Oceanic Linguistics, 48*(2), 148–171 (June 2009).

Svalberg, A. M.-L., & Fatimah Chuchu. (1998). Are English and Malay worlds apart? Typological distance and the learning of tense and aspect concepts. *International Journal of Applied Linguistics, 8*(1), 27–60.

Van Minde, D., & Tjia, J. (2002). Between perfect and perfective: The meaning and function of Malay Ambonese *su* and *suda*. *Bijdragen tot de Taal-, Land- en Volkenkunde* (*Journal of the Humanities and Social Sciences of Southeast Asia*), *158*(2), 283–303.

Vendler, Z. (1957). Verbs and times. *The Philosophical Review, 66*(2), 143–160.

Part III
Language Choice

Chapter 8
The Attitudes of University Students Towards Their Native and Non-native English Speaking Lecturers in Brunei

Debbie G.E. Ho

8.1 Introduction

Despite the observation that many language classrooms around the world today are taught by non-native English speaker teachers, native English speakers often still express surprise when they encounter a non-native English speaker teacher in the language classroom. At a language teaching conference some years back, a native English speaker came up to me after my presentation and said that he found the presentation to be surprisingly enlightening, especially since it was from a non-native speaker of English. I believe that experiences such as this are not uncommon for non-native teachers of English in many places. There appears to be a lack of confidence in non-native English speaker teachers and language teaching, and this has led many such teachers to start questioning their credibility as language teachers, despite the years of training and teaching experience.

It also leads me to ponder on the notions of 'native speaker' and 'non-native speaker', and how they affect non-native educators in educational institutions. How do my students perceive me, a non-native speaker of English, as a lecturer in the English language and linguistics programme in a local university? This question was the motivating factor behind this study. Furthermore, studies that explore the differences between native speaker and non-native speaker teachers of English have been scarce (Braine 1999; Llurda 2009), and this is particularly true for the ESL (English as a Second Language) context. Given the fact that more and more, as non-native English speaking teachers and lecturers are being employed as language teachers in both English and non-English speaking countries, contribution to this pool of research literature should be encouraged.

D.G.E. Ho (✉)
FASS/UBD, Universiti Brunei Darussalam, Jalan Tungku Link,
Gadong BE1410, Brunei Darussalam
e-mail: debbie.guan@ubd.edu.bn

This study attempts to explore ESL undergraduate students' perceptions about their native and non-native English speaker lecturers in a local university. It is hoped that such a study will not only help contribute to the pool of research literature on the subject, but also provide important insights into the native speaker and non-native speaker distinction. Working in a university which hires both native and non-native English speaking lecturers and with a largely ESL (English as Second Language) student population, I was very interested in finding out how students perceive their native and non-native English speaking lecturers in terms of academic knowledge and other qualities such as friendliness and acting as a role model via the variety of English used. It is noted that there have been arguments about the usefulness of using terms such as native and non-native speaker, and so we need to first consider whether the native/non-native speaker dichotomy is still viable today among researchers and writers of applied linguistics and language teaching.

8.1.1 The Pervasive Influence of the Native/Non-native Speaker Distinction in Language Teaching

Despite arguments in the field of applied linguistics advocating the abandonment of any reference to 'native speaker' or 'non-native speaker' because of positive connotations attached to the former and negative perceptions of the latter (Jenkins 2009; Matsuda 2003; Davies 1991, 2003; Piller 2002; Kachru 1992; Paikeday 1985), the native/non-native speaker dichotomy is still very much alive in English language teaching today. There is the implicit assumption that native speakers are ideal for promoting articulate communication, and that they should naturally be preferred over non-native speaker teachers (Llurda 2009). In the language teaching context, it is quite clear that native speaker teachers are assumed to be worth more than non-native speaker teachers, and only non-native speakers with native-like proficiency can aspire to enjoy some kind of prestige in the profession.

When asked in an interview to comment on the discrimination against non-native English speakers in job advertisements that required specifically native English speaker teachers, Kirkpatrick (2009) argued that hiring a person based on his/her linguistic birthright or colour of skin is highly discriminatory. But he also claims that non-native speakers are prejudiced against non-native speaker teachers, despite the fact that the native speaker model is less relevant in today's world where value is placed more on ability to communicate with other second language users (2010).

Medgyes (1992, 1994) brought the issue into the open by highlighting non-native speakers of English and thus challenging assumptions about who was actually worth more as a teacher. For the first time, attention was given to the non-native speaker teacher, and in a sense, some sort of visibility to the non-native speaker in the arena of language teaching which had been absent up until then. It has to be noted that research on native/non-native speaker teachers is still lacking in many aspects. This study attempts to address this gap in the research literature and hopefully provide further insights into the pool of current research.

It is argued that the purpose of highlighting non-native English speaking teachers is not to show up their inadequacy or inferior quality but to both appreciate non-native speakers without degrading native speakers. According to Derwing and Munro (2005), the issue should not be about whether a teacher is a native or non-native speaker, but about whether s/he is pedagogically trained and has proficient knowledge of the language being taught.

8.1.2 Perceptions of Native and Non-native English Speaking Teachers by Educators and Students

According to Braine (1999), empirical studies that explore the differences between native and non-native teachers of English have been scarce. In native English speaker contexts, students' perceptions of non-native speaker teachers have tended to be negative. The assumption that an English teacher has to be a native speaker of English to be able to teach may be something non-native educators in inner circle countries come up against repeatedly. Thomas (1999) describes how her native English speaking students in the United States found it difficult to accept her as the English teacher in their classes. She went on to say that she felt, as did many of her non-native English teachers, like 'strangers on the periphery' (p. 5). They were not taken seriously as professionals. Furthermore, and similar to the earlier claim by Kirkpatrick (2010), discrimination may also come from non-native English speaking students, many of whom claim that they did not spend a lot of money to come to the US to be taught by non-native lecturers, a sentiment echoed by school principals in the UK (Medgyes 1994).

Medgyes (1994) circulated a questionnaire to a few hundred native and non-native speaker teachers in both English and non-English speaking countries and found that teachers perceive differences between the two groups of speakers in terms of linguistic competence and sensitiveness to students' needs. The common perception is that, in terms of linguistic competence, the non-native teacher is viewed negatively. This has resulted in low self-esteem among non-native English speaking teaching professionals. These teachers were, however, perceived to be more sensitive to students' difficulties and were more able to estimate their students' potential in learning compared to their English native speaking counterparts.

Perhaps the problem lies with the non-native speakers themselves. According to Llurda (2004), many non-native speaker teachers themselves are still very much anchored to the old native-speaker dominated framework of teaching which adheres to British and American norms, even though they themselves have adequate levels of language proficiency to perform their tasks. They carry with them the mentality that, despite their ability to be very good language teachers, they are still not good enough unless they exhibit native speaker norms, which often proves to be a difficult thing to do. Jenkins (2007) pointed out that the standard native speaker English ideology is still very powerful today as both native and non-native English speakers see it as the language of success.

Cheung and Braine (2007) carried out a study to gauge the attitudes of university students towards their non-native speaker English teachers in Hong Kong. Overall, students have positive attitudes towards these teachers and perceive them as being more sensitive to student needs, efficient, aware of student language problems, able to code-switch but very reliant on textbooks. In a sense, his study supports Medgyes' (1994) findings. The majority of the students also claimed that both groups are successful in their teaching. They did not think that native English speaker lecturers were in any way superior to their non-native counterpart. These students put success in teaching down to the lecturer being able to deliver the goals of a programme and to his/her individual personality and skills as a teacher.

In a joint study carried out on student viewpoints about their native and non-native English language teachers in Vietnam and Japan (Walkinson and Oanh 2014), it was found that students perceived their native English teachers to be good models of pronunciation and correct language use, but poor at teaching grammar. They also felt uncomfortable around these teachers due to a clash of cultures. On the other hand, students felt that their local non-native English speaking teachers were good at teaching grammar and were able to code-switch when students encounter problems in their language learning. Also these teachers have better rapport with their students because of a shared culture.

8.1.3 Perceptions of Native and Non-native Educators in the Brunei Context

In Brunei (see Chap. 1 for a detailed description), English plays a vital role in the school system and is the medium of instruction at the secondary and tertiary levels of education. Most, if not all, young Bruneians are bilingual in Malay and English. Moreover, Brunei schools employ a substantial number of native English speaker teachers from the inner circle countries such as the UK, Australia and New Zealand, specifically to teach the English language. The language curriculum in the country has all along been based on standard British English (Jones 2007, 2009). While it is not clear if there exists a colloquial variety of English in Brunei equal to that of Singlish for Singapore, many Bruneians speak a standard form of Brunei English based on native speaker grammar and vocabulary but with a local accent.

The main university in the country offers English medium programmes taught by lecturers from native and non-native English speaking countries. The bulk of the student population is made up of local students who are from non-native English speaking homes.

The first study directly related to this topic was carried out some twenty years ago (Cane and Hjh Rosnah 1996). Since then there have been two other studies on non-native teachers in Brunei, including at the university, that are relevant to the present study. Noor Azam (2000) conducted a nationwide survey of non-native teachers which found that Bruneian teachers saw themselves performing all three roles identified by Kirkpatrick (1998): as providers of the regional model of English; as providers of learner models; and as teachers who can maximise linguistic resources in the classroom. The study also found that Bruneian teachers too experienced the problems faced by nonnative teachers in the USA, but:

> these problems do not occur in isolation; rather they are interrelated: lack of support and language inadequacy lead to feelings of isolation and powerlessness… There is an irony in that while some Bruneian teachers are uncomfortable with the fact that they do not have native command of the English language, it is this very ability to speak the language well enough alongside their mother tongue that they draw their confidence and pride from (Noor Azam 2000, p. 47).

In a study of codeswitching practices among nonnative Bruneian teachers at the university, Noor Azam et al. (2014) found that the teachers were perceived favourably by the students because they felt they could relate to them more easily:

> The students, it would seem, feel encouraged to [codeswitch] because they share the same L1 as the teacher, or they are fully aware of the fact that they and their teachers are 'Cultural natives'—with shared views of how and to what extent [codeswitching] can be used in the Bruneian classroom (Noor Azam et al. 2014, p. 155).

Both these studies found that a Bruneian model of English seemed to be preferred by both the students and the teachers. These studies add to the findings of Cane and Hjh Rosnah (1996) on which this present study is based.

The study by Cane and Hjh Rosnah (1996) was a small study aimed at finding out which variety of English trainee teachers would model themselves after in their classrooms. Among other things, students were asked to assess their native and non-native lecturers and their varieties of English in terms of comprehensibility, social prestige, friendliness and academic knowledge. Half the students claimed that they found the native English speaker variety to be easiest to understand because they were more familiar with the accent. The majority of them said that they would use standard Brunei English in their classroom where, apart from accent, grammar and vocabulary would be based on the native English speaker variety. Standard Brunei English was also perceived to have the highest social prestige by 92 % of the students, with the lowest social prestige given to the colloquial variety. Students also felt most comfortable with the non-native English speaking lecturers due to cultural similarity and ease of interaction. In terms of academic knowledge, 72 % of the students said that they preferred to have native English speaker lecturers in their linguistics classes. They thought that these lecturers could clearly present their lectures, they spoke in a style that the students could understand, and that they were more knowledgeable compared to the non-native English speaking lecturers. It is not clear if student perceptions today would be consistent with the findings then. The current study revisits this issue.

8.2 Purpose and Research Questions

The purpose of this study is to gauge the perceptions of university students on two aspects of the native/non-native speaker distinction—their attitudes towards (i) the different varieties of English used by their lecturers and (ii) their native and non-native English speaking lecturers based on a range of professional qualities. The language varieties addressed here are of three types: the native English variety spoken by people from the inner circle countries such as the UK, USA, Australia and so forth; the non-native standard English variety that has native English speaker grammar and vocabulary but is spoken with a local accent; and the non-native colloquial variety that has non-standard grammar, vocabulary and pronunciation. All students were from the second and fourth year English language programmes in the university.

Based on the purpose of the study, the following questions are posited:

(i) Which variety of English do students perceive as having the highest social prestige?
(ii) Which variety of English do students perceive to be more intelligible?
(iii) Which variety of English would students model themselves after if they were lecturers?
(iv) Which group of lecturers do students perceive to have more academic knowledge?
(v) Which group of lecturers do students perceive to be more friendly and approachable?

8.3 Methodology

8.3.1 Sample

The sample for the study consists of 55 male and female second, third and fourth year undergraduate students from the English medium programmes such as English Language and Linguistics and Professional Communication and the Media. It was thought that these students were the most appropriate group as they have all been taught or are currently being taught by both native (NSE) and non-native English speaking (NNSE) lecturers. First-year students were not included as they may not have been adequately exposed to the lecturing practices at tertiary level. Moreover, all 55 students are ESL speakers from Brunei and the surrounding regions such as Malaysia and Indonesia.

8.3.2 Data Collection

A questionnaire (see Appendix 1) was distributed to all fifty-five students to complete. The semi-structured questionnaire consists of 12 items, each of which requires the respondents to indicate the appropriate choice and then state a reason(s) for their choice. Included among the items is a Likert scale that requires students to rank the varieties of English on a scale of social prestige. All specialist terms were clearly defined in the questionnaire and students were allowed to ask the questionnaire administrator to explain the instructions if need be. A pilot study was carried out with a small group of students to gauge the clarity of the questionnaire items. Based on the feedback from these students, revisions were made to the questionnaire before distributing it to the actual respondents.

Following from the questionnaire, focus group interviews (see Appendix 2 for interview guide) were conducted with three groups of student volunteers from those who participated in the questionnaire. Third year students were not included in the focus group interviews as all were out doing their internships in the community or studying in universities abroad at the time of the interviews. Focus group interviews have been increasingly employed in the social sciences (Krueger and Casey 2000; Morgan 1988; Barbour and Kitzinger 1999) and more recently in language education (Ho 2012). The focus group interview was preferred over other types of interview here because it was thought to be the most appropriate method to collect rich, spontaneous and varied responses to questions and issues about a complex topic. Moreover, students were more likely to give "natural" responses in an interactive group discussion. In this study, all were mixed-gender groups. Two focus groups consisted of six students while one had five students. Each interview lasted between 35 and 40 min and was audio-recorded. The interviews were facilitated by the researcher as moderator and were recorded using a voice recorder and then transcribed and described. Each interview lasted between 30–35 min.

8.3.3 Data Analysis

Data from the questionnaire were subjected to a frequency count and the results were tabulated. Transcription from the focus group interviews were subjected to data indexing following Frankland and Bloor (1999). An analytic induction method of analysis, via data indexing, was used to analyse and interpret the transcribed interview data. It was thought that data indexing makes it possible for including, rather than excluding, all possible interpretations of data at the initial stages of analysis. The researcher first read through each interview transcript as a whole. She then re-read the transcript, attaching index-code words or phrases that relate to the content of the different parts of the transcript. The index-codes were quite broad and general at the start and became more defined and specific. New index codes emerged in the later parts of the transcript. These index codes were then collated, categorised and interpreted. Thus categories were not pre-determined but emerged from the data itself. A final interpretation was arrived at only after comparing each coded data item with the total number of codes over the entire transcript.

8.4 Results

8.4.1 Results of the Questionnaire

The results of the questionnaire items are categorised under four main categories that correspond to the research questions posited at the beginning of this paper—to gather student perceptions about the NSE and NNSE varieties, their attitudes towards their NSE and NNSE lecturers, and their rapport with their NSE and NNSE lecturers. Figure 8.1 shows the students' perceptions of the NSE and NNSE varieties in terms of intelligibility. NSE refers to native speakers of English, while NNSE refers to non-native speakers of English. Furthermore, NNSE varieties are divided into two types: NNSE1 which has non-standard native English speaker accent but with NSE grammar and vocabulary, and NNSE2 which has non-standard native English speaker accent, grammar and vocabulary.

When asked which variety they found easiest to understand, 17 (31 %) out of a total of 55 respondents claimed that they found the NNSE1 variety to be easiest to understand. This is the variety with the non-NSE accent, but with standard grammar and vocabulary. The main reasons have to do with familiar accent and a shared speaking manner:

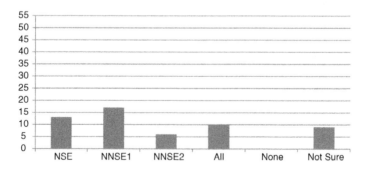

Fig. 8.1 Responses to: 'The group of lecturers I find easiest to understand'

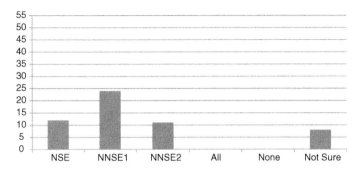

Fig. 8.2 Responses to: 'The variety of English I would prefer to speak if I had a choice'

(1) *"their English is without thick accent"* [C12]
(2) *"their accents are easier to understand"* [C16]
(3) *"it is because NNSE1 tends to speak using simple and understandable English"* [C35]
(4) *"I guess the NNSE1 are people from Asian regions and speak in the same way. it's different with how NSE can talk too fast for my pace to understand"* [C44]

From the reasons given, it is quite clear that students are more comfortable with the NNSE1 accent as many of the NNSE1 lecturers come from the surrounding countries and therefore speak in similar ways to these students. It is interesting to note that a similar question posed to students some 20 years ago yielded a different result (Cane and Hjh Rosnah 1996). At that time, students thought the NSE variety the easiest to understand for similar reasons given above: that they were familiar with the NSE accent, that the NSE lecturers tended to use simple grammar and vocabulary and that the NSE lecturers spoke slowly.

It was also found that students have positive attitudes towards the NNSE varieties, particularly the NNSE1 variety (see Fig. 8.2). Although more than half of the students (64 %) thought the NSE/variety to have the highest social prestige (see Fig. 8.3), 69 % claim that they would use the NNSE1 as a model if they were a lecturer, and 47 % claim that they prefer to speak the NNSE1 variety if they had a choice:

(5) *"I would like to speak non-standard English accent but using correct grammar and vocabulary as the NSE"* [C24]
(6) *"I like to keep my accent, don't feel like I have to sound like a native speaker"* [C06]
(7) *"I do not see the need to try and be like NSE"* [C38]
(8) *"NNSE1, because I'm non-native speaker of English language"* [C49]

It appears that students want to express and maintain their local identity via their use of English, that they are non-native English speakers. However, the examples above also showed that, apart from accent, they want to be considered NSE when it

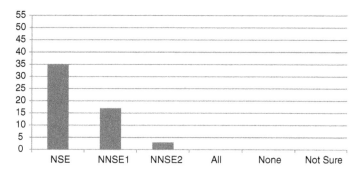

Fig. 8.3 Responses to: 'The variety of English I think that has the highest social prestige'

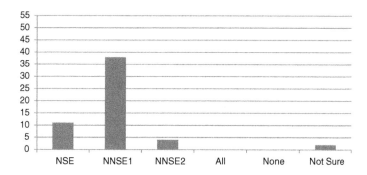

Fig. 8.4 Responses to: 'The variety I would model myself after if I was a lecturer or teacher'

comes to grammar usage and vocabulary. This is evident in Figs. 8.2, 8.3 and 8.4 where NNSE2 scored lowest in terms of role model, social prestige and language choice.

It is noted, however, that the NNSE variety these students aspire to model themselves after is the standard, non-native variety of English where, apart from accent, the grammar and vocabulary adhere to the NSE variety. From the chart, only 5 % of the students rated the NNSE2 variety as prestigious, while only 7 % claim they would use it as model for teaching and only 20 % say they would use it if given a choice. In the focus group interviews following the questionnaire, students also rated NNSE2 lowly as a model to use in the classroom. They have negative attitudes towards the use of colloquial English because "*I think that if you like speak locally er. it's like what kind of lecturer you are*" (FG3:S3).

However, their positive attitudes towards the NNSE1 variety appear not to extend towards NNES lecturers in the classroom. Figures 8.5, 8.6 and 8.7 present results of students' attitudes towards their NSE and NNSE lecturers. Although 47 % of the students felt that NNSE lecturers should use the NNSE1 variety in the classroom, 67 % of them claimed that they prefer a NSE lecturer in their English

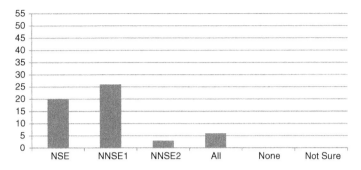

Fig. 8.5 Responses to: 'The variety of English I think NNES lecturers should speak in the classroom'

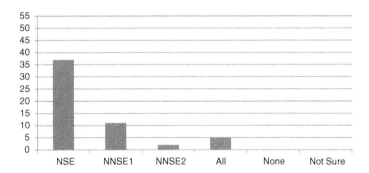

Fig. 8.6 Responses to: 'The lecturer I would prefer in my English language proficiency course'

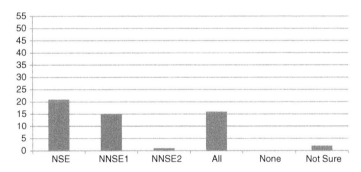

Fig. 8.7 Responses to: 'The group of lecturers that I think should be found more in the English Department and Language Centre'

language proficiency courses and 38 % of them think there should be more NSE lecturers in the English department and the Language Centre. This finding concurs with that found by Cane and Hjh Rosnah (1996).

Apparently, the reasons offered for their preference for NSE lecturers in the classroom have to do with the assumption that these lecturers have better knowledge of the grammar and are highly accurate language users, a sentiment echoed by students in the United States (Thomas 1999). The following are some reasons offered by the questionnaire respondents:

(9) *"(NSE) because I want to be as accurate as possible"* [C08]
(10) *"I believed most of them (NSE) would know their own language better... [C07]*
(11) *"they presumably the most knowledgeable in grammar and other stuff"* [C06]
(12) *"...because the foundation of correct English speaking comes from them"* [C48]
(13) *"it's preferable and favourable to have more NSE because they are more native"* [C42]
(14) *"I can improve my English language from them"* [C43]

The motivation here is more extrinsic than intrinsic, in the sense that their preference was based more on improving their English skills than a desire to assimilate the target language culture. Therefore, in a way, the results show not so much positive or negative attitudes towards both groups of lecturers but the desire for improving their standard of English.

With regard to the last category on lecturer-student rapport, Figs. 8.8, 8.9, 8.10 and 8.11 show that when it comes to identifying with their lecturers, students feel that they identify more positively with their NNSE1 lecturers. Twenty out of 55 students (36 %) claim that they relate better with their NNSE1 lecturers and 35 % claim they feel more comfortable with their NNSE1 lecturers.

The reasons given for their choice appear to be related to their familiarity with the NNSE1 variety and also a shared culture:

(15) *"they're (NNSE) the most like me"* [C06]
(16) *"...sense of belonging..."* [C18]
(17) *"I tend to understand their accent more and they sound familiar"* [C02]

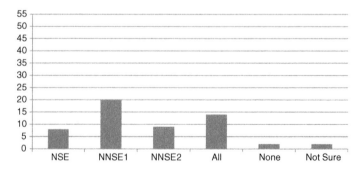

Fig. 8.8 Responses to: 'The group of lecturers I can relate to or identify with more easily'

8 The Attitudes of University Students Towards Their Native ... 109

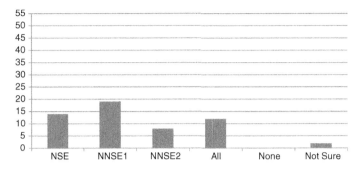

Fig. 8.9 Responses to: 'The group of lecturers I feel most comfortable with in the classroom'

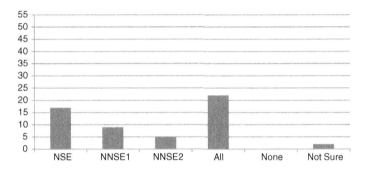

Fig. 8.10 Responses to: 'The group of lecturers that I find to be more helpful generally'

In terms of friendliness, 40 % of the students said that they find all their lecturers to be friendly, regardless of what variety of English they speak, and 38 % of them say they go to all both the NSE and NNSE lecturers for academic advice. Apparently, students do not equate knowledge with the variety of language spoken. This is evident in their reasons provided:

(18) *"they all are the same—can rely on" [C30]*
(19) *"any lecturer who can help me understand would be fine with me" [C01]*
(20) *"depending on how well the lecturer handle my academic problem" [C51]*
(21) *"I intend to look for help and advice from any lecturers who are best in their fields, regardless their capability to speak English" [C42]*

These findings do not appear to support that found by Cane and Hjh Rosnah (1996), who reported that students thought their NSE lecturers to be both more friendly and approachable. They were also able to identify more positively with their NSE lecturers compared to the NNSE lecturers.

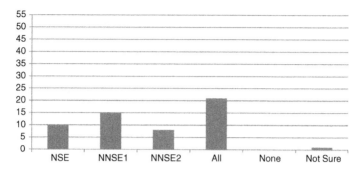

Fig. 8.11 Responses to: 'The group of lecturers I go to if I have an academic problem'

To summarise, the results from the questionnaire show that the majority of students found the NNSE1 variety to be the easiest to understand because they are familiar with the accent and the way their NNSE lecturers speak, particularly those from the surrounding regions. And although a high percentage of the student respondents claim that the NSE variety has the highest social prestige, they would prefer to speak the NNSE1 variety, for which apart from the accent, the grammar and vocabulary are of the NSE variety. This is because they wish to express their local identity through the way they speak. Furthermore, while these students claim that they would use the NNSE1 variety as a model if they became lecturers, only a very small percentage say they would use the NNSE2 variety, both in the classroom and if given a choice. Apparently, they rated the NNSE2 variety lowest in terms of prestige. And despite students' positive attitudes towards the NNSE1 variety, a higher number of them say that they prefer a NSE lecturer in their English language courses and that there should be more NSE lecturers in the English language and linguistics department, the main reason being that the NSE lecturer presents a model for them to attain a high proficiency in English for their future careers. When students were asked which group of lecturers they feel most comfortable with, and the group they can identify most with, a higher number of student respondents claim that they relate better to their NNSE lecturers. However, in terms of friendliness, a high percentage of respondents say that they found both groups to be equally friendly. As for which group of lecturers they would go to for academic advice, these students claim that they would go to any lecturer who they think can help them with an academic problem, regardless of the variety of English they speak. Thus, students do not actually equate language variety with friendliness and academic knowledge. Finally, the results from the questionnaire did not support the findings of a similar study by Cane and Hjh Rosnah (1996) in a number of significant areas, an indication that perhaps student attitudes towards the NSE and NNSE varieties and lecturers have changed over the years.

8.4.2 Results of the Student Focus Group Interviews

Following from the questionnaire, three student focus group interviews were conducted to provide deeper insights into students' perceptions of their NSE and NNSE lecturers. Apart from probing into questions raised in the questionnaire findings, the interviews also provided a platform for students to talk freely about the professional qualities of the two groups of lecturers. These interviews were carried out with students in their second and fourth years of undergraduate study. All are in English medium programmes in the Faculty of Arts and Social Sciences, and all have been and are being taught by both NSE and NNSE lecturers. Focus Group 1 (henceforth FG1) consists of five fourth-year undergraduates. Focus Group 2 (henceforth FG2) consists of six second year undergraduates and Focus Group 3 (henceforth FG3) consists of six fourth year undergraduates.

Data from the interviews covered six areas of student attitudes towards the NSE and NNSE varieties and the two groups of lecturers: intelligibility, prestige, knowledge, intelligence, friendliness and desired role model in the classroom. The results will be via excerpts of data taken from the interview transcripts based on the following transcription conventions

Transcription conventions	
S1	Individual student
SS	Students
M	Moderator
[	Overlap
(.)	Short pause
…	Longer pause
?	Question
[nod]	Non-verbal behaviour
(non-native)	Extra information

On the subject of intelligibility of their NSE and NNSE lecturers, all three focus groups agree that their NNSE lecturers are less intelligible because of their strong accent. However, from the examples below, it appears that students may not find all NNSE lecturers difficult to understand, but only those from some countries.

(22)   S3   …*sometimes I do have problems (.) like with mainland Chinese accent*   (FG3)
                (.) a bit difficult to understand
      S1   *their accent is super strong*
      S3   *yah*

(23)   S2   …*some lecturers are actually (.) when they speak for example an*   (FG2)
                African native speaker (.) they're they're really speaking in a faster (.)
                faster pace than English but then er it actually makes (.) when they

speak English (.) actually makes (.) they speak English (inaudible) so sometimes they're hard to catch

(24) S3 *I think the reason why is because the non-native English speakers,* (FG2)
when they speak English (.) their structure (.) of their structure of English is sort of like (.) Malay [laughs] like for instance for native speakers they go from a to b um in Malay there's no structure (.) like a z and then like so (.) oh (.) like you need to have a lot of background knowledge to understand them

Students in FG1 and FG2 claim that NNSE lecturers talk too fast and those in FG2 and FG3 said they found NNSE lecturers lacking in confidence when speaking in English. Of the three groups, FG2 appears to be most critical of NNSE lecturers when it comes to intelligibility.

With regard to the topic of which variety the students perceive to be more prestigious, all three groups agree that the NSE variety is more prestigious:

(25) S1 *I think I personally have a very very stereotypical point of view (.) especially in linguistics when I see a native speaker teaching a module (.) I'll be more (...) more*
      S3 *more inclined*
      M   *you mean more attentive*
      S1 *I think so...I think it comes down to the whole prestigious (.) even though [inaudible] I think everyone has it in you (.) almost*
      S4 *I don't know (.) I'm more inclined to the native English speakers (.) I* (FG1)
don't know (...) to me they're easier to understand (.)

(26) S3 *I think it's (their prestige) got to do with their culture (.) where they* (FG2)
come from (.) like Australia (.) it's like (.) cos I lived in Australia for 3 years...

However, there is also the perception among the students in two of the focus groups that prestige depends not so much on language variety but on the status and qualifications of the speakers of that variety. Moreover, as students in FG3 pointed out, any standard English is prestigious, regardless of variety:

(27) S1 *it's the first language (.) not exactly (.) just because you speak (.) you're a first language speaker of English doesn't mean you're all (.) I mean (.) just because they come from a culture where English is their mother tongue (.) um (.) it's like we all (.) it's their mother tongue (.) it's their language and we (.) we (.) can speak like them (.)*

		we think that we're as good as them (.) it's always the case (.) like when (.) yeah (.) it's like standard for us...	
	S3	*but as time goes on (.) you (.) you have to accept that accent or no accent (.) you're still (.) as long as you're able to (.) if you're able to speak it in British pronunciation or Bruneian*	
	M	*so (.) so (.) you don't think that it is prestigious (.) it is like any other variety*	
	S3	*I think the prestige is not related to the speakers ...*	
	S4	*other varieties have prestige as well*	(FG3)

When asked which group of lecturers students perceive to be more knowledgeable, all three groups claim that there is no relationship between knowledge and language variety spoken. Students feel that the basis for knowledge lies with factors such as the qualifications and subject expertise of the lecturers, regardless of which language variety they speak:

(28)	S2	*I think for me (.) depends on the subject (.) cos (.) most (.) some subjects are open for discussion...*	
	S4	*the thing is like based on experience (.) usually they (NNEs) [explain*	
	S2	*[usually at the*	
		end of the class (.) whether we understand or not	
	M	*so you would not equate knowledge with linguistic competence*	
	SS	*no*	(FG2)
(29)	S4	*I don't think a language defines [er*	
	S1	*[yeah*	
	S4	*er knowledge (.) because you could be a non-native speaker (.) could be more knowledgeable than a native speaker (.) but just because it's the language (.) not being able to express themselves...*	(FG3)
(30)	S4	*it depends on individual (.) where they got their Ph.D.*	(FG3)
(31)	S1	*I think it's not very consistent though (.) based on experience (.) hard to measure [laugh] some (NNEs) are much more knowledgeable (.) depending on how they teach (.) again...*	
	M	*what about the rest of you? What do you think?*	
	S3	*I think in terms of knowledge, they're the same (.) no difference*	(FG1)

In terms of friendliness, all three groups perceive their NNSE lecturers to be less open, friendly and approachable, especially the local lecturers. This finding does not support Braine's (1999) findings in a similar study carried out among non-native English speaking students with regard to the two groups of lecturers. The reasons given in this study are as follows:

(32)	S1	it comes down to the culture (.) because the culture (.) here (.) here (.) is more enclosed...they try not to be so... yeah (.) they're conservative here (.) compared to ... the thing is (.) they (NEs) are more approachable... in my opinion	
	S3	yes (.) they seem more approachable	(FG1)
(33)	S3	specifically locals	
	M	specifically locals?	
	S3	yeah (.) teachers from China or Japan (.) like (.) um (name of lecturer) I think she's more friendlier compared to the locals	(FG1)
(34)	S3	we have a lot of lecturers who are native speakers (.) they tend to be more friendly and open like somehow (.) yah	
	S2	yah (.) I remember once I was in my LE class (.) it was easier to talk to the lecturer then say in the biology class where there's a non - native English speaker	
	S4	I think one factor is they're (NEs) in a totally foreign country and so that I think they're open to students because it (.) it's non-native (.) non-native (.) they tend to know the minds of the students (.) so they tend to (.) I don't know (.) somewhat somewhat familiar (.) they don't really need to say as much	
	S3	the native speakers (.) they tend to talk to us more because they want to know us	
	S2	we probably need to think about the culture	(FG2)
(35)	S1	depends on the background (.) if it's Malay lecturers (.) frankly speaking (.) they should not speak (.) they're not very approachable to us (.) take for example (name of lecturer) (.) is he friendly?	
	SS	ooh! [laugh]	
	S1	sorry (.) like in terms of friendliness (.) his English (.) I mean ... yeah (.) he's a non-native speaker (.) he uses English	
	M	you think he's friendly enough?	
	SS	[laugh]	(FG3)

However, even though these students perceive the local lecturers to be less friendly, they claimed that they would go to both groups for academic help. In other words, they do not favour one group over another when it comes to academic knowledge:

(36) S1 *if you ask me to choose (.) I don't think it matters (.) it can be anyone though (.)*
    S5 *each has their own expertise*
    S2 *it depends on what you're looking for (.) like (.) if you're asking well (.) linguistics (.) we might just go to you (a non-native speaker of English) (.) or others we know*
    S1 *there's no ...*
    SS *na (.) na* (FG3)

(37) S3 *if I have an academic problem it would be (.) would be both*
    SS *yah*
    S3 *depends on who holds the position* (FG2)

Finally, students were asked which variety of English they would use if they were lecturers in the university. All three groups said they would use standard Brunei English, a similar finding to the questionnaire responses. By that they mean a variety which has the standard native English speaker grammar and vocabulary but with a local accent and pronunciation. Reasons given for this preference have to do with keeping the local identity and that trying to sound British or American may be tedious and unnatural:

(38) S3 *I'll use the standard*
    S1 *yeah (.) I'll use the standard*
    SS *non-native speaker standard*
    M *why?*
    S1 *it's easier*
    S6 *yeah (.) we won't like to speak like someone else* (FG3)

(39) S2 *yes (.) standard English. I mean don't have to follow other people's accent (.) er (.) we have our own identity (.) our own ways as Bruneians (.) so...* (FG1)

Students in FG1 and FG3, however, would not use colloquial English in the classroom. They regard a colloquial English speaker as unintelligent: *"I think if a lecturer teaches a module in English (.) but um (.) the lecturer has broken English I would tend to think that she's er less intelligent"* (R1, FG1) and someone people do not take seriously: *"I think if you like speak locally er (.) it's like what kind of lecturer you are (R3, FG3).*

In summary, results from the focus groups interviews show that all three groups of students perceive their NNSE lecturers to be less intelligible than their NSE lecturers. However, they qualified this by saying that not all NNSE lecturers are unintelligible, only those who come from certain countries like mainland China and Africa. They found their strong accents particularly difficult to understand. While all three groups perceive that the NSE variety has the highest social prestige, students also pointed out that prestige may not be dependent upon language variety, but on the status and qualifications of the speakers. They claimed that any standard variety of English is prestigious, regardless of variety. As for which group of lecturers was more knowledgeable, all groups agreed that there is no relationship between knowledge and language variety used. The basis for knowledge lies more with the qualifications and subject expertise of the lecturer. In terms of friendliness, all three groups of students felt that NNSE lecturers are less friendly, less open and less approachable, particularly local lecturers. They thought these lecturers to be very conservative and reserved, compared to their NSE lecturers, and they found their NSE lecturers easier to talk to. Despite the NNSE lecturers being less friendly and less approachable, students claimed that they would go to both groups for academic advice. In the area of academic knowledge, students do not appear to favour one group over another. Finally, when students were asked which variety of English they would use if they were lecturers in the university, all three groups claimed that they would use standard Brunei English. This is because it is one way to maintain their local identity and that it would be unnatural to sound British or American. Colloquial English is not the preferred choice for these students.

8.4.3 *Further Thoughts on the Results and Discussion*

From the above results, it was noted that there were a number of instances of conflicting viewpoints in the data between the student questionnaire and focus group interviews. One was the question about which variety of English students found to be most intelligible. Respondents from the questionnaire claimed they found the non-native English variety, particularly the local standard variety, to be most intelligible, while students in the focus group interviews tended to think the non-native varieties of English to be less easy to understand, especially those from outside the South-East Asian region, such as mainland China and Africa. While data from both sources show that students generally agree that native English speaker varieties have higher social prestige, students in the interview groups also pointed out that prestige may not lie in the language variety itself but on the qualifications and status of its speakers. While both the questionnaire respondents and student interviewees agree that they would approach both groups of lecturers for academic help and that they do not equate variety of English spoken with intelligence, students in the group interviews claimed that they found the local Bruneian lecturers to be less intelligent. Furthermore, these students differed in their viewpoints when it came to comparing the two groups of lecturers in terms of friendliness. The questionnaire respondents claimed that their NNSE lecturers were friendlier than the NSE lecturers. In the interviews, students claimed that their NSE lecturers are friendlier because they are more open and approachable. Moreover, they found the local non-native English speaking lecturers to be least friendly.

These differing perceptions provide two important insights into research related to issues of native and non-native speakers and language varieties. One is that it highlights the difficulty of pinpointing what or who exactly a native or non-native speaker is. It is quite clear from the student respondents in this study that there are different types of non-native speakers and that each type may be perceived differently by different people. Frequently, in the interviews, the moderator had to clarify or seek clarification about the particular group of non-native speakers under discussion. Even in discussing native speakers of English, students pointed out that they perceive Australian native English speakers differently from British English speakers. Thus, the native/non-native speaker dichotomy is ambiguous. The other insight that emerged in the study is that a substantive discussion from any research work can only come about via a triangulation of data collection and analysis methods. Questionnaires alone, or interviews alone, will not yield satisfactory results. Questionnaire responses highlight certain issues which are then probed more deeply via interviews where students appear to express themselves more freely, resulting in differing or even conflicting viewpoints. These should be accepted and embraced as natural conclusions drawn from such studies.

8.5 Conclusion

The purpose of this study was to examine ESL students' perceptions about the native and non-native English speaker varieties and their attitudes towards these two groups of lecturers in the classroom. To answer the question posed earlier in this chapter about the extent to which the findings in this study would differ from a similar study carried out some twenty years ago, it could be said that students today are less critical about their non-native lecturers' academic competence, but they are more critical about the perceived lack of openness and approachability of the local lecturers. However, it has to be noted that there were also conflicting viewpoints from students when it came to expressing their opinions about the two groups of lecturers on various aspects of professional qualities such as their degree of openness and friendliness and even intelligence. In addition, this study also highlights the methodological complexity and challenges in carrying out research work on the issues, due mainly to ambiguous interpretations of what constitutes a native and non-native speaker of a language or even how one can define a native and non-native variety of English. And yet, it is recognised that there should be more extensive research on the topic considering the fact that there is an increasingly large number of non-native English speaker teachers and lecturers in the language classrooms, and particularly in ESL contexts.

Acknowledgments I am grateful to my colleagues in the English language and linguistics programme for their constructive and relevant feedback to this chapter: Professor David Deterding, Associate Professor Noor Azam Haji-Othman and Dr. James McLellan. Thank you.

Appendix 1

Questionnaire
Please read the instructions carefully before doing this questionnaire.

(1) Please CIRCLE only one letter for each item, unless otherwise stated. Circle the choice that you find to be most important.
(2) In this questionnaire the following acronyms are used:

- **NSE** = *Native Speakers of English (standard English accent, grammar* and, *vocabulary). This includes speakers from English speaking countries, e.g. U.K., U.S.A., Australia, New Zealand.*
- **NNSE 1** = *Non-native Speakers of English (non-standard English accent, but NSE grammar* and *vocabulary). This includes speakers from non-English speaking countries, e.g. India, Japan, Malaysia, Singapore.*
- **NNSE 2** = *Non-native Speakers of English (non-standard English accent, grammar* and *vocabulary). This includes speakers from non-English countries as in NNSE 1*

1. Of the groups of lecturers in UBD I find it easier to understand [Circle your choice]

    (a) NSE.
    (b) NNSE 1.
    (c) NNSE 2.
    (d) all of the above.
    (e) none of the above.

Give reason(s) for your choice
....
....

2. I think NNSE lecturers should speak English [Circle your choice]

    (a) in the same way as NSE (standard English accent, grammar and vocabulary).
    (b) in the same way as NNSE 1 (non-standard English accent, but NSE grammar and vocabulary).
    (c) in the same way as NNSE 2 (non-standard English accent, grammar and vocabulary).
    (d) I have no preference.

If your answer is (d), please give reason(s)

....
....

3. The variety of English in Brunei is different from the NSE variety.

   (a) Agree.
   (b) Disagree.
   (c) Don't know.

   If your answer is (a), give some examples of the differences:

   ....
   ....

4. Which variety of English would you prefer to speak if you had a choice? Why?

   ....
   ....

5. The table shows the different varieties of English spoken by NNSE in Brunei. Tick in the appropriate box where 1 indicates lowest social prestige and 5 highest social prestige. (Social prestige here refers to a variety you highly admire and respect.) Tick in the DON'T KNOW box if you are not sure.

Varieties of English	Scale of social prestige					
	1	2	3	4	5	Don't Know
NSE (standard English accent, grammar and vocabulary).						
NNSE 1 (non-standard English accent, but NSE grammar and vocabulary).						
NNSE 2 (non-standard English accent, grammar and vocabulary)						

6. The group of lecturers I feel more comfortable with in the classroom is [Circle your choice]

   (a) NSE.
   (b) NNSE 1.
   (c) NNSE 2.
   (d) I have no preference.

Reason(s) for your choice

....
....

7. If I have to take an English language proficiency course, I would prefer the lecturer for the course to be [Circle your choice]

    (a) NSE.
    (b) NNSE 1.
    (c) NNSE 2.
    (d) I have no preference.

   Reason(s) for your choice
   ....
   ....

8. I think that in the English Department and the Language centre at UBD, there should be [Circle your choice]

    (a) more NSE than NNSE lecturers.
    (b) more NNSE 1 than NSE lecturers.
    (c) more NNSE 2 than NSE lecturers.
    (d) I have no preference.

   Reason(s) for your choice
   ....
   ....

9. If I had an academic problem, I would go to

    (a) NSE lecturers.
    (b) NNSE 1 lecturers.
    (c) NNSE 2 lecturers.
    (d) all of the above.
    (e) none of the above.

   Reason(s) for your choice
   ....
   ....

10. The group of lecturers I generally find more helpful towards students is

    (a) the NSE group.
    (b) the NNSE 1 group.
    (c) the NNSE 2 group.
    (d) I have no preference.

   Reason(s) for your choice
   ....
   ....

11. If I became a lecturer or teacher, I would like to model myself on
    (a) the NSE variety (standard English accent, grammar and vocabulary).
    (b) the NNSE 1 variety (non-standard accent, but NSE grammar and vocabulary).
    (c) the NNSE 2 variety (non-standard accent, grammar and vocabulary).

Reason(s) for your choice
....
....

12. I can relate to or identify with more easily with
    (a) the NSE.
    (b) the NNSE 1.
    (c) the NNSE 2.
    (d) all of the above.
    (e) none of the above.

Reason(s) for your choice
....
....

Thank you for your co-operation

Appendix 2

Focus group interview guide
Student attitudes towards NES and NNES varieties and lecturers in UBD
Possible topics for discussion:

1. You hear about NES and NNES. Do you think the two varieties are different/similar? In what ways are the two different/similar?
2. Have you experienced difficulty understanding your lecturers' English? Which variety do you find difficult to understand? Why?
3. It is generally accepted that NSE variety (e.g. British English, American English) is more prestigious. Do you agree? Why/why not?
4. How do you view your NSE lecturers and your NNSE lecturers in terms of (i) knowledge, (ii) intelligence and (iii) friendliness?
5. If you were a lecturer in UBD, which variety would you use? Why/why not?

References

Barbour, R. S., & Kitzinger, J. (1999). *Developing focus group research*. London: SAGE.
Braine, G. (1999). *Non-native educators in English language teaching*. Mahwah, NJ: Lawrence Erlbaum Associates.
Cane, G., & Hjh Rosnah Hj Ramly (1996). Factors influencing the choice of a role model for trainee English teachers in Brunei Darussalam. In P. W. Martin, C. Ożóg & G. Poedjosoedarmo (Eds.), *Language use & language change in Brunei Darussalam* (pp. 133–155). Athens, Ohio: Ohio University Center for International Studies.
Cheung, Y. L., & Braine, G. (2007). The attitudes of university students towards non-native speaker English teachers in Hong Kong. *RELC Journal, 38*(3), 257–277.
Davies, A. (2003). *The native speaker: Myth and reality*. Clevedon: Multilingual Matters.
Davies, A. (1991). *The native speaker in applied linguistics*. Edinburgh: Edinburgh University Press.
Derwing, T. M., & Munro, M. J. (2005). Second language accent and pronunciation teaching: A research-based approach. *TESOL Quarterly, 39*(3), 489–511.
Frankland, J., & Bloor, M. (1999). Some issues arising in the systematic analysis of focus group materials. In R. S. Barbour & J. Kitzinger (Eds.), *Developing focus group research* (pp. 144–155). London: SAGE.
Ho, D. G. E. (2012). The focus group interview: rising to the challenge in qualitative research methodology. In G. Walden (Ed.), *Focus group research* (pp. 295–310). New Delhi: SAGE Publications.
Jenkins, J. (2009). *World Englishes: A resource book for students* (2nd ed.). London: Routledge.
Jenkins, J. (2007). *English as a lingua franca: Attitude and identity*. Oxford: Oxford University Press.
Jones, G. (2009). The evolution of language-in-education policies in Brunei Darussalam. In K. Kosonen & C. Young (Eds.), *Mother Tongue as bridge language of instruction: Policies and experiences in Southeast Asia* (pp. 49–61). Singapore: SEAMEO.
Jones, G. (2007). 20 years of bilingual education: Then and now. In D. Prescott (Ed.), *English in Southeast Asia: Varieties, literacies & literatures* (pp. 246–258). Newcastle: Cambridge Scholars Publishing.
Kachru, B. B. (1992). World Englishes: Approaches, issues and resources. *Language Teaching, 25*(1), 1–14.
Kirkpatrick, A. (2010). *English as a lingua franca in ASEAN: A multilingual model*. Hong Kong: Hong Kong University Press.
Kirkpatrick, A. (2009). Non-native English speakers in TESOL of the month blog: Thomas Andrew Kirkpatrick. Retrieved 16 October, 2015, from http://nnesintesol.blogspot.com/2009/09/.
Kirkpatrick, A. (1998). Language, culture and the development of regional varieties of English: who owns the varieties? *Asian Englishes, 1*(2), 76–86.
Krueger, R. A., & Casey, M. A. (2000). *Focus groups*. London: SAGE.
Llurda, E. (2009). The decline and fall of the native speaker. In L. Wei & V. Cook (Eds.), *Contemporary applied linguistics* (Vol. 1, pp. 37–53). London/New York: Continuum International Publishing Group.
Llurda, E. (2004). Non-native-speaker teachers and English as an international language. *International Journal of Applied Linguistics, 14*(3), 314–323.
Matsuda, P. K. (2003). Proud to be a non-native speaker. *TESOL Matters, 13*(4), 15.
Medgyes, P. (1994). *The non-native teacher*. London: Macmillan Publishers.
Medgyes, P. (1992). Native or non-native: who's worth more? *ELT Journal, 46*(4), 340–349.
Morgan, D. L. (1988). *Focus groups as qualitative research*. London: SAGE.
Noor Azam Haji-Othman. (2000). Bilingual and nonnative teachers of the English language: A study of Bruneian teachers' roles and their concerns. Unpublished Masters thesis, Cardiff University.

Noor Azam Haji-Othman, Hajah Zurinah Haji Yaakub, Dayangku Liyana Putri Pengiran Abdul Ghani, Hajah Suciyati Haji Sulaiman, & Saidai Haji Hitam (2014). In R. Barnard & J. McLellan (Eds.), *Codeswitching in university English-medium classes: Asian perspectives* (pp. 144–155). Bristol: Multilingual Matters.

Paikeday, T. M. (1985). *The native speaker is dead!*. Toronto: Paikeday Publishing.

Piller, I. (2002). Passing for a native speaker: Identity and success in second language learning. *Journal of Sociolinguistics, 6*(2), 179–206.

Thomas, J. (1999). Voices from the periphery: Non-native teachers and issues of credibility. In G. Braine (Ed.), *Non-native educators in English language teaching* (pp. 5–27). Mahwah, NJ: Lawrence Erlbaum Associates.

Walkinson, I., & Oanh, D. H. (2014). Native and non-native English language teachers: Student perceptions in Vietnam and Japan. *SAGE Open*, April–June 2014, pp. 1–9.

Chapter 9
Patterns of Language Choice and Use in Interactions Among Foreign Workers in Brunei Darussalam: A Preliminary Study

Fatimah Chuchu and James McLellan

9.1 Introduction

The construction industry in Negara Brunei Darussalam (henceforth Brunei) has long depended on overseas short-term migrant labour. The same also applies to service industries such as retail stores. Major sources of migrant workers include Thailand, Indonesia, the Philippines, Malaysia and Bangladesh. As noted by bruneiresources.com (2005), foreign workers currently make up over one-third of the nation's workforce. On construction sites they form a large majority of the total workforce. In retail trade outlets such as supermarkets and department stores a substantial majority of the staff, especially at lower levels, are from overseas.

In workplace contexts, where safety considerations are paramount, miscommunication and failure to understand instructions can have serious economic consequences such as increased health and safety risks, budget overruns and delays in project completion. These have deleterious effects on development, on diversification from dependence on oil and gas, and thus on national development. Similar communication problems may reduce the efficiency and timeliness of house construction, and may affect levels of customer service, cleanliness and sales in department stores and supermarkets.

Fatimah Chuchu (✉) · J. McLellan
FASS/UBD, Universiti Brunei Darussalam, Jalan Tungku Link, Gadong BE1410, Brunei Darussalam
e-mail: fatimah.chuchu@ubd.edu.bn

J. McLellan
e-mail: james.mclellan@ubd.edu.bn

© Springer Science+Business Media Singapore 2016
Noor Azam Haji-Othman et al. (eds.), *The Use and Status of Language in Brunei Darussalam*, DOI 10.1007/978-981-10-0853-5_9

9.2 Background to the Study

Migrant workers on construction sites in Brunei Darussalam may not have full proficiency in the languages used by their supervisors and overseers. Anecdotal evidence from those working in the construction industry, as well as the research conducted in Brunei by Santoso (2009), suggests that workplace multilingualism and the need for effective communication in a lingua franca may have linguistic consequences, such as the development of pidginised or simplified speech forms. There may also be negative economic consequences arising from workplace miscommunication: delays in project completion, and substandard work arising from instructions that are not fully understood.

This study investigates language choice and use among a convenience sample of over 110 migrant workers in a variety of workplaces, using qualitative methods, mainly semi-structured interviews and observations, in order to generate narratives. A website, maintained by a senior Brunei government officer, summarises the official position as follows:

> Recognizing the constraints of the small workforce in the country, the Government of His Majesty The Sultan and Yang Di-Pertuan of Negara Brunei Darussalam practises a flexible policy to allow companies to recruit foreign workers to man their operations. Foreign workers, mainly from Malaysia, Thailand, Philippines, Indonesia and South Asia, account for over a third of the total workforce in Brunei Darussalam.
>
> (bruneiresources.com 2005)

9.3 Brief Literature Review

There are studies of workplace language choice and use in other multilingual contexts. Examples include the research by Holmes and associates in New Zealand workplaces, under the Language in the Workplace Project (e.g. Holmes 2007, 2009). Holmes's research suggests that effective use of language in workplaces involves diverse strategies and competencies to achieve workplace objectives, and that the language used in workplaces also has interpersonal functions such as building rapport. Handford and Matous (2010) study interactions in lingua franca English between Japanese engineers and Chinese workers at Hong Kong construction sites. These research studies from different socio-cultural contexts provide models for our research design and methodology.

Santoso (2009) is a case study of a Brunei dam construction site in a remote up-country location, where the majority of engineers and supervisors were Thai, but the workforce comprised both Thais and Indonesians. From focus-group discussions with groups of Indonesian workers, Santoso reports that there were communication problems between them and their Thai foremen owing to the lack of a shared lingua franca: The Indonesians spoke no Thai, and the Malay abilities of the Thai staff were rudimentary. Mediation was conducted through more experienced

Indonesians who had worked longer on the project site, and through a southern Thai employed as driver for the site manager who had many years of experience in Brunei and spoke fluent Malay (Santoso 2009, p. 532). The sections of Santoso's study dealing with issues of communication between construction workers of different nationalities and language backgrounds offer a powerful justification and rationale for the present study which focuses on issues of language use and choice.

The specific question of workplace language use by foreign workers has yet to be addressed in a sociolinguistic study in the context of Brunei. Previous studies undertaken by researchers based at Universiti Brunei Darussalam investigated local university graduates' language use in government departments (Swan et al. 2003), in particular whether they tended to use more English or more Malay in specific workplace situations such as meetings with superiors and colleagues. They found variability between predominantly English and predominantly Malay departments and ministries.

9.4 Aim and Objectives of Current Research

This study covers three different though comparable contexts: construction sites, retail shops and food outlets. We initially expected to find examples of pidginised or simplified language use, in line with patterns of communication that occur worldwide as contact phenomena, wherever workplaces require contact and communication between speakers of different languages, who have only limited competence in the workplace lingua franca (whichever that may be). This investigation is thus a scoping study which can uncover some initial findings, which can then be further investigated through in-depth case studies. We believe that the sociolinguistic and economic perspectives in combination constitute a strong justification and rationale for this research project.

The initial objectives are descriptive, in the form of linguistic and sociolinguistic accounts of workplace communication practices, including comparison and contrast between construction sites and other workplaces.

9.5 Methodology

Primary data was obtained from interviews with 10 foreign workers from two construction sites at Kampung Tungku and Kampung Kilanas, both located within 10–12 km of the national capital, Bandar Seri Begawan. The owner and the assistant manager of the construction company undertaking these projects were also interviewed. The data collection was then extended to other workplaces, a food stall in a major shopping mall, and a health spa with several branches. For these, the owner and the workers of the stall and spa were interviewed. Apart from the interviews, a questionnaire survey was carried out. The questionnaires were distributed among foreign workers who worked at grocery shops, computer shops, cleaning services and similar workplaces. 120 questionnaires were distributed and 115 of these were returned.

9.6 Main Findings

9.6.1 Baseline Data

A total of 115 workers agreed to take part in the survey by supplying the information in answer to the questions shown in Table 9.1.

The gender balance of respondents was 73 male (62.9 %) and 43 female (37.1 %). Their nationalities are shown in Table 9.2.

This sample represents a valid cross-section of the total of foreign workers currently employed in Brunei Darussalam. The female participants are from only two countries, Indonesia and the Philippines, whilst the males come from a wider range of national backgrounds. In the next section of the analysis the participants are grouped according to their nationality and where relevant, gender.

Table 9.1 Questions asked for baseline data collection

	Questions for employees
1.	What is your job?
2.	How long have you worked here?
3.	What nationality are you?
4.	What language(s) do you use with your employer/boss?
5.	What language(s) do you use with your clients/customers?
6.	What language(s) do you use with your colleague(s)?
7.	Any other issues concerning communication with your employer/clients/colleagues?

Table 9.2 Nationality and gender of survey participants

Country of origin	Number of participants	% of total
Indonesia	37 (20 male, 17 female)	31.9
Philippines	34 (8 male, 26 female)	30.2
Bangladesh	13 (13 male, 0 female)	11.2
India	12 (12 male, 0 female)	10.3
Vietnam	7 (7 male, 0 female)	6.0
Malaysia	4 (4 male, 0 female)	3.4
Nepal	2 (2 male, 0 female)	1.7
Pakistan	2 (2 male, 0 female)	1.7
Thailand	2 (2 male, 0 female)	1.7
Egypt	2 (2 male, 0 female)	1.7

9 Patterns of Language Choice and Use in Interactions … 129

Table 9.3 Number of years working in Brunei by the participants

Years of working in Brunei	Number of participants	% of Total (%)
Less than 12 months	28	24.1
1–4 years	60	51.7
5–10 years	20	17.2
More than 10 years	8	6.9

The females from the Philippines, 26 in number, are mostly sales assistants and cashiers. Most of them are trilingual in Tagalog (Filipino), English and Malay. A minority (6 out of 26) report they have little or no fluency in Malay. In all cases, this is because they are recent arrivals, having been in Brunei for less than 1 year. In answering the open question (no. 7 in Table 9.1), several of them explain that they learnt basic Malay from their friends and workplace colleagues. The most common response to this question by Filipinas is 'No problems' The Indians, Indonesians, Bangladeshis and others, provide various responses such as 'No problem', 'Learning from friends', 'Previously it was a problem but now it is alright'. However, they share the most common response 'No problem'. The 'No problem' response is connected to their years of working in Brunei. This response is obtained from the workers who have been working for 1–4 years, 5–10 years and more than 10 years. Their years of working in Brunei are shown in Table 9.3.

From these figures we infer that those who are recent arrivals in Brunei experience the most serious workplace communication problems.

9.6.2 Interviews

We conducted in-depth interviews with the manager of a food stall located in a modern shopping complex in Bandar Seri Begawan, the owner of a health spa with branches in two major hotels, and the Assistant Manager of a major housing construction company.

(i) The supervisor of the food stall is Indonesian, of Chinese ethnicity. He is able to speak Hokkien, Mandarin, Bahasa Indonesia (which is largely the same as both the Standard and the Brunei varieties of Malay). He uses Hokkien with his immediate family, and mainly Bahasa Indonesia and Malay with customers. His staff are Indonesian and Filipino, and they mostly use Bahasa Indonesia to communicate with him. Consistent with our findings from interviews with other Filipino workers, he reports that they pick up basic communicative Malay quickly after starting work in Brunei. For taking outside catering orders over the telephone he uses mainly Malay and sometimes English, in accordance with customers' language preferences. He does not report any particular communication problems, neither with his staff nor with customers, because of the range of available language choices, which "also include sign language ('bahasa isyarat') when customers speak no Malay and no English". As observed during our visits to the food stall, language mixing, mostly between Malay and English, is a common occurrence (McLellan and Noor Azam 2012).

(ii) The owner/manager of both the food stall and spa therapy business is Bruneian of Chinese ethnicity. The business employs four workers from Indonesia and the Philippines for her food stall; for her spa she employs thirteen therapists from Indonesia, the Philippines and Thailand. Customers are mostly Bruneian. Communication with staff and between staff and customers is in Bahasa Indonesia/Malay and English. Newly-arrived staff with low or no proficiency in Malay and English are mentored by their more experienced colleagues who share the same language background. She explains that "usually we get the seniors to teach and brief the new ones, in their own language. Eventually, they will learn." There can be problems with Thai staff, who take longer to acquire the basic communication skills in Malay and English from their Thai colleagues, compared to the Indonesian and Filipino staff who are already multilingual and thus have fewer problems adding further languages to their repertoire.

(iii) The Assistant Manager of a major housing construction company is a Malaysian of Chinese ethnicity who has worked in Brunei since 1982 and has been with this company for the past 6 years. He pointed out that the company employs over 300 construction workers, mostly from Indonesia, but also from Thailand, Bangladesh and Malaysia. Instructions to workers are conveyed through site foremen who share the same language background, so a Bangla-speaking foreman will give instructions to Bangla-speaking workers. It is company policy to employ Bangladeshi workers who have previous experience of working in Malaysia and who have therefore picked up basic Malay during their time spent working there. In communication between workers of different nationalities, simplified or pidginised Malay is the default code choice. This was confirmed by our on-site interviews with workers from this company. Thai staff in this company, according to the Assistant Manager, "occupy skilled positions and have experience from doing similar jobs in their home country. They can understand and interpret architects' plans and design specifications, but may need to use simplified Malay and some sign language in order to convey instructions to non-Thai workers".

These in-depth semi-structured interviews with business owners and managers, supported by our own observations as customers in supermarkets, department stores and small retail shops, demonstrate the capacity for multilingual negotiation for the achievement of work-oriented goals, whether preparing and serving food, providing therapy services or building houses. Tasks and associated interactions tend to be repetitive and formulaic, making it easier for newly-arrived foreign staff to be mentored into the required interactional routines by their more experienced colleagues.

9.7 Conversational Data Extract from a Private Company Office

To support the survey and interview findings, the short extract (Table 9.4), obtained by Siti Norhaziqah Omar (2013) and used with permission, shows code-mixed Malay-English operating as the default choice in an interaction involving a Bruneian and three foreign office workers.

Table 9.4 Workplace conversation extract (*Source* Siti Norhaziqah Omar 2013)

MC	*Betul* ↑ *macam* client *ku tengok ku marah diam terus*
	'True, like when my client sees me get mad, they keep quiet'
MM	*Siapa*?
	'Who'
MC	Client *ku*
	'My client'
MM	↑ *Yaa-kah*? (laughs)
	'Really?'
MC	(0.3) ohh-kay *lah*
BM	Oh-kay *lah aku pergi kerja lah semula aku pergi aku punya* table
	'OK I'm going back to work I'm going to my table'
MM	↑ Oh-kay ↓
	'OK'
F	I need {to go first
MC	{okay
MM	↑ You already the server?
F	No not yet *bah*. I go first
MM	Bye-ee

Participants:
MC—Malaysian Chinese
MM—Malaysian Malay
BM—Bruneian Malay
F—Filipino
Transcription key:
'…..'—free translations of speech in Malay
betul—italics for Malay speech
client—normal font for English speech
↑—Rising intonation
↓—Falling intonation
{—Overlapping speech

The predominant code choice is initially Malay, but there are switches to English for the single nouns 'client' and 'table'. In the final four turns, when the Filipino joins the conversation, English becomes the main language, but he inserts the Brunei Malay *bah* particle in his reply to the Malaysian male's question in the penultimate line. This demonstrates acquisition of Bruneian norms of politeness in conversation, with the multifunctional *bah* particle serving here as a 'softener' following the negative reply to the question, as described previously by Ożóg and Martin (1996, pp. 243–244).

9.8 Discussion: Language Choice and Use in Interactions Among Foreign Workers

Based on the returned questionnaires and on the extract in Table 9.4, the interactions among these foreign workers are not limited to their own native languages, but the data show more complex patterns. For instance, a majority of these migrant workers choose either Malay or English when they converse with their seniors. Their employers are mainly citizens of Brunei, so to converse in Malay and English is crucial in order to increase mutual understanding among them. This concurs with Gunn's (1997) affirmation that Brunei Malay has continued to retain its role as a general 'lingua franca' in Brunei and the importance of English as having instrumental value in this country. In their responses, supported by the conversational data transcript from which the above extract is taken, the participants also reported that they code-switched between the languages within their repertoire to facilitate communication with their co-workers and their employers. The language choice with their employers or seniors is shown in Table 9.5.

Table 9.5 shows considerable differences in the language choices reported by the overseas workers. In upward communication (with employer/boss) Malay or English are the most common choices, together amounting to 71 %, with code-mixed language choices reported to occur less often, accounting for a total of just 22 % of the total. In contrast, with clients and customers, code-mixing between Malay and English (26 %) and various other kinds of code-switching (22 %) account for nearly half of the language choices. In their interactions with workplace colleagues, participants report far greater use of their own native languages, both alone and code-mixed with Malay, or code-mixed with both Malay and English.

The usual proviso about the risks of over-reliance on self-report data in sociolinguistic language choice surveys must be considered here. However, the researchers and the research assistants agree that these findings about foreign workers' language use concur with their own observations in the various Brunei workplaces which were part of this study.

Table 9.5 Language choices (%) with various interlocutors

With	NL	M	E	NL + M	NL + E	M + E	E + C	NL + M + E	NL + M + C	na
Employer/Boss	3	37	34	6	4	9	1	1	1	4
Clients/Customers	2	24	6	10	2	26	8	1	1	20
Colleagues	65	1	13	13	1	7	0	7	0	0

NL Native Language, *M* Malay, *E* English, + shows code-mixing, *na* no answer

9.9 Conclusion

Most of the migrant workers do not report any problem or issues in their workplace communication. While more than 80 % of these respondents stated there is 'No Problem', a minority of them report that they do encounter problems, which can be summarised thus:

(a) Recent migrants normally have some trouble comprehending all varieties of Malay. This applies even to Indonesians who come with fluency in Bahasa Indonesia but experience initial problems adjusting to Brunei's predominant lingua franca, Brunei Malay, which is related, as noted above, but not the same as Bahasa Indonesia.

(b) Some foreign workers are not fluent in English, which serves as Brunei's second lingua franca. Several of the respondents who are recent arrivals in Brunei report that they have to use sign language to achieve their communicative goals;

(c) Issues in communicating might arise at the early stage after arriving in Brunei, but these are later lessened by the migrants' willingness to learn and accommodate their language capabilities to local speech styles.

Our findings concur with those of Handford and Matous (2010, p. 98). Unlike, for instance, the legal discourse of the law courts (Masmahirah, this volume, Chap. 10), the interactions in the workplaces chosen for our Brunei-based study are 'symbol-dominated' rather than 'word-dominated'. The communicative purposes of customers and sales staff, of spa therapists and their clients, and of construction site managers, foremen and workers are all largely self-evident in their particular workplace contexts.

This initial scoping study of Brunei workplace communication patterns reveals multilingual communicative practices on a higher scale than initially assumed. It opens up possibilities for more in-depth research requiring regular site visits for lengthy periods of observation and more in-depth interviews.

Note

This chapter is a revised and updated version of an article published in *Humanities and Social Sciences Review 3* (3) under the title 'Language Choice and Use in Interactions among Foreign Workers in Brunei Darussalam', ISSN 2165-6258. Accessible via http://www.universitypublications.net/hssr/0303/html/toc.html.

References

bruneiresources.com. (2005). Foreign workers information. Retrieved 30 October, 2015, from http://www.bruneiresources.com/foreignworkers.html

Gunn, G. (1997). *Language, power, & ideology in Brunei Darussalam*. Athens, Ohio: Ohio University Center for International Studies.

Handford, M., & Matous, P. (2010). Lexicogrammar in the international construction industry: A corpus-based case study of Japanese-Hong-Kongese on-site interactions in English. *English for Specific Purposes, 30*(2), 87–100.

Holmes, J. (2007). Monitoring organisational boundaries: Diverse discourse strategies used in gatekeeping. *Journal of Pragmatics, 39*, 1993–2016.

Holmes, J. (2009). Disagreeing in style: socio-cultural norms and workplace English. In C. Ward (Ed.), *Language teaching in a multilingual world: Challenges and opportunities* (pp. 85–102). Singapore: SEAMEO Regional Language Centre Anthology Series.

McLellan, J., & Noor Azam Haji-Othman. (2012). Features of the Brunei Darussalam variety of English. In E.-L. Low & Azirah Hashim (Eds.), *Englishes in South East Asia: Features, policy and language in use* (pp. 75–90). Amsterdam: John Benjamins.

Ożóg, C., & Martin, P. W. (1996). The *bah* particle in Brunei English. In P. W. Martin, C. Ożóg & G. Poedjosoedarmo (Eds.), *Language use and language change in Brunei Darussalam* (pp. 236–249). Athens, OH: Ohio University Centre for International Studies.

Santoso, D. S. (2009). The construction site as a multicultural workplace: A perspective of minority migrant workers in Brunei. *Construction Management and Economics, 27*(6), 529–537.

Siti Norhaziqah Omar. (2013). Office conversation. Data submitted for assignment for Analysing Talk module (AC-2204), Faculty of Arts and Social Sciences, Universiti Brunei Darussalam.

Swan, J., Elgar, A., Wood, A., & Sharifah Nurul Huda Alkaff (2003). The role of English in the Brunei workplace: The influence of communication, identity, power and education factors. *Universiti Brunei Darussalam Department of English Language and Applied Linguistics Occasional Papers in Language Studies, 8*, 115–149.

Chapter 10
Courtroom Discourse: A Case Study of the Linguistic Strategies in Brunei Courtrooms

Hjh Masmahirah Hj Mohd Tali

10.1 Introduction

This chapter explores the role of language in the Brunei Magistrates' Court and High Court. It illustrates the linguistic strategies employed by the various courtroom participants—judges, counsels, defendants and interpreters—to effectively serve their purpose in attempting to ensure that justice is done in these courts. The methodology is based on in situ observations: eleven sets of data were collected from courtroom sessions, and interviews were also conducted. Turn taking, repetition, discourse markers, language choice, code-switching and questioning sequences are among the main issues investigated in this chapter. In addition, there are other strategies employed by the participants, including the use of non-verbal communication (paralinguistic features), the tactics used by the counsels and the roles of the judge and the interpreter in the specific domain. Similarly, the unequal power status is brought to light among other interesting findings emerging from this study of language use in courtrooms. The roles of each participant are highlighted based on their choice of language and on the strategies they use to deliver their message in the institutionalized setting of the courtroom.

From a linguistic perspective, there are a number of studies on the analysis of interactions in the courtrooms in our neighboring country, Malaysia—by David (2003), Noraini Ibrahim (2008), Azirah Hashim and Norizah Hassan (2011) and Powell (2012) among others. These studies have analyzed the instances of code-switching, investigated strategies adopted by the counsels, and studied interactions in the *Syariah* courts.

The only study on courtroom discourse in Brunei prior to this one is by Powell (2009) who stated that there is 'a limited degree of code switching, and dispensing

---

Hjh Masmahirah Hj Mohd Tali (✉)
No. 19 Spg 422 Kg Lambak Kanan, Jln Berakas BB1714,
Brunei Darussalam
e-mail: masmahirah@gmail.com

© Springer Science+Business Media Singapore 2016
Noor Azam Haji-Othman et al. (eds.), *The Use and Status of Language in Brunei Darussalam*, DOI 10.1007/978-981-10-0853-5_10

with interpretation has also been observed in a monolingual Bruneian court' (p. 136). Initially, this gives the impression that the language that is used in the Brunei courtroom is *Bahasa Melayu* (Malay) only—since Brunei has the national philosophy of MIB (*Melayu Islam Beraja*, 'Malay Islamic Monarchy'), by which everyone must acknowledge the status of Islam as the official religion and be loyal to the country's ruler, and they are encouraged to use the official language, *Bahasa Melayu*, even though English is the dominant second language (Jones 2007). However, this is not the case in the Brunei civil law courts as it has been reported that '…Brunei Darussalam continue[s] to operate thoroughly Anglophone (English speaking) systems of law in which local languages are admitted only through translation' (Powell 2009, p. 136).

Additionally this is reinforced by Article 5A of the Language of the Supreme Court found in the Laws of Brunei (1984a), which was amended in 2004 and which clearly states, 'All proceedings in the Supreme court shall be in the English language (provided that the court may in the interest of justice allow the giving of evidence by a witness in any other language)' (p. 4).

Therefore it is important to distinguish the role of language in Brunei courtrooms, specifically exploring the types of linguistic features and strategies employed by the different courtroom participants, namely the judge, counsels, defendants, witnesses and interpreters, during courtroom sessions. The findings highlight the need for a better understanding of the 'workings, strengths and weaknesses of the court' (Azirah Hashim and Norizah Hassan 2011, p. 333).

10.2 Overview of Brunei Legal System

There are two major formal legal systems: the common law system originating from England, which is found in most of the countries it colonized; and the civil law system, which originated in continental Europe (Eades 2010, p. 18). Brunei courts have adopted the former, which is 'similar to that in the rest of northern Borneo, even though British suzerainty there never amounted to formal colonization' (Powell 2012, p. 246). Moreover, common law is 'predominantly adversarial with two sides arguing their case in front of a judge or jury' (Eades 2010, p. 18).

Despite the fact that Brunei regained its full independence in 1984, it has been noted that English law and the English language still dominate the Brunei legal system (Powell 2012, p. 246). Powell's study of the Malaysian legal system notes that 'many Malaysian lawyers express fears that changing the medium of the law risks changing the substance of the law and the integrity of the legal profession and would prefer resources be spent on improving translation and interpreting rather than on language shift' (Powell 2012, p. 260).

Additionally, changing the medium of the law to local languages would cause a number of problems not only because this would affect the spoken discourse in the courtroom, but also because written legal language is of equal or greater importance than spoken language, as official written records must be maintained by the courts, and many indigenous languages such as Brunei Malay are not generally written.

Translation in legal areas, especially in written form, is slow due to a number of factors—there are very few competent bilingual legal interpreters, and the quality of translation work is poor. As a result, legal texts are sometimes literally translated without understanding the true meaning, there is no uniformity in terminology or legal jargon (e.g. 'complaint' in Malay is *komplen* or *aduan*), there are inaccuracies in the translation, and the translated texts follow the structure of the source text but ignore the structure of the target language (Zaiton and Ramlah 1991, cited in Noraini Ibrahim 2012, p. 3). This might explain why Malay countries such as Malaysia and Brunei still openly accept the use of English law and the English language in their courtrooms. Due to this, according to Powell (2012, p. 246), 'while the majority of judges are now Bruneian, many others who are appointed from the benches of the UK or other commonwealth countries are not required to know Malay', as court proceedings and records are in English.

In addition, Brunei has a separate system that 'draw[s] for its sources of law on religious texts rather than judicial decisions or legislation which is known as Islamic Shari'a (*Syariah*) law, based primarily on the Koran' (Eades 2010, p. 18). It can be seen that Brunei has a dual system of courts; the civil court which is the main focus of this chapter (dealing with laws that include contract, tort, crime and constitutional and administrative cases), and the *Syariah* court which deals mainly with Islamic family law with jurisdiction over Muslims (Azirah Hashim and Norizah Hassan 2011, p. 335).

10.3 Methodology

The choice of methodology is based on observation of eleven interactions among the courtroom participants in the Magistrates' court and the High Court in Bandar Seri Begawan, the capital of Brunei Darussalam. Informal interviews with people in different positions, such as registrars, the Chief Interpreter and a few of the magistrates, were also conducted to obtain clarifications and validations regarding the data compiled with the permission of the Court Registrar.

10.4 Data Analysis

As no recordings are allowed in the Magistrates' Court, the data used in this study consists of eleven transcripts that were transcribed orthographically in full, by detailed writing out what took place in the courtroom. This allows the possibility of identifying emergent themes to examine the linguistic strategies employed by the participants. The eleven sets of data (in the Appendix) are thus authentic, and the cases included in this study vary from drugs cases to penal code violations.

All the data excerpts follow the conventions of the Transcription Key (Table 10.1), adapted from Powell (2009, p. 149). In addition to the symbols shown

Table 10.1 Transcription key (from Powell 2009)

Code	Meaning
J	Justice (judge, magistrate)
C	Counsel (DPP = Deputy Public Prosecutor; DC = Defence Counsel)
I	Interpreter
D	Defendant
W	Witness
//	Overlap
…	Short pause
xxx	Inaudible
italics	Languages other than English
( )	English translation
[ ]	Stage directions
_____	Names that have been omitted

in the table, the numbers are found on the right side of the data for ease of referencing to indicate the turns by the participants.

For instances from the data where the interpreter expressed word-for-word from one language to another, the English translation is not provided to avoid redundancy. Names of the participants have been omitted for ethical reasons.

10.4.1 Turn-Taking and Power Inequality

It was noted that a 'single question and answer sequence between a judge or lawyer and defendant or witness is usually initiated with a question', in which the ones who are obliged to respond are the defendant or witness and that the role of the judge is to listen and he/she may interrupt at any time (Azirah Hashim and Norizah Hassan 2011, p. 342).

In Excerpt 10, there is a power struggle for the floor reflected in the turn taking between the defendant and the judge, who compete for the floor from lines 12–13 and 18–19. However, due to the powerful role of the judge, the defendant's turn is interrupted: as stated by Noraini Ibrahim (2007a) with reference to Malaysian courtrooms, 'full control of the interactions still lies with the judge who still has absolute authority to redirect the issues or change the topics' (p. 26).

From Excerpt 10

J	Where does he work?	5
I	*Di mana kita bekerja?*	6
D	Zed and Zee, Gadong.	7

(continued)

(continued)

J	As a?	8
I	*Sebagai apa?*	9
D	Car washer	10
I	Car wash, your honor.	11
D	*Saya…//*	12
J	// I personally have no problem in extending the fine but I am abide to the law.	13
I	*Tuan Hakim mengatakan, dia tiada raguan untuk menambah hari pembayaran tetapi hukum itu sudah ditetapkan.*	14
D	*Saya merayu, saya ada dua anak*	15
I	Your honour, I am pleading. I have two children.	16
J	Personally, I have no problem…	17
D	*Tapi boleh saya…//*	18
J	// But…	19
I	*Tetapi…*	20
J	The law is clear	21
I	*Hukum itu sudah ditetapkan*	22
J	The law cannot be extended	23
I	*Hukum itu tidak dapat di ubah*	24
D	*Saya faham, kalau boleh saya mencari duit…*	25
I	Your honour, if I may, your honour, he will find the money by today	26
J	I'm sorry that's what the magistrate states. I have no problem but the law is there.	27
D	*Jadi cemana?*	28
I	What can I do, your honour?	29

10.4.2 Repetition

In Excerpt 10, there are many instances of repetition from the judge. The repetition is either exact or with a variation giving rise to a series of linked pairs in which words or phrases from the first question are repeated in the second (Azirah Hashim and Norizah Hassan 2011, p. 350). Lines 13 and 17 are an instance of repetition where the judge repeats that she personally has no problem in extending the deadline for the defendant to pay the fine. However, from lines 21, 23 and 27, the judge continues to emphasize that although she does not have any problem to extend the deadline of the fine, the law is clear and she must abide by the law. This shows that no one is an exception to the law—not even the judge, let alone a mere defendant.

In Excerpt 8, lines 1 and 3, there is also an instance of repetition by the judge to the counsel. The reason for this is to get information from the counsel, who does not answer the judge the first time in line 2.

From Excerpt 8

J	So, the investigation is complete?	1
C	The investigation obtained…xxx	2
J	My question just now is that, is the investigation complete?	3
C	But the analysis is not…	4
J	Except for the analysis?	5
C	Yes, your honor.	6
J	How does it respond?	7
C	xxx… to the DSS	8
J	Not at this moment, not future tense!	9
	You require it? …xxx… How long?	10
C	Two weeks your honor. And we request for the defendant to be remanded in the Jerudong prison	11
J	Alright, thank you very much.	12

Even after the judge repeats herself in line 3, the counsel only manages to answer her by using elliptical instances with negative polarity '[Yes, the investigation is complete] but the analysis is not…' This in turn results in the judge repeating another question based on the counsel's choice of words in line 4, 'Except for the analysis?' (line 5). The judge uses repetition in line 5 in order to get clarification from the counsel whose answers are unclear. Moreover, due to the lack of cooperation from the counsel, the judge is seen to lose her patience in lines 7 and 9, as she is not satisfied with the counsel's answer in line 8. As a result, the judge's utterances of line 9 have a rising intonation and she stresses the negation 'not' to indicate her annoyance towards the counsel. Usually, rising intonation at the end of an utterance would change it into a question, but in this context it changes a particular statement into a signal of annoyance.

10.4.3 Linguistic Discourse Markers

The linguistic discourse markers that are consistently found in the data are; 'alright', 'so' and 'now' which have different functions respectively. The judge uses 'alright' in most of the data as a closure to the issue (line 12), which is reinforced by the politeness strategy of 'thank you very much'.

From Excerpt 8

C	Two weeks your honor. And we request for the defendant to be remanded in the Jerudong prison.	11
J	Alright, thank you very much.	12

There are also instances where the counsel uses 'so' to summarize, for example: 'Taken from 3rd to 5th June… the result is negative. So, he has paid the fine' (Excerpt 1, line 5). Another discourse marker used by the judge to ask a question is 'alright': 'You pleaded not guilty. On Tuesday, 2 pm, see DPP, he is going to extend you the documents, alright?' (Excerpt 2, line 16). The discourse marker here acts as a tag question to check for confirmation. In another question asked by a judge: 'So, what's the application?' (Excerpt 3, line 6), the discourse marker 'so' acts as a so-prefaced question (Noraini Ibrahim 2007b) and there are other instances where it is adopted to show a resolution has been reached, for example, in Excerpt 4:

From Excerpt 4

DPP	Erm, Your Honor, I wish to bring to the court's attention to xxx justice also a corruption case… err, act. Where 18 months of conviction after trial, the defendant was arrested in January 2009, I understand he was charged in 2011. So in terms of reduction, in sentence, there should be xxx as a delay xxx in court before.	22

Additionally, the judge uses a temporal marker 'Now' as a topic shift at the beginning of the sentence to indicate the introduction of a new topic in the line of questioning (Noraini Ibrahim 2008, p. 41), as in Excerpt 2:

From Excerpt 2

J	Now (name of interpreter), please inform *Mohd* _____, ask him to stand properly, not to put his hands on the table!	4

In this excerpt, the judge uses an indirect imperative form to show that the role of the judge is not only to pass judgment (Noraini Ibrahim 2008, p. 30), but also to reinforce all the participants to follow the courtroom etiquette.

Although these three discourse markers ('so', 'alright', 'now') used in the courtroom may seem to serve similar purposes to ordinary conversation, it is important to consider the context in which they are used as well. Discourse markers can be found in any conversation (spoken, written, formal or informal) and for this particular domain, the judge utters most of the discourse markers. This not only illustrates the use of discourse markers as a common strategy to link ideas but also highlights the power of the judge to shift topics from one important issue to another in the courtroom.

10.4.4 Language Choice

Calculations are carried out to determine which language dominates the courtroom proceedings. An utterance is a single turn-at-speaking. The eleven data sets were classified according to their language choice: L1 indicates Malay only; L2 is for English only; and CS is for Malay-English code-switched utterances. L2 has the highest number of utterances from each data set except for Excerpt 11. This shows that English is the dominant language choice in the courtroom in this data, which is consistent with Article 5A on the Language of Supreme Court.

However, in Excerpt 11 there are more CS utterances than either L1 or L2. Excerpt 11 below illustrates the situation in which instances of code-switching are made by the judge who switches from English to Malay to get the message across to the Malay defendant. This can be seen in lines 11–13, where she expresses her irritation because the defendant is slow to respond to the previous turn. '*Awangku* (title)_____, *pandai kita becakap? Bila kana tanya, mesti dijawab, faham?*' (Can you talk? When you are asked a question, you must answer! [Do you] understand?) The judge seems to code-switch in order to press the defendant. When the defendant still does not respond, the judge code-switches back to English and orders the interpreter to 'ask him again!' in line 14.

Excerpt 11 reveals that the judge code-switches to 'emphasize the responsibility of the witness (defendant) as a civil servant to answer the question' (David 2003, p. 17). This is an instance of informality in the language of the judge in lines 13 and 14, which shows that the judge has authority and control of the courtroom discourse and is also meant to 'make herself (the judge) clear to the other party' (Azirah Hashim and Norizah Hassan 2011, p. 344). David (2003, p. 9) states that the mixing of two languages is a common feature of conversation that can be found in a bilingual community. Since Brunei is a bilingual country, it is not surprising to find the mixing of two languages in many domains, including in the courtrooms.

From Excerpt 11

J	Two charges, yeah?	1
	All right, application is?	2
	Well done.	3
I	...xxx *hukumnya ialah*...xxx *kita faham apa yang saya baca kan ini?*	4
D	*Faham.* [nods]	5
I	Your Honor, the defendant understood the... xxx	6
	Faham dengan tuduhan yang ke dua ini?	7
D	*Faham*	8
I	...xxx second charge...xxx	9
J	I'm gonna fix this case for further mention... on the 27th October, sorry, September, 2 pm for assigned...xxx Before that, *Awangku* _____, do you understand? *Awangku* _____, *pandai kita becakap?* *Bila kana tanya, mesti dijawab, faham?* Ask him again!	10
I	*Faham kita apa yang dicakapkan oleh Puan Hakim?*	11
D	*Faham*	12
J	Now, DPP, how fast can you process the documents?	13

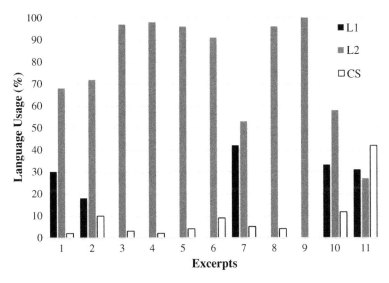

Fig. 10.1 Percentage of *L1* (Malay), *L2* (English) and *CS* (code-switched) utterances in the 11 data sets

Figure 10.1 shows that L1 (Malay) utterances are found only in five of the data sets. The highest number of L1 utterances is 42 %, which is found in Excerpt 7 due to the amount of translation done by the interpreters, speaking for the defendant and the judge alternately. The second highest number of utterances is 33.2 % in Excerpt 10, where the interpreter is not the only one who converses in Malay but also the defendant who is pleading with the judge in a request for the fine to be extended. The use of Malay by the defendant emphasizes that *Bahasa Melayu* is the official language in Brunei and the fact that the defendant works as a car washer (line 10) stresses his inability to speak English fluently in the courtroom.

The use of L1 indicates that there is a connection between choice of language and socio-economic standing. David (2003, p. 12) also notes this, observing that Malay was used by witnesses from the civil service who did not hold senior positions, as opposed to government witnesses of a higher standing who gave evidence in English.

Excerpt 9 is a cross-examination session in the High Court, and only the L2 (English) is used by the participants. Surprisingly the interpreters even utter the command 'All rise' in English without translating it into Malay '*Sila bangun*', which is usually said in the lower courtrooms. Moreover, the counsel speaks English throughout the session and it is not translated for the witness/defendant. This is due to the fact that the defendant holds a senior position of Inspector in the Royal Brunei Police Force; she is educated and can speak English fluently without the need for an interpreter.

10.4.5 Code-Switching

The eleven data sets were also tabulated according to who code-switches the most and were classified according to their language choice using McLellan's (2005, p. 68) five categories of CS below:

E-   monolingual English, i.e. with no Malay words
ML-E   main-language English, where English dominates in terms of word- and group-count
=LA   equal language alternation
ML-M   main-language Malay, where Malay dominates in terms of word- and group-count
M-   monolingual Malay

However, for this section, E- and M- will be excluded for the purpose of focusing on utterances that have both languages in a single turn. According to McLellan (2005, p. 69), the method of establishing if an extract contains equal language alternation or not: if the total Malay outnumbers both the English and mixed code, then it is classified as Main-Language-Malay (ML-M). Likewise, if the English outnumbers both the Malay and the mixed code, then it is Main-Language-English (ML-E). If however, there are sufficient mixed for neither of these patterns to occur, then the text is labeled as equal language alternation (=LA).

Examples of ML-E
From Excerpt 2

J	He was charged xxx by waving a *parang* (machete) on xxx in a public xxx... servant on duty that was previously charged against xxx...	6

In an interview with the Senior Magistrate referring to Excerpt 2, she explained that she used the Malay word *parang* instead of the term 'machete' because both the defendant and herself are Malays—it is easier to understand the Malay word instead of the English one. The Senior Magistrate emphasized the defendant's lack of English vocabulary, as the word 'machete' itself is historically of Spanish origin, borrowed into English. (Alternatively, one might regard 'parang' as a word of English.)

In Excerpt 7, the Senior Magistrate uses the Malay term *empat ekor* instead of the literal meaning 'four tails' to connote the idea of 'four digits' to make the defendant understand that the crime he has committed is gambling. The term *empat ekor* is commonly used to refer to the four-digit lottery which is legal in neighbouring Malaysia but not in Brunei.

From Excerpt 7

J	Alright, Mr _____, you have previous conviction… *empat ekor*…xxx where he was confined.	15

The extract from Excerpt 11 is classified as ML-E overall, even though the fourth and fifth lines are M-.

From Excerpt 11

J	I'm gonna fix this case for further mention… on the 27th October, sorry, September, 2 pm for assigned…xxx Before that, *Awangku* _____, do you understand? *Awangku* _____, *pandai kita becakap?* *Bila kana tanya, mesti dijawab, faham?* Ask him again!	10

The Senior Magistrate code-switches from English to Malay in this excerpt due to the fact that the defendant did not answer her previous questions. She adds that the defendant was being rude by not answering the questions asked by the judge who is a very important person in the courtroom. The defendant should know that every verbal statement said in court can and will be taken as evidence, and by being uncooperative the defendant's behaviour might influence the judge's decision on imposing a heavier sentence. The defendants sometimes do not follow the courtroom etiquette because the court does not have the time and human resources to brief the defendants before a courtroom session begins.

Examples of ML-M

In Excerpt 6, it is hard to determine whether there is code-switching or not.

From Excerpt 6

I	*Kalau kita sain sini* [points] *keputusan kita* negative [points]. [If you sign here your result is negative]	24

When interviewed about Excerpt 6, the Acting Chief Interpreter stated that although *sain* is derived from the English word 'sign', it is understandable and accepted by most people in Brunei. Furthermore, he noted that the standard Malay *tandatangan* would be considered too formal, so he preferred to use the word *sain* because it is less formal and this helps make the courtroom process faster. In fact, the Brunei Malay dictionary (DBP 2007, p. 275) lists *sain* as a word of Brunei

Malay and glosses it as *tandatangan* in standard Malay, which is why this use of *sain* might be regarded as colloquial usage rather than switching into English.

It is similarly difficult to determine whether 'negative' is English or Malay. Collins (2013) lists the standard Malay equivalent of 'negative' as *negatif*, and the only difference from the English word is whether the final consonant is [v] or [f], so it is very difficult to determine whether this word in Excerpt 6 is English of Malay. One might note that, in a local context, this word in Malay would typically be pronounced with [p] rather than [f] at the end. The absence of a [p] at the end in this case is why it is here treated as a word of English, but it could equally be treated as a word of standard Malay.

A similar example is shown in Excerpt 10, in which the English word 'fine' occurs.

From Excerpt 10

I	*Kalau boleh kita membayarkan* fine *kita sebelum pukul empat petang hari ini....* [If possible you pay your fine before 4 pm today]	33

In this example, 'fine' is used instead of the standard Malay *denda* as the word 'fine' is a common word in the field of courtroom discourse. One might note that the *pain* is listed as a word of Brunei Malay, as DBP (2007, p. 231) glosses it with the standard Malay *denda*; however, the use of [f] rather than [p] at the start of the word in Excerpt 10 suggests that, in this case, it is an English word, not Brunei Malay. However, as noted by the Acting Chief Interpreter, one might alternatively say that the use of 'fine' is informal usage in the domain of the court.

Two utterances which are classified as involving equal language alternation (=LA) are found in Excerpts 1 and 7.

From Excerpt 1

I	All rise. *Sila bangun.*	19

From Excerpt 7

J	Mr. _____, do you understand Malay?	4
D	[nods] Malay *saja.* [Malay only]	5

These consist of an equal number of Malay and English words. Excerpt 1 is a typical courtroom routine by the interpreter to announce the arrival of the judge.

The command, expressed in both English and Malay, directs all the people in the courtroom to stand up as a sign of respect towards the judge.

In Excerpt 7, the defendant answers 'Malay *saja*' when he is asked if he prefers the charge to be read to him in Malay or English. He probably says 'Malay' instead of '*Bahasa Melayu*' because he is repeating the words from the utterance by the Senior Magistrate. Furthermore, referring to *Bahasa Melayu* would be rather formal. Presumably he does not say 'only Malay' because he is not confident in his English skills.

10.4.6 Questioning Sequences

Other types of questioning process from the data include; information-seeking wh-questions, yes/no questions, imperatives and requests (Azirah Hashim and Norizah Hassan 2011, p. 346). Besides that, there are questions in the form of tag constructions and directives which serve as questions as they have a rising intonation (Azirah Hashim and Norizah Hassan 2011, p. 346). It must be remembered that questions have various functions and objectives (Gibbons 2003, cited in Azirah Hashim and Norizah Hassan 2011, p. 347) and that they play a major role in the courtroom, as they are the central structuring feature in an adversial legal system. In Brunei, the accused must produce evidence orally by going through a questioning process that comes under the purview of Criminal Procedure Code of Procedure at Preliminary Inquiries (The Laws of Brunei Darussalam 1984b) as well as the Evidence Act of 1939 (The Laws of Brunei Darussalam 1984c). This is a legacy of the common law system of England that has been adopted by the Malaysian legal system (Noraini Ibrahim 2007a, p. 1) as well as in Brunei.

Atkinson and Drew (1979, cited in Noraini Ibrahim 2007a), stated 'the courtroom questioning process is akin to a conversation but in reality it has its own procedural constraints depending on the context' (p. 3). In his study of responses to questions, Raymond (2003, cited in Azirah Hashim and Norizah Hassan 2011, p. 347) found two types of responses: those that are type-conforming and consist of variations of 'yes' or 'no', and those that are type-disconforming and resist a yes or no answer. Additionally, the structures of questions in general are of two types: information seeking and information confirming (Noraini Ibrahim 2007a, p. 19).

In information-seeking wh-questions, the use of interrogative words such as 'what', 'why', 'when', 'where' and 'how', are used at the start of the utterances and these type of questions are lower in terms of degree of control (Azirah Hashim and Norizah Hassan 2011, p. 348).

On the other hand, information confirming questions are realized in this case by yes/no question structures such as 'Are you going to get a lawyer?' and 'Do you understand?' Moreover, agreement questions are type-conforming and 'function mainly to elicit particular types of answers within the constraints allowed in this domain' (Azirah Hashim and Norizah Hassan 2011, p. 348). An example of this type of question is found in Excerpt 7:

From Excerpt 7

J	Now, do you agree that this… this… gambling…this… traffic light thingy is called gambling?	34
I	*Adakah kita mengaku bahawa perjudian….yang…lampu isyarat ini dikirakan menjudi?*	35
D	[nods] *ya.*	36
J	It's gambling, is it?	37
D	*Ya*	38
I	Yes	39

In this extract, both the questions in turns 34 (translated in turn 35) and also turn 37 require either a 'yes' or 'no' answer, which shows there is some form of control over the parties to whom the questions are asked (Azirah Hashim and Norizah Hassan 2011, p. 348).

10.5 Paralinguistic and Pragmatic Features

Aside from analyzing linguistic strategies, it is important to note that there are other types of strategies employed by the counsel and the defendant. In the courtroom, non-verbal communication can take place between all participants, including gaze, gesture, facial expression, prosodic features and other non-verbal vocalisations (Azirah Hashim and Norizah Hassan 2011).

Examples in the data include a defendant who was seen to be weeping in front of all the participants present in the courtroom (line 25 of Excerpt 4). This can be seen as a strategy of the defendant to seek sympathy from the judge in order to be given leniency in the sentence when passing judgment. Moreover, this is also an indication that the judge has the power in the courtroom where his/her 'words play a vital role and make a major impact on life and death, freedom or imprisonment' (David 2003, p. 11).

10.5.1 The Counsel's Tactics

The strategy of seeking sympathy from the judge is also used by the counsel to represent the defendant. In line 8 of Excerpt 5, the counsel displays his competence in the language by using specific lexical choices to gain sympathy from the judge to avoid punitive punishment for the defendant. The counsel uses lexical chains (highlighted in bold) that depict the defendant as a victim rather than as an accused criminal.

From Excerpt 5 (line 8)

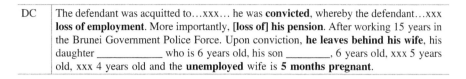

DC	The defendant was acquitted to…xxx… he was **convicted**, whereby the defendant…xxx **loss of employment**. More importantly, **[loss of] his pension**. After working 15 years in the Brunei Government Police Force. Upon conviction, **he leaves behind his wife**, his daughter _____ who is 6 years old, his son _____, 6 years old, xxx 5 years old, xxx 4 years old and the **unemployed** wife is **5 months pregnant**.

This clearly shows the counsel's strategies by listing the defendant's family members, his steady commitment to working in a respectable job and by embedding further appeals to mercy by emphasizing that the defendant's wife does not have a job to support her children and herself while she is pregnant. Additionally, before the session started, the counsel urged the family members to be present in court and to sit in the front row of the gallery. This can be seen as a persuasive strategy employed by the counsel in order to get a reduced sentence for the defendant from the powerful judge. All of this information is manually recorded by the judge in writing and 'what is taken down by the judge will comprise the notes of proceedings and this feature of the legal system has been cited as the cause of the huge backlog of cases in courts' (Noraini Ibrahim 2008, p. 43).

10.5.2 Role of the Interpreter

The role of the interpreter is to translate for both the judge and the defendant and act as a middle person in the interaction. The way a judge is addressed in court reflects on the standing of the judge and denotes their position in the hierarchy. Interestingly, the interpreters show that they are aware of the courtroom etiquette as illustrated by the form of address to the judge by saying 'Your Honour' at the beginning or at the end of their utterances. This invites speculation on whether this is a deliberate strategy to reduce tension when the interaction between the judge and defendant is heated. Moreover, not surprisingly defendants are sometimes unaware of the courtroom etiquette—this can be seen especially in the non-use of proper forms of address to the judge. Nevertheless, there are some defendants who address the judge in Malay with *Tuan/Puan Hakim*, maybe due to previous courtroom appearances or the defendant having been told to follow the courtroom etiquette and address the judge properly, or else from exposure to media representations of the courtroom.

10.5.3 Role of the Judge

In addition to hearing all courtroom cases and passing judgment, the role of the judge is not only confined within the courtroom, as they also connect with the outside world.

According to the Chief Interpreter, the judge goes to the crime scene when it is deemed necessary, for instance when a defendant explains a particular situation where something seems to be illogical to the judge. In one example, it was impossible to imagine the defendant being able to see someone stealing a bag through a concrete wall. The defendant stated that he was leaning on a wall, and that is why he could see that someone was stealing the bag. As a result, the judge went to the crime scene to verify the defendant's account of the truth, and the judge found out that he was giving a very credible testimony. This shows that not only does the judge have to hear from all sides of the courtroom cases, but also sometimes goes to the scene itself if necessary before passing judgment.

Furthermore, it is evident from the data that the judge records manually and this is further highlighted when a judge commands a witness to speak louder in the courtroom:

| C | Can you please not whisper? Speak up. | 1 |
| J | From now on, any evidence that I cannot hear, I will not record. | 2 |

The short extract above shows that the counsel is addressing the defendant who does not know the courtroom etiquette, instructing him to speak louder and not to whisper to the interpreter who was sitting next to him. It is clear from line 3 that the judge is not able to manually record any testimony (evidence) from the witness that is inaudible in the courtroom.

On another occasion, the judge commanded a different defendant, 'I need you to speak up louder. This is a communication between you and the court'. This shows the importance of clear-cut communication of what the defendant has to say (evidence) and of what the court will record (according to the judge's notes).

10.6 Conclusion

The data excerpts analyzed in this chapter confirm Powell's (2009) observation that 'a limited degree of code switching and dispensing with interpretation has also been observed in a monolingual Bruneian court' (p. 136). It also shows the complex roles and importance of linguistic strategies in the courtroom where each participant has to be careful in their usage in order to please the judge, as his or her decisions during the sessions determine the outcome for the other parties involved. What is more, the bilingual community, in which alternating between two languages occurs regularly, magnifies the extremely difficult position of every participant, as their language choice will determine their power status in the legal domain. English continues to dominate the Brunei legal system, and interpretation into Malay plays a secondary role in enabling laymen to understand the complex legal jargon.

Appendix

Excerpt 1

I	Criminal case number CC/9xx/2012, *Hj* _____ *bin Hj* _____.	1
C	Review of drug case dated… xxx	2
J	Is this my case?	3
	Was the… xxx	4
C	Taken from 3rd to 5th June… the result is negative. So he has paid the fine.	5
J	He has paid the fine yesterday. [J writes manually]	6
I	*Hari ini kita menjelaskan pembayaran.*	7
J	Today you will be paying four thousand and nine hundred.	8
I	*Kita membayar empat ribu sembilan ratus.*	9
J	You are under the investigation of the Narcotic Bureau.	10
I	*Kita nanti dalam pengawasan Biro.*	11
J	May I remind you this is your first offence, hopefully you do not get involve again.	12
I	*Ini amaran yang pertama untuk kita ni ah.*	13
J	Second offence is three thousand dollars.	14
I	*Kesalahan kedua akan di denda sebanyak tiga ribu ringgit.*	15
J	You will be prosecuted if you are caught again.	16
I	*Kesalahan kita di denda kalau di buat lagi.*	17
J	xxx… Court is adjourned.	18
I	All rise. *Sila bangun.*	19

Excerpt 2

J	Give me a second, yeah?	1
	By a new charge under section xxx… draw previous charge under section xxx… not among…xxx the application for… xxx	2
	(name of interpreter), you get my… xxx	3
	Now (name of interpreter), please inform *Mohd* _____, ask him to stand properly, not to put his hands on the table!	4
I	*Tuan Mohd* ____, *cuba berdiri tegak dan jangan menaruh tangan kita di meja.*	5

(continued)

(continued)

J	He was charged xxx by waving a *parang* (machete) on xxx in a public xxx... servant on duty that was previously charged against xxx...	6
I	*Kita telah melakukan kesalahan untuk melayang-layangkan parang abiskita kepada orang ramai xxx... pegawai kerajaan telah memberi tindakan sebelum ini terhadap kesalahan kita xxx...*	7
J	Now, new charge will be read to you and will be recorded. Understand? Start the recording.	8
I	xxx [reads the charges to the defendant]	9
J	Yes, (name of interpreter)?	10
I	Your Honor, *Mohd* _____ xxx pleads not guilty.	11
J	Pleads not guilty. Alright. Further mention xxx.	12
	Are the facts similar?	13
C	xxx	14
J	Alright, different witnesses. Thank you.	15
	Hold on _____, yeah. You pleaded not guilty. On Tuesday, 2 pm, see DPP, he is going to extend you the documents. Alright?	16
	Are you going to get a lawyer?	17
D	*Inda.* (No)	18
J	No. Defendant is not going to have a lawyer.	19
	So, read the documents. Make sure you read every single document before you come to court... xxx	20
	Alright? Understand? 27th September. Extended. Yes, thank you. Next.	21

Excerpt 3

I	All rise. *Semua bangun.*	1
	Call no._____	2
DC	Good afternoon your honor...xxx	3
	Accusation against the defendant...xxx	4
	Your honor, prosecution state...xxx hopefully extended... There are now 2 charges section 353 xxx number of people previously 3 person. First charge is xxx	5
J	So what's the application?	6
DC	I just talked to my learned friend... xxx	7
J	Yes?	8
DPP	13th of September xxx //normal documents... we have not received anything	9
J	//13th September?	10
DPP	Yes...xxx	11
J	You're not objecting to...xxx?	12
DC	No objection, your honor.	13

(continued)

(continued)

J	Nor ___, you are now face with 2 charges. Do you understand?	14
	Can you speak?	15
	Do you understand?	16
D	xxx	17
J	Did he say yes or uh-huh?	18
I	He said yes.	19
J	Thank you. Alright. Penalty record.	20
I	[reads charges to the defendant]	21
J	How long are you asking Mr._____?	22
DPP	We are gonna discuss, is it convenient xxx your honor xxx?	23
J	You mean 1 month?	24
	Why do you need until slightly over a month?	25
DPP	I'll be away from 22nd Sept to 24th Oct… if you can have //	26
J	//Do you have any objection on the 27th Mr.___?	27
DC	No judge, no objection.	28
J	No further mention… xxx 27th October 2012, 2 pm, *Md* _____…	29
	Ah, before that how fast can you discuss… xxx	30
DC	I can discuss xxx would surely take a week	31
	Your honor, in this matter wish to be xxx	32
	Sure it would take a week xxx	33
	xxx different section xxx	34
	Yes, your honor xxx with regards xxx aside it happened on the same area and at the same time xxx	35
	Yes, your honor, thank you. Thank you, you honor.	36

Excerpt 4

I	*Bangun*. All rise.	1
	Case number _____ public prosecutor vs. _____	2
DPP	Your honor, _____ on a maternity leave… xxx final submission… xxx my learned friend…. xxx	3
J	Yes [judge records manually]	4
	First of all, I would like to apologize… xxx… sore throat… xxx… having some medication… xxx	5
	The judgment I won't go through every page. The judgment… xxx… the defendant faces four charges, 2 charges under… xxx… 1 charge under 165…	6
	The burden of proof… xxx	7
	If the Prosecution fails… prosecution case pursuing to an anonymous call from… xxx… on 2nd April 2008	8

(continued)

(continued)

	CSI *Mohd* _____ assigned to… set up…xxx… the director bureau… xxx… filing …xxx…. corrupt activities… profiling was made for all custom officers	9
	I request… in order to help and operation *opsjarum* initiated from Miri, Sarawak… xxx	10
	The role of K_____, resides in Tawau, moved to Limbang 2007 to collect debt and same year, smuggled diesel fuel from Brunei to Miri. Sabah 2 cars, 3 times a week. He was… xxx…. July 2007 by preventing him… xxx… *Hj M*_____ suggested him to move his activities to Limbang… xxx… Mr _____, S_____ and A_____… xxx shipped diesel to Brunei to… xxx	11
[J spoke for a long period of time- summarizing the case]		
J	Conclusion, Mr K_____ by his own testimony dubious fact due to the nature and his main role in playing… xxx However… xxx, More importantly, xxx… I can only come to one conclusion, with the support of the video evidence, the defendant cannot deny the evidence…	12
	In summary, the defendant… xxx	13
DPP	xxx obliged your honor	14
	By way of investigate your honor, the defendant, 45 years old, has 5 children, who are still schooling and married, and his wife is a teacher. As your honor is well aware, the defendant may lose his benefits. May I ask your honor to consider that as a punishment already.	15
	Your honor, I've spoken with the defendant on this. He is extremely remorseful of what happened and regret his actions. With regards of first and second charges, although they are different… xxx… that also regards with third and fourth charges, although they are separate charges…	16
	So your Honor, we have 2 charges here, your honor. And I think that would be the correct method, the question arises as to with regards, I would urge your honor, in this sense…	17
	Your honor, would consider a concurrent sentence because they formed a sense of similar offences revolving same participants of the same personalities. They were in time wise, very close in approximity.	18
	Also, your honor, for such offence, it would seem that a term of imprisonment of 6 to 9 months would be a norm…	19
	Your honor, the xxx the prison gates is something … for your honor to consider as well, that will most probably happen in this case xxx	20
	Your honor, in reconsidering this, your honor, the defendant had to endure since this incident and going to this matter as… xxx maybe regarded as some sort of punishment as well. Your honor, I would plea with your honor to consider these issues and to impose a xxx sentence of 6 months	21
	Erm, your honor, I wish to bring to the court's attention to xxx justice also a corruption case… err, act. Where 18 months of conviction after trial, The defendant was arrested in January 2009, I understand he was charged in 2011. So in terms of reduction, in sentence, there should be xxx as a delay xxx in court before.	22
DPP	Would your honor be interested in the copy of the case?	23

(continued)

(continued)

J	No, it's alright. I have to bring attention to both parties that the charges xxx third and fourth charges xxx I believe it is a xxx that is with the amount it is… I think since xxx, we went through trials xxx I am concern with the xxx	24
	The figure is alright but the words are … xxx My judgment would reflect, I wouldn't follow that. I have corrected it. We will stand down for half an hour and to give the defendant to compose himself. It is important that he gained composition before this sentence and let him regain his dignity.	25
I	*Bangun*. All rise.	26
*NB: The defendant was already crying as pointed out by the judge in line 25.		

Excerpt 5

I	All rise. *Bangun*.	1
I	Code no. CC/2x/2011, _____ Bin _____	2
J	Yes?	3
DC	xxx…. Thank you for giving us time to prepare the litigation… xxx	4
J	Okay	5
DC	May I be permitted?	6
J	Yes	7
DC	The defendant was acquitted to…xxx… he was convicted, whereby the defendant…xxx loss of employment. More importantly, his pension. After working 15 years in the Brunei government Police Force. Upon conviction, He leaves behind his wife, his daughter _____ who is 6 years old, his son _____, 6 years old, xxx 5 years old, xxx 4 years old and the unemployed wife is 5 months pregnant.	8
[J records manually]		
J	xxx… any solution you like to comment?	9
DPP	Erm your honor, I have not researched on sentencing xxx I can do it in 2 days time, if you want me to…	10
J	Erm its open to prosecution… xxx.. open to defence… xxx	11
DC	Yes your honor, I've researched and xxx… penalty of 30 years and 30 strokes, your honour.	12
J	Similar to case… xxx	13
DC	But section… xxx	14
J	Sub section of…xxx Minimum of 8 years, the authorities… xxx	15
DC	Yes, your honor. This is where we are appealing for utmost leniency	16
DPP	I leave it to the court to do the sentencing authorities	17
J	I leave it to you to decide	18
DPP	xxx	19
J	Tomorrow Thursday	20
DPP	Very well, your honor.	21
DC	I will not be available.	22

(continued)

(continued)

J	Not available?	23
DC	I have to go back to KB for my colleague… xxx Give us ample time…	24
J	When are you available?	25
DC	xxx	26
J	What time can you make it?	27
DC	3.30 or 3 to be on the safe side	28
[J writes down]		
J	Adjourned to 3.30 and the assignment will give the authorities… xxx	29
I	*Bangun.* All rise.	30

Excerpt 6

I	All rise. *Semua bangun.*	1
J	Good afternoon.	2
C	Good afternoon, your honor.	3
	xxx	4
J	Application?	5
C	The defendant is further remained at the police station, your honor.	6
J	Reason?	7
C	Reason with the assistance…xxx with the defendant…	8
J	Right.	9
C	He has mentioned… police needs his help to recover some items.	10
J	You require one more week?	11
C	Yes, your honor.	12
J	Is that all your application?	13
C	Yes, your honor.	14
J	If you can… due to certain information… this application for the mention of 1 week from today.	15
[The Judge records manually]		
J	Do you understand? Is that all?	16
C	Yes, your honor.	17
[The defendant goes to the door]		
J	Alright, who's next?	18
I	*Awg* _____, *silakan.*	19
J	So what is the status?	20
C	Court proceeding…xxx defendant case no… xxx	21
J	Has the defendant paid the fees?	22
C	Yes, the defendant has on the 28th August 2012	23
[Counsel passed the paper to the Interpreter who then passed it to the defendant to sign]		
I	*Kalau kita sain sini* [points] *keputusan kita* negative [points].	24
D	Okay	25

(continued)

(continued)

C	Alright. Result is negative. So in this case… xxx… we've been undergoing… xxx	26
J	Alright. Okay. That's it. That's all. Thank you very much.	27

Excerpt 7

I	Criminal case number…xxx	1
C	Good afternoon your honor xxx	2
	xxx the defendant is present xxx	3
J	Mr. _____, do you understand Malay?	4
D	[nods] Malay *saja*.	5
I	He prefers Malay, Your Honor.	6
J	You prefer Malay. Charge will be read to you in Malay then.	7
I	[reads charge in Malay to the defendant] Your Honor, for Mr _____, xxx…charge…xxx…pleaded guilty. [continue to read the charge in Malay to the defendant]	8
	… duit sebagai…-	9
J	*-Main judi.*	10
I	*Main judi*…xxx	11
I	*Kita setuju dengan apa saya bacakan adalah betul?*	12
D	*Setuju*	13
I	Your Honor…xxx	14
J	Alright, Mr _____, you have previous conviction… *empat ekor*…xxx where he was confined	15
J	Can you confirm that?	16
I	*Baiklah tuan____, kita telah ada kesalahan yang dulu… empat ekor…x dimana kita telah di masukkan.*	17
J	What do you wish to say to the court?	18
I	*Apa yang kita hendak cakapkan di depan mahkamah ini?*	19
D	*Wang berjumlah seribu ringgit…adalah kepunyaan saya*	20
I	Your Honor, the sum of $1000 is…belong to him	21
J	But you said the sum $730 was used for gambling	22
C	xxx the rest of total is different xxx	23
J	$1000 and $5 was personal. Own money.	24
C	Yes, your honor.	25
D	*Ya.*	26
I	Yes.	27
J	What do you want to say?	28
D	*Tolong kurangkan bebanan hukuman saya*	29
I	Your Honor, …xxx most leniency to minimize the sentence…	30
J	Are you applying for…xxx?	31
D	*Ya, Puan.*	32

(continued)

(continued)

I	Yes, Your Honor.	33
J	Now, do you agree that this… this… gambling…this… traffic light thingy is called gambling?	34
I	*Adakah kita mengaku bahawa perjudian….yang…lampu isyarat ini dikirakan menjudi?*	35
D	[nods] *ya.*	36
J	It's gambling, is it?	37
D	*Ya.*	38
I	Yes	39
J	All right.	40
J	Alright, Mr _____, this is your second offence… xxx	41
I	*Baiklah tuan ____, ini kesalahan kita kali kedua…xxx*	42
J	First offence was…xxx and the current offence… xxx common gaming house.	43
I	*Kesalahan pertama ialah masa….xxx dan kesalahan yang masa kini…xxx dengan rumah perjudian*	44
J	The…xxx is 6 months	45
I	*….xxx adalah enam bulan*	46
J	In view that you pleaded guilty, saves the court's time.	47
I	*Dalam masa perkara tersebut yang kita mengaku salah, mahkamah ini telah dapat memberi keluangan masa*	48
J	I hereby sentence you to a fine of $1000 in default to 1 month.	49
I	*Kita telah disabit denda sebanyak seribu ringgit dalam tempoh sebulan mesti di bayar.*	50
J	The $730 and $5 which the defendant used for gambling will be given to the state.	51
I	*Yang tujuh ratus, tiga puluh ringgit dan lima ringgit yang abiskita pakai untuk perjudian akan di alehkan ke pejabat kerajaan*	52
J	$1000 and $5 will be given back to the defendant.	53
I	*Wang Seribu ringgit dan lima ringgit abiskita akan di bagi balik*	54
D	Okay	55
J	When can you pay your fine Mr.____?	56
D	*Dalam tempoh seminggu*	57
I	1 week, Your Honor.	58
J	Fine to be paid by 27th September, before 3 pm. The defendant is released at court bail at $1000.	59
I	*Pembayaran kesalahan kita harus di bayarkan pada 27 haribulan September, pukul tiga petang. Kita di lepaskan dengan jaminan mahkamah sebanyak seribu ringgit.*	60
J	Step down.	61
J	Any other application, DPP?	62
C	That will be all your honor, thank you.	63

Excerpt 8

J	So, the investigation is complete?	1
C	The investigation obtained…xxx	2
J	My question just now is that, is the investigation complete?	3
C	But the analysis is not…	4
J	Except for the analysis?	5
C	Yes, your honor.	6
J	How does it respond?	7
C	xxx… to the DSS	8
J	Not, at this moment, not future tense!	9
	You require it? …xxx… How long?	10
C	Two weeks your honor. And we request for the defendant to be remanded in the Jerudong prison	11
J	Alright, thank you very much.	12
J	[address the interpreter] Good afternoon Mr ____	13
I	Good afternoon, your honor.	14
J	DPP require the time to analyze the evidence so they are asking for 2 weeks	15
I	[translating what the Judge said to the defendant in tagalog]	
J	…to be remanded in the Jerudong prison	16
I	[translating what the Judge said to the defendant in tagalog]	
J	To be continued 19th September, 2 pm	17
I	[translating what the Judge said to the defendant in tagalog]	
J	The defendant in Jerudong prison. Do you understand?	18
I	xxx	
J	Mr _____, make yourself available on the 19th September	19
I	Okay	20
J	Any other application?	21
C	No, your honor.	22
J	That would be all	23
I	Court adjourned. *Bangun*. All rise.	24

Excerpt 9

I	All rise	1
C	Yes, xxx I would like to xxx the investigation what you did in your investigation xxx of assistance of one xxx, 2 recorded one statement from xxx, 3 recorded one statement from xxx and 4, sorry, 4 obtain xxx contract, 5 recorded a statement from xxx and 6 took two xxx of the neighbour's balcony and the exterior of the defendant's balcony xxx	2
W	xxx photographs…	3
C	Which were already obtain during the investigation. Is that xxx?	4

(continued)

(continued)

W	Yes	5
C	Just now, xxx with regard of the issue xxx if necessary xxx can assist looking at xxx to you dated 5th November 2011, in question 7, you confirmed she was not forced to xxx?	6
W	Yes	7
C	In question 4, you confirmed with Ms —' she applied xxx and she did work as a maid in Brunei xxx	8
W	Yes	9
C	Question 17, in question 17, you confirmed with Ms_ that her term with being employed by agent xxx were the same as the Brunei xxx? That her term with being employed by agent xxx were the same as the Brunei xxx?	10
W	Yes	11
C	Question 14, you confirmed with xxx that she xxx her salary is xxx?	12
J	Confirmed?	13
C	Travelling that her salary will be cut, yes?	14
W	Yes	15
C	Question 15, just looking at that question, you confirmed with xxx that she received by the agent known as xxx?	16
W	[slow to answer] Yes	17
C	Question 39, you confirmed ... that she did not think she was cheated by xxx. She was not cheated by xxx, yes?	18
W	Yes	19
C	Question 4 confirmed ... that she did not think she was cheated by the Brunei agent?	20
W	Yes	21
C	Question 41, confirmed with xxx that she xxx human trafficking?	22
W	Yes	23
C	I'll come back to this xxx but I want to deal with xxx Yesterday	24
	Do you have it? You don't have it?	25
	My first question. Can I take it, you did not draft this charge?	26
W	Yes	27
C	Can I take it that, u did not have the say in how this charge was drafted?	28
W	Yes	29
C	In fact, xxx that the first time you heard this charge was in court after both defendants were charged with this charge, yes?	30
W	Yes	31
C	I know you didn't help draft this charge ... xxx Yesterday you called, yesterday I recall, that you wanted to clarify that xxx so my question xxx wanted to clarify xxx date 2009. I'm asking you why ... xxx. I think the rest of us have issues. Do you agree that was no recruitment that xxx November 2009?	32
C	xxx	33
W	The recruitment was stop ... did not happen in November 2009.	34

(continued)

(continued)

C	Based on your investigation, there was also no evidence that in November 2009, of any force labour that xxx was forced to work against her will xxx. My question is there is no evidence that xxx is force to work against her will.	35
W	Yes	36

Excerpt 10

D	*Aku alum bayar*	1
I	I have not paid	2
J	It is not up to me to give extension	3
I	*Tuan Hakim mengatakan, bukan atas kuasanya untuk memberi tempoh masa baru*	4
J	Where does he work?	5
I	*Di mana kita bekerja?*	6
D	Zed and Zee, Gadong.	7
J	As a?	8
I	*Sebagai apa?*	9
D	Car washer	10
I	Car wash, your honor.	11
D	*Saya…//*	12
J	//I personally have no problem in extending the fine but I am abide to the law.	13
I	*Tuan Hakim mengatakan, dia tiada raguan untuk menambah hari pembayaran tetapi hukum itu sudah ditetapkan.*	14
D	*Saya merayu, saya ada dua anak*	15
I	Your honour, I am pleading. I have two children.	16
J	Personally, I have no problem…	17
D	*Tapi boleh saya…//*	18
J	//But…	19
I	*Tetapi…*	20
J	The law is clear.	21
I	*Hukum itu sudah ditetapkan*	22
J	The law cannot be extended	23
I	*Hukum itu tidak dapat di ubah*	24
D	*Saya faham, kalau boleh saya mencari duit…*	25
I	Your honour, if I may, your honour, he will find the money by today.	26
J	I'm sorry that's what the magistrate states. I have no problem but the law is there.	27
D	*Jadi cemana?*	28
I	What can I do, your honour?	29
D	*Kalau boleh karang kul 3 atau 4…*	30

(continued)

(continued)

I	If possible, 3 to 4 pm today…	31
J	I have to give you an order… but while the paperwork is being prepared, if you can pay the fine before 4 pm today…	32
I	*Kalau boleh kita membayarkan* fine *kita sebelum pukul 4 petang hari ini…*.	33
D	*Bah boleh… faham.*	34
J	xxx	35
I	*Sila bangun.* All rise. The court is adjourned.	36

Excerpt 11

J	Two charges, yeah?	1
	All right, application is?	2
	Well done.	3
I	…xxx *hukumnya ialah*…xxx *kita faham apa yang saya baca kan ini?*	4
D	*Faham.* [nods]	5
I	Your Honor, the defendant understood the… xxx	6
	Faham dengan tuduhan yang ke dua ini?	7
D	*Faham.*	8
I	…xxx second charge…xxx	9
J	I'm gonna fix this case for further mention… on the 27th October, sorry, September, 2 pm for assigned…xxx Before that, *Awangku* _____, do you understand? *Awangku* _____, *pandai kita becakap?* *Bila kana tanya, mesti dijawab, faham?* Ask him again!	10
I	*Faham kita apa yang dicakapkan oleh Puan Hakim?*	11
D	*Faham*	12
J	Now, DPP, how fast can you process the documents?	13

References

Azirah Hashim and Norizah Hassan. (2011). Language of the legal process: an analysis of interactions in the Syariah court. *Multilingua: Journal of Cross-cultural and Interlanguage Communication, 30*(3), 333–356.

Collins (2013). *Collins easy learning English-Malay dictionary.* Glasgow: Harper Collins.

David, M. K. (2003). Role and functions of code-switching in Malaysian courtrooms. *Multilingua, 22*(2), 5–20.

DBP. (2007). *Kamus Bahasa Melayu Brunei [Brunei Malay Dictionary]* (2nd ed.). Bandar Seri Begawan: Dewan Bahasa dan Pustaka Brunei.

Eades, D. (2010). *Sociolinguistics and the legal process.* London: MPG Books Group.

Jones, G. (2007). 20 years of bilingual education: Then and now. In D. Prescott, Azirah Hashim, I. P. Martin & A. Kirkpatrick (Eds.), *English in Southeast Asia: Varieties, literacies and literatures* (pp. 246–258). Newcastle-upon-Tyne, UK: Cambridge Scholars Publishing.

The Laws of Brunei Darussalam. (1984a) Chapter 5: Supreme Court Act. Article 5A. Amendment in 2004. Bandar Seri Begawan, Brunei: Government Printer.

The Laws of Brunei Darussalam. (1984b). Chapter 17: Criminal Procedure Code. Preliminary inquiries into cases triable by the high court. Bandar Seri Begawan, Brunei: Government Printer.

The Laws of Brunei Darussalam. (1984c). Chapter 108: Evidence act 1939. Bandar Seri Begawan, Brunei: Government Printer.

McLellan, J. (2005). Malay-English language alternation in two Brunei Darussalam online discussion forums. Unpublished Ph.D. thesis, Curtin University of Technology.

Noraini Ibrahim. (2007a). Building a credible and believable narrative: The role of direct examination in expert witness testimony. *3L Journal of Language Teaching, Linguistics and Literature, 13*(2), 1–27.

Noraini Ibrahim. (2007b). Whom should you believe? Strategies of counsels and witnesses in a Malaysian courtroom. *Malaysian Journal of Law and Society, 11*(1), 133–148.

Noraini Ibrahim. (2008). Language(s) in the judicial process: Tempering justice with 'mercy'. *TESOL Law Journal, 2*(1), 26–44.

Noraini Ibrahim. (2012). Lecture Notes. SKBE 3013 Language and the Law. Universiti Kebangsaan Malaysia.

Powell, R. (2009). Language alternation in Malaysian courtrooms and comparisons with other common law jurisdictions. In M. K. David, J. McLellan, S. Rafik-Galea & A. N. Abdullah (Eds.), *Code switching in Malaysia* (pp. 135–149). Frankfurt: Peter Lang.

Powell, R. (2012). English in Southeast Asian law. In Ee-Ling Low & Azirah Hashim (Eds.), *English in Southeast Asia: Features, policy and language in use* (pp. 241–266). Amsterdam: John Benjamins.

Part IV
Discourse

Chapter 11
Politeness Strategies of Bruneian Malay Youths in Compliment Speech Acts

Kamsiah Abdullah

11.1 Introduction

Compliments are complex multi-functional speech acts which aim to establish, maintain and consolidate social relationships. Holmes (1986) defined a compliment as a speech act which explicitly or implicitly attributes credit to someone other than the speaker, for some 'good' possession, characteristic, or skill which is valued by both the speaker and the hearer. Brown and Levinson (1987) refer to compliments as positive politeness strategies which are directed at approving the appearance, personality, possessions and needs of people and at their desire to be treated as members of a group rather than as individuals. Compliments are often described as social lubricants that increase rapport among people, though they are also recognised as essential in special ceremonial functions in addition to their ability to bring about the feel-good factor for the giver or the receiver. In some societies, compliments are given freely and directly in everyday conversations, while in others they are more often implicitly given or realised through non-verbal actions.

In Malay society, as in all cultures, the realisation of compliments is governed by societal norms and values. There are certain standard practices and routines as to whom, what, when and how one can give a compliment and how one should respond if compliments are given. For example, a man will generally not praise an unmarried woman directly, and a younger person normally will not direct his personal praise to an older respected person (although the reverse can be expected). Self-praise is taboo, and sometimes even accepting praise or agreeing to a deserved compliment can be regarded as violating the maxim of to be *rendah diri* (literally 'lower oneself', often translated as 'humbleness and modesty').

Kamsiah Abdullah (✉)
FASS/UBD, Universiti Brunei Darussalam, Jalan Tungku Link, Gadong, BE1410, Brunei Darussalam
e-mail: kamsiah.abdullah@ubd.edu.bn

Compliments in conversation are closely linked with the notion of *kesantunan* ('politeness' or 'etiquette') in using language, which in Malay is encompassed in the deeply rooted concept of *budi bahasa* ('refined speech') and *budi pekerti* ('cultured behavior') of a person who is courteous, graceful and uses language appropriately in accordance with the Malay way of life. Central to this notion is politeness in speech or etiquette termed *bahasa halus* ('soft language') or *bahasa dalam* ('palace language'), which originated in the *istana* ('palaces'). Asmah (2002) proposed that pragmatic rules in speech be directed at using effective language which is polite and appropriate to the situation or context. She defined a compliment as a speech act which delights the recipient and should be aligned to the use of polite everyday speech, speech which does not create any tension, anger or feeling of distress for the hearer, and thereby aligns the giving and acceptance of compliments as essential social skills. In education, praise is often used to reinforce desired socially accepted values and behavior.

Compliment behavior as speech acts has often been studied under the pragmatics of politeness, which entails expressing respect towards the person you are talking to by using appropriate respectful strategies and language. In studying politeness strategies in English, Brown and Levinson (1987) discussed ways of showing concern for people's face or self-image, and this has various facets in different cultures. They mentioned two types of face: positive face, which reflects the desire of every individual to be well-thought of and admired; and negative face, which reflects the desire to be independent, have freedom of action and to be unimpeded by others. In general, the notion of face and the universality of politeness theory with regards to its relevance to culture has not been refuted by other researchers studying different language communities. For example the nature of positive and negative face in interactions among Chinese (Mao 1994) and Malay (Normala 2011) speakers has been shown to be different from western practices, although their concept of face is also very much linked to the notion of politeness. The Chinese credit good name and dignity to one's face in relation to one's standing in a community, so to 'save face' and to 'lose face' involve others more than the individual (Mao 1994). Normala (2011) suggests that Malays perceive compliments as a threat to negative face and not contributing to positive face as native English speakers do.

There has been considerable research on compliment realisation in specific language communities, and Jucker (2009) observes that it is culture-specific and sociologically conditioned. Pomerantz (1978), Narjes (2012), and Yousefvand et al. (2014) have all demonstrated that speakers of different languages and language varieties follow different patterns when responding to compliments.

The study of complimenting behavior is particularly interesting because it poses a politeness dilemma for the recipient (Jucker 2009). Leech (1983) developed a politeness principle, and he proposed six maxims of indirectness in language use. These are mostly motivated by the will of interlocutors to be polite in order to maintain social equilibrium and friendly relations. His Maxims of Politeness are as follows:

- **Tact Maxim**: minimise the expression of beliefs which imply cost to the hearer; maximise the benefit to the hearer
- **Generosity Maxim**: minimise the expression of beliefs that express or imply benefit to self; maximise the expression of beliefs that express or imply cost to self
- **Approbation Maxim**: minimise the expression of beliefs that express dispraise of others; maximise the expression of beliefs that express approval of others
- **Modesty Maxim**: minimise the expression praise of self; maximise dispraise of self
- **Maxim of Agreement**: minimise the expression of disagreement between self and others: maximise the expression of agreement between self and others
- **Maxim of Sympathy**: minimise antipathy between self and others: maximise sympathy between self and others

Further research on the function of speech acts referring to politeness, especially in complimenting, was conducted by Pomerantz (1978) and also Herbert (1986). There are two parts to the act of complimenting: giving the compliment; and receiving the compliment. Pomerantz (1978) stated that the act of responding to a compliment is governed by two general conditions: agree with the speaker; and avoid self-praise. The addressee's dilemma is how to agree with the speaker and not to seem to praise oneself (Narjes 2012).

Herbert (1990) focused on strategies used to respond to compliments by the different genders of Americans in the ways compliments are expressed and responded to. Four main strategies were found to be commonly used: agreement or acceptance; agreement but non-acceptance; non-agreement; and request interpretation. These were further categorised into 12 strategies.

A. Agreement/Acceptance
1. Appreciation token: A verbal or nonverbal acceptance of the compliment (e.g. Thanks; Thank you; [nod])
2. Comment acceptance: Addressee accepts the compliment and offers a relevant comment on the appreciated topic (e.g. Yeah, it's my favorite, too)
3. Praise upgrade: Addressee accepts the compliment and asserts that the compliment force is insufficient (e.g. Really brings out the blue in my eyes, doesn't it?)

B. Agreement/Non-acceptance
4. Comment history: Addressee offers a comment on the object complimented but shifts the force from the addressee (e.g. I bought it for the trip to Arizona)
5. Reassignment: Addressee agrees with the compliment assertion, but shifts the force to some third person or object (e.g. My brother gave it to me; It really knitted itself)
6. Return: As with (5) except that the praise is returned to the first speaker (e.g. So's yours).

C. Non-agreement

7. Scale down: Addressee disagrees with the complimentary force, pointing to some flaw in the object or claiming that the praise is overstated (e.g. It's really quite old)
8. Question: Addressee questions the sincerity or the appropriateness of the compliment (e.g. Do you really think so?)
9. Disagreement: Addressee asserts that the object being complimented is not worthy of praise; the first speaker's assertion is in error (e.g. I hate it)
10. Qualification: weaker than (9). Addressee merely qualifies the original assertion, usually with *though, but, well,* etc. (e.g. It's all right, but Len's is nicer)
11. No acknowledgement: Addressee gives no indication of having heard the compliment or responds with an irrelevant comment [topic shift or no response]

D. Request interpretation

12. Request interpretation: Addressee, consciously or not, interprets the compliment as a request rather than a simple compliment; it is not actually a compliment response (e.g. You wanna borrow this one, too?)

There are gender and cultural differences in complementing behaviours. Speakers in the east are said to show different ways in giving and responding to a compliment. Generally people in the east, such as Chinese people, respond to praise with non-acceptance (Gu 1990). Chen (1993) also made a comparative study between the American speakers of English and Chinese speakers by using the Politeness Principles of Leech (1983) and found that Americans are more likely to accept praise than Chinese. Acceptance of praise is among the characteristics of Americans during complimenting behaviour, whereas Chinese prefer rejection of praise, probably due to modesty.

Chen (2003) analyses praise among Mandarin speakers in Taiwan. She recorded 29 strategies within seven super strategies, namely Accepting, Returning, Mitigating, Rejecting and Denigrating, Accepting and Mitigating, Mitigating and Rejecting, and Accepting and Rejecting. She found that use of the Accepting strategy in general is significantly higher in the situation in which the complimenter is of equal status while the use of the Rejecting Strategy is more frequent in the situation in which the complimenter is of higher status. Another point of difference is in the Returning strategy, which is used significantly less often in the former situation, which indicates that compliments rarely go upwards.

The functions of praise in American and Chinese culture are dissimilar: among Americans, praise acts as an opening to talk and it builds rapport and solidarity, but in Chinese communities, especially among those who come from different social backgrounds, praise is likely to be more genuine and more sincere. Americans are also found to prefer to praise someone about external features or their ownership of material things, while Chinese tend to prefer to offer praise about a person's ability or performance (Yu 2005).

More recently, Chen and Yang (2010) did a follow-up study with Chinese speakers from the same location as the earlier study by Chen (1993), i.e. in Xi'an,

China, and they reported that the ways speakers respond to compliments have changed—they are now more likely to accept than refuse compliments that are given. This finding has been linked by researchers to influence from the expanded role of English in Xi'an, as more English is now used in education and the dissemination of knowledge.

However, the study of complimenting behaviour in compliments in Malay or in the context of Malay speakers is sparse. Two studies will be discussed here: Sari (2009), and Normala Othman (2011).

In investigating compliment responses in English used by Indonesians, who have similar cultures as Malaysian Malays, Sari (2009) found that tokens of appreciation were the most frequently used responses by her subjects. This selection was limited to the simple 'Thank you'. However she acknowledged that it could be due to the subjects' limited sources and exposure to variations of the types of compliment responses. An interesting feature of her research is the inclusion of a new semantic formula or a new type of compliment response whenever Herbert's taxonomy of compliment responses could not be adequately employed for her data. She added four new categories in her data: Joking, Promise, Hope, and Apology.

Joking was treated as humour which might assume agreement with the compliment given. Thus by joking, the addressee could maintain the solidarity and intimacy with the addressor rather than offend the addressor's positive face, thus reflecting the need for everyone to be desirable to at least some others (Brown and Levinson 1987).

Promise was mentioned whenever a subject or subordinate made some kind of promise to improve beyond what had been praised, especially when this praise was by people of higher status. Thus promise is not just a return of the compliment, as also found earlier by Ibrahim and Riyanto (2000, cited by Sari 2009). This is peculiar to Indonesians and not the Americans in their study and may reflect an Indonesian value in exchanges between those of higher and lower social status.

Hope is another category suggested by Sari (2009). She explained that it indicates that the subjects might think that it was the right of superiors to expect their subordinates to work well. This was found only among Indonesian superiors and not among their American respondents.

The last new strategy of compliment responses is called Apology. This might occur because of some kind of mistake made because of a lack of ability to do the work, indicating that there may be some kind of weakness that the complimentor failed to recognise when giving the praise. This aspect is clearly different from the 'scale down' response proposed by Herbert (1986).

Normala Othman (2011) investigated compliment responses in Malaysia, and she noted that, in dealing with positive and negative face, Malay speakers have begun to adopt western ways of responding to compliments, by accepting and appreciating rather than maintaining the eastern style of rejecting and denying. She concluded that this is due to a change in the motivation for politeness in speech. For English native speakers, praise is seen as a positive issue (wanting their own desires be desirable to others), while praise for Malay speakers was traditionally seen as an instance of negative pressure (wanting to be free from imposition and distraction) and therefore should be declined. This is because the recipient of praise becomes indebted to the giver of the praise for their good deed. But the situation now, according to Normala, is changing: response to praise is no longer seen as a negative threat to the face of the speaker. This shows shifting norms in speech behaviour in Malay society.

The purpose of the current study is to investigate the politeness strategies of complimenting among young Brunei Malays. Speech acts during compliment exchanges are indicative of how Bruneians practice polite speech in acts of complimenting.

11.2 Methodology

The researcher enlisted the help of university students to collect compliment exchanges among Malays in Brunei Darussalam. Two phases of data collection were conducted, one in 2013 and another in 2014. This was easily and quickly done, as the collectors were asked to be on the look-out for 'praiseworthy' situations. They worked in pairs or in small groups, one recording the interaction and the others acting as the complimenter or observer. (The consent of the participants was obtained later during a brief interview to find out their background.)

Altogether 41 and 61 compliment acts were collected in 2013 and 2014 respectively. They were then transcribed and analysed, firstly based on Leech's (1983) Politeness Maxim and later using Herbert's (1986) Response Strategies to Compliments. Sari's (2009) new Indonesian compliment response categories were also utilised in the last stage of analysis. As no difference was found between the results for the 2013 and 2014 data, they are combined in this analysis.

11.3 Findings

The results of the two phases of data collection show that most of the complements involved the appearance or physical aspect such as face and hair-dos. These covered 50 % of the speech acts. Another 30 % dealt with attire such as clothing and head-scarfs. Compliments on skills and work in education and other matters comprised 12 and 8 % respectively.

11.4 Leech's Politeness Maxims

The following are examples of speech acts which were categorised using the six maxims of Leech's Politeness theory.

11.4.1 Tact Maxim

The Tact Maxim, according to Leech, involves minimising the cost and maximising the benefit for the speaker/hearer. It applies to Searle's (1979) directive and commissive Speech Acts which are only applicable in illocutionary functions classified as 'impositive' e.g. ordering, requesting, commanding, advising, and recommending, and 'commissive' e.g. promoting, vowing, and offering. The Tact Maxim focuses more on the hearer/recipient normally by appealing to solidarity and using a modifying hedge.

Example 1

A: *Lawa jua Pik baju mu ah…tu ah.* (It's pretty Pik, your dress.)
B: *Alhamdulillah, Terima kasih.* (Praise to Allah, thank you.)

Example 2

A: *Di mana kau membali? Ani bah? Lawa tia karang.* (Where did you buy it? This one? It will be pretty later.)
B: *Nada eh…Si Fatin ni membagi. Nada ku makai bejalan ni..inda ku pernah.* (No… Fatin gave it to me. I don't use it to go out, ever.)

Example 3

A: *Sukaku eh…bajumu ..cantik..* (I like your dress.)
B: *Terima kasih.* (Thank you.)

Example 4

A: *Lawa jua Diyana ah tudung ah.* (The head-scarf is pretty, Diyana.)
B: *Tadi awal-awal aku pakai yang bulat atu.* (Earlier today I used the round one.)

Example 5

A: *Lawa jua suaranya ..atu.. merdu lagi, tinggi lagi tu, eh, cik cik.* (Your voice is nice .. it's melodious, it's also high, eh, chik chik.)
B: *Awu, yatah, lantang lagi kan.* (Yes, it's also clear, isn't it?)

In Example 4, Speaker A praises Speaker B's *tudung* ('head-scarf'), but Speaker B is tactful in not responding directly to the praise and deflects it to the type of *tudung* she was wearing earlier.

11.4.2 Generosity Maxim

The Generosity Maxim involves minimising the benefit and maximising the cost to self. The generosity maxim focuses more on the speaker or complimenter. It is only applicable in impositives and commissives. Some examples in our data are shown below:

Example 6

A: *Lain kali a...makin lawa jua ku lihat. Jauh bezanya dari dulu.* (Next time, ah.. you are prettier, I see. Very different from the last time.)
B: *Yakan, hihihi terima kasih eh, inda ku ada usin pacah ne.* (Is it? Hi hi hi, thank you, I don't have any small change.)

Example 7

A: *Patut tah lawa.* (You are pretty.)
B: *Biasa, terima kasih. Esok ku membagi gula-gula.* (It's just usual. Thank you. Tomorrow I will give out sweets.)

Both these examples show generosity by the receiver of praise. In Example 6, the compliment recipient mentions her intention to give a token of reward (money) to the complimenter, and in Example 7, the recipient of the compliment proposes to distribute sweets because of this event (the praise given to her).

11.4.3 Approbation Maxim

The Approbation Maxim involves minimising dispraise and maximising praise to the speaker/hearer. This maxim is only applicable in illocutionary functions classified as 'expressive' such as thanking, congratulating, pardoning, blaming, praising and condoling, and 'assertives' such as stating, boasting, complaining and reporting. The Approbation Maxim is close to a politeness strategy of avoiding disagreement.

Example 8

A: *Banar lawa ...* (True, it's pretty.)
B: *Hehe, terima kasih. Kau pun lawa.* (Hehe, thank you. You are also pretty.)

By saying the word *banar* ('true'), the speaker is maximising the degree of the compliment—it is really true, not just plain talk. The recipient of the praise responds by returning the compliment, so both of them are appreciating one another.

Example 9

A: *Di mana kita membali? Baru ku pernah meliat kita makai. Tepakai banar ku lawa designnya.* (Where did you buy it? I've never seen you wearing it. I like its design, it's pretty.)
B: *Au batah udah ni ku membali di Nazmi masatu. Lawa kan, nampak muda aku makai atu hehehe.* (Yes, I bought it long ago at Nazmi then. It's pretty, isn't it, and I look young when I wear it, hehehe.)

Example 10

A: *Nini si Silah yang membuat kueh lenggang ani lai aa.* (Silah's grandmother is the one who made this cake, my dear.)
B: *Mana tah kan inda, tangan rang tua-tua.* (Of course, the hand of an old person.)

Example 11

A: *Yai, aku suka liat begmu aa.. ne lawa.. aku kelewaan.* (Yai, I like your bag, I think it's nice.)
B: *Ramai orang kelawaan.. kawanku jua.* (Many people like it, my friends too.)

In these examples, the speakers are maximising praise to one another, showing approval, consent and admiration to the compliment.

11.4.4 Modesty Maxim

The Modesty Maxim involves minimising praise and maximising dispraise of oneself. This maxim is only applicable in expressive and assertives. The Modesty Maxim is found in self-deprecating expressions. There are numerous examples of this maxim.

Example 12

A: *Lawa kau hari ane eyh.* (You look handsome today.)
B: [smiling].. *nadalah..biasa-biasa saja.* (No, it's just normal.)

Example 13

A: *Ma… baseri seri muka kita ha, awet muda tah banar…* (Ma … you look radiant ha, you look young, truly.)
B: *Mana ada, biasa saja bah.* (No, it's just ordinary.)
A: *Banar ma, kawanku berista tadi…krim apa mamamu pakai ah?* (True ma, my friend told me just now… what cream did your mother (=you) use, ah?)

In Example 13, even though she is the mother of the speaker, the recipient of the praise is very modest and she downplays the praise to herself. In fact it looks like she is denying the fact that she looks young when she replies that she looks normal.

Example 14

A: *Putih mua mu ah. Lawa eh.* (You are fair. You are pretty.)
B: *Lawa kan? Inda jua. Tua dah ni.* [Smiling]. (Pretty? No. I'm already old. [Smiling])

11.4.5 Agreement Maxim

The Agreement Maxim involves minimising disagreement and maximising agreement between self and other. The agreement maxim is only applicable in assertives.

Example 15

A: *Lawa jua suaranya atu.. merdu lagi, tinggi lagi tu.. eh, cik cik..* (Your voice is nice .. it's melodious, it's also high, eh, chik chik.)
B: *Awu yatahkan, lantang lagi kan.* (Yes, it's also clear, isn't it?)

Example 16

A: *Wah! Kurus jua kau.* (Wah! You are thin.)
B: *Awu aku jogging saja.* (Yes, I go jogging only.)

The examples above show minimising disagreement and maximising agreement; but at the same time they show an element of what, in Malay culture, would be regarded as pride, conceit, vanity or immodesty.

11.4.6 Sympathy Maxim

The Sympathy Maxim involves minimising antipathy and maximising sympathy between self and other. The sympathy maxim is only applicable in formal expressions or assertives, and it can be found in polite speech acts like congratulating or expressing condolence.

Among Malays, sympathy is not often expressed directly and it is difficult to find instances of the concept of sympathising in everyday situations. To express condolence formally, one uses *takziah* ('commiseratons'), a word borrowed from Arabic, instead of the Malay word *kasihan*, which has an implicit notion of love tied to it. In the analysis, it was found that there were no instances that could be categorised under this maxim.

11.4.7 Violations of Leech's Maxims

There were a few apparent violations of Leech's maxims, which we discuss below.

Example 17

A: *Baru sudah mobile nya.* (Your mobile is new.)
B: *Iyalah.* (Yes, of course.)

In Example 17, the Maxim of Tact seems to have been violated; but one might also analyse it as a violation of the Maxim of Modesty, as speaker B accepts the compliment rather than deflecting it. Examples 18 and 19 are clearer instances of the violation of the Maxim of Modesty.

Example 18

A: *Eh lawa dangan hari ani.* (You look pretty today.)
B: *Biasalaaa.. siapakan ne?* (It's like that always… it's me.)

Example 19

A: *Nyaman eyh ayam bbq kakamuti buat aa.* (It's delicious, the bbq chicken cooked by your sister.)
B: *Apakan tidak, mestilah. It is from Secret Recipe.* (Why not, it should be. It is from Secret Recipe [a well known brand name].)

It seems that in Examples 18 and 19 the person who is complimented fails to follow the Modesty Maxim, which is valued in Malay culture. However, looking further into the contexts, it may be that in each case Speaker B is only joking.

In Example 20, Speaker B similarly seems to violate the Modesty Maxim.

Example 20

A: *Kamu kelihatan cantik hari ini.* (You look pretty today.)
B: *Jadi yang kemarin kemarin tu beda ya.* (So, the last time it was different?)

Speaker A is being polite in giving praise, but Speaker B violates the maxim of modesty by inferring that looking pretty is normal for her, implying she always looks pretty.

One more apparent violation is in Example 21, in which the response by Speaker B seems to indicate that her dress being pretty is expected.

Example 21

A: *Eeh lawa baju ya.* (Your dress is pretty)
B: *Bila jua indak?* (When was it not?)

In all these examples using Leech's Modesty Maxim as the criterion might lead one to interpret the act of responding to compliments as violations of the politeness maxim. However, looking further into the context of Malay culture suggests that these Malay speakers are instead using jokes as a strategy to avoid self-praise, and they are not being impolite. In fact, they are adhering to the Malay value of *budiman* ('refined culture').

Be that as it may, Example 22 is one clear instance of a violation of the Modesty Maxim where a joke is not used.

Example 22

A: *Anak kita semua anu pandai-pandai. Kelulusan tinggi-tinggi saja.* (Your children are all clever. They have high qualifications.)
B: *Awu, anak ku semua kelulusan tinggi. Anakku tua, atu kelulusan tinggi dari London. Anakku sorang lagi atu Master. Ikut bapanya.* (Yes, all my children have high qualifications. My eldest, he has a high qualification from London. My other child, he has Masters degree. They follow their father.)

Table 11.1 Frequency of each of Leech's Politeness Maxims

Maxim	Instances
Tact	9
Generosity	2
Approbation	11
Modesty	55
Agreement	48
Sympathy	0
Total	125

11.4.8 Overall Results Using Leech's Maxims

On analysing all the data using Leech's Politeness Maxims, it was found that most of the complimenting speech acts follow the maxims, as shown in the Table 11.1. However, there are a few compliments and responses to compliments that violated the Politeness Maxims.

Instances of five of the six categories in the taxonomy could be identified. The maxim that is most frequently followed is the Modesty Maxim, followed closely by the Agreement Maxim. There are fewer instances of Approbation and Tact, and just two instances of the Generosity Maxim were found.

The only category that could not be identified in our data is the maxim of sympathy. Perhaps utterances of sympathy are not appropriate in complimenting behaviour, at least in the data that was collected for the current study.

In total, there were 13 apparent violations of the maxims.

11.5 Herbert's Strategies

An analysis was conducted on the compliment data using Herbert's Strategies on Compliment Response. In this classification, twelve strategies categorised under the four main headings of Agreement + Acceptance, Agreement + Non-Acceptance, Non-Agreement, and Request Interpretation were considered.

Examples of categorisation from our data are shown below:

11.5.1 Agreement + Acceptance

Example 23

Appreciation—A verbal or nonverbal acceptance of the compliment.
A: *Awu ... lawa jua bajumu. Warnanya lagi lembut saiz dengan kulitmu yang putih.*
(Yes your dress is pretty. The colour is soft and suitable for your fair skin.)
B: *Owh .. terima kasih.* (Oh … thank you.)

Example 24

Comment acceptance—Addressee accepts the complimentary force and offers a relevant comment on the appreciated topic.
A: *Inda jua over tapi manis menawan.* (It's not too over, but sweet.)
B: *(smiling) Manis atu yang mahal tu, sekali sekala bukan selalu.* (The sweet one is expensive, once in a while, not often.)

Example 25

Praise upgrade—Addressee accepts the compliment but asserts that the force of the compliment is insufficient.
A: *Lawa jua barang kau bali. Mestilah mahal kali ah.* (It's pretty, the thing you bought. It must be expensive, ah.)
B: *Urang pandai memilih barang, bisai bah aku ani.* (A person who is clever at choosing, I'm good at that.)

11.5.2 Agreement + Non-acceptance

Example 26

Comment history—Addressee offers a comment on the object complimented, shifting the force from the addressee.
A: *Lawa ah, bajumu. Macam mana ko tu .. di mana ko buat?* (It's pretty your dress. Where did you do it?)
B: *Oh ane dari India.* (Oh this is from India.)

Example 27

Reassignment—Addressee agrees with the compliment assertion, but shifts the force to some third person or object.
A: *Handal banar ia main atu a.* (It's great, the way he plays.)
B: *Kau cerita arahku inda jua ku tahu, bila jua ku minat main anu .. melihat orang main bola.* (You tell me what I don't know, when did I have interest in that game .. in watching people playing football.)

Example 28

Return—As with Reassignment, except that the praise is returned to the first speaker.
A: *Lawa bajunya, he he.* (Your dress is pretty, he he.)
B: *Hehe, thank you.. kau pun sama jua, lawa.* (Hehe, thank you. Yours is also pretty.)

11.5.3 Non-agreement

Example 28

Scale down—Addressee disagrees with the complimentary force, pointing to some flaw in the object or claiming that the praise is overstated.
A: *Shawlmu pun lawa matching dengan baju, ada manik-manik lagi, mahal kali harganya.* (Your shawl is pretty, matching with your dress, it has beads, maybe it's expensive.)
B: *Nadalah ... shawl murah saja ni.* (Not so, the shawl is cheap.)

Example 29

Question—addressee questions the sincerity or the appropriateness of the compliment.
A: *Eh, lawa kita hari ni!* (Eh, you look pretty today.)
B: *Well, hehe ... lawakan?* (Well hehe ... Am I pretty?)

Example 30

Disagreement—Addressee asserts that the object of the compliment is not worthy of praise; the first speaker's assertion is in error.
A: *Oh ... patutlah bergaya.* (Oh ... no wonder you look stylish.)
B: *Prasanku inda pun bergaya.* (I feel it's not stylish.)

Example 31

Qualification—Weaker than Disagreement. Addressee merely qualifies the original assertion, often with 'though', 'but', 'well', etc.
A: *Lawa bajunya.* (Your dress is pretty.)
B: *Hehe..sshhh baru tadi ku menyampati membali.* (Hehe..sshhh, I bought it only just now.)

Example 32

No acknowledgement—Addressee gives no indication of having heard the compliment, responding with an irrelevant comment or topic shift or giving no response.
A: *Lawa masuk dengan kulit kita putih melepak eh.* (Pretty, it suits your fair skin.)
B: [gives no answer and only raises her eyebrow]

11.5.4 Request Interpretation

Example 33

Request interpretation—addressee, consciously or not, interprets the compliment as a request rather than a simple compliment; it is not a real compliment response.
A: *Lawaa ni.* (Very nice.)
B: *Ada satu saja.* (There is only one.)

11.5.5 Overall Results Using Herbert's Taxonomy

The frequency of responses is tabulated in Table 11.2.

The result of analysing the data and subjecting it to Herbert's (1986) taxonomy of responses towards compliments shows that the largest category, 32 %, is Accept. The second category is Scale down, with 12.3 % of the responses. The third highest responses are in the category of Questioning (11.3 %), followed by Praise upgrade (10.4 %) and Appreciation token (9.4 %). Other strategies such as Comment history, Reassignment, Disagreement, Qualification, Return of compliment and Request interpretation were not often employed. The least commonly employed

Table 11.2 Results of analysis using Herbert's Response Strategies towards compliments

Agreement/acceptance	Instances
1. Appreciation token	10 (9.4 %)
2. Comment acceptance	34 (32 %)
3. Praise upgrade	11 (10.4 %)
Subtotal	*55 (52 %)*
Agreement/non-acceptance	
4. Comment history	6 (5.7 %)
5. Reassignment	6 (5.7 %)
6. Return	2 (1.8 %)
Subtotal	*14 (13.2 %)*
Non-agreement	
7. Scale down	13 (12.3 %)
8. Question	12 (11.3 %)
9. Disagreement	5 (4.7 %)
10. Qualification	3 (2.8 %)
11. No acknowledgement	1 (1 %)
Subtotal	*34 (32 %)*
Request interpretation	
12. Request interpretation	3 (2.8 %)
Subtotal	*3 (2.8 %)*
Total	106

strategy was No acknowledgement with just one token, indicating that there was nearly always at least some form of response from the person being given the compliment.

11.6 Utilising Sari's Four Additional Categories

An attempt was made to review whether our data can be described under the four additional categories suggested by Sari (2009) for Indonesians speaking in English: Joking, Promise, Hope, and Apology.

11.6.1 Joking

Our analysis suggests that the category that we earlier categorised under Praise upgrade in Herbert's response strategies and Leech's Modesty Maxim could also be placed under Sari's Joking category. Four examples are shown again below:

Example 18 (repeated)

A: *Eh lawa dangan hari ani.* (You look pretty today.)
B: *Biasalaaa.. siapakan ne?* (It's like that always... it's me.)

Example 19 (repeated)

A: *Nyaman eyh ayam bbq kakamuti buat aa.* (It's delicious, the bbq chicken cooked by your sister.)
B: *Apakan tidak, mestilah. It is from Secret Recipe.* (Why not, it should be. It is from Secret Recipe [a well known brand name].)

Example 20 (repeated)

A: *Kamu kelihatan cantik hari ini.* (You look pretty today.)
B: *Jadi yang kemarin kemarin tu beda ya.* (So, the last time it was different?)

Example 21 (repeated)

A: *Eeh lawa baju ya.* (Your dress is pretty)
B: *Bila jua indak?* (When was it not?)

11.6.2 Promise

An example that was earlier described under Leech's Generosity Maxim might be classified under the Promise strategy:

Example 7 (repeated)

A: *Patut tah lawa.* (You are pretty.)
B: *Biasa, terima kasih. Esok ku membagi gula-gula.* (It's just usual. Thank you. Tomorrow I will give out sweets.)

In addition to being classified under Leech's Generosity Maxim, this example was included under Herbert's Agreement strategy. It is clear the agreement to a compliment in this case is strengthened with a promise to give something (in this case sweets) as a positive return or reward for the complimenter.

11.6.3 Hope and Apology

Instances of Sari's two additional strategies, Hope and Apology, were not found in our data.

11.7 Conclusion

This paper documents attempts to investigate politeness strategies in compliment speech acts by Brunei Malays. In our small-scale study, we have utilised three different types of instruments to probe into politeness strategies: Leech's maxim of politeness; Herbert's strategies of compliment response; and Sari's categories for compliment response (originally developed for Indonesian).

In Leech's six maxims of politeness, it was found that 90 % of the responses follow the maxims, and only in a few cases were the maxims violated, indicating that a large majority of the respondents practice the expected politeness strategies in their compliment behavior. Therefore Leech's maxims were able to portray whether the compliment behaviour is classified as generally polite or otherwise.

In the case of Herbert's twelve compliment response strategies, two strategies, in our opinion, can be interpreted as 'not so polite' in Malay culture, that is No acknowledgement (showing heedlessness or unconcern), and Praise upgrade (under which traces of arrogance might be detected). Our results showed that those were the two least common responses adopted by the respondents when receiving compliments. Most respondents utilised positive and polite compliment responses in line with Malay values. This shows that Herbert's strategies can provide a more detailed explanation of the compliment strategies used by our respondents than those suggested by Leech's general politeness maxims.

Finally, using Sari's new categories, we managed to identify two extra strategies, that is Joking and Promise, to explain self-praise, which otherwise might be seen as arrogance, something which should be avoided in Malay culture. We found that such tactics were used to deflect some of the negative effect of accepting compliments. We therefore conclude that Sari's compliment strategies are appropriate to explain Malay/Indonesian compliment behavior.

The present study therefore provides evidence that traditional norms of politeness in compliment speech acts are maintained by Bruneians; but more research linking politeness theories and strategies in realising politeness behaviour in speech and interaction should be attempted before conclusive results can be obtained. In particular, it is hoped that more informal conversational data can be obtained to allow us to evaluate the various strategies young Malay people adopt to ensure that their interactions are perceived to be polite.

References

Asmah Haji Omar. (2002). *Setia dan Santun Bahasa*. Tanjong Malim, Malaysia: Universiti Pendidikan Sultan Idris.
Brown, P., & Levinson, S. C. (1987). *Politeness: Some universals in language usage*. Cambridge: Cambridge University Press.
Chen, R. (1993). Responding to compliments: A contrastive study of politeness strategies between English and Chinese Speakers. *Journal of Pragmatics, 20*(1), 49–75.
Chen, R., & Yang, D. (2010). Responding to compliments in Chinese: Has it changed? *Journal of Pragmatics, 42*(7), 1951–1963.
Chen, S-H. E. (2003). Compliment response strategies in Mandarin Chinese: Politeness phenomenon revisited. *Concentric: Studies in English Literature and Linguistics, 29*(2), 157–184.
Gu, Y. (1990). Politeness phenomena in modern Chinese. *Journal of Pragmatics, 14*, 237–257.
Herbert, R. K. (1986). Say 'thank you'—or something. *American Speech, 61*(1), 76–88.
Herbert, R. K. (1990). Sex-based differences in compliment behavior. *Language in Society, 19*, 201–224.
Holmes, J. (1986). Compliments and compliment responses in New Zealand English. *Anthropological Linguistics, 28*(4), 485–508.
Jucker, A. H. (2009). Speech act research between armchair, field, and laboratory: The case of compliments. *Journal of Pragmatics, 41*, 1611–1635.
Leech, G. N. (1983). *Principles of pragmatics*. London: Longman.
Narjes, Z. (2012). Translation on the basis of frequency: Compliment and compliment response. *Journal of Translation 16*(3). Retrieved October 22, 2015, from http://www.translationjournal.net/journal/61compliment.htm.
Mao, L. M. R. (1994). Beyond politeness theory: 'Face' revisited and renewed. *Journal of Pragmatics, 21*(5), 451–486.
Normala Othman (2011). Pragmatic and cultural considerations of compliment responses among Malaysian-English speakers. *Asiatic 5*(1), 86–103. Retrieved April 26, 2013, from http://asiatic.iium.edu.my/article/Asiatic%205.1%20pdf%20files/Normala_Othman.
Pomerantz, A. (1978). Compliment responses: Notes on the cooperation of multiple constraints. In J. Schenkein (Ed.), *Studies in the organization of conversational interaction* (pp. 79–112). New York: Academic Press.
Sari, Y. (2009). Compliment responses used by Indonesians learning English based on the compliment topics and social statuses. *Celt, 9*(2), 126–149.
Searle, J. R. (1979). *Speech acts: An essay in the philosophy of language*. Cambridge: Cambridge University Press.

Yousefvand, E., Yousofi, N., & Abasi, M. (2014). The study of compliment speech act responses: A study based on status and gender in Persian. *Journal of Applied Environmental and Biological Sciences, 4*(3), 182–196.

Yu, M.-C. (2005). Sociolinguistic competence in the complimenting act of native Chinese and American English speakers: A mirror of cultural value. *Language and Speech, 48*(1), 91–119.

Chapter 12
The Discourse of Online Texts in Brunei: Extending Bruneian English

Alistair Wood

12.1 Introduction

Everyday language use among Bruneians in the twenty-first century is very different from what it was only twenty years ago. Like many others around the world, young Bruneians especially are avid users of the Internet and much of their language use occurs online, whether in reading articles in an online newspaper, texting their friends, updating their Facebook page, or commenting on a video on YouTube. Examination of language use in Brunei, therefore, would be seriously incomplete if it overlooked the use of language online by Bruneians, since so much language use now occurs in cyberspace rather than in the offline world.

As other chapters in this book make clear (see especially Chap. 1 for an overview of the language situation in Brunei), for such a small country, language use in Brunei is exceedingly complex. Most of the population is at least bilingual in Malay and English, and that bilingual use also tends to involve more or less fluent command of more than one dialect of Malay (Brunei Malay and Standard Malay) and varying levels of fluency in English (Deterding and Salbrina 2013; Wood et al. 2011). English is used not only in fields like education, where it is the language of the classroom for much of the time (Jones 2012), but, largely because of this use in education from an early age, also outside of the classroom in daily life.

As McLellan (2005, 2010), Noor Azam (2007) and Noor Azam and McLellan (2014) among others have demonstrated, not only is English use common in Brunei, but English is commonly used via code-switching along with Malay. Young educated Bruneians in particular commonly code-switch in everyday speech, although it is extremely difficult to estimate how much of everyday language is in fact code-switched, due to obvious difficulties in collecting

---
A. Wood (✉)
Universiti Brunei Darussalam, FASS/UBD, Jalan Tungku Link,
Gadong BE1410, Brunei Darussalam
e-mail: alistair.wood@ubd.edu.bn

© Springer Science+Business Media Singapore 2016
Noor Azam Haji-Othman et al. (eds.), *The Use and Status of Language in Brunei Darussalam*, DOI 10.1007/978-981-10-0853-5_12

data on casual conversation and extrapolating to the whole population. The majority of young Bruneians of Malay ethnicity speak Brunei Malay as their everyday language rather than English, and to speak only English would appear snobbish (McLellan 2005). On the other hand, to speak only Malay, with not even intra-sentential use of English words for particular terms, would be very unusual in normal speech and would be evidence of a purist tendency that is not so common, among younger English-educated Bruneians at least. Because of their English educational background, young educated Bruneians frequently use English terms like *exam* as these terms are far more common and easily used than the Malay equivalent *peperiksaan*.

This chapter therefore investigates how online language use by young educated Bruneians may reflect this offline language usage and to what extent it is specific to online use. More particularly it investigates to what extent it makes sense to separate online and offline language use and whether in fact online use can be seen more fruitfully as an extension of offline language use. The data for the study is taken from a number of student theses investigating such features as status updates on Facebook (Nurdiyana Daud 2012), WhatsApp chat (Syaza 2013), tweets on Twitter (Siti Saleha 2013) and online gamers' discussion on a gaming bulletin board (Muhammad Nazmi 2014). These different types of online data are chosen so that it might be possible to discern more general tendencies than would be found for example in a study of just text messages, such as that by Tagg (2012) in the UK.

12.2 Language Use Online

The topic of language use online is one which has attracted a lot of attention, and much of it tends to focus on those features which differentiate online from offline language, as encapsulated in such titles as Crystal's *Txtng: The gr8 db8* (2008). However, it would seem more profitable to consider not only the extent to which online language is *sui generis*, but also how it shares features with the offline language use of the society concerned. Since the initial work on online language by people like Crystal (2001, 2008), Herring (2001) or Baron (2008) was by scholars in the UK and US, there was a tendency to contrast online language as a whole with offline language as a whole. Both offline and online language were assumed to be monolingual and in English, which was reasonable enough in the early days of the Internet when English ruled the world of cyberspace.

Nowadays, however, other languages are increasingly used online, so although English is still the main language, it is by no means the only one. The latest statistics date only from December 31, 2013, so the tendency for non-English usage is likely to have increased since then, but these show only 28.6 % of users of the Internet using English, followed by Chinese at 23.2 %. The rate of growth of users from 2000–2013 is much greater for languages like Chinese (1,910 %), Arabic (5,297 %), Russian (2,722 %) and even Malay (1,217 %) than for English (469 %) (Internet World Stats 2015b). English, therefore, although still the most widely used, no longer dominates, and increasingly the Internet is seen as a multilingual domain (Danet and Herring 2007).

Given this growth online of languages other than English, we might expect that analysis of the language of the Internet would have taken account of the multiplicity of language use online. Although to some extent this is the case, and there is recognition that online language use is complex and can involve multiple language use and code-switching, as is the case offline (e.g. Androutsopoulos 2007, 2014; McLellan 2005, 2010), theorizing about language on the Internet still tends to take monolingual use as the norm. Thus Crystal (2001) talks about the language of the Internet as 'Netspeak', and even the influential classification scheme of Herring (2007) only includes choice of code as one of the eight situation factors.

It would seem that online language use is generally taken, therefore, to be something rather different from offline use. In the latest update of her widely cited CMDA (Computer Mediated Discourse Analysis) model, Susan Herring (2013) focusses on four main levels of CMDA, i.e. structure, meaning, interaction management and social phenomena. The first three of these focus on the more technical and structural aspects of CMC (Computer Mediated Communication), while only the final one looks at factors which are more specific to the society concerned. My analysis of the Bruneian online data will examine whether it is possible to differentiate so clearly between offline and online discourse.

12.3 Use of Different Languages Online in Brunei

Since Brunei is a multilingual society, it would be somewhat surprising if Bruneians online were not also multilingual. In societal terms of course, multilingualism does not necessarily correlate with widespread individual bilingualism, but in Brunei this is certainly the case. Except for some older Malays, the vast majority of the population is bilingual, having been educated in the *dwibahasa* or bilingual system that has been in place since 1985 (Jones 2009). Since the average educated young Malay Bruneian is bilingual in Malay and English, we would expect that the everyday use of the two languages would also be found online. Certainly, previous studies of online use such as that of McLellan (2005), who studied the language of online discussion in the sites Brudirect and Bruclass, have indicated that Malay, English and code-switched Malay and English texts are used by Bruneians online. This investigation of Brudirect was then replicated by Deterding and Salbrina (2013), who looked at the replies to English posts on Brudirect in Chap. 8 of their book.

However, in a sense this kind of use of online language is atypical. Such postings and replies to postings are a tiny subset of online language use of the types that have become common in recent years. Only a small number of people ever post on these sites in comparison with the tens or rather hundreds of thousands of Bruneians who send text messages, tweet and use sites like WhatsApp and Facebook every day. Brunei has a fairly high Internet penetration rate of 65.59 %

(Internet Live Stats 2015), and social media use is very high. Worldwide some 500 million tweets are sent every day, and although Bruneians do not send anywhere near that number, Brunei is in fact number three in the world in the number of tweets sent per capita (Mocanu et al. 2013). Similarly, in terms of Facebook usage, for figures valid at the end of 2012, Brunei ranked number one in Asia in terms of Facebook usage per Internet user (Internet World Stats 2015a). For young educated Bruneians like university students, the figures are probably over 90 %, as the present author uses Facebook for each of his classes and in a class of over 60 normally only one or two people do not have a Facebook account.

Rather than looking at an online site where only a few people actively post, it makes more sense, therefore, to look at the typical kind of application that young Bruneians actively use on a daily basis, such as Twitter, Facebook and WhatsApp. The data from these three sources all show that the types of language use typical for Malays in Brunei take place online, i.e. Malay only, English only and code-switched English/Malay. However, the proportions of each are rather different in the various sources of data for each because of the different way that the applications are used.

The Twitter data (from Siti Saleha Binti Jabar 2013) is a corpus of 1,022 tweets collected over a period of one month. The tweeters were all Malay Bruneians, deliberately restricted to that group, using the hashtag #brunei. One might expect, therefore, given that demographic and the known pattern of language use offline, that we would get a pattern of English only, Malay only and a mix of Malay and English. In fact, the data was much more complicated with the data comprising the following language patterns: Malay only, English only, Arabic only, Japanese only, Korean only, a mix of Malay and English, a mix of Malay and Arabic, a mix of English and Arabic, a mix of Malay, English and Arabic, and others (English and Japanese mix, English and Korean etc.) That makes a total of ten categories (in fact even more since some minor categories like English/Korean were collapsed together). How can so many different language patterns be explained?

It should be remembered (Saxena 2011) that Arabic is also used in Brunei, along with Malay and English, as a medium of education, and Arabic is also the sacred language of Islam, the national religion of Brunei. As such, it should not be too surprising that Arabic tweets are also found, e.g. 'Alhamdulillah #brunei'. (For the purposes of analysis '#brunei' was ignored in all tweets.) In fact, all the Arabic or Arabic mixed with other languages had Arabic in a religious context or an Arabic phrase that has religious connotations, as in the one quoted. It might be argued that these are not Arabic but in fact Malay, since they are used by all Malays, but this would be a misreading of the data, since they have an easily available translation but the Malay translation would never be used, and Bruneians would recognise these Arabic words as being Arabic and being used because of religious tradition. It would seem sensible to take them as being Arabic in line with this feeling.

More problematic is the presence of Korean and Japanese, either by themselves or mixed with English. This is first of all connected with the high regard in which Japanese and Korean pop culture is held among young people in Brunei. Japanese and Korean culture societies are popular at Universiti Brunei Darussalam and

Korean pop videos are a nightly feature of TV, along with complete TV channels, with recently even a package of several Korean channels becoming available on satellite television. This explains the ability of some young Bruneians to understand and write Japanese or Korean, at least to a certain level, but it does not explain why they do so in their tweets. The answer might be that the hashtag #brunei also has a non-Bruneian audience whose native languages are Japanese or Korean and the tweets in those languages are targetted at those speakers, although they may be using the languages for other Bruneians who speak them.

It seems therefore that in considering language use in Brunei online we have to consider the potential audience. Since the Internet is used all over the world, messages online potentially at least have an international audience and we can therefore expect a wide variety of languages to be used. The author's personal Facebook feed, for example, has messages not only in English and Malay, but also in Welsh, Swedish, Thai and Vietnamese among others, despite my lack of facility in these languages, and the reader can no doubt supply similar instances.

In terms of the analysis of Internet language use, this is an interesting feature, as it shows the interaction between the purely technical aspects of the Internet and the social. Interestingly, though, this characteristic of audience distribution is not captured by any of Herring's (2007) medium factors, which do not include any feature which captures the idea that the potential audience of a message is in fact worldwide. Similarly, the characteristics of CMDA enumerated in Herring (2004) or Herring (2013) do not include this. What we have here, though, is not simply a technical feature, but one which interacts with the social, and without the social basis the technical potential would not be activated. It is the ability of Bruneian tweeters to tweet in at least basic Korean or Japanese which enables these tweets to be sent. This in its turn relies on the place that Korea and Japan have built in Bruneian youth culture so that the Korean wave breaks internationally in the form of tweets in Korean. In other words the technical side provides the basis, but the seed that sprouts is embedded in the society that produces the tweet.

12.4 Code-Switching and Monolingual Use Online in Brunei

As noted already, code-switching is a ubiquitous feature of both offline and online texts in Brunei, but examination of more popular texts helps to bring to light some additional features that might not have been so apparent in previous work. In his analysis of online language on two discussion forums, McLellan (2005) in a corpus of 211 texts found 39.3 % English-only and 10.9 % Malay-only, making roughly a fifty:fifty split between monolingual and code-switched posts. In their replication of this study, Deterding and Salbrina (2013) found 41 English-only and 20 Malay-only out of 102 postings, so 40.2 and 19.6 % respectively, substantially in agreement. In the Twitter study cited above, the number of monolingual tweets was somewhat higher at 779 out of 1,022 tweets, or around 76 %, with the English-only making up about 66.4 % and the Malay-only being only around 7 %. This greater number of both monolingual and English texts can be explained probably by two factors. The first is the Twitter limit of 140 characters, which makes the opportunity to code-switch proportionately less, and the second is the potential international character of the audience, as was discussed above. But it may also be due to the character of Twitter as a technological, contemporary and international medium, which may have encouraged the use of English, perhaps perceived as a more appropriate language for such a platform.

If we turn now to another study, that of 240 Facebook status updates (Nurdiyana Daud 2012), we find that, in this case, the proportions of monolingual use were very close to those of the Twitter study, i.e. 60.3 % English only and 8.8 % Malay only. So in the data from Facebook and Twitter, we find that there is roughly 50 % more monolingual English use and about half the amount of monolingual Malay use that was found in the discussion forum texts. Again, Facebook updates, as with the tweets, tend to be a lot shorter than posting on the discussion forum, so the opportunities to code-switch are less. However, it is still quite possible, even in a short update, e.g. '- book heaven at pesta buku: D ♥♥♥' (Nurdiyana Daud 2012, p. 158).

The potential international audience is not such a factor in this case, since these were all personal status updates which would be seen mostly by fellow Bruneians. It would seem to be the case, therefore, that the anonymous posters on the online discussion forums seem to be more inclined to code-switch and less likely to use monolingual English posts than the Twitter and Facebook users.

It is interesting, nevertheless, that these Facebook and Twitter users were so comfortable using monolingual English such that it constituted more than 60 % of the posts. This suggests that Bruneians, or at least young educated Bruneians, are becoming more comfortable with using English and are happy to use just English for at least short stretches of language use. This can be the case even when the context would not suggest monolingual English, e.g. 'is on the way to send some fishes and extra rice to grandparent's house =)' (Nurdiyana Daud 2012, p. 154). Deterding and Salbrina (2013) suggest that Brunei English is in the third phase of English, nativization, in terms of Schneider's five-phase model of the stages a variety of English goes through in its development (Schneider 2007). This would seem to be the case, but the extent of monolingual English use in this data would suggest that perhaps Brunei English is moving fairly rapidly along the road to phase four, termed endonormative stabilization, given the unproblematic status that monolingual English use seems to enjoy online in this kind of context.

12.5 Code-Switching Online in Brunei

We have seen that there is a preponderance of monolingual texts, the majority in English, in the Twitter and Facebook data we have examined above. In this section, we will look at code-switching in the Twitter and Facebook data already looked at, as well as in an additional corpus on code-switching in WhatsApp, a total of 4013 messages, of which 1465 were code-switched. This means that 36.5 % of the messages in WhatsApp were code-switched, with the rest being monolingual Malay or English (Syaza Hj Taib 2013). This is a higher proportion of code-switched messages than the Twitter or Facebook data, which have 24 and 31 % respectively, but it is not as high as the McLellan figure, 48.8 %, or the 40.2 % in the Deterding and Salbrina data. Since the discussion forum data contained longer texts, it is likely that this would lead to a greater proportion being code-switched, since only a few words out of a very long text would mean that it was counted as code-switched.

As noted in the discussion of the Twitter data, there were a number of tweets which were code-switched, but not between English and Malay, switching between these two languages making up 12.4 % of the total tweets. A number of the tweets code-switched between Malay and Arabic (1.7 %) and between English and Arabic (5.8 %) or Malay, English and Arabic (0.9 %). The Facebook status updates had a 25.5 % total for English and Malay, but also 1.3 % in English and Arabic, 2.1 % in Malay and Arabic and 2.1 % in Malay, English and Arabic. We can see, therefore, that a small proportion of code-switching, between 5 and 9 % roughly, involved Arabic.

An interesting aspect of the data on Twitter and Facebook is the comparison possible between men and women as regards their use of code-switching. Among the tweets, those by men were more likely to be monolingual with 80 % monolingual as opposed to 71 % among women, so 29 % of tweets by women were code-switched as compared to 20 % of tweets by men, though the differences were not statistically significant. In the Facebook data, women also code-switched more than men, 37 % of status updates by women being code-switched, as opposed to 25 % by men, which was marginally significant at the 0.1 level ($\chi^2 = 5.4$, df = 2, p = 0.066) (Nurdiyana Daud 2012, p. 86).

It is well established in the sociolinguistic literature that women tend to use more prestige forms than men (Coates 2004), so this finding regarding code-switching raises the intriguing possibility that code-switching is prestigious in Brunei. As women are also usually in the forefront of language change (Labov 2001), then this might be another factor, with code-switching becoming more common. Certainly, it would seem to be the case that lack of ability to speak English in Brunei would be looked down on as indicating lack of education (Jones 2002), while speaking only in English would be considered somewhat snobbish. Therefore, it would seem logical that ability to command both Malay and English would be seen as prestigious. If this is the case, then what would better indicate a facility in both languages than the ability to switch appropriately between them? Since the type of data analysed is at least in principle asynchronous, participants would have the time to avoid the use of a particular language if they wanted to, so the fact that they chose to code-switch would seem to indicate that it was not because of inability to find the correct form in one language or another.

It is of course often very difficult to decide on the reasons for a particular language switch in code-switching between a pair of languages, as Deterding and Salbrina admit in their discussion of language mixing (2013). In the WhatsApp messages an attempt was made to establish the reason for the code-switching and the majority (1869 out of 3506 switches or 53 %) were carried out to emphasise a point (with Malay usage indicated by *italics*) (Syaza Hj Taib 2013, p. 65), e.g.

> *kita bagi yang* the agreement letter *saja jua ia minta bukan* the one *yang* in the blue envelope *kan*
> We give the agreement letter only not the one in the blue envelope

Lack of facility would not seem to be a common reason for code-switching, as most of those involved would be reasonably bilingual in both Malay and English, as educated young adults. One counter-example to this may be the fact that in the WhatsApp data, the most common one-word element that was code-switched when the matrix language was Malay and the switch was into English was the discourse particle, the most common of which was the particle *bah*, which is practically impossible to translate adequately into English (c.f. the well-known use of *lah* in Singaporean English). On the other hand, this could be said to be less lack of facility on the part of the writer, but rather lack of adequate translation equivalence between English and Malay. This particle is actually often found in Bruneian English, so it is a question in itself whether this is code-switching when used in an English text (Ożóg and Martin 1996; Deterding and Salbrina 2013).

12.6 Features of Online Language

Code-switching is one area where women seem to be going further than men in their use of language. Another area could be their use of emoticons. A feature of online language that is commonly noted as being highly typical of the medium is the use of non-standard language, punctuation and emoticons (e.g. Crystal 2008; Tagg 2012). The status updates on Facebook showed quite a high proportion of emoticon use, with just over one-third of status updates including one or more emoticons. Interestingly, there was a significant difference between men and women in their emoticon use, with the 120 status updates by males having a 26.7 % emoticon use, while the same number by females had a 44.2 % emoticon use, reflecting a highly significant difference ($\chi^2 = 8.03$, df = 1, p = 0.0046) (Nurdiyana Daud 2012, p. 89). Women not only used more emoticons than men, but they used a greater variety (22 vs. 18) and had four different emoticons used more than four times, as opposed to only the basic smiley, used more than four times by the men. This confirms the findings of previous researchers like Wolf (2000) and Kapidzic and Herring (2011) who found that women used more emoticons than men, especially the more positive ones.

The reasons for this may be that women are stereotypically more concerned with relationships and their upkeep than men, as evidenced by the fact that 63.3 % of women's status updates had some emotional content, as opposed to only 46.7 % of men's. But it may also be related to the fact that women are commonly in the forefront of linguistic change (Labov 2001). Since online language is rapidly changing, it is a very good site for the analysis of linguistic change and this kind of data can be useful in this regard. Women's greater use of emoticons, therefore, would correlate with their greater use of code-switching as being emblematic of a greater willingness to push the boundaries of language use.

Non-standard spellings are a common feature of online language use, at least in the popular imagination (Baron 2008; Tagg 2012). In fact, most of the status updates, 77.1 %, used standard spellings, which means that only a relatively small number conformed to the stereotype of non-standard use. However, men were found to use non-standard spellings in their Facebook status updates significantly more often than woman, 29.2 % of the time versus 16.7 % of the time ($p < 0.05$, $\chi^2 = 5.307$, df = 1, $p = 0.021$). There would seem then to be a difference in the type of non-standard use of language between men and women, with women using more emoticons but men using more non-standard spellings, with both differences being significant. The difference can perhaps be put down to the fact that women are extending the standard use of language by using emoticons, which are a new type of language which has grown up online to avoid possible ambiguities because of the limitations of online language. By using emoticons, therefore, women are not breaking rules, they are following new rules. Men, on the other hand, are actively breaking offline spelling rules. This is in line with the well-known rules for covert prestige among men in using non-standard forms (Coates 2004; Trudgill 1975), and explains why women follow some rules but seemingly 'break' other ones regarding emoticons.

12.7 Creative Language Use Online

Deterding and Salbrina (2013) and Deterding (2014) have argued that new varieties of English, including Brunei English, may in fact be leading the way in bringing about language change in areas like the pronunciation of unstressed vowels as full vowels, syllable-timed rhythm and use of count and non-count nouns. Clearly online data of the type that we have been examining cannot shed much light on pronunciation, but another set of data has some interesting and novel language of the type that can be found online. Muhammad Nazmi (2014) looked at the language used on a bulletin board of Brunei gamers playing League of Legends, an online fantasy game. He found in his data a number of new coinages, words that had been invented by players of the game, though not necessarily by Bruneians. These new words, however, had been taken up and used frequently by the Bruneian gaming community in their online discussions, showing that they were comfortable with very new terms. These new terms were often used very frequently, the top term, *jungling*, being used 294 times in 1 year, with six terms being used over a hundred times (*jungling, laning, tanky, gank, jungler(s), imba*). This term, and the associated term, *jungler*, are unusual in that they break normal word formation rules of English, since the *-ing* suffix is normally added to a verb, not a noun like *jungle*, and the *-er* agentive suffix is also added to a verb, not a noun. These game players, therefore, seem comfortable with a level of new word formation that is outside the norm, as there were a total of 14 words like this that were identified as coinages in the data.

The practice of creative language use, however, was not limited to the coinages of new words by gamers. The Facebook data demonstrated a number of variant spellings that are deliberate and not due to carelessness or lack of knowledge. These included not only standard offline contractions like *uni* but conscious playing with words, as in the use of letter/number homophones like *l8ter* or *2getha*. Tagg (2012) points out that the rationale behind such use of numbers is not just to save space, but is also creative play with language in many cases. Unconventional spellings like *wivout* found in the Facebook data are not due to lack of knowledge of the correct spelling but the writer taking on a particular persona for the purposes of the communication they are involved in.

An interesting unconventional spelling practice found in the Facebook data, which is also commonly found in textese, or SMS data, is the habit of repeating letters for emphasis, as in *gooooooood* As Tagg notes, this cannot possibly be due to an intention to shorten the communication, which is often taken to be the reason for unconventional texting spellings like *shld*. In any case, on Facebook there is no need to contract for reasons of lack of space or character limit, as there would be on Twitter. Here the extension of the vowel is a kind of iconic representation of the emphasis, with the number of repeated letters seeming to represent the extent of the quality described. As Tannen (2013) points out, however, reduplication of letters need not have a phonetic equivalent, so that, for example, the Facebook data has forms like *muscleeee*. Here the repetition of 'e' at the end of the word does not have a phonetic equivalent, but just seems to be a visual equivalent of a stressed vowel for emphasis. In this case it is stressing how sore her muscle is feeling: 'sakit muscleeee because of the early work this morning' ('muscle sore because of the early work this morning').

This ludic quality of the Facebook updates is not limited just to English of course, and there are numerous examples of playfulness with language also in Malay, e.g. '- Come on 5th March! can't wait for my appointment, *arrghhhhgatalsudahsanasini*!!!!!!' ('arrghhhh itchy already here and there!!!!!!') (Nuridayana Daud 2012, p. 158). Here we not only have English-Malay code-switching, but also an interjection 'arrghhhh' with reduplicated letters, which is joined to a Malay 'word' which is actually four words. Online language seems to give a licence to play and be playful with words, something which was also found by Tagg (2012), who argued that much of her data could not be explained on the grounds of efficient communication, but that the communication was phatic, keeping up social connections and friendships. The phatic nature of the communication was also found to be paramount in the WhatsApp data, with almost half (48 %) of the code-switches judged to be due to phatic reasons.

12.8 Conclusion

We have identified a number of interesting features of online language in Brunei which reflect various characteristics of language in Brunei. As is the case offline, Bruneians online make common use of code-switching, the data examined here confirming what previous researchers such as McLellan (2005, 2010) have established. Our everyday experience in living in Brunei makes it clear that Bruneians code-switch as a matter of course offline, but it is rather difficult to gather everyday conversational data on code-switching, involving as it does a great deal of painstaking effort in transcribing the data. In addition, this tends to mean that conversational code-switched data will be rather limited, which in turn brings problems of representativeness. Online data avoids these pitfalls and can be completely natural. Thus the WhatsApp data quoted here were extracted from an archive of messages which had been collected naturally with no thought that it would be used for linguistic analysis. The tweets too were gathered from publically available data, thus avoiding the pitfalls of the observer paradox. Thus online data reflects the society offline, but can be gathered more easily and is more naturalistic.

This illustrates an important feature of the use of online data to investigate language use in Brunei. Online data reflects the more general society, so that we can use it as a lens through which to survey Bruneian life overall. This suggests, however, that we must test what we find against what we know of Bruneian society offline, so that we do not exaggerate what we find. But in this case, for example, the prevalence of code-switching offline is quite established, having even been claimed that it is the default state of conversation among young educated Bruneians (McLellan 2005). It makes sense, therefore, to use online data to make an argument about language use in the society outside since the users of online language are also the users of offline language in the wider society.

Online language, therefore, is social and emblematic of the society in which its users have their origin. However, in many cases it is more than just a reflection of that society, but in fact it acts as a magnifying glass which helps to highlight features of language use in that society. Language use online in some respects helps to bring into sharper focus facets of offline language use. Thus Brunei is a multilingual country with a number of different languages in regular use, not only the expected Malay and English, but also other, perhaps less expected languages. For example, the Twitter and Facebook data showed that Arabic was also used reasonably frequently, sometimes with English, sometimes with Malay, sometimes with both. This serves to highlight the multilingual nature of Bruneian society, something which is emphasized by the Korean and Japanese data on Twitter. It is not claimed that use of such languages is by any means commonplace in Brunei, but it would be very difficult to find use of such languages as Korean or Japanese if we restricted ourselves to the typical traditional offline small-scale conversational data (e.g. Ho 2012). Language use online therefore brings into focus aspects of offline use which are present offline, but which appear in sharper outline online.

This reflection of online language in the wider society brings us to another important point about the use of online data. Such data should always be seen in societal terms, so that we do more than talk about online data as emblematic of a technological, global cyberspace that floats free above more earthbound societies, as is sometimes suggested by terms like Crystal's 'Netspeak', which seem to be divorcing online language use from offline societies. My point here is that online use is not just technological and connected to abstract concepts like CMC or CDMA (Herring 2004), but is rooted in the society where the users of the Internet have their everyday existence. So at all times I have endeavoured in this analysis to show how Internet language is also Bruneian language, Bruneian language which is used on the Internet, not Internet language which happens to be used in Brunei. Much of the work on language on the Internet is focused naturally enough on what makes the language of the Internet distinctive and the framework of the analysis is that of cyberspace. Thus work like that of Sherry Turkle (1995), Naomi Baron (2008) and much of Susan Herring's work (e.g. Herring 2004) seeks to explain phenomena that are Internet phenomena. The focus of even quite recent work like that of Herring (2013) is on characterising Internet language, in this case in terms of whether the discourse is 'familiar', 'reconfigured' or 'emergent', the framework being used 'to highlight the structural reshaping of some discourse phenomena that takes place in Web 2.0 environments' (p. 8). Similarly, even Androutsopoulos (2015), when talking about using Facebook, places such use in a networked framework. Such an analysis of online language in terms of how it can explain the new structures online is of course valuable, but if this is the only way we analyse online language, we miss the fact that it is also a reflection of real life offline. Online language, it is argued here, is primarily representative of the society its users come from, rather than the place where it appears, cyberspace.

This chapter, therefore, has served as a plea for researchers to remember that online data is local as well as part of the global Internet, and that we lose a lot if we think of the Internet as having just characteristics which are inherent in it as a global network. If we remember that the Internet is also local, we not only give a more accurate picture of language online, but we can also use it as a prism which brings into focus local language practice.

References

Androutsopoulos, J. (2007). Bilingualism in the mass media and on the Internet. In M. Heller (Ed.), *Bilingualism: A social approach* (pp. 207–230). Basingstoke: Palgrave MacMillan.

Androutsopoulos, J. (2014). Moments of sharing: Entextualization and linguistic repertoires in social networking. *Journal of Pragmatics, 73*, 4–18.

Androutsopoulos, J. (2015). Networked multilingualism: Some language practices on Facebook and their implications. *International Journal of Bilingualism, 19*(2), 185–205.
Baron, N. (2008). *Always on: Language in an online and mobile world.* Oxford: Oxford University Press.
Coates, J. (2004). *Women, men, and language: A sociolinguistic account of gender differences in language.* Oxford: Pearson Education.
Crystal, D. (2001). *Language and the internet.* Cambridge: Cambridge University Press.
Crystal, D. (2008). *Txtng: The gr8 db8.* Oxford: Oxford University Press.
Danet, B., & Herring, S. C. (Eds.). (2007). *The multilingual Internet: Language, culture and communication online.* New York: Oxford University Press.
Deterding, D. (2014). The evolution of Brunei English: How it is contributing to the development of English in the world. In S. Buschfeld, T. Hoffmann, M. Huber & A. Kautzsch (Eds.), *The evolution of Englishes. The dynamic model and beyond* (pp. 420–433). Amsterdam: John Benjamins.
Deterding, D., & Salbrina, S. (2013). *Brunei English: A new variety in a multilingual society.* Dordrecht: Springer.
Herring, S. C. (2001). Computer-mediated Discourse. In D. Schiffrin, D. Tannen & H. Hamilton (Eds.), *The handbook of discourse analysis* (pp. 612–634). Oxford: Blackwell.
Herring, S. C. (2004). Computer-mediated discourse analysis: An approach to researching online behavior. In S. A. Barab, R. Kling & J. H. Gray (Eds.), *Designing for virtual communities in the service of learning* (pp. 338–376). New York: Cambridge University Press.
Herring, S. C. (2007). A faceted classification scheme for computer-mediated discourse. *Language@Internet 4*(1), 1–37.
Herring, S. C. (2013). Discourse in Web 2.0: Familiar, reconfigured and emergent. In D. Tannen & A. M. Trester (Eds.), *Discourse 2.0: Language and new media* (pp. 1–25). Washington, DC: Georgetown University Press.
Ho, D. G. E. (2012). *Code-Switching in the spontaneous speech of a Brunei Malay-English bilingual speaker: A case study.* Paper presented at the 11th International Borneo Research Council Conference at Universiti Brunei Darussalam, Bandar Seri Begawan, June 12, 2012.
Internet Live Stats. (2015). *Internet users by country (2014).* Retrieved 30 October, 2015 http://www.internetlivestats.com/internet-users-by-country/.
Internet World Stats. (2015a). *Asia marketing research, internet usage, population statistics and Facebook information.* Retrieved 30 October, 2015 http://www.internetworldstats.com/asia.htm.
Internet World Stats. (2015b). *Internet world users by language.* Retrieved 30 October, 2015 http://www.internetworldstats.com/stats7.htm.
Jones, G. M. (2002). Bilingual education equals a bilingual population? The case of Brunei Darussalam. In D. W. C. So & G. M. Jones (Eds.), *Education and society in plurilingual hubs* (pp. 128-142). Brussels: Brussels University Press.
Jones, G. M. (2009). The evolution of language-in-education policies in Brunei Darussalam. In K. Kosonen & C. Young (Eds.), *Mother tongue as bridge language of instruction: Policies and experiences in Southeast Asia* (pp. 49–61). Singapore: SEAMEO.
Jones, G. M. (2012). Language planning in its historical context in Brunei Darussalam. In E. L. Low & Azirah Hashim (Eds.), *English in Southeast Asia: Features, policy and language use* (pp. 175–187). Amsterdam: John Benjamins.
Kapidzic, S., & Herring, S. C. (2011). *Gender, communication, and self-presentation in teen chatrooms revisited: Have patterns changed?* Paper presented at the Georgetown University Round Table on Languages and Linguistics, Washington DC, March 11, 2011.
Labov, W. (2001). *Principles of linguistic change: Social factors.* Oxford: Blackwell.
McLellan, J. (2005). *Malay-English language alternation in two Brunei Darussalam on-line discussion forums.* Unpublished PhD thesis, Curtin University of Technology, Perth.
McLellan, J. (2010). Mixed codes or varieties of English? In A. Kirkpatrick (Ed.), *The Routledge handbook of World Englishes* (pp. 425–441). London: Routledge.

Mocanu, D., Baronchelli, A., Perra, N., Gonçalves, B., Zhang, Q., & Vespignani, A. (2013). The Twitter of Babel: Mapping world languages through microblogging platforms. *PLoS ONE* 8 (4). Retrieved 30 October, 2015 http://journals.plos.org/plosone/article?id=10.1371/journal.pone.0061981.

Muhammad Nazmi Bin Puasa. (2014). *Word formation and lexical use among online gamers in Brunei*. Unpublished MA research exercise, Universiti Brunei Darussalam.

Noor Azam Haji-Othman. (2007). English and the bilingual Bruneian. In K. Dunworth (Ed.), *English in South East Asia: Challenges and changes* (pp. 59–70). Perth: Curtin University of Technology.

Noor Azam Haji-Othman, & McLellan, J. (2014). English in Brunei. *World Englishes, 33*(4), 486–497.

Nurdiyana Daud. (2012). *UBD Undergraduates' use of code-switching, non-standard forms and other features on the online social networking site Facebook*. Unpublished MA thesis, Universiti Brunei Darussalam.

Ożóg, A. C. K., & Martin, P. W. (1996). The *bah* particle in Brunei English. In P. W. Martin, A. C. K. Ożóg, & G. Poedjosoedarmo (Eds.), *Language use and language change in Brunei Darussalam* (pp. 236–249). Athens: Ohio University Center for International Studies.

Saxena, M. (2011). Reified languages and scripts versus real literary values and practices: Insights from research with young bilinguals in an Islamic state. *Compare: A Journal of Comparative and International Education, 41*, 277–292.

Schneider, E. W. (2007). *Postcolonial Englishes: Varieties around the world*. Cambridge: Cambridge University Press.

Siti Saleha Binti Jabar. (2013). *Investigating the use of code-switching by Malay Bruneians on Twitter*. Unpublished MA research exercise, Universiti Brunei Darussalam.

Syaza Hj Taib. (2013). *The occurrences of code-switching in WhatsApp*. Unpublished MA research exercise, Universiti Brunei Darussalam.

Tagg, C. (2012). *The discourse of text messaging: Analysis of SMS communication*. London: Continuum.

Tannen, D. (2013). The medium is the metamessage: Conversational style in new media interaction. In D. Tannen & A. M. Trester (Eds.), *Discourse 2.0: Language and new media* (pp. 99–117). Washington, DC: Georgetown University Press.

Trudgill, P. (1975). Sex, covert prestige and linguistic change in the urban British English of Norwich. *Language and Society, 1*(2), 179–195.

Turkle, S. (1995). *Life on the screen: Identity in the age of the internet*. New York: Simon and Schuster.

Wolf, A. (2000). Emotional differences online: Gender differences in emoticon use. *CyberPsychology and Behavior, 3*, 827–833.

Wood, A., Henry, A., Malai Ayla Surya Malai Hj Abdullah, & Clynes, A. (2011). English in Brunei: "She speaks excellent English"—"No he doesn't". In L. J. Zhang, R. Rubdy, & L. Alsagoff (Eds.), *Asian Englishes: Changing perspectives in a globalized world* (pp. 52–66). Singapore: Pearson.

Chapter 13
Identity Representation in Press Releases of a Brunei-Based Banking Institution

Mayyer Ling

13.1 Introduction

The nature of press releases requires institutions to respond to the changes in their stakeholders' environment. It is, therefore, logical to expect that the organisations can switch roles at different times and in different situations (Thomas et al. 1999).

Unpredictable changes in the stakeholders' environment resulting in a number of variations in the role of an institution make the definition of identity difficult to pin down. In this chapter, identity is defined as the 'organisational self-perception, projections of this self-perception, and beliefs about others' views of the organisation' (Gilpin 2010, p. 267). This definition captures the notion of fluidity of identity reflected in a press release. The current study will focus on how a Brunei-based banking institution shapes their identity with the use of lexis in their press releases.

13.2 Indicators of Identity and Institution-Public Relations in Press Releases

One method for gathering identity data is semantic network analysis. Comrey and Lee (1992) recommend a threshold value of 300 words as being adequate for analysis to capture the identity of an institution. Gilpin (2010) extracted the 300 most frequently occurring words used by an organisation called Whole Foods and analysed them from various communication channels. Some examples of the identity constructed for Whole Foods using this analysis include how familiar the institution is with the local

---

Mayyer Ling (✉)
No. 207, Kg Kuala Tutong, Tutong, Brunei Darussalam
e-mail: mayyer.ling@ubd.edu.bn

environment by mentioning specific places known to the local communities, and how well it is performing in the global marketplace by mentioning names of countries where the institution supplies luxurious, organic and cost-effective products to.

Other language indicators that have been analysed in press releases include pronouns (Kim 2009). These are termed 'reader-involvement evoking act[s]' (p. 2088) because they make the interaction between the author and readers more direct, and he reported that first person pronouns were preferred in a Korean corpus. This is probably due to the collectivistic nature of Eastern Asian cultures (Hofstede 2001). It was concluded that the choice of pronouns used in texts is due to socio-cultural influences from the attitude of the writers and the norms of the community for whom the text is written. Therefore, in order to yield a rich analysis, it is worth investigating texts along with the socio-cultural background of the author and the readers. In the current study, the use of proper nouns and honorific titles in press releases will be investigated.

In Brunei, Islam is the main religion and it plays a major role in the everyday lives of the citizens living in the sultanate. As noted by Deterding and Salbrina (2013, p. 92), it comes as no surprise that 'a wide range of words originating from Arabic are incorporated into Brunei English'. The Arabic lexis is only sometimes glossed as there may be no equivalent in the English language for the terms. An example to demonstrate this is *Zikir Nation* which can be loosely translated as a 'chanting nation'. However, in the Brunei context this phrase refers to a mission that the monarch has set for the population to always do good deeds and to follow Allah's guidance. Thus, one of the main elements that will also be considered in this paper is Arabic-derived lexis.

13.3 Methodology

This section is divided into two subsections, data collection and data analysis. Data collection focuses on the corpus used for this study. Data analysis discusses the analysis of the 300 most frequently used words from press releases from the chosen banking institution.

13.3.1 Data Collection

The banking institution that was chosen for this study is known as Bank Islam Brunei Darussalam (henceforth, BIBD) which has a tagline of being 'Bruneian at Heart'. BIBD is the largest Islamic financial institution in Brunei Darussalam. It was established in 1981 and currently has fifteen branches at strategic locations across all four districts in the sultanate. The bank has enjoyed a respectable reputation at both the national and international levels reflected in a number of international awards and also a series of local recognitions that it has received. As a result, this institution is often featured in local media including newspapers.

100 Press releases from the media section of BIBD's website were gathered to form the corpus used for analysis. This corpus contains 39,674 words with each press release having between 125 and 1329 words.

13.3.2 Data Analysis

In the analysis, the program used was Antconc Build 3.2.4, which is software created by Laurence (2011) specifically for corpus analysis research. The procedure for the production of the 300 most frequently occurring lexis started with the press releases from the BIBD corpus being input into Antconc. Then a stoplist was created to be used as a filter. The stoplist is the product of taking a list of the 1000 most-frequent lemmas in the English language from the British National Corpus, identifying the function words and removing them. This disallows function words such as determiners, conjunctions, prepositions, pronouns, auxiliary verbs, modal verbs and quantifiers from being detected in the corpus when the generation of the 300 most-frequent words is carried out. What were left to be detected from the corpus were content words.

The list containing the 300 most-frequent words was divided into three word categories, namely Financial, Institutional and National. Lexis in the Financial category comprises of vocabulary words that were used to identify the nature of the institution that issues the press releases. This includes words such as *debit*, *credit*, *mortgage* and *loans*. Lexis in the Institutional category was found uniquely in the environment of the issuing institution. This includes the names of staff members of BIBD (such as *Javed Ahmad*) and the products that it offers (including *CE-ALAF*, which is a community outreach program carried out by BIBD). Lexis in the National category, on the other hand, contains words associated with the location of the institution in a particular setting or country such as *Brunei Darussalam* which is the specific name of the place where BIBD is located, or the citizens in the country (*Bruneians*). In addition, proper nouns which are not necessarily associated with the institution but belong to a particular local group or local individual (i.e. the names of customers, names of sponsors) such as *Hj* (which is an abbreviation for *Haji*, an honorific title for someone who has undertaken a pilgrimage to Mecca), *Bin* (which means 'the son of') and *Minister* (often preceding the proper name of the minister of an institution). These words are then analysed in the context of the respective press releases to interpret how they contribute to the identity representation of BIBD.

Table 13.1 Extract from 300 most-frequently occurring word list

Lexis	Occurrences in corpus	Word category	Example
BIBD	1221	Institutional	*BIBD* would also like to inform the public that prayer tents will be provided for Subuh Prayers
ALAF	218	Institutional	Launched earlier in the year, the *ALAF* initiative is an extension of BIBD's contribution towards its strong belief in the importance of early childhood education …
Islamic	99	Institutional	The aim of the visit was to provide the students with an insight and understanding of *Islamic* Banking…
Barakah	52	Institutional	The '*Barakah* 4' campaign is open to all new and existing BIBD customers
Rahnu	24	Institutional	Bank Islam Brunei Darussalam's (BIBD) exciting promotion for Ar-*Rahnu* micro-financing is coming to a close soon
Yang	74	National	The 5 km event continued and was flagged off by *Yang* Mulia Awang Junaidi bin Haji Masri, Assistant Managing Director, Brunei Investment Agency (BIA) …
Hjh	49	National	The fourth prize went to *Hjh* Hindun Bte Dato Paduka Hj Noordin represented by her daughter Siti Haziqah binti Marzuke
Mulia	47	National	Present as the guest of honour at the prize giving ceremony was Yang *Mulia* Dr Abdul Manaf bin Hj Metussin, Acting Chief Executive Officer
Shariah	30	National	The Sukuk will be used to refinance debt and support capital expenditure, for working capital and general corporate purposes which are *Shariah*-compliant
Pehin	28	National	The recital of Surah Yassin, tahlil and doa arwah was led by Yang Dimuliakan Begawan *Pehin* Khatib Dato Paduka Hj Hamidon bin Begawan *Pehin* Siraja Khatib Dato Paduka Seri Setia Hj Mohd Hamid
Bank	895	Financial	The systems upgrade is required to further improve the *bank*'s service delivery channels…
Finance	514	Financial	The customer's ownership of the property will gradually increase over time by way of purchasing BIBD's share over the period of *finance* through
Card	190	Financial	The lucky draw winners were chosen from BIBD customers who used the BIBD Debit *Card* or BIBD Credit *Card* at any retail outlet during the promotional period
Capital	59	Financial	Ar-Rahnu is a suitable avenue for customers who wish to have short-term financing, perhaps to be used as working *capital* for their small businesses …
Account	43	Financial	The entries will be submitted automatically upon approval or activation of the facility or *account*

The key words are italicised in the table, but they are not in italics in the corpus.

13.4 Results

Table 13.1 lists some of the words that were found in the 300 most frequently occurring words in the BIBD corpus. Five words have been selected from each of the three categories, Institutional, National, Financial, to demonstrate the context in which they were found.

13.5 Discussion

This section will first consider proper nouns found in the corpus, then the use of honorary titles, and finally the occurrence of lexis derived from Arabic. This part of the discussion mainly focuses on how BIBD portrays its identity as a Brunei-based institution with practices and norms suitable for the sultanate. This includes terms of addressing its stakeholders and important persons, and the lack of gloss for some Arabic-derived lexis. Due to the nature of BIBD, the last part of the section will briefly discuss how BIBD identifies itself as a financial institution with the use of lexis in its press releases that specifically reflects its core banking identity. These lexical items are not specific to the Bruneian context and will be understood by general members of financial institutions.

13.5.1 Proper Nouns

> **Examples from data set**: Haji/Hj, Hajah/Hjh, Bin, Binti/Bte, Javed Ahmad, Nurul Akmar.
>
> **Examples from the corpus**:
> The guest of honour at the event was *BIBD* Managing Director *Javed Ahmad*, who was accompanied by *BIBD's* Head of Institutional Banking *Hj Minorhadi Hj Mirhassan*.
>
> Present to give away the prizes was the Deputy Head of Consumer Banking Division *Hjh Nurul Akmar bte Hj Mohd Jaafar*.

The proper names italicised above (the managing director's name *Javed Ahmad*, the name of a member of staff *Hj Minorhadi Hj Mirhassan*, and the organisation's abbreviated name *BIBD*) all belong to the institution of BIBD. It should also be noted that abbreviated lexis is abundant in the corpus. Examples include proper names *Hj* (for *Haji*), *Hjh* (for *Hajah*) which refer to men and women respectively who have performed their pilgrimage to Mecca. These references have become part of the names of the respective individuals and thus were classified under proper names (in contrast with the use of honorary titles presented in the discussion below). The institution's abbreviated name *BIBD* is also found in abundance when compared to the full form, *Bank Islam Brunei Darussalam*. This suggests a level of understanding and familiarity between the issuer of the press releases and the readers. Many of these lexical items would not be comprehensible to readers who are not familiar with the discourse in Brunei Darussalam. These shared lexical items have a function that is seen to be similar to those labelled as reader-involvement evoking acts in the analysis of Korean texts by Kim (2009), especially the use of *we* which was often used to refer to the Korean community (i.e. national community) and was seen to signal in-group membership at the national level. The use of these proper nouns in the BIBD corpus serves a similar purpose to the use of *we* in Kim's (2009) analysis which is to signal a sense of national community and also that the writers of the press releases in BIBD are primarily addressing readers who are familiar with the naming conventions in Brunei Darussalam. In other words, it seems as though the target audience for BIBD is primarily those who are in Brunei, which is the primary catchment area for the institution. The audience is assumed to already be familiar with the bank, and the bank is aware of the conventions and norms practised in the nation.

Furthermore, proper names reflect the importance of identifying people in this part of the world. The highlighting of named people in press releases is prominent as it gives credit to those who have been involved in the success of BIBD's efforts towards corporate social responsibility. This suggests gratitude on behalf of the institution as part of its way of thanking its customers, sponsors and various stakeholders personally in press releases throughout their involvement in the banking arena. This being said, it seems as though even when the press releases were issued by BIBD and sponsorship for the programme highlighted in the text was provided by BIBD, the institution still foregrounded individuals who were the driving force behind the success in their corporate social responsibility efforts with the use of proper nouns. They, surprisingly, did not take all the credit for the success events. The sense of appreciation might serve a more powerful tool in harnessing the support of its customers as opposed to blatantly advertising itself as being a successful institution for all that it has achieved thus far.

13.5.2 Honorary Titles

Examples from data set: Yang Mulia, Dato Seri Setia, Dato Paduka, Pehin Orang Kaya, Yang Berhormat.

Examples from corpus:
Present was *Yang Mulia Dato Paduka* Awang Haji Bahrin bin Abdullah, Deputy Minister of Finance cum BIBD Chairman along with other BIBD Board of Directors, *Yang Mulia* Awang Junaidi bin Haji Masri, Assistant Managing Director of Brunei Investment Agency (BIA), *Yang Mulia* Dr Abdul Manaf bin Haji Metussin, Deputy Chief Executive Officer of The Brunei Economic Development Board …

Present as the guest of honour was *Yang Berhormat Pehin Orang Kaya Seri Kerna Dato Seri Setia* Haji Awang Abu Bakar bin Haji Apong, Minister of Education, who consented to present the scholarships to the selected recipients.

The italicised lexical items above represent honorary titles that are commonly found in Bruneian contexts to signify respect for the individuals that are mentioned in the press releases. It is apparent that these honorary titles take up a significant amount of space in press releases and the generated list of most frequently occurring words includes many honorary titles. This suggests that BIBD balances the need to inform and conform. The press releases are used to inform the public of the institution's progress, products and corporate social responsibility activities. They also reflects caution about conforming to the national norm of showing respect through the use of honorary titles irrespective of the space in the press release that has to be allocated to the purpose of providing information. It should also be noted that the institution's tagline of being 'Bruneian at Heart' comes into play especially in the inclusion of honorary titles which are uniquely found in Brunei Darussalam. This suggests that BIBD wants to adhere to the norms that are present in the sultanate by offering a service that is moulded to the norms of address in the nation. This act of conforming to the norms is what Hofstede (2001) described as being a collectivistic intention. This is a different technique in demonstrating such collectivistic nature of East Asian societies, which includes Brunei Darussalam, than the use of reader-involvement evoking acts (Kim 2009), but it serves the same function. Giplin's (2010) semantic analysis captures this phenomenon, and it seems that BIBD issues press releases not only as a token of gratitude (as was discussed in the section on proper nouns), but also to show respect and share the unique honorary title system in Brunei Darussalam. A similar system of titles is also commonly found in Malaysia (Lim 2001, p. 133). Indeed, there is a wide range of honorary titles in Brunei Darussalam and these titles represent various hierarchical ranks for the person who holds them. For instance, *Pehin* and *Dato* are titles bestowed by the Sultan of Brunei (McLellan 1996) while *Yang Mulia* ('the honourable') is used before names generally to signal respect for the referent. *Pehin* is also a title that is only bestowed by the Sultan to ministers in Brunei with no other rank. BIBD does well in conforming to these conventions and adhering to its tagline of being 'Bruneian at Heart'. Therefore, instead of promoting the tagline at all times, the institution can use other form of identity-projection strategies. This includes resorting to other Bruneian ways of identification via the use of honorary titles many of which are only present in the Bruneian social environment.

13.5.3 Lexis Related to Islam and Arabic Words

Examples from data set: Islam, Barakah ('blessing'), Shariah ('Islamic law'), *Ar-Rahnu* ('Islamic concept of pawn-broking'), Sirah Amal ('the head of charity').

Examples from corpus:
Ar-Rahnu is an Islamic pawn-broking concept based on the principles of Wadiah Yad Dhamanah and *Ar-Rahnu*, and represents a comprehensive and hassle-free avenue for Bruneians to obtain micro-financing with their gold items or precious stones.

BIBD today held a prize presentation ceremony for its monthly 'Barakah 4' winners.

As was noted by Deterding and Salbrina (2013, p. 92), Arabic lexis occurs widely in Brunei English and some words such as *doa* ('prayer') are often not glossed, as the meanings are assumed to be understood. There are similar occurrences in the BIBD corpus because a wide range of Arabic words are found in the corpus. These Arabic words are sometimes not glossed because readers are expected to understand their meaning and a brief explanation is only occasionally given. When a customer would like more information on the product, they have access to information that can be supplied by representatives of BIBD and this information is supplied in Malay or English depending on the preference of the customers. However, in the context of the press releases that were analysed, lexical items that have become familiar to the population such as *Barakah*, *Sirah Amal* and *Shariah* are never glossed nor given any explanation. This manner of using Arabic words as if they are part of English shows how Arabic influence, which results from the practice of Islam in the sultanate, has prominent effect on the language system used by contemporary establishments such as this banking institution. Interestingly, the lack of gloss is also an indication of another form of promotional device used by BIBD, as the use of Arabic words not only stimulates the interest of the intended audience but also encourages them to get in touch with BIBD to learn more about the products and services offered.

Another incidence of Arabic influence in written discourse in the sultanate was noted by Coluzzi (2012), who investigated the use on shop signs of Jawi, the Arabic-based script that can be used to write Malay. Therefore, the presence of Arabic influence is not a new phenomenon in the written discourse found in the sultanate.

13.5.4 Finance and Banking-Related Lexis

> **Examples from data set**: bank(ing/s), finance(ial/ing), card(s), investment, credit, capital, account(s).
>
> **Examples from corpus**:
> The region represents 24 % of the global *investable* universe, a significant portion of well-diversified, shariah-compliant investments opportunities.
>
> The Sukuk will be used to refinance debt and support capital expenditure, for working *capital* and general corporate purposes which are Shariah-compliant.

It is expected that when an institution is as established as BIBD, there will many words that allow readers to identify the issuer with the financial community. Language has always been a distinct, yet subtle, manner of defining group membership. Well-known studies in which language variation is an indicator for stratification and grouping of individuals include those by Labov (1972) focusing on r-pronunciation, Milroy (1980, cited in Wardhaugh 1986) on final cluster simplification, and Jones (1999) on vocabulary choices.

The current study is not concerned with spoken discourse, but the elements found in the written press releases are quite similar in concept. Despite the fact that BIBD is an institution that is claimed to be truly 'Bruneian at heart', it still uses press releases to identity itself with the rest of the banking-financing community worldwide. This is done by means of the inclusion of lexis in the financial category which will be familiar to readers in the banking industry. Therefore, although as noted above there are Arabic-derived concepts in abundance in the press releases issued by BIBD, international readers can assume that these lexis are Islamic banking concepts and that it is a type of service uniquely offered by BIBD. At the same time, the financial category lexis also allows the portrayal of BIBD as an institution that is not too different from contemporary banks, apart from the Shariah-compliant nature of its operations. This allows customers who are unfamiliar with the nature of Shariah concepts in the bank to at least have some familiarity when doing business with BIBD. To some extent, it can be assumed that BIBD is indeed an institution that aims to provide banking services to all walks of life present among the diverse population of the sultanate.

13.6 Conclusion

The linguistic representation of identity indicators investigated in this study suggests that BIBD is an institution that expresses gratitude to its respective stakeholders with the use of proper nouns with conventions that can only be fully understood by readers who are familiar with the discourse in the sultanate. BIBD is also a conformist institution which seeks a balance between informing the public, which is the primary function of press releases, and conforming to the manner of addressing the hierarchical system in Brunei Darussalam. This has enabled the institution to stay 'Bruneian at heart' as its tagline suggests.

The institution adheres closely to Islamic banking concepts that are applicable to a society in which Islam is the dominant religion. However, despite the Shariah-compliant nature of BIBD, as reflected in the inclusion of Arabic-derived lexis, there is also financial category lexis that is assumed to be understood by contemporary banking customers in general.

We must not forget that BIBD is still an institution that needs promotional devices to attract the attention of its stakeholders. Even when BIBD does not directly advertise itself, they use other methods to carry out this function. These include the use of familiarity-signaling devices such as the use of abbreviated forms of proper names, appreciative gestures such as foregrounding figures who are responsible for the success of their programmes, and also interest-stimulating Arabic words to encourage their intended audience for consultation in any of their branches.

References

Coluzzi, P. (2012). The linguistic landscape of Brunei Darussalam: Minority languages and the threshold of literacy. *South East Asia: A Multidisciplinary Journal, 12*, 1–16.

Comrey, A. L., & Lee, H. B. (1992). *A first course in factor analysis* (2nd ed.). Hillsdale, NJ: Lawrence Erlbaum Associates.

Deterding, D., & Salbrina, S. (2013). *Brunei English: A new variety in a multilingual society*. Dordrecht: Springer.

Gilpin, D. R. (2010). Organizational image construction in a fragmented online media environment. *Journal of Public Relations Research, 22*(3), 165–287.

Hofstede, G. (2001). *Cultural consequences: Comparing values, behaviors, institutions, and organizations across nations*. Thousand Oaks, CA: Sage Publications.

Jones, J. 1999. Language and class. In L. Thomas, S. Wareing, I. Singh, J. S. Peccei, J. Thornborrow & J. Jones (Eds.), *Language, society and power: An introduction* (pp. 117–134). Abingdon: Routledge.

Kim, C.-K. (2009). Personal pronouns in English and Korean texts: A corpus-based study in terms of textual interaction. *Journal of Pragmatics, 41*, 2086–2099.

Labov, W. (1972). *Sociolinguistic patterns*. Philadelphia, PA: University of Pennsylvania Press.

Laurence, A. (2011). Antconc (Build 3.2.4) [Computer program]. Retrieved February 11, 2014, from http://www.antlab.sci.waseda.ac.jp/antconc_index.html.

Lim, G. (2001). Till divorce do us part: The case of Singaporean and Malaysia English. In V. B. Y. Ooi (Ed.) *Evolving identities: The English language in Singapore and Malaysia* (pp. 125–139). Singapore: Times Academic Press.

McLellan, J. (1996). Some features of written discourse in Brunei English. In P. W. Martin, C. Ożóg & G. Poedjosoedarmo (Eds.), *Language use and language change in Brunei Darussalam* (pp. 223–235). Athens, OH: Ohio University Center for International Studies.

Thomas, L., Wareing, S., Singh, I., Peccei, J. S., Thornborrow, J., & Jones, J. (1999). *Language, society and power: An introduction* (2nd ed.). London: Routledge.

Wardhaugh, R. (1986). *An introduction to sociolinguistics* (p. 7). Padstow: T.J. Press Ltd.

Chapter 14
Similar Story, Different Angles? A Comparative Study of 'Hard News' Texts in the Malay and English Print Media in Brunei Darussalam

Sharifah Nurul Huda Alkaff, James McLellan
and Fatimah Chuchu

14.1 Introduction

In this chapter we compare texts from two Brunei Darussalam newspapers, the English-language *Borneo Bulletin* and the Malay-language *Media Permata*. The comparative focus is on 'hard news' texts: reports of current events that are considered newsworthy. We use a modified Critical Discourse Analysis (CDA) framework to analyse the texts as product, investigating which aspects and actors are given prominence, e.g. through topicalisation, and whether there are differences in prominence and topicalisation between the English and Malay texts. The initial comparison of reports covering the same story in Malay and English sheds light on whether any translation occurs in the process of preparing the reports for publication, as well as on editorial decisions about what to include and what to leave out of the Malay and English texts. In order to achieve a measure of triangulation, we also present findings from semi-structured interviews conducted with journalists and editors of the two newspapers. These interviews offer insights into the processes involved in the production of print media texts in English and Malay.

The English and Malay text corpora also enable the research team to explore aspects of discourse transfer: whether, for example, Malay media reports reflect the canonical structure of English media reports, or whether they display structures that are distinct and that reflect canonical Malay discourse patterns. We hypothesise that there is a canonical structure of news media reports in English which constrains

---

Sharifah Nurul Huda Alkaff (✉) · J. McLellan · Fatimah Chuchu
Universiti Brunei Darussalam, FASS/UBD, Jalan Tungku Link,
Gadong BE1410, Brunei Darussalam
e-mail: sharifah.alkaff@ubd.edu.bn

J. McLellan
e-mail: james.mclellan@ubd.edu.bn

Fatimah Chuchu
e-mail: fatimah.chuchu@ubd.edu.bn

© Springer Science+Business Media Singapore 2016
Noor Azam Haji-Othman et al. (eds.), *The Use and Status of Language in Brunei Darussalam*, DOI 10.1007/978-981-10-0853-5_14

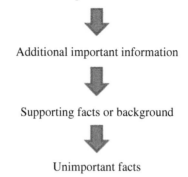

Fig. 14.1 Inverted pyramid model of news report structure (adapted from Faure 2001, p. 358)

writers to produce short paragraphs in descending order of importance in terms of content: the inverted pyramid structure (Bell 2014; Faure 2001, p. 358; Richardson 2013; Thomson et al. 2008; see Fig. 14.1). One reason for this is practical: editors are likely to cut texts from the bottom whenever space is limited. The rhetorical and propositional structure of the texts are thus analysed using notions of salience, foregrounding (Huckin 2002, p. 9) and newsworthiness.

We seek to uncover the extent to which Malay news reports in *Media Permata* follow this canonical structure which, as noted by Manning (2011), may run counter to normal chronological order, as the order of reporting is determined by importance rather than sequentially.

14.2 Overview of Related Research Studies from Brunei and Elsewhere

Bell and Garrett (1998) acknowledge that studies in media discourse have long been a focus amongst those working with language and communication, as well as others working within the broader field of media studies. Apart from the pragmatic reason that the media are a rich source of readily accessible data for research, they also attribute interest in the media among researchers to the fact that it can tell us a great deal about a society's values and its expressions of culture, politics and social life. It is for these reasons that the media have become a popular research field now. However, previous studies on media discourse have primarily focused on media texts in English only. Studies that utilise a cross-linguistic comparative approach to media texts are relatively few in number. Thomson et al. (2008, p. 212) suggest that it is about time that 'our gaze' should be cast 'more widely to consider the situation in the news reporting discourses of other languages and cultures'. Similarly, Hallin and Mancini (2004, p. 1) state that 'though there have been attempts, particularly since the 1970s, to push the field in the direction of comparative analysis, such a research tradition remains essentially in its infancy'.

One such study that does employ a comparative analysis of news stories is Knox and Patpong's (2008) analysis of the reporting of violence in southern Thailand by two daily newspapers in Thailand, one in Thai and the other in English. The results show that the same news story was reported very differently in these two newspapers. The authors suggest that the two languages provide different resources for making meaning and that these meanings are developed by newspapers 'to reflect their audience, political alignment, institutional values, economic imperatives, institutional story-telling traditions and news-gathering practices' (p. 198). Another study that investigates media accounts of the same event by newspapers in different languages is Wang's (1993) analysis of the coverage of the failed Soviet coup in 1991 by the *New York Times* and by China's Communist Party newspaper, *Renmin Ribao* (People's Daily). Wang discovers that the coverage of this event by the two newspapers was both structurally and quantitatively different. The *New York Times* coverage was found to be structurally more complete while *Renmin Ribao* omitted all background and contextual information. Wang suggests that the differences in the reporting of this event were not just due to linguistic differences but were culturally, ideologically and politically situated.

Scollon et al. (1998) also analyse accounts of similar stories in Chinese and English newspapers in Hong Kong, primarily in terms of the rhetorical structure employed within these texts. Their main conclusion is that Chinese language news texts do not necessarily favour the classical Chinese *qǐ-chéng-zhuǎn-hé* (起承轉合, 'opening, development, change, and conclusion') or inductive structure over the inverted pyramid deductive structure of English news texts. They conclude that 'clear contrasts can only be sustained by artificially excluding significant data from analysis' (p. 298).

With reference to Brunei Darussalam, there are as yet very few studies of media discourse. Among these few is David and McLellan's (2007) study which investigates nativised varieties of English in news reports in Malaysia and Brunei Darussalam. Their findings show that, despite the discourse being in written form, code-switching occurs often, either as flagged or unflagged items. McLellan and Noor Azam (2012, pp. 83–85) analyse an English-language print media report on the visit of a foreign Head of State to Brunei Darussalam, and they note the near-complete absence of any pronominal references to His Majesty the Sultan of Brunei, with a strong preference for phrases such as 'His Majesty', 'the Monarch', and 'the benevolent ruler'. However, the report has regular third-person pronominal references to the visiting Head of State. McLellan and Noor Azam claim that these textual features reflect 'an observance of the Malay practice in which *he* (*dia/ia/beliau*) seems acceptable for dignitaries other than the Brunei ruler' (p. 85). Hence this may be a case of discourse transfer from Malay.

Nurkhalisah Mustapa (2013) reveals some interesting findings regarding Malay newspaper texts versus English newspaper texts in Brunei. She finds that, contrary to popular belief, reports of the same stories in English media texts are often longer than Malay texts, and she notes many omissions in the Malay texts, which she feels could be due to the contexts of the stories. In one particular example of an incest case, the details were omitted in the Malay text, possibly due to the sensitive nature of the case. She quotes Abdullah and Ainon (2001) who state that one of the classifications of taboo topics in Malay culture is sex, while others are fecal matters, disasters and death. She also finds that the Malay texts she analysed have a higher morpheme count, even though they are not necessarily longer than the English texts by word count.

All the previous studies on media discourse cited above focus on textual analysis only. As CDA requires us to go beyond the text to investigate processes surrounding the production of texts, this study incorporates an analysis of text with qualitative data obtained from interviews with editors and journalists. Thus, this study is novel in two ways: first, it is one of the few studies on media discourse that utilises a cross comparative approach; and second, unlike other studies in the area, a mixed methods approach is adopted, in which textual analysis is carried out together with interview data from the media practitioners.

14.3 About the Newspapers

The *Borneo Bulletin* and *Media Permata* are both published by Brunei Press Sendirian Berhad (Private Limited Company), a subsidiary of QAF Brunei, a Brunei-based holding company linked to the Royal Family. The *Borneo Bulletin* is the leading English daily in the country. It was first published by Brunei Press in 1953 as a weekly community newspaper for expatriates. In September 1990, it became a daily newspaper in Brunei Darussalam. It currently has more than 100,000 daily readers. *Media Permata*, on the other hand, was launched by Brunei Press in 1995, 'focusing on local news and features for the Malay literate'. With a tagline of *Akhbar Harian Unggul Negara Brunei Darussalam* (Brunei Darussalam's Premier Daily Newspaper), it is currently the only Malay language daily in the country with close to 90,000 daily readers (Brunei Press Sdn Bhd—QAF-Brunei.com 2006).

14.4 Research Methods

The approach and methodology adopted for this study are both quantitative and qualitative. Parallel corpora of hard news reports covering the same events were compiled from four consecutive issues of the English-language *Borneo Bulletin* (henceforth BB) and the Malay-language *Media Permata* (henceforth MP) from 8th to 11th December 2014. Thus the sampling was purposive. There were a total of fourteen parallel texts appearing in both newspapers over these 4 days. All of these texts were written by Bruneian journalists; none were from overseas press agencies.

From these fourteen parallel texts we selected two dealing with royal events, two covering crimes and accidents, and two which reported local events. Most of the local hard news reports in Bruneian newspapers fall within these three categories. The parallel texts were then placed side-by-side to enable comparison of length and depth of coverage. This approach also enables us to investigate what ideas or issues are being foregrounded or given prominence in the texts. The main way this is achieved in texts is through topicalisation, which is defined by Huckin (2002, p. 8) as 'the positioning of a sentence element at the beginning of a sentence so as to give prominence' or at the beginning of a main clause.

A quantitative approach to textual product is used to establish the degree of parallelism between Malay and English media texts reporting the same story: counting the number of words, and establishing the degree of translation equivalence. This enables us to find out which information is included in the Malay but not in the English version, and vice versa. It also enables investigation of the hypothesis that Malay texts tend to be longer, more explicit and more complex than equivalent English texts: Nurkhalisah Mustapa's (2013) initial research, as noted above, casts doubt on this.

On the qualitative side, semi-structured interviews were conducted with journalists and editors, enabling us to discover what policies and processes are involved in the production of Brunei print media texts; e.g. whether the original text is drafted in Malay then translated into English, or vice versa, and the ways in which the source language influences the target language.

This mixed-methods approach thus facilitates comparisons between the English and Malay textual products and the processes of text production. It also allows for validation of the journalists' and editors' stated views through the application of a modified CDA with specific focus on topicalisation and topic prominence, and on translation equivalence. This novel approach has only rarely been applied to news media texts in bilingual and multilingual contexts such as Brunei Darussalam.

14.5 Findings from the Textual Data

Table 14.1 shows the word count in six parallel texts in the three categories. It also shows the numbers of photographs accompanying each news report. (The full set of six parallel texts discussed in this section can be found in Appendix A.)

The two royal reports analysed (Reports 1 and 2) are longer in Malay than English, and they have more photographs. For crime and accident reports (Reports 3 and 4), no fixed pattern emerges. In reports covering local events (Reports 5 and 6), the two English texts are longer than the Malay texts. Hence our preliminary finding in terms of text length is that it depends on the subgenre of the news report rather than on the language of the report.

Within the six parallel news reports, variation is found in the topicalisation and information structure, starting with the headlines as shown in Table 14.2.

Table 14.1 Word count and number of photographs in six parallel hard new reports

Report	A: MP (Malay)	B: BB (English)	No. of photos MP	No. of photos BB
1. Strong ties with Korea	827	666	5	3
2. HM departing from Korea	438	286	5	1
3. Street scuffle	100	89	1	0
4. Drowning	88	109	0	1
5. Air accident investigation unit	283	423	1	2
6. Bid for bridge construction	561	633	1	1
Average word length	383	368	–	–

Table 14.2 Headlines of six parallel hard news reports

	A: MP (Malay) headline	B: BB (English) headline
1	*Brunei-Korea perkukuh hubungan* [names] AV-strengthen relation	Brunei hails strong energy cooperation with Korea
2	*Berangkat tinggalkan Seoul* AV-leave AV-leave [name]	Sultan leaves Seoul after state visit
3	*Pergaduhan di tengah jalan* Brawl in middle road	Police investigating cause behind scuffle
4	*Mayat wanita ditemui terapong* Body woman VPASS-find floating	Body of local woman found at Tutong beach
5	*Bengkel siasatan kemalangan udara berakhir* Workshop investigation accident air AV-end	DCA plans to set up independent air accident investigation unit
6	*CRCC bida jambatan Temburong* [name] bid bridge [name]	Chinese company bids for Temburong bridge project

The first pair of parallel texts, 1A and 1B, show a contrast right from their respective headlines: the MP headline makes no reference to energy, only to strengthening cooperation. In contrast, the BB report headline is thus more specific. Furthermore, the first paragraph of the BB report refers to 'energy partnership' and 'energy cooperation'. These are not mentioned in the initial paragraph of the MP report, which focuses more broadly on the strengthening of Brunei-Korea relations through the Sultan's 3-day state visit. Energy is only mentioned as one of a number of areas of cooperation in the final sentence of paragraph 2 of the MP report, along with education, agriculture and people-to-people ties.

The two texts, 2A and 2B, which report the Sultan's departure from Seoul, show a grammatical contrast in the headlines: the MP headline has no subject, whilst the BB report headline uses the term 'Sultan'. Pro-drop (null subject) structures are grammatical in Malay, but this is not generally so in English (Deterding and Poedjosoedarmo 2001, p. 216). This usage also reflects the strategy of avoidance of pronominal reference to the Brunei monarch in Malay texts, as noted by McLellan and Noor Azam (2012), discussed above. The need for brevity in the BB headline obliges the use of the noun 'Sultan', whereas the MP is able to avoid this problem by using the pro-drop structure. The order of information in these two texts is similar, presumably because the reports were constructed on the basis of a press release provided in Malay by the Sultan's Press Liaison Office. The substantial difference in length between the MP and BB reports (see Table 14.1) is because of the dual listing of names of the Bruneian Ministers accompanying the Sultan on the visit, firstly in attendance when the Sultan left the hotel in which he stayed, then at the air base from which his flight departed. The list of names and full titles is less complete in the BB report.

A contrast in terms of focus and topicalisation is evident in texts 3A and 3B, which report a brawl or 'scuffle' (*pergaduhan*) which took place in public in the middle of a road and was captured on video and shared via social media. The MP report includes details which do not appear in the BB report, including the fact that the three protagonists were all from the same family. The MP report also includes a photograph showing the actual scuffle which was also shared via social media. The BB report is less detailed, with no photograph, and right from the headline it focuses more on the investigative action taken by the police.

In the short reports of a drowning case (texts 4A and 4B), the headlines of both the MP and BB reports begin in similar factual fashion, but the MP headline ends with the word *terapong* ('floating'). More differences appear in the respective second paragraphs, in which the MP report gives the full name of the victim and the village she lived in, whilst the BB only identifies her as 'a 48 year old local woman'. There is once again a greater focus on the actions of the police in the BB report, supported by a photograph showing 'the police personnel securing the area' as stated in the caption. This photograph does not appear in the MP report.

There is also a contrast in the headlines in the MP and BB reports (texts 5A and 5B) covering an air accident and safety workshop held in Brunei. The MP report topicalises the workshop itself as an event, whereas the BB report foregrounds a decision made and announced at the conclusion of the workshop to set up an independent Air Accident Investigation unit. This is not reported at all by the MP, which instead focuses on the participants and the presentation of certificates to them.

Texts 6A and 6B report a bid made by a construction company from the People's Republic of China for a major bridge project in Brunei, connecting the capital with Temburong District. Whilst the headlines are similar, the MP report follows the inverted pyramid structure by referring to the bid by the Chinese company in its first paragraph. In contrast, the BB report begins with background information about the bridge project and its significance for national development, only referring to the bid in the third paragraph. Hence this BB report does not follow the inverted pyramid structure. In paragraphs 15 and 16 of the BB report, information is given about Temburong District, including details of how to reach it. This is not found at all in the MP report.

Based on the analysis of these six parallel hard news texts and others published between 8th and 11th December 2014, we note that the inverted pyramid structure is invariably followed in the MP reports, but not necessarily followed in the BB: Text 6B on the Temburong bridge, as noted above, begins with background information rather than with the most important event or message. Hence we can challenge the claim of universality made by Thomson et al. (2008, p. 218) for the canonical English-language inverted pyramid model.

14.6 Findings from the Interview Data

To obtain information about the policies and processes involved in the production of BB and MP hard news reports, semi-structured interviews were conducted with journalists and editors of both papers. The Chief Editors of the BB and the MP as well as five journalists from each of the sister papers agreed to be interviewed. The BB interviews were conducted in English while the MP interviews were in Malay and later translated into English. All the interview data, except for two with the MP journalists, were audio-recorded and then transcribed. The two MP journalists who were not interviewed face-to-face provided written answers to the interview questions posed (refer to Appendix B).

One of the main themes that appears prominently in the interview data is that although both are sister papers within the same organisation and operating from the same floor of the *Brunei Press* building, the MP and BB claim to work independently from each other. According to the BB Chief Editor, 'only on occasions' is there collaboration, as 'they write the way they think, we write the way we think. So it's a totally different angle, yes, totally independently'. This was echoed by the MP Chief Editor who concedes that they occasionally translate articles from the BB into Malay but they ensure that these are 'rearranged according to suitability'. Apart from translating and re-writing texts that appear in each other's papers, this collaboration can also extend into sharing the sources of information. As explained by the BB Chief Editor,

> The editor (MP Chief Editor) will share with me about the good story happening, and I give the details to my journalists. Then BB journalists would not just copy but make some calls like the police or any relevant parties or something and that's how we write the stories. So that's how the cooperation is.

Thus, it is clear that although these two papers do on occasions choose to collaborate with each other on producing news reports, the prevalent feeling is that each has a distinct identity and a well-defined target audience and these influence how their news reports are created. The BB Chief Editor further elaborated, 'The Malay editor does quite different, you know, he keeps the Malay readers in his mind, and he goes about the story the way he perceives it to be right.' This was echoed by the MP Chief Editor when he said that, unlike the BB whose reports he believes are more 'open' and 'international', the readers of the MP are mostly Malays and Muslims. Thus, the news reports that are published in the MP are directed more towards 'the aspirations of the traditions and cultures of the Malay/Muslim community'.

The fact that each of the papers caters to a different target audience, based primarily on language choice, is another recurrent theme in the interview data. It appears that the journalists of the MP and BB are well aware of this too. One MP journalist is of the opinion that the BB 'is more international than MP, which caters locally' focusing more on local content for news; another states that

> as we are the *Media Permata*, our readers are among the Malays as well. We don't cover news on the praying of people at the [Chinese] temples. Borneo Bulletin does that, as their readers involving those populations of Chinese and Westerners in Brunei.

A BB journalist, on the other hand, attributes the difference in emphasis of BB and MP news reports to what she perceives as 'different cultures' at work for both Malay and English newspapers. By this she means that unlike MP, BB has a competitor in the English language daily newspaper market in the country, that is, the *Brunei Times*. Thus the BB has to constantly 'find the best angle to attract the readers' attentions' while the MP, she feels, tends to 'just report' the facts as they appear.

The BB perceives that its readers include not just Malay-English bilingual Bruneians but also expatriates residing in Brunei and foreigners living outside of Brunei. Hence another finding emerging from the interviews is that the BB journalists feel that it is necessary to provide background information when drafting their news reports. This is especially true when there are local or Islamic or Malay references in their reports that they assume will not be familiar to non-Muslim and non-Malay readers. One BB journalist attributes this to the advice given to her by the former Chief Editor of the BB when she first started:

> When I first started, he would say things like when you write your story make sure you have to write it in a way that people know what is going on. So we always have to – for me at least, even if it's not given in the speech or press release I always give background knowledge of what's currently going on to give the readers an idea, 'Okay, this is what she's talking about.

The interviews also reveal that almost all of the journalists claim to have knowledge of the basic structure of a news report, despite the fact that the majority are not formally trained in journalism. They mention that they follow the inverted pyramid deductive structure of English news texts, even though this matter was not specifically raised during the interviews. The MP journalists also claim to practice this when drafting their news reports, as stated clearly by one of them:

> The first paragraph will be filled with most important point, in order to attract readers. It will cater to the most important point of the news. Next important points will be put in the second or third paragraph. They're important too but not as important as the one in the first paragraph. The point in the first paragraph will usually sum up all aspects at the event. That's how it's usually done.

However, as noted by the Chief Editor of the BB, even though he instructs his journalists specifically to 'follow inverted pyramid format of reporting', there are occasions when it doesn't happen, it still goes into the paper... So when they go start writing like this, and the copy is not re-written, it so happens you get a headline but the headline is not corroborated to the story until you come to the seventh or eighth paragraphs. Then, you said, 'Oh so this is the headline.'

The interviews also reveal that media practitioners in Brunei are very much aware of what may or may not be allowed to be published. Although there are no official written instructions pertaining to this matter, most respondents say that they practice self-censorship. One BB journalist states that 'we regulate ourselves. We have some kind of rule—in-house rules that we shouldn't cross the line' while another, also from the BB, summarises that 'we will not include things that we think would be culturally wrong or probably frowned upon by the readers or something that the readers would consider distasteful'. This very careful approach applies to not just obviously sensitive topics pertaining to the MIB philosophy (see Chap. 2 of this volume) and all matters attendant to it, but also to reports about crime and accidents. Reports under this category that appear in Bruneian newspapers generally do not contain personal details of the victims or the perpetrators. According to the Chief Editor of the BB, 'we generally tell the journalists to be careful... We are very concerned when it comes to crime reports for libel'. Apart from pragmatic reasons such as avoiding libel, this reluctance to be explicit about this type of news could be due to the fact that Brunei is such a small country and people generally know each other well, so more explicit coverage will be deemed 'distasteful'. One BB journalist is of the opinion that of late, the paper has been more cautious in their reporting of crime and accidents: 'now I notice we try not to name the victim but we give age, where is he from, to give the audience an idea on who the victim is.' When these reports are published, they generally include a 'deterrent' statement, normally placed at the end of the report. In the words of one BB journalist

> over the years, I have learned that I have understood that the criminal justice system in Brunei, they want some effects of – what do we call that – deterrence, in our reports. They want some deterrence to take effects.

Another BB journalist confirms that

> we will end up putting the gender of the victim, the age, how the accident happened. And the end note would usually be the police would like to call out to the public to be more sensitive about this issue and stop spreading this on the Whatsapp or Facebook.

The MP journalists also report that they generally adopt a cautious approach to stories about crime and accidents. However, there is a tendency for MP reports to include more specific information and details about crime and accident cases. The MP journalists reveal that, for crime cases, once an individual is sentenced by the courts, they normally identify the wrong-doer in their reports. One MP journalist also cited a recent example of a rape case in Tutong District in which not just the name of the rapist was revealed but also information about the victim's nationality and place of residence where the crime took place, 'except for the witnesses, normally, the witnesses are not fond of their names being revealed'. The BB report of this case, on the other hand, did not include as many details.

Perhaps the more direct approach to news reports in the MP can be attributed to the paper's re-branding exercise about 2 years ago. According to our MP respondents, the paper is now focusing on covering more news of the local community, since a readership survey carried out in relation to the re-branding strategy revealed that most readers prefer the MP to focus more on local and community news. Additionally, the current policy of the paper is to have more photos to accompany their reports. This was shared by one MP journalist:

> normally, as we are *Media Permata* and want more people to buy our paper, we will focus the pictures of the publics or the audiences…if these publics found out their faces were on the paper, they will definitely buy a copy to treasure them.

Another recurrent theme from the interviews concerns the Sultan's *titah* ('speech'). As the Sultan is also the country's Prime Minister, he gives speeches regularly on many matters relating to the country and its ties with foreign countries. Our respondents inform us that the usual practice is for the Sultan's Office to provide the media with full-text copies of his speeches which are in the Malay language. His speeches which are delivered in a foreign country or in an international setting would be in English. An MP journalist comments that

> As for the *Media Permata*'s style, when it comes to the *titah*, for every *titah*, one full text will be used for one story. We will not change any of the speech. We re-type the whole text and publish it.

However, he notes that for subsequent reports based on the same *titah*, the MP will either 'provide a summary' based on the *titah*, or they will interview people to get their reactions to the monarch's speech:

> For the second story, we will provide a summary of the *titah*. Thus, we have to pick the best, the most important and make it a news format – to make it extra special… If we're keen to do so, we will come up with interviews for the summarised text's story, as a follow-up news.

Another MP journalist explains that '…all we have to do is copy and paste the *titah*'s text and add "His Majesty says" with it'. She also adds that they refrain from making additional comments.

However, the BB seems to have a slightly different practice with regards to the Sultan's *titah*. As his speeches are mostly in Malay, the BB does not have the option of reproducing the whole text in full. Instead of translating the text into English word-for-word, their normal practice is to decide on the most important point of the ruler's speech and to then produce a news report based on this. However, they stress that even though they may take the liberty of re-arranging his speech, they ensure that none of the content of the *titah* is left out. This was confirmed by the Chief Editor of the BB:

> Even His Majesty's *titah* doesn't go accordingly to what he says by order, but every His Majesty's *titah* and ministers speeches, everything generally go in full, we don't cut anything. But, we take the important ones and take it to the top and go down from there. We take everything. We don't cut down on anything. Most of the *titah* is taken, we generally don't leave out anything.

In the following section we seek to make connections between the textual and the interview data.

14.7 Findings from the Textual Analysis and from the Interview Data

Our initial assumptions about Malay hard news texts being lengthier and more detailed is partially confirmed, but we find there is a need for a more nuanced analysis of three different sub-genres of hard news reports: the MP royal reports are longer and more detailed than those in the BB, as they normally report the whole text of the Sultan's *titah* ('speech') in the original language and the order in which it was delivered. The MP also takes care to follow Brunei protocol by giving the full titles, sometimes repeated, of high-ranking officials present or participating in an event. The BB on the other hand, has a policy of selecting and highlighting points from the Sultan's *titah*, and reporting these in order of importance, mindful of both their Bruneian and expatriate readership. They feel able to do this since they are writing and publishing in English, hence they are under less of an obligation to remain faithful to the original Malay text of the *titah*.

In the crime and accident reports there are differences of focus, but not of length, between the MP and BB reports. Contrary to our prior assumptions, it is the Malay reports in the MP which contain more graphic detail and more specific information about victims and perpetrators, e.g. names of accused persons and place of residence of victims. One common feature of both MP and BB, which shows the close rapport of the journalists with the police and other authorities, is the deterrent message, which tends to come at the end of a crime report, as shown in texts 3a and 3b, and the reassurance that the authorities have matters under control, as seen in 4a and 4b.

In the third category of hard news reports, local events, the BB English reports are lengthier and contain more detail, in part because of the non-Bruneian international readership who are perceived to require more background information to be included, such as in text 6b about Temburong District.

The interview data provided by the journalists and Chief Editors provide a valuable rationale and justification for the patterns of inclusion and exclusion found in the report texts. Recurring themes in the interviews are sensitivity towards the readership of the respective newspapers, combined with an understandable commercial concern to sell more of their product by maximising the appeal of the newspapers to readers, including the large number of photographs and details about who was present at any gathering or event. The MP texts, addressed to Malay-speaking Bruneians, include *ciri-ciri KeBruneian* ('Bruneian features', as in the final paragraph of text 6A), whereas the BB texts often contain background information, especially on matters relating to Islam and to Malay culture, for the benefit of non-Malay Bruneians, expatriates residing in Brunei, and international readers.

14.8 Conclusion

The findings from this research study are tentative and have obvious limitations. Space and time constraints only permit close analysis of a small sample of Brunei hard news reports in Malay and English, and there is scope for further in-depth research which may support or challenge our initial findings. Nonetheless we maintain our claim that this study of comparative media discourse of hard news reports across languages breaks new research ground in its application of a revised CDA format to the textual product and the processes of production of Malay- and English-language reports in the print media of Brunei Darussalam. As mentioned earlier, studies that utilise a cross-linguistic comparative approach to media texts are relatively few in number. Thus, the findings from this study, although limited in scope, can provide significant insights into a relatively unexplored area of media discourse.

Acknowledgements The research described in this chapter is funded by Universiti Brunei Darussalam, research grant number UBD/PNC2/2//RG/1(287), and forms part of the project 'A multidisciplinary investigation of media texts in Malay and English in Malaysia and Brunei Darussalam'. The co-authors would like to record their most sincere thanks to the editors and journalists of the *Media Permata* and the *Borneo Bulletin* who gave of their valuable time to be interviewed for this study. In order to ensure respondent validation and to avoid any misquotation or misrepresentation they were invited to comment on a draft of this chapter.

Appendix A

Text 1A	Text 1B
Tajuk: Brunei-Korea perkukuh hubungan	**Title: Sultan hails strong energy cooperation with Korea**
Posted date: December 10, 2014	December 10, 2014
(1) SEOUL, Republik Korea, 9 Dis— Kebawah Duli Yang Maha Mulia Paduka Seri Baginda Sultan Haji Hassanal Bolkiah Mu'izzaddin Waddaulah, Sultan dan Yang Di-Pertuan Negara Brunei Darussalam memulakan Keberangkatan Negara selama tiga hari ke Republik Korea ke arah memperkukuhkan lagi hubungan dan kerjasama rapat yang sedia terjalin antara kedua-dua buah negara	(1) His Majesty the Sultan and Yang Di-Pertuan of Brunei Darussalam lauded the strong energy partnership between Brunei Darussalam and Korea spanning over the past 20 years, as energy cooperation remains the core of economic engagement between both countries
(2) Bertitah pada Majlis Santap Malam Negara yang berlangsung di Bangunan Yeong Bin Gwan, Cheong Wa Dae, Seoul malam ini, Baginda Sultan menekankan bahawa Negara Brunei Darussalam dan Republik Korea telah menikmati kemajuan	(2) His Majesty expressed his pleasure that the LNG contract between the countries has been extended until 2018

(continued)

(continued)

yang berterusan dalam kerjasama dua hala yang meliputi pelbagai bidang termasuklah tenaga, pendidikan, pertanian dan perhubungan di antara rakyat kedua buah negara	
(3) Kebawah Duli Yang Maha Mulia sangat gembira melihat Negara Brunei Darussalam dan Republik Korea mengukuhkan lagi pencapaian yang sedia ada dengan penandatanganan tiga perjanjian semasa Keberangkatan Negara ini	(3) The monarch was delivering a titah at a State Banquet hosted by Park Geun-hye, President of the Republic of Korea, in conjunction with the State Visit of His Majesty from December 8–10
(4) Baginda bertitah melahirkan keyakinan bahawa hubungan dua hala di antara Negara Brunei Darussalam dan Republik Korea akan bertambah-tambah kukuh untuk manfaat bersama bagi rakyat Negara Brunei Darussalam dan Republik Korea	(4) The State Banquet was held at the Yeong Bin Gwan Hall, Cheong Wa Dae, Seoul
(5) Majlis Santap Malam Negara tersebut dihoskan oleh Presiden Republik Korea Puan Yang Terutama Park Geun-hye	(5) His Majesty was greeted on arrival at the Cheong Wa Dae by the President of the Republic of Korea. Before the State Banquet commenced, President Park was introduced to Brunei Darussalam's delegation followed by His Majesty to the special guests of President Park *(photo: His Majesty the Sultan and Yang Di-Pertuan of Brunei Darussalam and President of the Republic of Korea, Park Geun-hye, share a light moment during the signing of an agreement to avoid double taxation.— PHOTOS: INFOFOTO)* *(photo: His Majesty shakes hands with Korean President Park Geun-hye)* *(photo: His Majesty delivers the titah)* *(photo: His Majesty the Sultan and Yang Di-Pertuan of Brunei Darussalam inspects a royal guard of honour at the Yeong Bin Gwan Hall, Cheong Wa Dae, Seoul)* *(photo: His Majesty and President Park Guen-hye witnessing the signing of the Agreement and Memoranda of Understanding. Signing on behalf of the Government of His Majesty the Sultan and Yang Di-Pertuan of Brunei Darussalam was Pehin Dato Seri Setia Awang Haji Abdul Rahman, Minister of Finance II at the Prime Minister's Office)* *(photo: His Majesty during the bilateral meeting with Korean President Park and their respective delegations)*

(continued)

(continued)

(6) Keberangkatan tiba Baginda di Cheong Wa Dae dialu-alukan oleh Puan Yang Terutama Park Geun-hye, Presiden Republik Korea	(6) The State Banquet began with the national anthem of both countries. President Park delivered an address welcoming His Majesty on the occasion of His Majesty's State Visit to the Republic of Korea
(7) Sebelum Majlis Santap Malam Negara dimulakan, Puan Yang Terutama Presiden Republik Korea diperkenalkan kepada delegasi Negara Brunei Darussalam. Kemudiannya, Kebawah Duli Yang Maha Mulia disembah-kenalkan kepada tetamu-tetamu khas Puan Yang Terutama Presiden Republik Korea *(gambar: Kebawah Duli Yang Maha Mulia semasa berkenan mengurniakan titah. – Gambar Infofoto)* *(gambar: Presiden Park Geun-hye menyembahkan ucapan bagi mengalu-alukan keberangkatan Kebawah Duli Yang Maha Mulia bagi Keberangkatan Negara ke Republik Korea. – Infofoto)* *(gambar: Baginda Sultan berkenan berangkat menghadiri Majlis Santap Malam Negara yang dihoskan oleh Presiden Park Geun-hye. – Infofoto)* *(gambar: Baginda Sultan berkenan disembah-kenalkan kepada tetamu-tetamu khas Puan Yang Terutama Presiden Republik Korea. – Infofoto)*	(7) In the titah, His Majesty said Brunei values Korea's assistance in the construction of vessels for Brunei's LNG consignments and is ready to continue working closely with Korea to further enhance the long-standing cooperation in this area
(8) Majlis Santap Malam Negara tersebut telah dimulakan dengan Lagu Kebangsaan kedua-dua buah negara	(8) His Majesty acknowledged Brunei and Korea have enjoyed steady progress in bilateral cooperation that extends to many areas including energy, education, agriculture and people-to-people exchanges
(9) Ini diikuti dengan ucapan Presiden Park Geun-hye sebagai mengalu-alukan keberangkatan Kebawah Duli Yang Maha Mulia bagi Keberangkatan Negara ke Republik Korea	(9) His Majesty was most heartened to see Brunei and Korea building on these existing achievements by signing three agreements during this visit. His Majesty expressed his confidence that the bilateral ties will continue to prosper for the mutual benefit of the peoples of Brunei and Korea
(10) Dalam titah, Baginda mula-mula melahirkan penghargaan yang mendalam kepada Puan YangTerutama Park Geun-hye, Kerajaan dan rakyat Republik Korea atas layanan yang baik kepada Baginda dan rombongan	(10) His Majesty also said Brunei appreciates Korea's continued efforts to promote youth exchanges, particularly through the Brunei-Korea Youth Exchange Programme. The people of Brunei, especially the younger generation, have developed a keen interest in the Korean language, food and culture, which has created strong bonds of friendship and understanding between the peoples

(continued)

(continued)

(11) Baginda juga melahirkan kegembiraan kerana dapat sekali lagi berangkat melawat Republik Korea	(11) At the same time, Brunei and Korea are also making great strides through the close partnership in the field of e-government, where Korea's assistance and expertise in developing Brunei Darussalam's ICT has been invaluable
(12) Kebawah Duli Yang Maha Mulia bertitah memaklumi bahawa Republik Korea telah mencapai pertumbuhan ekonomi yang begitu pesat sejak beberapa dekad yang lalu	(12) Brunei also appreciates the contributions of Korean companies in Brunei's development efforts and continues to warmly welcome them to the Sultanate, His Majesty further added
(13) Pada hari ini Republik Korea terkenal sebagai sebuah ekonomi terkemuka dengan industri bertaraf dunia, serta dikenali dalam kemajuan teknologi. Segala pencapaian ini merupakan inspirasi kepada banyak orang di merata dunia	(13) His Majesty noted Korea has achieved rapid economic growth over the past few decades. Today, Korea is widely regarded as a leading economy with world-class industries, well-known for their technological advancements. Korea's achievements are an inspiration to many around the world
(14) Baginda seterusnya bertitah bahawa Negara Brunei Darussalam berharap untuk mempelajari dari pengalaman Republik Korea terutama dalam usaha Negara Brunei Darussalam mencapai Wawasannya pada tahun 2035	(14) His Majesty stated that Brunei hoped to learn much from Korea's experience, especially as Brunei move towards 2035 in pursuit of Brunei Darussalam's own development vision
(15) Kebawah Duli Yang Maha Mulia juga bertitah bahawa Negara Brunei Darussalam dan Republik Korea telah menikmati kerjasama yang kukuh dalam bidang tenaga sejak 20 tahun yang lalu	(15) His Majesty noted that this year is a special occasion for relations between Asean and Korea, which now enters its 25th year of excellent cooperation and reaffirmed Brunei's commitment to continue working closely to further enhance the Asean-Korea partnership
(16) Kerjasama tenaga masih kekal sebagai teras utama penglibatan ekonomi antara kedua buah negara dan Baginda melahirkan kegembiraan bahawa kontrak LNG telah dilanjutkan sehingga tahun 2018	(16) His Majesty looked forward to celebrating 25 years of Asean-Republic of Korea dialogue relations and wished President Park and Korea much success in hosting the Asean-Republic of Korea Commemorative Summit in Busan
(17) Brunei Darussalam juga menghargai bantuan Republik Korea dalam pembinaan kapal-kapal bagi pembekalan LNG, dan Negara Brunei Darussalam terus bersedia untuk bekerjasama rapat dengan Republik Korea bagi meningkatkan lagi kerjasama yang sudah lama terjalin dalam bidang ini, tambah Baginda	(17) In closing, His Majesty again thanked the president, the government and people of Korea for the friendship and goodwill that has been extended to Brunei and its people. His Majesty also looked forward to strengthening the warm and close friendship so happily enjoyed by the peoples of Brunei and Korea
(18) Kebawah Duli Yang Maha Mulia juga bertitah bahawa Negara Brunei Darussalam menghargai usaha-usaha berterusan Republik Korea untuk mempromosikan pertukaran	(18) Accompanying His Majesty at the State Banquet were Pehin Orang Kaya Laila Setia Dato Seri Setia Awang Haji Abdul Rahman bin Haji Ibrahim, Minister of Finance II at the Prime Minister's Office; Pehin Orang Kaya

(continued)

(continued)

belia khususnya melalui Program Pertukaran Belia Brunei-Korea	Pekerma Dewa Dato Seri Setia Lim Jock Seng, Minister of Foreign Affairs and Trade II; and Pehin Datu Singamanteri Colonel (Rtd) Dato Seri Setia (Dr) Awang Haji Mohammad Yasmin bin Haji Umar, Minister of Energy at the Prime Minister's Office
(19) Titah Baginda, rakyat Negara Brunei Darussalam, khususnya generasi muda, telah menaruh minat yang mendalam kepadabahasa, makanan dan budaya Republik Korea, yang mana telah mewujudkan hubungan persahabatan dan persefahaman yang kukuh diantara rakyat kedua buah negara	
(20) Pada masa yang sama, Negara Brunei Darussalam dan Republik Korea juga telah melangkah jauh melalui perkongsian yangrapat dalam bidang e-kerajaan, di mana bantuan dan kepakaran Republik Korea untuk memajukan bidang ICT di Negara Brunei Darussalam amatlah dihargai	
(21) Negara Brunei Darussalam juga menghargai sumbangan syarikat-syarikat dari Republik Korea dalam usaha pembangunan Negara Brunei Darussalam dan terus mengalu-alukan mereka ke Negara Brunei Darussalam	
(22) Kebawah Duli Yang Maha Mulia bertitah memaklumi bahawa tahun ini merupakan tahun yang istimewa bagi hubungan di antara ASEAN dan Republik Korea, yang sekarang memasuki 25 tahun kerjasama yang cemerlang, dan menyuarakan semula komitmen Negara Brunei Darussalam untuk terus bekerja rapat ke arah mempertingkatkan lagi perkongsian ASEAN-Republik Korea	
(23) Kebawah Duli Yang Maha Mulia bertitah mengalu-alukan sambutan 25 tahun hubungan dialog ASEAN-Republik Korea dan berharap semoga Puan Yang Terutama dan Republik Korea akan mencapai kejayaan menjadi Tuan Rumah Sidang Kemuncak Komemoratif ASEAN-Republik Korea di Busan	
(24) Di akhir titah, Kebawah Duli Yang Maha Mulia sekali lagi menyampaikan penghargaan kepada Puan Yang Terutama, Kerajaan serta rakyat Republik Korea di atas	

(continued)

(continued)

persahabatan dan hubungan muhibah yang telah dihulurkan kepada rakyat dan Negara Brunei Darussalam	
(25) Baginda juga berharap untuk mengukuhkan lagi persahabatan yang mesra dan rapat yang dinikmati oleh rakyat Negara Brunei Darussalam dan Republik Korea	
(26) Mengiringi keberangkatan Kebawah Duli Yang Maha Mulia Paduka Seri Baginda Sultan dan Yang Di-Pertuan Negara Brunei Darussalam pada Majlis Santap Malam Negara tersebut ialah Menteri Kewangan II (Kedua) di Jabatan Perdana Menteri, Yang Berhormat Pehin Orang Kaya Laila Setia Dato Seri Setia Haji Abd. Rahman bin Haji Ibrahim; Menteri Hal Ehwal Luar Negeri dan Perdagangan II (Kedua), Yang Berhormat Pehin Orang Kaya Pekerma Dewa Dato Seri Setia Lim Jock Seng dan Menteri Tenaga di Jabatan Perdana Menteri Yang Berhormat Pehin Datu Singamanteri Kolonel (Bersara) Dato Seri Setia (Dr.) Haji Mohammad Yasmin bin Haji Umar	

Text 2A	Text 2B
Tajuk: Berangkat tinggalkan Seoul	**Title: Sultan leaves Seoul after State Visit**
Posted date: December 11, 2014	December 11, 2014
(1) SEOUL, Republik Korea, 10 Dis – Kebawah Duli Yang Maha Mulia Paduka Seri Baginda Sultan Haji Hassanal Bolkiah Mu'izzaddin Waddaulah, Sultan dan Yang Di-Pertuan Negara Brunei Darussalam berkenan berangkat meninggalkan Seoul, Republik Korea pagi ini setelah selesai menamatkan Keberangkatan Negara selama tiga hari mulai 8 hingga 10 Disember 2014	(1) HIS Majesty the Sultan and Yang Di-Pertuan of Brunei Darussalam yesterday morning consented to leave Seoul, Republic of Korea after concluding a 3-day State Visit from December 8–10, 2014
(2) Sebelum berangkat meninggalkan Hotel Grand Hyatt Seoul, Doa Selamat dibacakan oleh Mufti Kerajaan Yang Berhormat Pehin Datu Seri Maharaja Dato Paduka Seri Setia (Dr.) Ustaz Haji Awang Abdul Aziz bin Juned	(2) Prior to leaving the Grand Hyatt Seoul Hotel, a Doa Selamat was read by Pehin Datu Seri Maharaja Dato Paduka Seri Setia (Dr) Ustaz Haji Awang Abdul Aziz bin Juned, the State Mufti
(3) Sejurus tiba di Pangkalan Udara Seoul, Seongnam, Kebawah Duli Yang Maha Mulia berkenan melintasi Kawalan Kehormatan Statik yang dianggotai oleh 22 anggota Tentera Udara Republik Korea sebelum berangkat menaiki pesawat khas	(3) Upon arrival at the Seoul Air Base, Seongnam, His Majesty walked past a static guard mounted by 22 personnel from the Republic of Korea Air Force before boarding a royal aircraft

(continued)

(continued)

(4) Berada di Pangkalan Udara Seoul, Seongnam bagi menyembahkan selamat berangkat Kehadapan Majlis Kebawah Duli Yang Maha Mulia ialah Timbalan Menteri bagi Hal Ehwal Ekonomi, Kementerian Hal Ehwal Luar Negeri Republik Korea, Ahn Chong-ghee; Ketua Pengarah bagi Hal Ehwal Protokol, Kementerian Hal Ehwal Luar Negeri Republik Korea, Lee Yong Soo; Duta Besar Republik Korea ke Negara Brunei Darussalam Tuan Yang Terutama Cho Won-myung dan Ketua Pangkalan Udara Republik Korea, Leftenan Jeneral Sung Hwan-ro serta para pegawai kanan Kerajaan Republik Korea *(gambar: Kebawah Duli Yang Maha Mulia berkenan menerima mengadap beberapa orang mantan Duta Besar Republik Korea yang pernah berkhidmat di Negara Brunei Darussalam.)* *(gambar: Baginda Sultan melambai tangan sebelum berangkat meninggalkan Seoul, Republik Korea setelah mengakhiri Keberangkatan Negara selama tiga hari.)* *(gambar: Sebelum Baginda Sultan berangkat meninggalkan hotel Grand Hyatt, Seoul doa selamat dibacakan oleh Mufti Kerajaan. – Infofoto)* *(gambar: Ketua Pangkalan Udara Republik Korea Leftenan Jeneral Sung Hwan-ro juga menyembahkan selamat berangkat Kehadapan Majlis Kebawah Duli Yang Maha Mulia. – Infofoto)* *(gambar: Kebawah Duli Yang Maha Mulia berkenan melintasi Kawalan Kehormatan Statik yang dianggotai oleh 22 anggota Tentera Udara Republik Korea sebelum berangkat menaiki pesawat khas. – Infofoto)*	(4) Present at the Seoul Air Base to bid farewell to His Majesty were Ahn Chong-ghee, Deputy Minister for Economic Affairs of the Ministry of Foreign Affairs of the Republic of Korea; Lee Yong-soo, Director-General for Protocol Affairs, Ministry of Foreign Affairs of the Republic of Korea; Cho Won-myung, Ambassador Extraordinary and Plenipotentiary of the Republic of Korea to Brunei Darussalam; Lieutenant General Sung Hwan-ro, Chief of Air Base of the Republic of Korea; and senior Korean government officers *(photo: His Majesty the Sultan and Yang Di-Pertuan of Brunei Darussalam is greeted by senior government officials before leaving Seoul.—INFOFOTO)*
(5) Turut hadir bagi menyembahkan selamat berangkat Kehadapan Majlis Kebawah Duli Yang Maha Mulia ialah Menteri Hal Ehwal Luar Negeri dan Perdagangan II (Kedua), Yang Berhormat Pehin Orang Kaya Pekerma Dewa Dato Seri Setia Awang Lim Jock Seng; Menteri Tenaga di Jabatan Perdana Menteri, Yang Berhormat Pehin Datu Singamanteri Kolonel (B) Dato Seri Setia (Dr.) Awang Haji Mohammad Yasmin bin Haji Umar dan Duta Besar Negara Brunei Darussalam ke Republik Korea Tuan Yang Terutama Dato	(5) Also present to bid farewell to His Majesty were Pehin Orang Kaya Pekerma Dewa Dato Seri Setia Lim Jock Seng, Minister of Foreign Affairs and Trade II; Pehin Datu Singamanteri Colonel (Rtd) Dato Seri Setia (Dr) Awang Haji Mohammad Yasmin bin Haji Umar, Minister of Energy at the Prime Minister's Office; Dato Paduka Awang Haji Harun bin Haji Ismail, Ambassador Extraordinary and Plenipotentiary of Brunei Darussalam to the

(continued)

(continued)

Paduka Awang Haji Harun bin Haji Ismail serta para pegawai Kedutaan Negara Brunei Darussalam di Republik Korea	Republic of Korea; and officers from the Embassy of Brunei Darussalam in Seoul
(6) Mengiringi keberangkatan Kebawah Duli Yang Maha Mulia ialah Menteri Kewangan II (Kedua) di Jabatan Perdana Menteri, Yang Berhormat Pehin Orang Kaya Laila Setia Dato Seri Setia Awang Haji Abd. Rahman bin Haji Ibrahim	(6) Accompanying His Majesty was Pehin Orang Kaya Laila Setia Dato Seri Setia Awang Haji Abd Rahman bin Haji Ibrahim, Minister of Finance II at the Prime Minister's Office
(7) Terdahulu, Baginda Sultan berkenan menerima mengadap beberapa orang mantan Duta Besar Republik Korea yang pernah berkhidmat di Negara Brunei Darussalam. Majlis Mengadap tersebut telah berlangsung di Hotel Grand Hyatt Seoul	
(8) Mereka ialah Tuan Yang Terutama Choi Bae-shik; Tuan Yang Terutama Huh Se-lin; Tuan Yang Terutama Choi Kwang-shik; Tuan Yang Terutama Sa Boo-sung; Tuan Yang Terutama Kim Dae-sik; dan Tuan Yang Terutama Kim Woong-nam	
(9) Turut hadir pada Majlis Mengadap tersebut ialah Yang Berhormat Pehin Dato Seri Setia Awang Haji Abd. Rahman bin Haji Ibrahim; Yang Berhormat Pehin Dato Seri Setia Lim Jock Seng; Yang Berhormat Pehin Datu Singamanteri Kolonel (Bersara) Dato Seri Setia (Dr.) Awang Haji Mohammad Yasmin bin Haji Umar dan Tuan Yang Terutama Dato Paduka Awang Haji Harun bin Haji Ismail	

Text 3A	Text 3B
Tajuk: Pergaduhan di tengah jalan	**Title: Police investigating cause behind scuffle**
Posted date: December 10, 2014	December 10, 2014
Oleh Yusrin Junaidi	By: James Kon
(1) BANDAR SERI BEGAWAN, 9 Dis – Pasukan Polis Diraja Brunei, baru-baru ini telah menerima panggilan kecemasan dari orang ramai mengenai pergaduhan di tengah-tengah jalan kawasan Jerudong, yang telah tersebar di media sosial WhatsApp dan Facebook	(1) THE Royal Brunei Police Force (RBPF) is investigating the cause of a scuffle, during which two locals, aged 32 and 36, were alleged to have been beaten up by a 38-year-old
(2) Kejadian yang berlaku pada 7 Disember lalu itu, melibatkan tiga orang dari sebuah keluarga, berusia 32 tahun, 36 tahun, dan 38 tahun, dan telah mengakibatkan kesesakan	(2) The incident happened in the vicinity of the Jerudong Mosque last Sunday morning

(continued)

(continued)

lalu lintas di kawasan jalan berdekatan masjid Jerudong	
(3) Pertengkaran keluarga ini masih disiasat dan punca sebenar juga masih dalam siasatan	(3) A picture of the scuffle had made its way onto the social media, showing a person who had been dragged onto the road
(4) Jika sabit kesalahan tertuduh boleh didakwa di bawah Seksyen 324 dan Seksyen 427 Kanun Hukuman Jenayah	(4) If found guilty, the accused will face punishment under Sect. 324, Chap. 427 under the penal code

Text 4A	Text 4B
Tajuk: Mayat wanita tempatan ditemui terapung	**Title: Body of local woman found at Tutong beach**
Posted date: **December 08, 2014**	December 08, 2014
Oleh Yusrin Junaidi	By Khal Baharulalam
(1) TUTONG, 7 Dis – Mayat seorang wanita tempatan berusia 48 tahun ditemui terapung di Pantai Seri Kenangan di sini kira-kira jam 2.45 petang ini	(1) THE body of a woman was discovered along the Seri Kenangan Beach yesterday afternoon by residents of the Tutong District. She was presumed to have drowned
(2) Mangsa dikenali sebagai Rohana Binti Haji Talip, 48 tahun dari Kampung Sengkarai, Tutong	(2) The Tutong District Police Station was informed and they immediately dispatched personnel to the scene
(3) Menurut polis, mereka menerima panggilan daripada orang ramai memaklumkan mengenai penemuan mayat tersebut	(3) They identified the victim as a 48-year-old local woman
(4) Mayat mangsa kemudiannya dibawa ke Hospital Duli Pengiran Muda Mahkota Al-Muhtadee Bollah, Tutong untuk dibedah siasat. Polis masih menjalankan siasatan lanjut berhubung kes itu dan hasil siasatan awal menunjukkan tiada sebarang perbuatan khianat	(4) There were speculations among the local communities as to how the victim had drowned after Whatsapp messages carrying the news went viral
	(5) However, the Royal Brunei Police Force in a statement said the cause of drowning is still under investigation, and added that there were no signs of foul play *(photo: A WhatsApp image shows people watching police personnel securing the area)*

Text 5A	Text 5B
Tajuk: Bengkel siasatan kemalangan udara berakhir	**Title: DCA plans to set up independent Aircraft Accident Investigation unit**
Posted date: December 11, 2014	December 11, 2014
Oleh Yusrin Junaidi	By: Khal Baharulalam
(1) BANDAR SERI BEGAWAN, 10 Dis – Bengkel tiga hari mngenai Penyiasatan	(1) AS CONCERNS arise following challenges that recently surfaced in the

(continued)

(continued)

Kemalangan dan Kejadian Pesawat anjuran bersama Jabatan Penerbangan Awam dan Biro Penyiasatan dan Kemalangan Udara Singapura, berakhir hari ini dengan majlis penyampaian sijil yang berlangsung di Bangunan Kementerian Perhubungan	aviation industry after a slew of global developments, the Brunei Department of Civil Aviation (DCA) is currently looking to set up an independent Aircraft Accident Investigation (AAI) unit, as a means to highlight the importance of aviation safety and aircraft accident investigations in the Sultanate
(2) Penyampaian sijil kepada seramai 30 peserta bengkel di majlis itu disempurnakan oleh Pemangku Pengarah Penerbangan Awam, Haji Abdul Karim bin Haji Abdul Wahab	(2) This was shared by Acting Director of the DCA Haji Abdul Karim bin Haji Abdul Wahab in an interview held during yesterday's conclusion of the DCA's AAI Workshop, which was jointly organised by the department with the Air Accident and Investigation Bureau of Singapore
(3) Dalam ucapannya, Haji Abdul Karim berharap dengan adanya bengkel ini, setiap agensi yang terlibat akan dapat menggunakan pengetahuan yang diperolehi dengan sebaik mungkin apabila pulang ke unit masing-masing	(3) The Acting Director, who attended the closing ceremony as guest of honour, elaborated that the initiative 'is still in the pipeline' adding that the inaugural AAI Workshop is only the beginning of the department's efforts in enhancing aviation safety and investigation resources locally
(4) Para peserta bengkel berkenaan terdiri daripada wakil-wakil dari Jabatan Penerbangan Awam, pihak berkepentingan dan pengendali, serta pelbagai agensi kerajaan termasuk Tentera Udara Diraja Brunei, Pasukan Polis Diraja Brunei dan Jabatan Bomba dan Penyelamat *(gambar: Antara yang hadir di majlis penutup di bengkel, kelmarin.)* *(gambar: Tetamu kehormat menyampaikan sijil kepada salah seorang anggota Angkatan Bersenjata Diraja Brunei yang menyertai bengkel berkenaan.)*	(4) 'We hope to form a unit that specialises in AAI—an independent body that reports directly to the minister,' said Haji Abd Karim, noting that involvement of all stakeholders—including that of which under the Royal Brunei Police Force and the Royal Brunei Armed Forces—in the Brunei Aviation industry could make this goal a success in the near future *(photo: The Acting Director of the DCA, Haji Abdul Karim bin Haji Abdul Wahab)* *(photo: A section of the participants)*
(5) Bengkel ini diadakan untuk membolehkan para peserta memahami punca-punca kemalangan pesawat dan kejadian, meningkatkan keselamatan dan mencegah kejadian di masa depan di samping memahami protokol antarabangsa bagi kemalangan pesawat dalam insiden penerbangan dan penyiasatan kejadian seperti menurut 'Standard and Recommended Practices' yang ditetapkan oleh Pertubuhan Penerbangan Awam Antarabangsa (ICAO)	(5) 'In a way, with plans to continue conducting AAI workshops (such as this), our locals will have a certain degree of qualification to carry out certain AAI duties
(6) Bengkel ini juga memenuhi sebahagian daripada Memorandum Persefahaman (MoU) mengenai Kerjasama Penerbangan	(6) It was explained that following the Memorandum of Understanding (MoU) on Civil Aviation Cooperation between Brunei

(continued)

(continued)

Awam di antara Negara Brunei Darussalam dan Singapura yang telah ditandatangani pada 27 November 2014 oleh Menteri Perhubungan Brunei Darussalam dan Menteri Pengangkutan Singapura	and Singapore recently, some DCA officers have been attached at the Air Accident and Investigation Bureau of Singapore for training, as part of realising the department's goals
(7) Selain itu, ia juga merupakan salah satu daripada usaha berterusan jabatan berkenaan untuk meningkatkan pengetahuan dalam Lampiran 13 mengenai Penyiasatan Kemalangan Pesawat, iaitu program untuk meningkatkan keselamatan penerbangan	(7) The 3-day workshop was initiated to enable participants to further understand the underlying causes of aviation accidents and incidents, to improve safety and instigate early prevention of future occurrences—all of which are in line with the international protocol in aircraft accident and incident investigation as per the Standard and Recommended Practices laid down by the International Civil Aviation Organisation (ICAO)
	(8) Meanwhile, commenting on her participating experience of the 3-day workshop, Major Siti Khadijah binti Haji Emran of the Royal Brunei Air Force, agreed that the cooperative efforts in fostering competencies in aircraft safety would bode the aviation industry well in incorporating skills and expertise in AAI, particularly in the local framework
	(9) Yesterday's ceremony also saw the presentation of certificates to some 30 participants from various government agencies, aviation stakeholders and operators

Text 6A	Text 6B
Tajuk: CRCC bida jambatan Temburong	**Title: Chinese company bids for Temburong bridge project**
8 Disember 2014	December 08, 2014
Oleh Sim Y.H.	By Aziz Idris in Beijing, China
(1) BANDAR SERI BEGAWAN, 7 Dis – Sebuah syarikat pembinaan terkemuka China mengesahkan menyertai tender bagi pembinaan Jambatan Temburong yang akan dibina tidak lama lagi	(1) THE proposed construction of a bridge linking Temburong and Brunei-Muara Districts across the Brunei Bay is not only a dream that will in a few years' time become a reality for the people of Brunei, especially residents in Temburong District, but also a milestone achievement for the Ministry of Development as the mega project will become a new landmark in the Sultanate
(2) China Railway Construction Corporation Limited (CRCC), yang disenaraikan sebagai syarikat teratas dari 250 kontraktor global dalam laporan ENR bagi 2013 berkata	(2) Bids for the construction of the mega project are being submitted; with various local and international contractors

(continued)

(continued)

mereka telah mengemukakan bidaan dan sebut harga tawaran bagi pembinaan jambatan berkenaan untuk semua pakej pembinaan yang dikeluarkan	participating in the tender to build the bridge, which has been divided into several packages
(3) Pengerusi Lembaga Pengarah CRCC, Meng Fengchao semasa pertemuan dengan peserta pertukaran media Asia Tenggara di ibu pejabat CRCC, Beijing, Republik Rakyat China, baru-baru ini berkata, CRCC mempunyai pengalaman luas dalam pembinaan jambatan penghubung yang besar dan pelbagai reka bentuk di China	(3)The project has also received the attention of an international construction company with vast experience in building mega projects in and outside of China—the China Railway Construction Corporation Limited (CRCC)—which has also submitted its bid for the construction of the bridge
(4) Dengan kepakaran dan pengalaman pelaksanaan projek-projek pembinaan jambatan mega menerusi projek-projekyang dilaksanakan di China dan juga di seluruh dunia beliau yakin ia dapat diguna pakai dalam pembinaan jambatan penghubungan Temburong nanti *(gambar: Meng Fenchao (tiga dari kanan_ dan Zhuo Lei (dua dari kanan) bercakap kepada media di ibu pejabat CRCC di Beijing baru-baru ini)*	(4) CRCC, which is listed in the 250 global contractors in ENR report for 2013, is confident that it will offer its best services, expertise and experience gained from bridge projects in China and across the world
(5) Pada masa yang sama, beliau berkata bahawa syarikatnya juga terus meneroka pelbagai peluang-peluang pembinaan di negara-negara anggota ASEAN termasuk di Malaysia dan Singapura dengan hasrat untuk menyertai tawaran bagi pembinaan laluan kereta api pantas menghubungkan Singapura dan Malaysia yang akan dilaksanakan	(5) The Chairman of the Board of Directors of CRCC, Meng Fengchao, said this during a joint meeting with the media from Southeast Asia at CRCC Headquarters in Beijing, China, recently. The mediapersons were there for an exchange programme. *(photo: Meng Fengchao, Chairman of the Board of Directors of CRCC (L) speaking at the joint meeting as Vice-President Zhuo Lei looks on.)*
(6) Beliau turut melahirkan keyakinan bahawa dengan pengalaman, kepakaran dan pengetahuan yang dimiliki oleh syarikatnya itu, ia mampu untuk membantu pertukaran ilmu pengetahuan itu kepada pekerja-pekerja tempatan di negara-negara ASEAN itu nanti	(6) He added that the company has extensive experience in the construction of bridges in sophisticated and diverse designs in China and believes that the experience could be applied in the construction of the bridge linking Temburong and Brunei-Muara Districts
(7) Menyentuh lanjut mengenai penyertaan tawaran CRCC dalam projek jambatan penghubung Daerah Temburong itu, Penolong Presiden CRCC, Pengerusi dan Pengurus Besar CRCC Intl. Ltd, Zhuo Lei berkata bahawa proses pembidaan bagi projek Jambatan Temburong itu dibahagikan kepada beberapa pakej dan CRCC menyertai	(7) At the same time, the chairman said that CRCC continues to explore various opportunities in construction in Asean member countries, including Malaysia and Singapore, where the company is spearheading the construction of a railway route linking the neighbours

(continued)

(continued)

atau menghantar bidaan mereka dalam kesemua pakej-pakej yang ditawarkan itu	
(8) Katanya, setiap pakej yang ditawarkan itu berada dalam pelbagai peringkat pelaksanaan dari peringkat awal hingga ke peringkat lanjutan. Keputusan bidaan dijangka dikeluarkan pada masa yang terdekat	(8) He noted that with the experience, expertise and knowledge the company has, CRCC will also be able to help transfer knowledge to local workers in Asean countries
(9) 'CRCC menaruh harapan akan diberi peluang oleh pihak Negara Brunei Darussalam untuk mengongsi pengalaman dalam pembinaan jambatan. Kami juga yakin dapat melaksanakan projek itu dengan jayanya'	(9) Vice-President of CRCC, Chairman and General Manager of CRCC Intl Ltd, Zhuo Lei said the bidding process for the Temburong bridge project was divided into several packages and CRCC has sent its bids for all packages offered by Brunei's ministry of development
(10) Mengulas mengenai penyertaan pekerja tempatan dalam projek itu, Zhuo Lei berkata syarikatnya meletakkan keutamaan untuk mendapatkan sebanyak mungkin tenaga kerja tempatan dalam projek-projek yang dilaksanakan di luar negara	(10) He explained that each of the packages offered was in various stages of implementation, from the initial stage to the advanced stage. The decision on bids/tender will be released soon
(11) 'Ia adalah prinsip utama kami dan klien-klien kami mengharapkan perkara itu dapat dilaksanakan dengan jayanya serta memberikan pulangan yang positif kepada penduduk setempat dari segi ilmu pengetahuan dan kepakaran'	(11) 'CRCC hopes to be given the opportunity by the government of Brunei Darussalam so as to share its experience in the construction of the bridge with Brunei. We also believe that we can implement the project successfully,' said Zhou Lei
(12) Tambah beliau, syarikatnya juga akan memastikan pelaksanaan projek itu dijalankan secara mesra alam yang mana adalah menjadi salah satu prinsip syarikat berkenaan untuk melaksanakan projek yang mempunyai pelan mesra alam yang terperinci supaya tidak mengakibatkan kerosakan teruk kepada alam semula jadi dan persekitaran projek	(12) Commenting on the participation of local workers in the project, he said the company's priority is to employ as many locals as possible in projects undertaken abroad
(13) Jambatan penghubung itu nanti akan merentasi perairan Brunei melalui jambatan sepanjang kira-kira 14 km dan menjadikan panjang keseluruhan jalan dan jambatan sejauh 30 km, menghubungkan Daerah Brunei Muara dan Daerah Temburong, bermula dari Jalan Utama Menteri hingga ke Labu Estet	(13) He also said CRCC will ensure the execution of the mega bridge project in an environmentally friendly manner, which is one of the core principles of the company
(14) Apabila siap nanti, ia akan mempercepatkan lagi perjalanan berulang-alik antara Brunei Muara ke Temburong dalam masa kira-kira 30 ke 40 minit sahaja	(14) 'CRCC ensures that while implementing any project, detailed plans emphasising on environmental friendly issues will be applied and will ensure minimal damage to nature and the environment,' he said
(15) Projek Jambatan Temburong itu juga bakal menjadi mercu tanda bagi Negara	(15) Temburong District is separated from Brunei's other three districts by Malaysian

(continued)

(continued)

Brunei Darussalam dan merupakan satu projek mega Kementerian Pembangunan	territory. Currently, the main modes of travel between Temburong and Brunei-Muara Districts are through a 45-min boat ride, or a 90-min journey by land
(16) Kementerian Pembangunan sebelum ini menyatakan yang ia sedaya upaya akan memastikan semua aspek projek jambatan itu dari reka bentuk yang menepati ciri-ciri KeBruneian hinggalah kepada kerja-kerja pembinaan dan kualiti jambatan yang siap itu nanti, benar-benar mencerminkan satu kerja kejuruteraan yang boleh dibanggakan	(16) The 30-km link will start from an interchange at Jalan Penghubung Mentiri, through a series of tunnels in Bukit Subok, before crossing the scenic Brunei Bay covering a distance of 14 km. Once completed, it will cut the travelling time to only 30–40 min' drive
	(17) The construction of the bridge will ensure that all aspects of the design meet the characteristics of the country, which will be one of the engineering marvels that Brunei can be proud of

Appendix B

Interview Questions (Editors)

1. What is your editorial policy regarding language use in
   (a) news reports;
   (b) reporting parliamentary and political speeches or debates;
   (c) crime reports?
2. What are the criteria for translating reports from Malay into English and vice versa?
3. Do your journalists translate word-for-word or are some features left out?
4. Are they differences in what is covered in the Malay newspaper produced by your company as compared to your English-language newspaper?

Interview Questions (Journalists)

1. How do you go about drafting reports?
2. How do you decide what to include or exclude in your reports?
3. Are the reports drafted in Malay or English?
4. Do you translate word-for-word or are some features left out?
5. What is your strategy or what are your strategies when drafting the following:
   (a) Current affairs news?
   (b) News regarding speeches of Ministers and other VIPs?
   (c) News about crime?

References

Abdullah Hassan and Ainon Muhamad (2001). *Teori dan teknik terjemahan*. Kuala Lumpur: PTS Publication.
Bell, A. (2014). News stories as narratives. In A. Jaworski & N. Coupland (Eds.), *The discourse reader* (pp. 236–251). Oxford: Routledge.
Bell, A., & Garrett, P. (1998). *Approaches to media discourse*. Oxford: Blackwell Publishers Ltd.
Brunei Press Sdn Bhd—QAF-Brunei.com. 2006. Brunei Press Sdn Bhd. Retrieved June 23, 2015 from http://www.qaf-brunei.com.bn/media/brunei_press.htm.
David. M., & McLellan, J. (2007). Nativised varieties of English in news reports in Malaysia and Brunei Darussalam. In D. Prescott, Azirah Hashim, I. P. Martin & A. Kirkpatrick (Eds.), *English in Southeast Asia: Varieties, literacies and literatures* (pp. 94–119). Newcastle-upon-Tyne, UK: Cambridge Scholars Publishing.
Deterding, D., & Poedjosoedarmo, G. (2001). *The grammar of English: Morphology and syntax for English teachers in Southeast Asia*. Singapore: Prentice Hall.
Faure, C. (2001). Newspaper production. In P. Fourie (Ed.), *Media studies: Content, audiences, and production* (pp. 341–381). Lansdowne, South Africa: Juta Education.
Hallin, D., & Mancini, P. (2004). *Comparing media systems: Three models of media and politics*. West Nyack, NY: Cambridge University Press.
Huckin, T. (2002). Critical discourse analysis and the discourse of condescension. In E. Barton & G. Stygall (Eds.), *Discourse studies in composition* (pp. 19–42). Cresskill, NJ: Hampton. Retrieved October 30, 2015 from http://www.writing.ucsb.edu/wrconf08/Pdf_Articles/Huckin_Article.pdf.
Knox, J., & Patpong, P. (2008). Reporting bloodshed in Thai newspapers: A comparative case study of English and Thai. In E. Thomson & P. White (Eds.), *Communicating conflict: Multilingual case studies of the news media* (pp. 173–202). London: Continuum International Publishing Group.
Manning, D. (2011). Traditional versus new media: Thinking about narrative. Mediabite.org. Retrieved October 30, 2015 from http://mediabite.org/2011/07/27/traditional-vs-new-media-thinking-about-narrative/.
McLellan, J., & Noor Azam Haji-Othman. (2012). Features of the Brunei Darussalam variety of English. In E. Low & Azirah Hashim (Eds.), *Englishes in South East Asia: Features, policy and language in use* (pp. 75–90). Amsterdam: John Benjamins.
Nurkhalisah Mustapa. (2013). Issues in translation between Malay and English. *Southeast Asia: A Multidisciplinary Journal 13*, 27–34.
Richardson, J. (2013). *Journalism studies: Theory and practice*. London: Routledge.
Scollon, R., Wong-Scollon, S., & Kirkpatrick, A. (1998). *Contrastive discourse in Chinese and English: A critical appraisal*. Beijing: Foreign Language Teaching and Research Press.
Thomson, E., White, P., & Kitley, P. (2008). 'Objectivity' and 'Hard News' reporting across cultures. *Journalism Studies, 9*(2), 212–228.
Wang, S. (1993). The New York Times and Renmin Ribao's news coverage of the 1991 Soviet coup: A case study of international news discourse. *Text, 13*(4), 559–598.

Part V
Literature and Language in Education

Chapter 15
Contemporary English and Malay Literature in Brunei: A Comparison

Kathrina Mohd Daud, Grace V.S. Chin and Maslin Jukim

15.1 Publishing in Brunei: Facts and Figures

Despite numerous initiatives and calls for action on the part of the government, notably through the National Language and Literature Bureau (*Dewan Bahasa dan Pustaka*, DBP), the state of Bruneian literature and publishing remains nascent. At the 2011 Globalisation and Translation conference in Kuala Lumpur, Abdullah (2011) stated that developed countries generate 1,000 new book titles per year per population of one million, including textbooks and translations. For Brunei, which has an estimated population of 406,000, that means that 400 new titles should be published annually in order to qualify as developed. In 2013, 49 new titles were reportedly published by the DBP for the year 2013, with only 15 of these classified as literary texts. In 2011, the number was 11; in 2012, 18. While the DBP is not the only publisher of texts in Brunei, it does represent a significant proportion. Additionally, other publishers work primarily with textbooks.

Sunny (2012) puts the average number of local literary texts being published per year as 20. Sales figures per title are estimated at well below 100 units, apart from the bestsellers, which generate sales from between 800–2000 per unit, and have been non-fiction in nature (Azlan 2013). This is partly due to the marginal presence that these texts have in local bookstores—many of these texts, published by the DBP, are available only at official government bookstores. These numbers are applicable only to Malay literature in Brunei, as almost without exception, all of the literary texts published by the DBP are in *Bahasa Melayu* or Malay; in contrast, English literature produced by Bruneians tends to be published by overseas agencies.

Kathrina Mohd Daud (✉) · G.V.S. Chin · M. Jukim
FASS/UBD, Universiti Brunei Darussalam, Jalan Tungku Link,
Gadong BE1410, Brunei Darussalam
e-mail: kathrina.daud@ubd.edu.bn

© Springer Science+Business Media Singapore 2016
Noor Azam Haji-Othman et al. (eds.), *The Use and Status of Language in Brunei Darussalam*, DOI 10.1007/978-981-10-0853-5_15

Since 1998, 11 English-language literary texts have been published that might be considered Bruneian literature: four novels, six anthologies of poetry, and one anthology of scripts (see the Appendix for a complete list of Anglophone Bruneian publications). Ten of these were published from 2009–2015, a significant upsurge in the past 6 years in the production of local English literature. However, only one of these texts was published by the DBP. At least four were self-published while two were published by local educational institutions. Furthermore, nine out of the ten were published abroad. A pattern of self-publication, overseas publications and one-off productions begins to emerge when discussing the production of English literature in Brunei, suggesting a lack of institutionalised national support which contrasts with the scale and treatment of Malay literature.

15.2 State Policies on Literature

The national support of Malay literature is rooted in the use of Malay as the national language. Since Brunei's independence in 1984, the importance of Malay language and literature has been formally recognised at the state level. The country's investment in Malay is highlighted by the role of the DBP, which is 'responsible for language and literary development and propagation, cultural research and documentation and book publication' (Rozan 2011). The DBP has in the past encouraged and supported local literary output through activities such as writing competitions. It organised the first national novel-writing competition in 1980 to encourage Bruneian writers, who tended to write poetry and short stories, to explore the form as well as increase literary production in Brunei. The two winners of this first competition, H.B. Mahmud for *Langit Semakin Cerah* ('The Sky Grows Brighter') and Leman Ahmad for *Menyerah* ('Surrender') penned two nationalist novels with anti-insurgency overtones, condemning rebellion and invoking national spirit. These first victories have since set the tone for future DBP novel writing competitions. In 1983, when it organised another competition to commemorate the first Bruneian Independence Day, the prize was taken by Norsiah Abd Gapar for *Pengabdian* ('Dedication'), another nationalistic novel which explores the patriotism of locals who return to Brunei after being educated in the West. Norsiah, who has since been acknowledged as the premier female Bruneian writer, became the first female Bruneian SEA Write Award winner in 2009. This award is notable because of its status in Brunei as a way for the DBP—and correspondingly, the state —to officially acknowledge national writers of note; each year since 1986, one of the key Malay literary figures in Brunei has been awarded this prize (Chin 2007). No corresponding recognition has been awarded to any English-language writer in Brunei.

More pertinently, the privileged status of Malay language and literature falls in line with the aims of the state ideology and discourse of *Melayu Islam Beraja* (MIB), or Malay Islamic Monarchy, a tripartite ideology which formalises three essential components that make up the national identity and state discourse:

(1) Malay language, cultural values and traditions, (2) the teachings of Islam, and (3) a monarchical government headed by the Sultan. Since its implementation in 1984, MIB has been legitimised through state policies, agencies and institutions, including the education system. MIB is not only considered one of the 'twin pillars' (Loo 2009, p. 153) of Brunei's education (the other being Islamic Religious Knowledge, or IRK), but is in itself a core compulsory subject in primary and secondary schools, as well as the higher education institutions. The significance of MIB as a national ideology and state discourse cannot be understated, for it corresponds with the rise of the 'active processes of both Islam-ization and Malay-icization' in the past decade, highlighting a 'general move towards a single national identity […] in conjunction with a growing national consciousness' (Noor Azam 2012, p. 176), of which Malay language and literature form a vital part.

This is reflected in the treatment of Malay and English literature in the national educational curriculum. Both languages are taught as compulsory core subjects at the primary and secondary school levels, from Year 1 to Year 10/11. It is only from Year 9 to Year 10/11 (when students have to sit for their GCE 'O' Level exams), that the literature of both languages appear as elective subjects in the *Sistem Pendidikan Negara Abad Ke-21* (SPN21) curriculum mentioned in the introductory chapter.

However, according to Haji Ramlee (2009), while Malay literature is an elective subject under the GCE 'O' Level syllabus, the subject has long been incorporated in the teaching of Malay language through which students generally learn the varying genres of poetry (*pantun, syair*), proverbs, folktales, and so on. Once students are able to take Malay literature as an elective subject in Year 9, they are introduced to local and regional Malay literary texts that have been carefully selected by the education board for their messages, morals and values; these texts should harmonise with the principles upheld by MIB in the building of a 'well-rounded Bruneian race' (Norhazlin 2014) and society (Haji Ramlee 2009). Typically divided into three categories—classic texts, modern prose, and modern poetry—Bruneian texts that have been included in the past GCE 'O' Level syllabi are *Hikayat Awang Kamaruddin* ('Tales of Awang Kamaruddin'), *Pengabdian* ('Dedication'), and *Antologi Cerpen Meniti Waktu* ('The Passing of Time: An Anthology of Short Stories'). At the university level, the Malay Literature programme offers a deeper study of the subject through a wider range and variety of local and regional Malay literary works in all genres.

As for the study of English Literature, a glance at the GCE 'O' Level syllabi from 2013 to 2018 reveals a heavier emphasis on British and American writers and texts in the major genres of novel, short story, drama and poetry. Western canonical figures such as William Shakespeare, John Donne, Thomas Hardy, E.M. Forster, W.H. Auden, Nathaniel Hawthorne, and Tennessee Williams form part of the staple list of authors in the syllabus every year. In contrast, Asian writers are seldom featured; the 2013–2018 syllabi only offer the following names: Asian American authors Jhumpa Lahiri and Shirley Geok-lin Lim, Indian writers V.S. Naipaul, Amit Chaudhuri and Anita Desai, and Singaporean-Australian poet Boey Kim Cheng. In short, the GCE 'O' Level English Literature syllabus does little to foster interest or understanding among Bruneian students toward Asian literature, much less Southeast Asian or Bruneian works. At the university level too, the English Literature programme leans toward Western writers and texts, with only two modules—*Postcolonial Literature* and *Southeast Asian Literature*—that focus on non-Western works of English literature.

Writers who wish to write in Malay will thus find some degree of cultural assistance and capital in the support provided by educational syllabi and national publishing houses. The official status of Malay literature and Malay language writers is not only protected by the national philosophy and discourse of MIB, but also developed and bolstered through language and education policies as well as state agencies such as the DBP. However, apart from small creative writing classes in English at the national university, no such formal support is accorded to local writers in English or their works, a factor that may well have influenced and will continue to influence the way in which the paths of both literatures have diverged in the nation space.

15.3 The Development of Modern Malay and English Literature: An Overview

Locally produced English literature is a fairly new development compared to Malay literature, which is rooted in a proud history of oral tradition, folklore, legends and myths. With the arrival of Islam in the 15th century, this tradition has been enriched by Islamic beliefs, values, teachings, as well as its literature (Ampuan 2001, 2010). Echoing Malaysia, the emergence of modern Malay literature in Brunei generally refers to post-1840s works, in particular with the publication of Pengiran Shahbandar Pengiran Mohd Salleh's *Syair Rakis* ('The Rakis Poems') in 1847. Although *Syair Rakis* takes the form of a traditional poem, scholarly consensus is that the content of the poem, which criticises the Bruneian rule and British influence in the region, marks an ideological break with pre-1840 literature. Pengiran Shahbandar's insistence on recognising the importance of a unique Bruneian identity and the preservation of the sultanate marks him as the father of Brunei Malay modern literature (Badaruddin 1967; Haji Hashim 1994).

Despite the efforts of the DBP, the novel form has historically had a late and disjointed presence in the development of Malay literature. The first Bruneian novel, *Bendahara Menjadi Sultan* ('The Chief Minister becomes Sultan') or *Mahkota Berdarah* ('Bleeding Crown'), was written by Yura Halim and published in 1951—one of the impetuses for this novel was the Japanese occupation of Brunei during World War II. *Mahkota Berdarah* was followed by H.M. Salleh's *Pemimpin Tunangan Bangsa* ('The Leader Betrothed to the Nation') in 1952. A three-decade drought would follow, until the publication of Mohd Salleh Abd Latiff's *Gegeran Se-Musim* ('A Season of Tremors') in 1981. (Gallop 2004 claims that the next novel actually appeared in 1968, but does not name it, putting the number of novels in

Brunei prior to 1981 at three.) For this breakthrough, Mohd Salleh was hailed as a survivor of novel-writing in Brunei (Maslin 1997).

The 1980s would see a significant increase in the production of Malay novels, with Mohd Salleh publishing *Meniti Hasrat* ('The Passing Aspiration') in 1982, followed by *Titian Semusim* ('The Passing of a Season') in 1986 and *Pahlawan Bendahara Sakam* ('Chief Minister Sakam the Warrior') in 1991. He would be joined by Muslim Haji Burut (known as Muslim Burmat), Chong Ah Fook (the first Bruneian Chinese writer of Malay literature), and Norsiah Abd Gapar. Other genres, particularly poetry and *cerpen* ('short stories'), have also continued to flourish during this period, thanks to both individual perseverance and the continuing efforts of the DBP and *Asterawani* (The Brunei Writers Association), which sustained high rates of literacy for the production of Malay literature in Brunei. Gallop (2004, p. 45) hypotheses that the marked preference for short stories and poetry over the novel form has its roots in a number of factors, including the relative ease of publication compared to a novel and the lack of a 'prior literate tradition' in comparison with neighbouring Malay-speaking countries Malaysia and Indonesia.

In English literature, novel production such as it is has developed at the same pace as the production of other genres. Due once again to the lack of a critical mass, it is impossible and unfruitful to make generalised statements about trends in Bruneian English literature. With such a small and under-marketed body of work to draw upon, writers often find themselves working in isolation, with little if any knowledge of other writers of the language. This is exacerbated by the fact that English language writers tend to have very little exposure to Malay literature. One also notes the influence of Western popular fiction, particularly American blockbuster fiction, in Amir Falique's *The Forlorn Adventure* (2013) and Christopher Sun's *Four Kings* (2011). The resulting work tends to be summed up in a comment that a local Anglophone writer made in email correspondence to one of the researchers of this chapter:

> Writing is only a solitary experience to a certain extent. I find myself longing to read English works by other Bruneian writers, to get a fuller and sharper perspective on home, to echo or challenge their voices in my own work, but that has not been possible...

He adds as an afterthought, 'well, until possibly now', in reference to the steady production of work since 2009.

Thematically, Gallop (2004, p. 47) claims that Bruneian literature, bolstered by the government's 'firm and stated commitment to a literature which will lead the country towards development' is 'expected to deliver a measure of fictional 'success' for the protagonists at the closure of the narrative in the form of satisfying, if not necessarily happy, resolutions' (p. 48). He also argues that Bruneian writers have needed to 'believe in their possession of a separate and distinct national identity' (p. 45). While Gallop is referring to Malay literature, this belief also seems to hold true for English literature.

Malay literature, in comparison with English, has had the time and space to grow in response to and in conversation with critical study and other local literary texts as well as texts from the Malay world. While thematically it tends to address social issues, writers have proven willing to experiment with narrative form, although a didactic style befitting the perceived moral role of literature in the national culture is often adopted. While the influences of the West are far more apparent in Bruneian English literature, traditional narrative dominates, with writers as yet unwilling to experiment with form. Thematically, however, the texts echo Malay literature in that they also insist on a unique and distinct national identity (apart from *Four Kings*, which is neither set in Brunei nor features a Bruneian protagonist): *The Wild Men of the East* is a political satire distinct to the Bruneian context; *The Forlorn Adventure* is a time-travel sci-fi adventure which features the first Bruneian astronaut and a vision of Brunei in 500 years in which the key tenets of MIB are still intact, manifested in the physical landscape (the Sultan Omar Ali Saifuddien mosque and the Water Village dominate a futuristic urban environment) and the continued governance of the Sultan; *Written in Black*, which covers a few days in the life of a Bruneian Chinese ten-year-old and pays homage to Mark Twain's *Huckleberry Finn*, draws heavily on local icons and curiosities, including *poklens* (members of a particular kind of Bruneian youth culture), black magic and national landmarks.

Despite the fewer constraints involved in writing for a publisher outside of Brunei, Bruneian English literature still seems ideologically invested in perpetuating a vision of Brunei in which MIB is central, and the unique features of Brunei are emphasised. This is in part due to a sense that local literature, because of its paucity, has to bear social responsibility that goes beyond artistic integrity, and is a common burden shouldered by writers from under-represented communities. In order to mitigate this responsibility, for example, K.H. Lim invites readers in *Written in Black*'s paratext to explore Brunei themselves, insisting that the Brunei he portrays is only one of many possibilities.

Across the languages, there is little evidence that the literatures engage with or are even aware of each other in any substantial way. It is worth noting that both *The Forlorn Adventure* and *Written in Black* engage in implicit commentary on Brunei's relationship with the West, a common theme in Malay literature (and particularly in the seminal text *Pengabdian*, 'Dedication') although again, it is impossible to extrapolate this occurrence into evidence of a trend.

Tracing the development of both literatures reveals a still-nascent literary situation struggling to build the critical mass of texts necessary to truly claim a national literary history or scene. The slowness of this literary development may also be attributed to the lack of a national culture of review or critique, other than in academic circles. Nevertheless, the sudden growth in productivity in the English sphere makes it clear that the lack of engagement across the literatures is, in the future, something that the Bruneian literary community will have to address if it is to prove inclusive rather than divisive. In this, the increasingly popular creative writing classes at Universiti Brunei Darussalam, offered separately in modules in the English literature and Malay literature programmes, may prove to play a significant role. Chin and Kathrina (2015), in their study of student scripts which engage in the telling and re-telling of Bruneian stories in English, note the encouragement in classes to retain the bilingualism of the students' lived experiences, thereby eroding the traditional divide between the languages in print. The resulting anthology of scripts by university students, *In the Spotlight: An Anthology of Bruneian Plays in English* (2012), retains this bilingualism (Chin 2014, pp. 134–137) and marks a significant step in the development of Bruneian literature; it is also the first anthology of its kind to make its appearance in the local English literary scene.

15.4 Digital Media: New Possibilities for Bruneian Literature

The advent of digital media has offered new possibilities for Malay and English literature in Brunei. Chin and Kathrina (2015, p. 105) suggest that some of the factors contributing to the low publishing rate have been 'the stringent policing of texts, the lack of financial support, and low readership numbers', referring to the government policy that all literature published in the country be vetted by a censorship board whose guidelines are reactive rather than proactive. Other factors include the poor sales figures of local texts and a worrying 'lack of proper reading habits among the Bruneian public' (Alwines 2013). To circumvent these limitations, local writers are increasingly turning to the Internet to find an audience for their stories. Online digital space still remains largely unmediated, as the government policy is to react as situations arise rather than actively seek out dissenting or controversial voices.

Following global trends, the production of Bruneian content specifically for the Internet gained popularity in the mid-2000s (Faiq 2013) with the emergence of bloggers. More recently, two websites of note have emerged showcasing Bruneian writing—one in English and one in Malay. *Songket Alliance*, which was 'initiated to encourage Bruneians who write to keep writing' by providing a space for content, was established in 2013 and managed to maintain, for a year, a schedule of three posts a week. While much of this content is non-fiction, with a focus on the personal essay, the stated purpose of the online magazine was also to provide a space for fiction, particularly poetry. It is notable as perhaps the first digital presence of its kind for Bruneian writers of English, especially as it has a particular emphasis on curating the stories of minorities in the nation. It is also perhaps worth speculating on the relationship between the emergence of a long-form blogging culture in the mid-2000s with the publication of *The Wild Men of the East* in 2009, and the Anglophone novels written over the subsequent five years.

More substantial and sustainable is *Mode Seram*, a Malay language website which curates and collates Bruneian horror stories. Established in 2010 and unapologetically pulpy, *Mode Seram* protects itself from controversy and critique by having the stated purpose of providing stories which are '*pengajaran, bahan bacaan dan hiburan untuk semua tanpa menganggu atau mengubah serta memsongkan akidah kita sebagai Ahli Sunnah Wal Jamaah*' ('educational, reading material and entertainment for all, without changing or affecting our faith as members of the Islamic faith'). *Mode Seram*, unaffiliated with sanctioned literary production in the country, functions as a space for creation as well as consumption since readers are encouraged to send in stories, thus blurring the line between creator and consumer. This model is familiar in the production of popular fiction globally and the website updates itself daily. Its quantifiable readership holds steady at 40,000 subscribers; in comparison, the daily circulation of the two local English newspapers ranges from 15,000–20,000, while the daily circulation of the two local Malay language newspapers ranges from 10,000–19,000. Using these figures gives a combined circulation figure of 65,000 copies daily in a population of 406,000 (Anjaiah 2013). However, these figures are contradicted by *The Report: Brunei Darussalam*, published by the Oxford Business Group (2011), which puts the daily circulation of the Malay language newspapers in the range of 40,000–76,000, including online readership. Nevertheless, this figure places *Mode Seram* as one of the most-read disseminators of local prose in the country, far outstripping traditionally published local texts, although of course the comparison is not an entirely fair one. Although it is hard to definitively attribute the popularity of *Mode Seram*, the familiarity and informality of the Brunei Malay used in the stories clearly make it easy for readers to enter into the interactive model which *Mode Seram* thrives on.

More significantly, *Mode Seram* provides an avenue for the proliferation of stories in *bahasa rojak* ('Malay infused with other languages'). *Bahasa rojak* is characterised as utilising abbreviations, text-speak and use of words from other languages, most notably English. Although the mission statement of *Mode Seram* is in standard Malay, the stories are in *bahasa rojak*. Linguistic purity is one of the key tenets of the MIB philosophy, as encapsulated in a 2012 press statement by the head of the Magazine and Journal Planning Department at the DBP, that the Malay language is in danger of dying out due to the rise of *bahasa rojak*:

> That's a very scary scenario…We have to hold onto the Malay language, because it is what differentiates Brunei from other countries. There are Bruneians who have studied abroad for several years [who] claim they can't speak Malay as fluent as before. The funny thing is those people who have only been living abroad for several years and they pretend they can't speak Malay or that they don't eat traditional food. Hopefully these kinds of people recall their roots. We are Malay. We are living in a Malay society that adopts the Islamic Malay Monarchy (MIB). We should prioritise the Malay language.
>
> (Rabiatul 2012)

Bahasa rojak is thus identified as a key threat to the national narrative and outside of the realm of publication sanctioned by the DBP and consequently, or simultaneously, the state. The usage of *bahasa rojak* in the popular *Mode Seram* and *Songket Alliance* signals the demand for prose which elides the traditional divide between the languages. These unmonitored online spaces offer possibilities for the dissemination of unaltered prose not subject to the local mediatory practices of traditional publishing. It will be interesting to see how such spaces might offer the opportunity for ideological critique, subversion and engagement in emerging literary forms and content.

15.5 Conclusion

The development of contemporary Bruneian Malay and English literature has been tied to publishing and educational policies which have privileged Malay language and literature as a core part of national identity. Nationalist themes such as support for the monarchy (*Syair Rakis* and *Mahkota Berdarah*), Islam and the importance of Malay culture and tradition (*Pengabdian*) abound in Malay literature.

In contrast, the emergence of English language literature in the last decade seems to have developed separately from Malay literature, in large part because of its marginalisation from state support and attention. Its development can perhaps be attributed to, or at least linked with, global trends and increased Bruneian presence online, particularly in the blogosphere. Despite this differing impetus, the themes, form and ideological concerns across literatures have not diverged significantly. The most recent English novels, for example *The Forlorn Adventure* and *Written in Black*, take the opportunity not to critique nationalist themes or ideology, but to reinforce them. Generally, support for the national ideology of MIB remains a strongly pervasive theme of local literature in both languages.

Ideologically, literatures online, while amateurish and raw, provide an interesting space for consideration of what Bruneian literature unmediated by the concerns of traditional print publishing might look like. This space, unregulated and largely not subject to considerations of state censorship, offers many intriguing possibilities for study. Additionally, while there is a similar lack of conversation across the languages online as there is in the printed literatures, the informal nature of online prose may provide scope for more cross-lingual possibilities.

Appendix: Anglophone Bruneian Texts

Year of publication	Title	Author	Publisher
Fiction			
2009	The Wild Men of the East	Selamat Munap	Raider Publishing
2011	Four Kings	Christopher Sun	CreateSpace Independent Publishing Platform
2013	The Forlorn Adventure	Amir Falique	Trafford Publishing
2014	Written in Black	K.H. Lim	Monsoon Books
Drama			
2012	In the Spotlight: An Anthology of Bruneian plays in English	Ed. Grace V.S. Chin	Creative Industries Research Cluster, Universiti Brunei Darussalam

(continued)

(continued)

Year of publication	Title	Author	Publisher
Poetry			
1998	Under the Canopy and Other Poems: English Poetry in Brunei	Ed. Vaughan Rapatahana	Center for British Teachers
2009	The Swan Scripts	Shai Omarali	CreateSpace Independent Publishing Platform
2009	Young Dreams	Izzati Jamil	Dewan Bahasa dan Pustaka
2012	Tribute to Brunei and Other Poems	John Onu Odihi	Trafford Publishing
2013	Streak of Colour	Winter Frostt	Trafford Publishing
2015	Moments of Nil	Flora Tavu	Partridge Singapore

References

Abdullah Hassan (2011). Publishing 26,000 New Titles a Year. In A. Jamil, N. I. Ramli & N. Abdul Aziz (Eds.), *Globalisation through translation: A catalyst for knowledge and technological excellence* (pp. 15–24). Kuala Lumpur: Malaysian Translators Association.

Alwines, A. (2013). Reading culture a sign of advanced society. *The Brunei Times*, April 24.

Ampuan Haji Brahim Ampuan Haji Tengah (2001). *Sastera Brunei sebagai entiti sastera nusantara*. Kuala Lumpur: Dewan Bahasa dan Pustaka.

Ampuan Haji Brahim Ampuan Haji Tengah (2010). *Kesusasteraan Brunei tradisional: Pembicaraan genre dan tema*. Brunei Darussalam: Dewan Bahasa dan Pustaka.

Anjaiah, V. (2013). Brunei, Timor Leste much better than RI. *The Jakarta Post*, February 25.

Azlan Othman. (2013). Research needed on level of reading culture in Brunei. *Borneo Bulletin*, March 1.

Badaruddin, H. O. (1967). *Puisi Melayu dan perkembangannya di Brunei. Bahana*. Brunei Darussalam: Dewan Bahasa dan Pustaka.

Chin, G. V. S. (2007). Malaysia, Singapore and Brunei Darussalam: A comparative study of literary developments in English. *Asian Englishes: An International Journal of Sociolinguistics of English in Asia/Pacific, 10*(2), 8–29.

Chin, G. V. S. (2014). Co-constructing a community of creative writers: Exploring L2 identity formations through Bruneian playwriting. In D. Disney (Ed.), *Beyond Babel? Creative writing in non-native English-language contexts* (pp. 119–138). Amsterdam: John Benjamins.

Chin, G. V. S., & Kathrina Haji Mohd Daud (2015). Negotiating difference: The trope of "anak derhaka" and ideological endings in Bruneian writings. *The Journal of Commonwealth Literature, 50*(2), 101–114.

Faiq Airudin (2013). November 27. Brunei Online: Platform Websites. Retrieved October, 15, 2015 from http://openbrunei.org/2013/11/brunei-online-platform-websites.

Gallop, C. H. (2004). Brunei Darussalam and the modern novel. *Journal of the Malaysian Branch of the Royal Asiatic Society, 77*(1), 43–52.

Haji Hashim Haji Abd Hamid (1994). *Riak sastera Darussalam*. Kuala Lumpur: Hikmat Enterprise.

Haji Ramlee Bin Haji Tinkong (2009). *Pendidikan kesusateraan Melayu dalam mendepani cabaran abad ke-21: Pengalaman Negara Brunei Darussalam.* Paper presented at the Seminar Dasar Malaysia, October 6–8, in Kota Kinabalu, Malaysia.

Loo, S. P. (2009). Ethnicity and educational policies in Malaysia and Brunei Darussalam. *SA-eDUC Journal, 6*(2), 146–157.

Maslin Jukim (1997). *Watak dan perwatakan novel terbenamnya matahari.* Academic Exercise. Brunei: University Brunei Darussalam.

Noor Azam Haji-Othman. (2012). It's not always English: 'Duelling aunties' in Brunei Darussalam. In V. Rapatahana & P. Bunce (Eds.), *English language as hydra: Its impacts on non-English language cultures* (pp. 175–190). Bristol, UK: Multilingual Matters.

Norhazlin Muhammad (2014). *The educational system in Brunei Darussalam: In the light of Al-Attas' philosophy of education.* Brunei Darussalam: UBD Press.

Rabiatul Kamit (2012). Bahasa rojak affecting Malay language. *The Brunei Times*, April 22.

Rozan Yunos (2011). Dewan Bahasa dan Pustaka. *The Brunei Times*, September 19.

Sunny, N. D. P. H. (2012). *Empowering a reading culture: A Brunei Darussalam perspective.* Paper presented at the TK Conference on Reading, May 10–11, in Bangkok, Thailand.

The Oxford Business Group. (2011). *The report: Brunei Darussalam 2011.* Oxford: Oxford Business Group.

Chapter 16
Bilingual Education Revisited: The Role of Ugama Schools in the Spread of Bilingualism

Noor Azam Haji-Othman

16.1 Introduction

This chapter considers the role of Islamic religious schools or Ugama schools (*ugama* lit. 'religion') in the development of bilingualism and bilingual education in Brunei Darussalam. Brunei's bilingual mainstream education system has long been the subject of studies which often, rightly to some extent, identify it to be the primary reason for Bruneians' widespread bilingualism in English and Malay. In particular the focus has been on the *Dwibahasa* ('two-language') system that was introduced in 1985 (replacing the dual Malay stream and English stream schools system) and ran until 2009, when it was then replaced by the 21st Century National Education System (SPN21), which was in fact not too dissimilar from its predecessor. Bruneian students mainly attend mainstream schools in the morning from 7.30 am to 12.30 pm. However, for the Malay Muslim majority population of Brunei, many actually concurrently attend an Islamic ('Ugama') school in the afternoon from 1.30 pm to 5 pm for at least 7 years, mainly in their formative and primary years of development. Most works published on bilingualism in Brunei have tended to study the mainstream education systems only (Dual-Stream, Dwibahasa and SPN21), because these are the comprehensive systems that all Bruneians must go through. Although some make reference to Ugama schools, these are often fleeting, and Ugama schools seem to be regarded as peripheral to the subject of English-Malay bilingualism in Brunei. In fact, Ugama schools are usually assumed to be linked to Arabic language development, which is not necessarily the case. The following discussion argue that the comprehensive curricula of the mainstream education provide mainly the English language input, and in fact relatively little Malay input to Bruneians' bilinguality. It will be argued that in fact the

---

Noor Azam Haji-Othman (✉)
FASS/UBD, Universiti Brunei Darussalam, Jalan Tungku Link,
Gadong BE1410, Brunei Darussalam
e-mail: azam.othman@ubd.edu.bn

Ugama schools, which teach entirely in Malay language and in Jawi (Arabic) script, actually provide most of the Malay input for a Malay-English bilingual Bruneian, and that it is time the roles that Ugama schools play are given due credit. This chapter asks whether critics of Dwibahasa were right all along.

16.2 Bilingual Education in Brunei

The CfBT Report written by Rigall (2014) which analysed the bilingual education policy concludes that three central features have contributed to Brunei's ability to manage its bilingual policy effectively. According to Rigall, the first feature is Brunei's continued commitment to a bilingual education policy amidst early external pressures. The second central feature in the development of mastery of two languages that is embodied in the perceived status of English as a key competency of the 21st century (including for special needs and different language needs). And thirdly, there has been increased awareness of the potential 'synergy' between English and Malay. The report states:

> [Brunei's] consistent focus on promoting bilingual education has proved a strength, encouraging stability and consistency in the priority accorded to promoting competencies in both English and Malay. This has supported recognition of Brunei's contribution to and ability to offer leadership from the lessons learned in the teaching and learning of English in the ASEAN region.

According to Rigall (2014), there is growing external recognition of Brunei's educational success internationally which reflects Brunei's track record of support for and investment in English and the consistent policy commitment to bilingual education, thus enhancing the quality of education and increasing participation rates. As a result of these, Brunei can boast an adult literacy rate of over 90 % with the total number of students enrolled in pre-primary, primary and secondary levels of (mainstream) schooling rising from 91,992 in 1998 to 101,686 in 2012. These figures become more significant in view of the decline in Brunei's annual population increase rate from 2.82 % in 1990 to 1.7 % in 2011, with likewise falling birth rates from 29 births per 1000 in 1990 to 19 births in 2011 (Rigall 2014).

However, most previous studies on and relevant to bilingualism and bilingual education in Brunei such as those by Jones (1996, 1997a, b), Jones et al. (1993), Martin (1999), Noor Azam (2005, 2007), and Noor Azam and McLellan (2014), as well as the CfBT report (Rigall 2014) cited above, have tended to focus on the impact of mainstream formal education on Bruneian students, with little or no mention of Ugama schools as a possible contributor to their resultant bilingualism. UNESCO-IBE's (2011) report does outline fairly extensively the development of Ugama schools in Brunei, but stops short of mentioning that instruction is in the Malay language. Even the government-published Brunei Darussalam Statistics Yearbook (2010) only lists the number of mainstream schools, teachers and students for the years 2006, 2007, 2008, 2009 and 2010, without the inclusion of statistics for the Ugama schools. Although published works by Bruneian writers such as Mohammad (2014a, b) and Tassim (2014) acknowledge the existence and long history of Ugama schools alongside mainstream schools, none has so far stated their potential contribution to the development of Bruneian students' bilingual abilities. In a nutshell, the discourse on formal education has tended to refer exclusively to secular and mainstream education, and to exclude any consideration of the role of Ugama schools.

16.3 Early History of Mainstream Formal Education

The development of education in Brunei was not a smooth journey at first, although it picked up speed after the Second World War. The first Malay vernacular school was opened in 1914 with an intake of 30 boys. By 1918 three more schools opened in Muara, Tutong and Belait, but the official report on Brunei, as cited by Gunn (1997, p. 71), stated that the public was not yet ready for universal compulsory education. This was an omen for the 1920s, which did not see much development in terms of formal education. In fact the schools in Muara and Belait had closed due to a lack of students, and the ones that remained open benefited only those living near major towns such as the Bruneis and the Chinese and disadvantaged those living in more rural areas.

In the 1930s the first Brunei Malay girls' school opened, alongside more new schools, resulting in growing attendance. This was due to the fact that all male children between seven and fourteen were now required by law (Enactment No 3. 1929) to attend school within a two-mile radius of where they lived. St. George's English School was opened in 1938, followed by four more similar English mission schools throughout Brunei. Indeed prior to the spread of war in the region in 1941, the number of schools in Brunei had increased to 32, consisting of 24 Vernacular Malay, 3 private English and 5 private Chinese schools. The number of pupils enrolled was 1,746, including 312 girls (Ministry of Education 2002).

However, up till the 1940s there was still no secondary education in Brunei. During World War II, Brunei was occupied by Japanese forces between 1941 and 1945. The Japanese administrators in Brunei however 'recognized the importance of education for social engineering even more than the British' (Gunn 1997, p. 98). They even introduced the *Rumi* or Romanized Malay script. When Allied forces liberated Brunei in 1945, schools were once again forced to close, but an important legacy had been left by the Japanese: they promoted Malay and raised awareness of the importance of education in Brunei (Jasmin 1987, p. 8).

In October 1951 a Brunei Town Government English school was opened in the capital, followed by the opening of a similar school in Kuala Belait a year later. In less than 3 years, the Government was able to introduce English-medium secondary education in the country. Malay-medium secondary education however only began in 1966.

The 1954 Five Year Development Plan for education created the infrastructure for what eventually became the Ministry of Education. New schools were planned, large numbers of teachers were trained and more expatriates were employed in the schools. By the completion of the Plan in 1959, there were 15,006 pupils enrolled in the State schools, 30 % of whom were girls. By now, Brunei had 52 Malay primary schools; 3 English schools (including one exclusively for girls that had been completed in 1958); 7 mission schools; 8 Chinese primary schools and 3 Chinese secondary schools (Jones 1994, p. 104). There were also 133 Bruneians at teacher training colleges overseas, and many at Brunei's own Teachers' College that had opened in 1956. With growing emphasis on education, it soon became apparent that expatriate teachers had to be recruited from Sri Lanka, India, Singapore, Malaya, the Philippines, the United Kingdom and Australia (Jones 1994).

In 1959, two Malaysians, Aminudin Baki and Paul Chang were appointed to advise the Brunei Government on general education policy and principles. Jones comments that:

> having spent only two weeks in Brunei, and using the Malayan Tun Razak Education Report of 1956 as the source of their recommendation, Baki and Chang presented their report'
>
> (Jones 1994, p. 106)

The recommendations of this report subsequently became Brunei's National Educational Policy of 1962. Jones states that the theme of 'national unity' was recurrent through both the Malayan and Bruneian reports, and he cites the Tun Razak Report:

> ...the ultimate objective of the educational policy ... must be to bring together the children of all races under a national educational system in which the national language is the main medium of instruction
>
> (Tun Razak Report 1956, cited in Jones 1994, p. 107)

This statement echoes the British Resident's report in 1939 that suggested 'linguistic assimilation' for educative purposes. But although the National Educational Policy of 1962 and the subsequent Report of the Education Commission in 1972 both recommended the use of Malay as the main medium of instruction in primary and secondary schools, subsequent events determined a change of emphasis in the final choice of language medium for the country's national education system. Political and diplomatic relations between Brunei and Malaysia, where Bruneian students and trainee teachers were sent, deteriorated in the 1970s. Jones states:

> Bruneians studying in Malaysia were recalled and the option of adopting a Malaysian System of Education was cancelled ... This experience seems to have had a decisive influence on the eventual choice of language medium for the National Education System... There is no doubt that the Education Commission of 1972 wanted and expected the System to use Malay as the medium of instruction, just as the Report of 1962 had recommended. Instead, through circumstance, English was adopted.
>
> (Jones 1994, pp. 115–116)

Perhaps the most radical move in the makeover of the old education system was the implementation of the bilingual *Dwibahasa* (Bilingual) education policy in 1985 for the newly independent country, replacing the old dual-stream system whose Malay-stream graduates were disadvantaged in a job market that increasingly preferred English-knowing candidates. The new bilingual system was meant to ensure that pupils attain a high degree of proficiency in both English and Malay, although Braighlinn (1992, p. 21) notes that 'the supposed development of the Malay language as a medium of literary expression and analytical thought [had] instead been thwarted by the introduction of the Dwibahasa system'. This contention is supported by Martin (2002) who says that while the rhetorical correctness of the government's official emphasises Malay, the system clearly legitimised English as the dominant language. But with the emphasis and official support given to Malay and English, it soon became apparent that 'the other languages [in Brunei] have been left to fend for themselves' (Martin 2002, p. 181). Yet despite these criticisms, and despite Jones' (1997a, b) suggestion that its birth was accidental, the Dwibahasa survived for 24 years with arguably great success in creating an English-knowing population. In fact Brunei became known internationally for its bilingual education efforts, as noted by Rigall (2014).

In 2009, some tweaking was felt to be necessary within the education system, particularly with the developments in ICT and universal move toward globalisation. Hence, *Dwibahasa* evolved into SPN21, retaining the use of both Malay and English but with new approaches in teaching and learning, and with the emphasis on creative and critical thinking skills to prepare students for challenges of the globalised world of the 21st century. SPN21 would equip students with the skills and knowledge considered necessary to enable them to compete successfully at the local and international levels while remaining loyal and committed to the country as responsible citizens who would contribute meaningfully to the future socio-economic progress and well-being of the community and the world at large. A key element in SPN21 is improved success rates among students, and their increased marketability in the job market. SPN21 was aligned to Brunei's long-term development plan Vision 2035 (*Wawasan* 2035) by shaping itself as a first-class education system to create 'an educated, highly skilled and accomplished people' (Jabatan Perancangan dan Kemajuan Ekonomi 2013). This would be done through instruction in English and Malay, much like the *Dwibahasa* system.

No doubt, the impact of mainstream education in Brunei up to now has been tremendous, as it has created a more biliterate and bilingual population. However, much of the discussion on formal education in Brunei has been framed within the mainstream formal education system that employs both Malay and English, but which by all accounts has been English-heavy. On the other hand the Ugama schools, typically taking place in the afternoon after secular school sessions in the morning, teaches a complete and comprehensive set of Islamic subjects for seven years fully in the Malay language.

16.4 History of Ugama Schools

Islamic religious education had always been offered privately, through mosques and prayer halls prior to 1931, the year which can be considered the starting point of the formal system of instruction via vernacular Malay schools (Mohammad 2014a).

As outlined above, formal education in the form of Malay schools had been introduced about 15 years ahead of the inclusion of Islamic religious education. This timing is 'surprising', according to Mohammad (2014a), given that the students of the Malay schools were mainly Muslim. However, a modern Ugama school system was only established in 1956.

Beginning in the early 1950s, Islamic education was taught as a subject in Malay and English schools two days per week (Thursday and Saturday) for an hour and a half (Abd. Aziz 1968). Ironically, after years of reluctance among Malay parents about sending their children to mainstream school, they began to relent after realising the importance of formal education, and more importantly due to the fact that the Malay and English schools had now begun to offer Islamic religious studies as a subject (Tassim 2014). But while appearing organised, the early Ugama school system was fraught with problems such as 'a weak, unsystematic, and ad hoc administration', 'a lack of teachers', and 'an absence of systematic measure (syllabus)' (Abd. Aziz 1977).

Mohammad (2014a, b) argues that in fact Ugama schools had already been built since 1913, but were unutilised or neglected by the British administrators in a bid to diminish religious education, Islamic law and Islamic practices in Brunei under the guise of non-interference in Islamic affairs and Malay culture.

In the first ten years of being established, government provisions and the number of students enrolled in Ugama schools are shown in Table 16.1.

Table 16.1 Students enrolled in Ugama schools

Year	No. of Ugama schools*	No. of teachers*	No. of Ugama students*	No. of mainstream students+	% of Ugama students out of total mainstream school students^
1956	7	9	283	–	–
1957	15	25	779	4943	15.76
1958	29	57	1271	5797	21.93
1959	32	65	1375	7164	19.18
1960	37	67	1606	8049	19.95
1961	45	110	3485	9934	35.08
1962	49	139	4218	11,377	37.07
1963	51	142	4263	12,369	34.47
1964	54	194	4763	14,399	33.08
1965	62	227	5813	15,118	38.45
1966	63	291	5546	15,918	34.84
1967	65	308	6816	16,630	40.97
1968	68	332	6935	16,194	42.82

+Data from Brunei Annual Report 1953–1960, Brunei Annual Report 1976
*Data from the Annual Report of Department of Religious Affairs 1971–1980
^Percentage calculation does not account for non-Muslim students attending Mainstream schools who would not normally be expected to be enrolled in Ugama schools

The percentage of students attending Ugama schools compared with the total number of students attending mainstream schools between 1956 and 1968 showed a steady increase every year in the first decade of its establishment. By 1968, the number of students in Ugama schools accounted for 42 % of the mainstream school student population. This would mean 58 % were exposed to Malay language instruction through mainstream schools only. This statistic is significant as it indicates the growing number of students who were exposed to Malay language as a medium of instruction in both mainstream as well as the Ugama school. Malay as a medium of instruction was therefore firmly grounded among these Muslim (Malay) students via two curricula. For generations of Bruneian students in 1970s, 1980s and 1990s, Ugama school became a rite of passage.

By 2006, the number of students who had graduated from Ugama school, having passed the Primary 6 public examination, stood at 65,234 (82.78 %) out of a total of 78,798 who had completed their schooling. Interestingly, out of 40,044 students registered in 2007, a total of 252 students were non-muslim Bruneians, usually comprising students from traditionally non-Muslim groups such as Dusun, Bisaya, Murut, Iban, or even Dusun-Chinese. Between 2010 and 2014, a total of 680 non-Muslim students were enrolled (Rabiatul 2014). This point is significant in that it emphasises the impact Ugama school Malay-language instruction has on students whose families traditionally speak another language. The latest available figures indicate that 5,102 new students were registered in Ugama schools in January 2015 (Pelita Brunei 2015), compared to 5,358 in 2014, and 5,036 in 2013.

Since 1956, Ugama schools developed rapidly to fit Bruneian needs. In 1966 the Hassanal Bolkiah Arabic Boys' Secondary School opened to accommodate students who wished to further their studies in Islamic knowledge, followed by the Raja Isteri Pengiran Anak Damit Arabic Girls' Secondary School in the following year, and the Seri Begawan Teachers' College in 1972. In 1990 the Ma'had Islam Brunei (Brunei Islamic College) was set up. Following the success of Islamic secondary education, in 1989 the Ministry of Islamic Religious Affairs set up the Islamic Studies Institute to take in tertiary level students, and the Faculty of Islamic Studies at the Universiti Brunei Darussalam in 1993 for undergraduate studies. These were merged in 1999 to form the Sultan Omar Ali Saifuddien Institute of Islamic Studies (SOAS-IIS). In 2007, Brunei's second university, Universiti Islam Sultan Sharif Ali (UNISSA) was created by absorbing most of UBD's SOAS Institute of Islamic Studies faculty. The latter has since been re-shaped into the Sultan Omar Ali Saifuddien Centre for Islamic Studies (SOASCIS) that focuses on research and postgraduate studies. In the same year, another Islamic university was established in the form of the Seri Begawan Religious Teachers University College (*Kolej Universiti Perguruan Ugama Seri Begawan*, KUPU-SB).

At this juncture, and to put it within the context of this study, it is worth noting that while the Arabic language is considered important, it has only been taught as a language subject in Ugama schools, and it is not used as a medium of instruction. Full Arabic-medium instruction is only found in specialised Arabic schools. According to Raghadah (2014), apart from the Hassanal Bolkiah Arabic Boys' Secondary School and the Raja Isteri Pengiran Anak Damit (RIPAD) Arabic Girls'

Secondary School that opened in 1966 and 1967 respectively, and the Ma'had Islam in 1990, a few other Arabic Preparatory schools have been opened since 1997. Students enrolled in these Arabic schools are a select group who have excelled in both lower primary mainstream schools, as well as in lower primary Ugama school. Graduates from Arabic preparatory school could then join Ma'had Islam, Hassanal Bolkiah Arabic Boys' School, or RIPAD Arabic Girls' school for Lower and/or Upper secondary education. In the higher education sector, in Brunei only UNISSA offers programmes that are taught entirely in Arabic.

16.5 The Two-Session Schooling System

Brunei Malay students typically attend mainstream school in the morning and Ugama school in the afternoon. In its infancy, between 1956 and 1958, 29 Ugama schools were opened for afternoon sessions with 1874 students (Mohammad 2014b). This pattern of two-session schools would become the norm for many Muslim Bruneians over the decades. But in February 2004, the Ugama school was merged with the morning schools in an experiment called *Sepadu* ('joint'), in its first phase. In January 2005 this was enforced fully for all Ugama schools. The structure of administration would be led by the Principal in the morning session and by the Deputy Principal in the afternoon session. As UNESCO-IBE (2011) observed, Sepadu attempted

> to integrate the curriculum by streamlining the contents of three curricula, that is, the religious school curriculum, one religious subject taught in the primary and secondary school curriculum, and Al-Quran and Islamic religious knowledge taught in several schools as a pilot project, into one curricular component of Islamic education within the integrated education system.

Due to insurmountable logistical problems and parents' concerns about students' well-being, His Majesty the Sultan ordered that this experiment be scrapped and schools should revert to the previous two-session format, thereby returning the Ugama schools to the full control of the Islamic Studies Department under the Ministry of Religious Affairs.

16.6 Compulsory Ugama School Enactment

The Compulsory Islamic Religious Education enactment was approved in 2012 and enforced in January 2013 (Azlan 2013). The rule requires all Bruneian Muslim children aged 7 up to 15 to be registered in Ugama pre-school and primary schools for up to 7 years. The penalty for parents who fail to register their children is a fine up to $5000, imprisonment up to one year, or both (Sect. 5). In January 2013, the number of students enrolled in Ugama school was 5036, while in January 2014 the figure was 5358, meanwhile in 2015 it was 5102 (Brudirect.com 2014; Pelita Brunei 2014, 2015).

The increase in enrolment figures from 5036 in 2013, to 5358 in 2014 does not appear too drastic for us to conclude it was a direct result of the enactment. Instead, it can be argued that annual new registrations have (always) remained consistently high (above 5000) with or without the new law—but not necessarily as a result of it. This could in fact be the result of a strong sense of duty among Muslim parents who see Ugama schools as an obligation to provide their children with proper religious education, which they themselves could not otherwise provide.

16.7 The Ugama Syllabus

In its early years in the 1950s the Ugama school syllabus included the following subjects from Primary 1 Ugama school until Primary 6 (final year): Al-Quraan, *Tauhid* (Divinity), *Ibadat* (Obedience), *Toharoh* (Hygiene), *Solat* (Prayers), *Zakat* (Tithe), *Puasa* (Fasting), *Hajj* (Pilgrimage), *Muamalat* (Commerce), *Munakahat* (Marriage), *Jinayat* (Crime), *Adab* (Civilisation), *Tarikh* (History), *Tajwid* (Quraanic elocution), *Faraid* (Property and probate), *Tasauf* (Spiritual purity), *Latihan Amali Ugama* (Religious practice), *Tulisan Jawi* (Jawi writing), *Dikir*

Table 16.2 The syllabus as of January 2015

Level	Subject
Pre-school	Al-Quraan
	Amali (Practical)
	Tauhid (Divinity)
	Adab (Manners)
	Introduction to Jawi
	Arabic language
Additional Modules in subsequent levels	
Primary 1	Ibadat (Religious obedience)
	Jawi writing
	Jawi reading
Primary 2	Tarikh (Islamic history)
Primary 4	Toharoh (Hygiene)
	Siam (Fasting)
	Tasauf (Spirituality)
	Dikir (Psalms)
Primary 5	Solat (Prayers)
	Zakat (Tithe)
	Haji (Pilgrimage)
	Mu'amalat (Commerce)
Primary 6	Munakahat (Marriage)
	Janayah (Crime and punishment)
	Faraid (Property and probate)
	Rawi (Narration)

(Psalms), *Rawi* (Narration), *Bacaan Jawi* (Jawi reading), *Rencana Jawi* (Jawi composition), and *Asuhan Agama* (Religious development). These classes are taught in 30-minute blocks. Tassim (2014) comments that these subjects are the basic foundations for Islamic studies. As stated above, the Ugama schools suffered growing pains in terms of administration and logistics in their infancy (Abd. Aziz 1977), but they soon overcame these issues with steady improvements over the years with a more organised and systematic syllabus and operations. The contents of the syllabus as of January 2015 as prescribed by the Department of Islamic Studies (Jabatan Pengajian Islam 2015) are shown in Table 16.2.

The scope of study has not changed much from the 1950s, as these are considered basic topics in Islamic education. But the modern syllabus is organised incrementally and suited to students' mental and academic growth: the intensity and level of difficulty of the study increases as the student approaches the final year of Ugama study—all using Malay as medium of instruction.

16.8 The Linguistic Intersection

While all these developments in the Ugama schools are taking place, we must not lose sight of concurrent developments in the mainstream school system. The Government mainstream Primary schools in Brunei were also mainly using Malay as the medium of instruction throughout the 1950s, 1960s and 1970s up to 1985 when *Dwibahasa* was introduced. As its name suggests, *Dwibahasa* involved the use of two languages (Malay and English) in formal instruction. In this system, all primary and secondary schools adopted a common curriculum prescribed by the Ministry of Education. From Pre-school level to Primary III, the medium of instruction for all subjects was Malay, except for English Language, which was taught as a subject. From Primary IV (Upper primary) onwards the pupils followed a bilingual system. Malay was used for teaching Malay language subject, Islamic Religious Knowledge, Physical Education, Arts and Crafts, Civics, and Malay Islamic Monarchy (MIB). The English language was used for teaching subjects such as Science, Mathematics, Geography and English Language itself. History has been taught in Malay since 1995. Observations by Braighlinn (1992), Martin (1996b), Jones (1993) and Noor Azam (2005) have suggested in general that the mainstream Primary school system was in fact English-dominant.

In comparison, according to UNESCO-IBE (2011) the SPN21 curriculum framework comprises eight key learning areas: languages; mathematics; sciences; humanities and social sciences; arts and culture; technology; Islamic religious knowledge and Malay Islamic Monarchy; and health and physical education. In addition, ICT and entrepreneurship are included across the curriculum, as well as co-curriculum and the community involvement programme. The new SPN21 curriculum has identified the smooth transition and continuity from preschool to the primary and secondary levels in a developmentally appropriate setting.

According to MOE (2009), in SPN21, Primary school students take the following subjects in Malay: Malay language, Islamic religious knowledge, Malay Islamic Monarchy, and Physical education. Meanwhile, subjects that are taught in English are: English language, Mathematics, Science, Social studies, ICT, Music and drama. As a whole, throughout the six years of Primary school, both English and Malay are used for instruction, but with slightly more use of English in the six subjects compared to the four subjects taught in Malay.

In secondary school, in Years 7 and 8, students then take the following Malay-medium subjects: Malay language, Islamic religious knowledge, Malay Islamic Monarchy, and Physical education. On the other hand, English-medium subjects include: Mathematics, Science, Social studies, Business and technology (including Design and Technology, Home economics and Agriculture); ICT, Commerce, and Music and Art (in Malay/English).

Meanwhile in Upper secondary (Years 9, 10 and 11), students must take Malay language, Malay Islamic Monarchy, Physical education and Co-curriculum, which are predictably taught in Malay. They are also required to take the following subjects in English: English language, Mathematics, Sciences (Physics, Biology, Chemistry or Combined science).

Elective subjects taught in Malay include Malay literature and Islamic religious knowledge. Other electives that are taught in English include English literature, Additional mathematics, Geography, History, Economics, Principles of accounts, Art and craft, Music, Design and technology, Computer studies/ICT, and Food and nutrition. There are also modern languages for the students to choose from: Arabic, French, and Mandarin.

One can see, perhaps not surprisingly and not too differently from *Dwibahasa*, that SPN21 students have more subjects taught in English compared to those taught in Malay. To some extent, the same criticisms towards *Dwibahasa* could apply to SPN21 as well. And if a student so desired, they could avoid all the Malay-medium electives altogether, thus completing an English-dominant secondary education.

Without clear differences, save a few new subjects, new methods of assessment and new approaches in teaching, SPN21 is unlikely to escape accusations of being a cosmetic change only. And much like its predecessor, SPN21 has been criticised for being English-heavy and being a 'valorization of English' (Noor Azam 2012). On these grounds, the two systems alone could not have supplied adequate Malay language input for Bruneians to achieve a balanced foundation in both Malay and English.

Of course Malay-English bilingualism among Bruneians cannot be the result of just the education system(s) that they go through as students. Certainly there are other factors such as social use and interactions as introductions and/or maintenance, and other social stimuli. But if we are going to attribute the bilingualism to an education system, surely the Ugama system must have had a role to play.

16.9 Conclusion

Seven years of full instruction in Malay in the formative years of a child (from age 7 in Ugama pre-school), in addition to Malay and English language instruction in the mainstream primary and lower secondary stages must have some degree of additive effect on the linguistic development of students. A limitation of this chapter is that it does not account for the linguistic impact on non-Malay and non-Muslim population who do not experience Ugama school; but within the context of Brunei, the Malay and Muslim population is predominant. So to accredit the success of bilingualism among the majority of the population to just the mainstream education system seems a little bit disingenuous; mainstream bilingual education cannot claim the credit alone. One could argue that it is in fact the Ugama school that provides most of the Malay language skills and opportunities for Malay Muslim students—thus cementing Malay's position as the 'language of the soul'.

References

Abd. Aziz Bin Juned (1968). *Buku kenangan berpuspa*. Bandar Brunei: JHEU.
Abd. Aziz Bin Juned (1977). *Ke arah pendidikan akhlak dan peribadi yang sempurna*. Bandar Brunei: JHEU.
Azlan Othman. (2013). Perintah wajib pendidikan agama. *Borneo Bulletin*, 2 January 2013.
Braighlinn, G. (1992). *Ideological innovation under monarchy: Aspects of legitimation activity in contemporary Brunei*. Amsterdam: VU Press.
Brudirect.com. (2014). 9 January 2014. Jumlah penuntut semakin meningkat. Retrieved October 13, from 2015 Brudirect.com.
Gunn, G. C. (1997). *Language, power and ideology in Negara Brunei Darussalam*. Athens, OH: Ohio University Press.
Haji Mohammad bin Pengiran Haji Abdul Rahman, Pengiran Dato Seri Setia. (2014a). Perkembangan ilmu Islam di Brunei: Peralihan dari sistem balai ke sistem persekolahan moden (1931–1956). In Ampuan Haji Brahim bin Ampuan Haji Tengah (Ed.), *Tradisi dan reformasi pendidikan: Merista jasa Sultan Haji Omar 'Ali Saifuddien Sa'adul Khairi Waddien, Vol.1* (pp. 1–18). Brunei: UBD & YSHHB.
Haji Mohammad bin Pengiran Haji Abdul Rahman, Pengiran Dato Seri Setia. (2014b). Perkembangan pelajaran agama di Negara Brunei Darussalam: Zaman pemerintahan Sultan Omar 'Ali Saifuddien III (1950–1967). In Ampuan Haji Brahim bin Ampuan Haji Tengah (Ed.), *Tradisi dan reformasi pendidikan: Merista jasa Sultan Haji Omar 'Ali Saifuddien Sa'adul Khairi Waddien, Vol. 1* (pp. 19–32). Brunei: UBD & YSHHB.
Haji Tassim bin Haji Abu Bakar. (2014). Kampong Ayer: Pusat pembelajaran ilmu agama Islam dan pemantapan sistem pendidikan forma'. In Ampuan Haji Brahim bin Ampuan Haji Tengah (Ed.), *Tradisi dan reformasi pendidikan: Merista jasa Sultan Haji Omar 'Ali Saifuddien Sa'adul Khairi Waddien, Vol. 1* (pp.47–58). Brunei: UBD & YSHHB.
Jabatan Perancangan dan Kemajuan Ekonomi. (2013). *Brunei Darussalam long-term development plan, Wawasan Brunei 2035*. Bandar Seri Begawan: JPKE.
Jabatan Pengajian Islam. (2015). *Sukatan pelajaran sekolah ugama Negara Brunei Darussalam*. Bandar Seri Begawan: Kementerian Hal Ehwal Ugama.
Jasmin Abdullah (1987). Bilingual education in Brunei: Problems in implementation. Unpublished Masters thesis. Singapore: SEAMEO-Regional Language Centre.

Jones, G. M. (1994). A Study of Bilingualism and Implications for Language Policy Planning in Negara Brunei Darussalam. Unpublished PhD Thesis. Wales: The University College of Abersytwyth.

Jones, G. M. (1996). Bilingual education and syllabus design: Towards a workable blueprint. *Journal of Multilingual & Multicultural Development, 17*, 280–293.

Jones, G. M. (1997a). The evolution of a language plan. *Language Problems and Language Planning, 21*(3), 197–215.

Jones, G. M. (1997b). Language planning in Brunel Darussalam: The role of accommodation & acculturation. *Multilingua, 16*(2/3), 217–232.

Jones, G. M., Martin, P. W., & Ożóg, C. (1993). Multilingualism and bilingual education in Brunei Darussalam. *Journal of Multilingual & Multicultural Development, 14*, 39–58.

Martin, P. W. (1999). Close encounters of a bilingual kind: Interactional practices in the primary classroom in Brunei. *International Journal of Educational Development, 19*(2), 127–140.

Martin, P. W. (1996b). Sociohistorical determinants of language shift among the belait community in the sultanate of Brunei. *Anthropos, 91*: 199–207.

Martin, P. W. (2002). One language, one race one nation: The changing language ecology of Negara Brunei Darussalam. In M. K. David (Ed.), *Methodological and analytical issues in language maintenance and shift studies* (pp. 175–190). Berlin: Peter Lang,

Ministry of Education. (2002). Retrieved August 13, 2002 from www.moe.gov.bn.

Ministry of Education. (2009). *Sistem pendidikan negara abad ke-21*. Bandar Seri Begawan: MOE.

Noor Azam Haji-Othman. (2005). *Changes to the linguistic diversity in Negara Brunei Darussalam*. Ph.d. Thesis. University of Leicester.

Noor Azam Haji-Othman. (2007). English and the bilingual Bruneian. In K. Dunworth (Ed.), *English in Southeast Asia: Challenges and changes* (pp. 59–70). Perth, WA: Curtin University of Technology.

Noor Azam Haji-Othman. (2012). Is it always English? 'Duelling Aunties' in Brunei Darussalam. In V. Rapatahana & P. Bunce (Eds.), *English language as hydra: Its impact on non-English language cultures* (pp. 175–190). Clevedon: Multilingual Matters.

Noor Azam Haji-Othman & McLellan, J. (2014). English in Brunei: Challenges and future directions. *World Englishes, 3*(4), 486–497.

Pelita Brunei. (2014). Perintah pendidikan ugama wajib 2012: Terap kesedaran dari peringkat akar umbi, Saturday, 11 January 2014.

Pelita Brunei. (2015). 5102 murid mendaftar ikuti persekolah agama, Thursday, 8 January 2015.

Rabiatul Kamit (2014). More new pupils in Brunei's religious schools. *The Brunei Times*, Thursday, 9 January 2014.

Raghadah Agus. (2014). Kenali pendidikan ugama dan Arab di Brunei Darussalam. *The Brunei Times*, Sunday, 11 October 2014.

Rigall, A. (2014). *Bilingual education in Brunei: The evolution of the Brunei approach to bilingual education and the role of CfBT in promoting educational change: Summary report.* Reading, UK: Centre for British Teachers (CfBT).

UNESCO-IBE. (2011). *World data on education, Vol. 7. 2010/2011*. Paris: UNESCO-IBE.

Chapter 17
Changing Patterns of Education in Brunei: How Past Plans Have Shaped Future Trends

Gary M. Jones

17.1 Introduction

In 1992 Brunei's Ministry of Education published a booklet *Education in Brunei Darussalam* that provided an outline of the continuing development of the primary, secondary and tertiary education systems in the country. It provides a snapshot of the time as well as a description of aspirations and plans for the future.

This chapter considers whether and to what extent the plans outlined then have been achieved. In the process it takes into consideration how a variety of factors have brought about change to education and society as a whole. Among the factors considered are population, economy, infrastructure, communications and policies.

17.2 Comparisons

Brunei has witnessed a rapid population increase over the last 23 years. Back in 1992 the population was 256,500, while today that figure has risen to 406,000. This enormous increase has resulted in a need for rapid expansion across all levels of education in the country. Class sizes have increased, as have the number and variety of schools. In turn, this has created a much bigger administrative burden on the Ministry of Education itself, which has also increased its staff numbers and positions.

In the meantime Brunei's economy has struggled to keep pace. In 1992 GDP per capita was US$27,500, but it has fallen to just above US$24,000 today. (Of course, GDP per capita does not tell the full economic story by any means, but it does

---

G.M. Jones (✉)
FASS/UBD, Universiti Brunei Darussalam, Jalan Tungku Link,
Gadong BE1410, Brunei Darussalam
e-mail: gary.jones@ubd.edu.bn

provide an indication of how the economy is faring. A falling GDP per capita must obviously have implications for future investment.) Interestingly, 1992 marked the high point for Brunei's GDP per capita adjusted for purchasing power parity (PPP). It is still high compared to most countries, nearly four times the world's average, but in 1992 GDP per capita PPP was US$78,688.42 while in 2013 it fell to its lowest recorded figure, US$69,474.1 (Trading Economics 2015). Perhaps most worrying of all is that the various GDP indicators now forecast a stagnant economy.

In 1992 Brunei's economy was largely dependent on oil and gas, and this is still the case today. However, while crude oil production averaged 160.79 barrels per day between 1994 and 2004, reaching a peak of 217 BPD in 2006, output fell to just above 100 BPD in 2014, with a low of 88 BPD in September 2013. This fall in production is compounded by the recent drop in global oil prices. Unsurprisingly, Brunei's balance of trade has been badly affected by oil production and price falls. Averaging B$1,178.99 million between 2005 and 2015, an all-time low was recorded in September 2013 of B$401 million (Department of Economic Planning and Development, Brunei).

It is clear from the above figures that Brunei's continued reliance on oil and gas has left the country's economy perilously exposed. This was just as much the case back in 1992 as it is now. The 1992 booklet states that 'priority is being given to the diversification of the economy through the development of agriculture and industry' (Ministry of Education 1992, p. 2). Unfortunately the country remains highly dependent oil and gas with very little real diversification in the economy. The International Monetary Fund has projected that Brunei's economy will shrink by 0.5 % in 2015 and that the sizable surpluses which the country has enjoyed over the last decade will be replaced by large deficits (Fitri Shahminan 2015). The IMF recommends freezing wages and employment in the government sector, dropping projects that require large capital expenditure, and encouraging private sector growth.

While the health of the economy is pertinent to this chapter, in particular the prospects for future economic development, perhaps the most telling observation when comparing 1992 with today is that, back then, Brunei had the means to implement strategy. It had a buoyant and robust economy, albeit one that relied on a single commodity, and could confidently plan major infrastructure change. Today there is much less certainty about future growth and income. It is hoped that new oil fields will be found and developed and that the price of oil will rebound. However, these are big ifs. In the meantime, on the positive side, investment in education has resulted in a literate, educated populace who have access to free schooling and universities. Inflation is low, there is no personal income tax, salaries are reasonable, healthcare is free, and crime rates are low. Perhaps the country is now in a better position to diversify its economy than it was in 1992, and maybe necessity will make this happen. Lawrey (2012) examines the diversification dilemma facing Brunei. He notes that investing income overseas should bring some reward but would do little to help the country's non-oil and gas related businesses, most of which are small and depend heavily on spending by the government and by officers and their families employed by the government, with the result that local industries are both directly and indirectly dependent on government spending.

Not all comparisons are negative. Positive developments between the two periods have been brought about by the benefit of healthy income from oil and gas and large budget surpluses, and this is particularly obvious from the country's infrastructure and communications.

17.3 Infrastructure

In 1992 detailed road maps were unnecessary because there were so few roads and it would have been very difficult to get lost, but this is certainly no longer the case today. There are many roads of all types and those in the urban areas are maintained. Fuel is heavily subsidised and cheap, so it is possible to get around the country easily and at no great expense. Private cars are common, but public transport much less so: given the number of cars, locals have little need to resort to public buses, so the majority of public transport users are low-income foreign contract workers.

The rising population has meant the need for more schools, hospitals, telephone exchanges and power sources. Again, the country has been able to afford and deliver all of these and increasingly they are staffed by locals who now have the relevant education and training. It will now be important to maintain what has been delivered. The years of rapid expansion, successfully implemented on budget surpluses, are now past. Consolidation, carefully considered investment, and maintenance of what has been delivered now need to be the priorities.

17.4 Communication

Together with the rest of the developed world, Brunei has enjoyed the benefits of a much improved communication structure. Developments in cell phone technology, satellite communication and the growth of the internet have resulted in a fully connected society. In 1992 there was limited television access, only home telephone lines (for those who had telephones) and no internet. In all sectors of the economy and society there has been a communication revolution, and this change has had an impact on education.

In 1992, and still today, children read very few books. However, the difference now is they have access to online sites that require reading skills—though children may not be reading novels, they are reading, albeit other genres, and importantly they have a need to read. In addition, a world of knowledge is at everyone's finger-tips with the result that digital-literate learners have access to information that would have been undreamt of in their parents' day.

17.5 Education

While the economy, infrastructure and communication have all impacted on education in one way or another, it is the Ministry of Education's policies, aims, systems and vision which are most central to this chapter.

17.5.1 Policy

The National Education Policy in 1992 very prominently stressed the role of religion, priority for the Malay Language and loyalty to the monarch and state (via the national philosophy, Malay Islamic Monarchy, or MIB). As well as actually teaching the religion, Islamic values and the Islamic way of life were integrated in the education system by means of an appropriate curriculum. The role of religion in today's policy remains unchanged, as do pledges of loyalty to the monarch and state.

Priority for the Malay Language is a different matter. In 1992 it officially played a leading role, 'while English Language is not neglected' (Ministry of Education 1992, p. 4). As will be shown below, Malay remains important as one of the pillars of society and as an important school language, but it no longer plays the leading role in education—that role is now played by English.

Other aspects of the Policy in 1992 remain the same today: offering at least 12 years of schooling, a common curriculum (albeit now a different one), opportunities to go for higher education for those pupils who are able, and provision for the development needs of the country.

17.5.2 Aims

Eight clear Aims were stated in 1992. In summarised form these were:

- Develop the individual.
- Ensure fluency in the Malay language while not neglecting English.
- Inculcate the teaching of Islam.
- Cultivate in each individual a sense of loyalty to the Monarch, the State and the Law.
- Cultivate values centred on the principle of MIB.
- Instil a love of peace, harmony and mutual help and unity.
- Mould in each individual the desire for progress, confidence, creativity, innovativeness and ability to adapt to change.
- Speed up capable, rational and responsible manpower resources.

The Ministry of Education's *Strategic Plan 2012–2017* does not have stated aims as such, and instead these have been replaced by Vision, Mission and Core Values. In effect, these state Ministry aims, but in a more detailed, concise and focused manner.

The stated Vision is *Quality Education towards a Developed, Peaceful and Prosperous Nation.* It goes on to explain an acknowledged relationship between education and economic performance, one that will equip children with moral, intellectual, physical, social and aesthetic values. In many ways this is similar to the first and sixth of the 1992 Aims, but with rather more detail.

Below are the various characteristics of the Vision (Strategic Management Unit 2012, p. 6):

- Moulding individuals within our society to be balanced and well rounded.
- Developing the personal attributes (spiritual, mental, physical and aesthetic values, leadership, entrepreneurship, morals) of the students.
- Producing team players, caring individuals, good communicators, accountable and responsible citizens.
- Producing an education system of international standard, which fosters valuable and marketable skills, and encourages a life-long learning orientation that will contribute to a harmonious and politically stable society.
- Setting the foundation for a knowledge-based economy.
- Improving students' learning achievements comparable with international standards.

In addition to these characteristics, a list of features was added, providing a far more detailed description of aims than had been the case in 1992.

The features are:

- A knowledge based economy
- Security assurance
- Political stability
- Civil service excellence
- Excellent human resources
- A balance of socio-cultural development
- High standards of health
- High quality sustainable environment
- The ability to compete in a globalised economy while retaining strong religious and social values, and national identity
- An entrepreneurial and resilient society.

The 2012 Mission is stated as to *Provide Holistic Education to Achieve Fullest Potential for all.* Holistic is a word that is now commonly used in education circles, suggesting that pupils should become all-round balanced learners. In Brunei the mission is to 'nurture students with spiritual strength; a healthy body and mind; high social, moral, aesthetic and cultural values together with excellent cognitive skills' (Strategic Management Unit 2012, p. 7).

To achieve all of the above, the core values to underpin this are considered to be:

- Accountability
- Integrity
- Leadership
- Honesty
- Respect
- Teamwork.

Comparing 1992s Aims with the Vision, Mission and Core Values of 2012, a number of observations are immediately apparent. Today, aims are not enough, so borrowing from industry and management practice, these have grown to become vision and mission statements, breaking down the contents in more detail. As a result, length and detail is the first difference, but despite lengthier descriptions it is the content itself that is clearly most important.

In 1992 far more emphasis was given to the place of Malay and Islam in education than in the later document. In 2012 there is mention of personal attributes that include spiritual values, but not specifically Islamic ones, but there is no mention at all of Malay. Language ability might be assumed to be considered as part of marketable skills for good communicators, and these are presented as characteristics. In Brunei this would include being able to use Malay and today English, especially with the emphasis given to competing in a global economy and reaching international standards. The aims of the 1992 document reflect the budding aspirations of a newly fully-independent nation. The aims address local issues and needs, the most apparent being to consolidate the place of religion and language in education and the wider community. The 2012 publication addresses different issues. It speaks of the need to be more accommodating and outward-looking while remaining true to traditional civic and spiritual values.

17.5.3 System

In 1992 the country was still using a mainstream bilingual education system, known locally as *Dwibahasa* (two languages). The development and evolution of this system has been described in detail in earlier publications (Jones 1990; Jones et al. 1993). Suffice to say, it was a bilingual education system that employed both English and Malay. All pre-school education was conducted in Malay and the use of Malay was dominant in the lower primary classes (years 1–3) as well, with only the English Language class being taught in English. A big change took place in year 4 at the start of upper primary school when, as well as the English Language, subjects such as Mathematics, Science, History and Geography were also taught in English. As described in the earlier publications, many children struggled with this abrupt change. This was particularly so back in 1992 when there was far less access to English outside the schools than there is today. For many children, English would have been a foreign language rather than a second one. (This is still the case for some children today, but far fewer given access to satellite television, the internet and various forms of social media.)

The trend of moving increasingly towards the use of English continued into secondary school, and by upper secondary only the Malay Language class itself was taught in Malay, all other compulsory and examinable subjects being taught in English. (Some optional classes such as Art and Craft and Malay Literature were also taught in Malay.)

When the bilingual education system was first introduced in 1985, it meant that many teachers had to switch the medium of their classes from Malay to English, which for most was difficult and for others impossible. Nevertheless, despite the early difficulties, eventually most children left school with an ability in both Malay and English. (Unsurprisingly, while the majority of children knew Malay well, reflected in a high pass rate for the Malay Language GCE Ordinary-level examination, the pass rate in the equivalent English Language examination was much lower. Nevertheless, even though they may have failed the examination, even these children could still use English to some extent.)

Brunei's journey from different medium education systems to one unified system has been well documented, and how this has affected language use among Bruneians has received scrutiny by local researchers. For example: McLellan (2010) shows that code-switching is exceptionally common in Brunei; Wood et al. (2011) report how ability in English varies considerably in the country, so children going to the best secondary schools have good English at the start and then steadily improve during their time at school, while those in less fashionable rural schools often start with rudimentary English and show little or no improvement during their time in secondary school; Noor Azam (2012) observes that the minority languages of Brunei, such as Dusun and Tutong, are being squeezed out by the two dominant languages, Malay and English; and Deterding and Salbrina (2013) report on developments in Brunei English in terms of phonology, syntax and lexis, so for instance it seems to be becoming rhotic with an [r] occurring wherever 'r' is found in the spelling, and there is extensive use of words borrowed from Malay such as *tudong* (head-scarf) and *titah* (royal speech) in the local English-language newspapers.

In 2009 the education system was changed and replaced by what is known locally as SPN21, or the National Education System for the 21st Century. This was the result of a thorough review of the type of skills future school leavers would need, as described earlier in the Vision and Mission statements.

The new system has attempted to borrow from best practice implemented elsewhere, including the idea of lesson-study from Japan where groups of teachers work together collaboratively to create new classroom material. In addition, far more emphasis is given to making classes pupil-centred rather than teacher-centred, creating a classroom environment where the child has more opportunity to explore and question rather than learn by rote. Of course, just as the earlier bilingual education system had created problems for the teachers, in 2009 teachers had to adjust what they did in the classroom, incorporating new teaching strategies and materials.

Perhaps the most significant change of all, however, involved the teaching medium at the primary level. Much greater emphasis was placed on English, with Mathematics and Science being taught in this language from year one. Of course, many Bruneian children enter school with very little English language ability, so the burden on them and their teachers is immense. Ideally, children should become literate in their home or mother tongue before moving on to learn and study in other languages. This is the policy advocated by ASEAN and the UN and a concept that, in theory at least, Brunei supports. (There is a problem in Brunei in determining which of the 'Mother Tongues' might be used if the country were to implement the policy. The country's official national language is Standard Malay, as used across Malaysia and in Brunei schools, but in Brunei the first language of most people is Brunei Malay—so for Bruneian pupils the language medium problem is compounded by their not being familiar with either of the school languages. For further discussion see (Jones 2009).)

The jury is still out among teachers about whether SPN21 is better than *Dwibahasa*. Teachers had become comfortable with the bilingual system and were therefore wary of change, as is normally the case with any change in a programme. Among teachers I have interviewed, there is broad agreement that the objectives of the system are admirable and will have a positive impact. However, it is clear that many teachers are still unclear of what is expected from them and are having difficulty adjusting their teaching methodology. Again, this is to be expected. The Ministry and schools provide regular workshops to assist them, although teachers can find these time-consuming and a burden, especially when the new system also requires more administrative paperwork. A common complaint is that all of this takes them away from teaching. One problem noted is that the textbooks used in the new system are more expensive and more numerous than previously and can be a serious financial burden for some families.

Introducing a new education system is unlikely ever to be universally popular and complaints from teachers and others who have to actually implement it are to be expected. To ensure the changeover is done as smoothly as possible, it is important that all parties understand the need for change and are well educated in the new processes. From talking to teachers it would seem that not all these considerations were taken into account.

17.5.4 Curriculum

As already described, the most obvious curriculum change between the previous and current school systems involved teaching more subjects in English from Year 1. Other changes included the introduction of an express stream in secondary school wherein selected pupils could complete the programme and take their GCE 'O' Levels after only 4 years instead of five. SPN21 also introduced a Specialised

Education Programme for gifted children in specific academic fields as well as a Special Educational Needs Programme for students with physical or other learning difficulties.

New textbooks were introduced (and have been introduced on a regular basis, with concerns about cost, as described earlier, raised by teachers and parents). The new books reflect the reorientation of SPN21 and are designed to promote better pupil self-learning as well as inculcate the specific attributes described in the Core Values.

In 1992 Brunei had only recently emerged from being a British Protectorate and was finding its feet regionally and globally. It was also a time of rapid change and expansion, with an inward-looking focus and an economy that was buoyed by strong oil and gas production and demand. By 2009 the country's role and position in the global economy was more widely appreciated and local issues were being increasingly subsumed by global ones. Globalisation was truly being felt in Brunei. The country had joined many international organisations and was thus tied to various treaties. Planning became longer term and global, rather than short term and local. National Development Plans are 5-year, but in addition the country is now working towards a Brunei Vision 2035, which includes the development and renovation of teaching institutes across the nation at all levels. SPN21 has a place within this Vision which recognises the incorporation of ICT at all levels of education, government and industry and a workforce that has the skills to adapt to new ways of thinking, to be flexible and to be receptive to change.

Compared with 1992, the curriculum has a new focus and more subjects are taught in English than before. Local thinking has given way to global thinking and greater consideration has been given to the type of world that today's school graduates will enter.

17.5.5 Strategic Plan 2012–2017

At the moment the country is mid-way through a 5-year Ministry of Education Strategic Plan. The planned outcome is to deliver 21st-century skills within nine different learning areas. The Plan encompasses issues such as professionalism and accountability, optimised funds and growth, and well-rounded and values-driven individuals. It is an ambitious agenda and the Ministry has identified nine critical success factors to ensure the success of its plan (Strategic Management Unit 2012, p. 37):

- Continuous and effective implementation and monitoring system
- Strong community support
- Effective communication
- Sufficient financial resources
- Adequate infrastructure
- Clear policy statement

- Effective research and planning
- Quality leadership
- Competent, quality and committed workforce.

To what degree these success factors are in fact successful would be going well beyond the scope of this particular chapter. All make perfect sense, but talking to teachers in particular, it is not immediately obvious that all have filtered down. My impression is that, at the school level, there is still much confusion and even some resentment about the amount of extra administrative bureaucracy that has resulted from the monitoring of teachers and their daily work. For the most part, individuals will have different experiences depending on who their line managers are, how well these managers have understood and can communicate objectives given to them, and how successful they have been in generating purpose and optimism.

17.5.6 Other Considerations

As has already been noted, the current education system uses more English than Malay, which may be at odds with the country's national MIB ethos in which the Malay language is supposed to be promoted. Indeed, Brunei's Language and Literature Bureau is meant to actively promote Malay and there are many signs around the country, in Malay naturally, telling the population to do just that. In the meantime the schools are promoting greater use of English, implicitly if not explicitly. The process has been gradual and mirrors what has happened in the wider society—more use and a greater acceptance of English.

From my own observations, previous generations rather reluctantly accepted a role for English because knowledge of it enabled greater access to education and wealth. Nevertheless, there was an underlying tension about this acceptance and a real desire that Malay could replace the roles being performed by English. This has never happened and English is now the world's de facto second language, which, given the command of English that most Bruneians enjoy, has actually put them in a privileged position. Among the younger generation, the tension appears to have dissipated and the majority of young Bruneians move easily between using both Malay and English. (It could be argued that code-switching between Malay and English and, for some, Chinese, is now the actual national language. It is certainly the norm.) The worry for the Malay lobby, given the wider use of English in schools and the community, must be for the long term health and vitality of the language. Unsurprisingly, this is a theme that has been commented by academic staff working on Malay language (Fatimah 2009; Exzayrani 2012).

17.6 Summary and Conclusion

Back in 1992 there were still very few Bruneian graduates and even fewer with post-graduate qualifications. In the intervening years, with the development of local universities and government scholarships for overseas studies, many Bruneians are educated up to and beyond graduate level. The majority have studied in English and many have travelled abroad to study. The need to be fully competent in English is obvious to them, as it is to employers. Language rivalry, the need to promote a language in the name of nationalism, seems increasingly a thing of the past, but inevitably some tensions and jealousies persist. The need for an English-knowing educated population is obvious at the personal level, but it should not be at the expense of losing national identity, so any future planning must take into consideration language as well as economic issues.

Brunei also needs to come to terms with the fact that large budget surpluses are a thing of the past and that government spending will have to be more prudent. The country's educated population can take on most of the jobs that were previously filled by foreign contract workers, and there needs to be a shift from a focus on the government to provide encouragement to greater entrepreneurship in the private sector. This is nothing new, but such calls in the past were made in times of full employment and a high oil price, so there was no real impetus for change. The scenario has now changed, the needs are more apparent and immediate, and the type of school leaver that SPN21 is meant to foster may well be able to meet the challenge.

References

Deterding, D., & Salbrina, S. (2013). *Brunei English: A new variety in a multilingual society*. Dordrecht: Springer.
Exzayrani Awang Sulaiman (2012). *Kajian tentang sikap masyarakat Melayu terhadap Bahasa Melayu*. (Project organised by MABBIM. A pilot study has been conducted on SMSMJA students and St. Andrews students). UBD, Tungku Link.
Fatimah Chuchu (2009). *Pengukuhan Bahasa Melayu: Bahasa Melayu harus berkembang dan maju bersama-sama dengan bahasa dunia lain, bukan disaingi*. Paper presented at Seminar Bahasa MABBIM ke-48, Rizqun International Hotel, Gadong, March 25–26.
Fitri Shahminan (2015). 6th June. Freeze public sector hiring, wage hikes: IMF. *The Brunei Times*. Retrieved October 30, 2015 from http://www.bt.com.bn/business-national/2015/06/06/freeze-public-sector-hiring-wage-hikes-imf.
International Merchandise Trade Statistics. (2015). http://www.depd.gov.bn/externaltrade.
Jones, G. M. (1990). How bilingualism is being integrated in Negara Brunei Darussalam. In R. B. Baldauf Jr. & A. Luke (Eds.), *Language planning and education in Australasia and the South Pacific* (pp. 295–304). Clevedon: Multilingual Matters.
Jones, G. M. (2009). The Evolution of Language-in-Education Policies in Brunei Darussalam. In K. Kosonen & C. Young (Eds.), *Mother tongue as bridge language of instruction: Policies and experiences in Southeast Asia* (pp. 49–61). Singapore: SEAMEO.

Jones, G. M., Martin, P., & Ożóg, C. (1993). Multilingualism and Bilingual Education in Brunei Darussalam. In G. M. Jones & C. Ożóg (Eds.), *Bilingualism and national development* (pp. 39–58). Clevedon: Multilingual Matters.

Lawrey, R. (2012). *Brunei economy*. In *The Far East and Australasia 2013. The Europa regional surveys of the world*. Oxford: Taylor & Francis (Routledge).

McLellan, J. (2010). Mixed codes or varieties of English. In A. Kirkpatrick (Ed.), *The Routledge handbook of world Englishes* (pp. 425–441). London/New York: Routledge.

Ministry of Education, Public Relations Section. (1992). *Education in Brunei Darussalam*. Ministry of Education, BSB: Brunei Government Printers.

Noor Azam Haji-Othman. (2012). It's not always English: 'Duelling Aunties' in Brunei Darussalam. In V. Rapatahana & P. Bunce (Eds.), *English language as hydra: Its impact on non-English language cultures* (pp. 175–190). Bristol: Multilingual Matters.

Strategic Management Unit. (2012). *The Ministry of Education strategic plan 2012-2017*. Ministry of Education: Brunei Government Printers.

Trading Economics. (2015). Brunei GDP per capita PPP. Retrieved October 31, 2015 from http://www.tradingeconomics.com/brunei/gdp-per-capita.

Wood, A., Henry, A., Malai Ayla Surya Malai Hj Abdullah, & Clynes, A. (2011). English in Brunei: "She speaks excellent English"—"No he doesn't". In L. J. Zhang, R. Rubdy, & L. Alsagoff (Eds.), *Asian Englishes: Changing perspectives in a globalized World* (pp. 52–66). Pearson: Singapore.

Index

A
Academic knowledge, 98, 101, 115, 116
Accent, 4, 41, 100, 101, 105, 110, 111, 113
Acceptance of praise, 170
Accommodation, 46, 51
Accomplishments, 76, 77, 79, 82, 84, 85, 89–91, 93
Achievements, 76, 77, 81, 84, 88, 90, 92, 271
Active knowledge, 22, 23
Activities, 76, 80, 84, 88, 89, 92, 93
Adau Gayoh, 22
Adversarial legal system, 136
Africa, 116
Airport Mall, 31
Allophones, 59, 68
Alveolar click (tsk), 53
Alveolar sibilants, 57
Amahs, 12
American English, 58
American norms, 99
Antconc, 203
Apical vowels, 59, 64
Apology, 171, 182, 183
Applied linguistics, 1, 98
Approachability, 117
Approbation Maxim, 169, 174
Approximants, 60
Arabic, 3, 14, 30, 44, 176, 190, 193, 202, 208, 209, 254, 259, 260, 263
Articles, 41
ASEAN, 10, 43, 234, 274
Aspect, 3, 75–78, 82–84, 86, 88–93
Aspect hypothesis, 83, 91, 93
Asterawani, 245
Atelic verbs, 76
Attitudes, 4, 100, 102, 105, 106, 110
Australia, 9, 12, 34, 100, 102, 112, 243, 256

B
Backchannels, 54
Bah, 132, 179
Bahasa dalam, 168
Bahasa halus, 168
Bahasa Indonesia, 129, 133
Bahasa Melayu. *See* Malay
Bahasa rojak, 5, 248
Baki, Aminudin and Chang, Paul, 256
Bandar Seri Begawan (BSB), 9, 29, 31, 127, 129, 137
Bangla, 12, 130
Bangladesh, 9, 12, 125, 128, 130
Bank Islam Brunei Darussalam (BIBD), 202, 204, 205
Banks, 209
Bario, 12
Bark scale, 65, 69
Baru, 75, 78, 80, 88, 89, 92
Beijing Dialect, 57
Beijing Language and Culture University (BLCU), 61
Belait District, 9, 12
Belait language, 17
Belait River, 12
Bilingual education system, 13, 272, 273
Bin, 203, 204
Bisaya, 11, 13, 17, 21, 259
Bookstores, 241
Borneo, 5, 9, 11, 12, 18, 136, 214, 223
Borneo Bulletin (BB), 211, 214, 219
Borrowing, 36, 272
British English, 58, 100, 117
British National Corpus (BNC), 203
British norms, 99
British protectorate, 10, 11, 275
Brudirect, 189, 260

Brunei Malay language, 10, 11, 20, 214, 242, 254
Brunei Malay people, 184
Brunei Mandarin, 2, 57, 64, 69, 72
Brunei-Muara District, 234, 235
Brunei Times, the, 21, 219
Bruneization, 18
Budi bahasa, 168
Budi pekerti, 168

C
Cantonese, 12, 58
Cell phones, 269
CfBT (originally 'Centre for British Teachers', now 'CfBT Trust'), 34, 254
Chief Editor, 218, 219, 222
China, 57, 116, 217
Chinese characters, 30, 62
Chinese language, 213
Chinese people, 170
Chinese schools, 14, 57, 62
Citis Square, 32
Civil law, 4, 136
Classrooms, 97, 117
Coarticulation, 72
Code-switching, 4, 11, 15, 135, 142, 144, 187, 189, 191, 193–195
Coinages, 195
Common law, 136, 147
Compliment speech acts, 184
Comprehensibility, 43, 101
Compulsory Islamic Religious Education, 260
Computer Mediated Discourse Analysis (CDMA), 198
Consonant clusters, 41, 43
Consonant reduction, 49
Construction sites, 125–127
Counsels, 135, 136
Count nouns, 195
Court Registrar, 137
Courtroom etiquette, 141
Creative writing, 6, 244, 246
Crime reports, 220
Critical Discourse Analysis, 211
Cultural shift, 18, 20
Culture, 6, 100, 108, 202, 212, 219
Curriculum, 100, 243, 260, 262, 270, 274
Cyberspace, 187, 188, 198

D
Dato, 204, 207
Debuccalisation, 49
Deductive structure, 213, 219
Defendants, 4, 135, 145

Denigrating, 170
Dental fricatives, 42, 50
Dewan Bahasa dan Pustaka (DBP), 33, 241
Dhivehi, 44
Dialect Shift, 19
Diaspora, 57
Digital Media, 247
Diglossia, 12
Diphthongs, 50, 58–60, 65, 66, 70
Disagreement, 169, 170, 174, 176, 180, 181
Discourse markers, 135, 140, 141
Discrimination, 98, 99
Discussion forums, 191
Diversification, 5, 125, 268
Dusun, 2, 3, 6, 9, 13, 18, 21, 22, 24, 259, 273
Dwibahasa, 10, 189, 253, 256, 257, 262, 263, 272

E
East Wind and the Sun (EWS), 63, 64
-ed suffix, 53
Education system, 10, 13, 243, 253, 256, 257, 260, 263, 267, 270–274, 276
Egypt, 128
Elision, 48
Emoticons, 194, 195
Employment, 268, 277
Endonormative stabilization, 192
English as a Lingua Franca (ELF), 41–43, 45, 47, 50
English as a Second Language (ESL), 97, 98, 103, 117
English language teaching, 98
English literature, 241–243, 245, 246, 249, 263
English-medium education, 13, 270
Ethno-Vitality Rating. *See* Vitality rating, 20
Euclidean distance, 65, 69, 73

F
F1/F2 plane, 58, 60, 64–67, 70
Face, 4, 168, 171, 172, 218, 221, 231
Facebook, 4, 187–189, 191–193, 195–198, 220, 230
FACE vowel, 41
Fast speech, 3, 46, 47, 49–51, 53, 54
Feedback, 42, 45, 47, 52, 103, 118
Fiction, 245, 247–249
Filipino, 129, 130
Focus groups, 103, 106, 111, 116
Folktales, 243
Food outlets, 127
Foreign workers, 4, 12, 125, 127, 128, 132, 133
Formants, 58, 60, 63, 65, 66, 72

France, 44, 52
French, 44, 66, 263
Friendliness, 98, 101, 109, 110, 114, 116, 117
Frustration, 53

G
Gaming, 4, 188, 195
GCE 'O' Levels, 274
General American. *See* American English, 51
Generosity Maxim, 169, 173, 178, 182
Globalisation, 34, 241, 257, 275
Glottal stop, 49
GOAT vowel, 41, 50
Grammar, 2, 3, 33, 100, 102, 104, 106, 108, 110, 115
Grammar teaching, 100
Grammatical aspect, 76, 87, 92
Gross Domestic Product (GDP), 268, 267
Gurkhali, 33

H
Haji, 203, 205
Hakka, 12, 57, 62
Hassanal Bolkiah Arabic Boys' Secondary School, 259
Headlines, 215–217, 220
Herbert's Response Strategies, 181, 182
High Court, 135, 137, 143
Hokkien, 12, 57, 62, 129
Hong Kong, 100, 126, 213
Honorary titles, 205–207
Hope, 171, 182, 183
Horror stories, 247

I
Iban, 11–13, 17, 21, 24, 259
Identity, 201, 203, 205, 207, 209
Imperatives, 141, 147, 213
Imperfective, 76, 78, 81, 84, 85, 88–93
Inchoative, 88
India, 12, 128, 179, 256
Indigenous languages, 12, 13, 17–21, 24, 136
Indonesia, 9, 18, 54, 103, 125, 128, 130, 245
Inductive structure, 213
Infrastructure, 10, 255, 267–270, 276
Initialisms, 36, 52
Inner Circle, 47, 99, 100, 102
Institute of Brunei Technical Education, 14
Institut Teknologi Brunei (ITB), 14, 61
Intelligibility, 2, 3, 42, 43, 46, 50, 53, 104, 111, 112
International Monetary Fund (IMF), 268
Internet, 34, 187–189, 191, 198, 247, 269, 273
Interpretability, 43
Interpreters, 135–138, 141–143, 145, 146, 150
Interruptions, 138
Interviews, 4, 5, 32, 35, 44, 98, 103, 106, 111, 116, 117, 126, 127, 129, 130, 133, 135, 137, 144, 145, 172, 211, 214, 215, 218, 219, 221–223, 232, 274
Intonation, 42, 52, 140, 147
Intonational nucleus, 41
Inverted pyramid model, 212, 218
Islam, 9, 14, 136, 190, 202, 207, 209, 222, 242, 244, 249, 259, 260, 262, 270, 272
Islamicization, 18
Islamic Religious Knowledge (IRK), 243, 260, 262
Islamic Studies, 14, 259, 260, 262
Italy, 30

J
Jalan Sultan, 30, 31, 36
Japan, 100, 114, 191, 273
Japanese, 54, 126, 190, 191, 197, 244, 255
Japanese occupation, 244
Jawi, 3, 30–32, 34–37, 208, 254, 261
Job advertisements, 98
Joking, 171, 177, 182, 183
Judges, 4, 135, 137

K
Kampung Air, 11
Kampung Bukit Udal, 22
Kedayan, 9, 11, 13, 17, 19, 21, 24, 33
Kelabit, 12
Kesantunan, 168
Kolej IGS Brunei Darussalam, 61
Kolej Universiti Perguruan Ugama Seri Begawan (KUPU-SB), 14, 259
Korea, 44, 191, 216, 223, 225–229
Korean, 44, 190, 191, 197, 202, 206, 224, 225
Kuala Belait, 9, 255

L
Lah, 25, 131
Lakat, 75, 78, 82, 83, 86, 89, 91, 93
Language acquisition, 2, 3
Language choice, 2, 4, 106, 126, 130, 132, 133, 135, 141, 151, 219
Language maintenance, 18, 20
Language policy, 1, 5, 30
Language shift, 3, 17, 19, 21, 24, 136
Laughter, 80
Law, 3, 4, 133, 136, 137, 139, 147, 258, 261, 270
Lecturers, 4, 12, 98–102, 104–106, 108–112, 114–117

Leech's Politeness Maxims, 172, 178
Legal jargon, 137, 151
Lenition, 49, 57
Let-it-pass strategy, 45
Lexical aspect, 76, 77, 83, 85, 89, 92
Lexical stress, 42
Lexis, 5, 19, 36, 47, 51, 201, 203, 205, 207–209, 273
Limbang, 9
Lingua franca, 11, 12, 15, 18, 20, 41, 42, 126, 132, 133
Lingua Franca Core (LFC), 42
Linguistic competence, 99, 113
Linguistic divide, 14
Linguistic Landscape (LL), 2, 3, 29–31, 37
Literacy rates, 254
Literature, 2, 5, 6, 242–246, 249, 263, 273
Lun Bawang, 9, 12, 17
L-vocalisation, 48

M
Ma'had Islam Brunei, 259
Magistrates' Court, 6
Malayicization, 18
Malay language, 10, 11, 14, 18, 20, 30, 214, 221, 242, 243, 247–249, 254, 257, 259, 262, 263, 270, 273, 276
Malay literature, 2, 14, 242–246, 249, 263, 273
Malay-medium education, 13
Malay people, 184
Malaysia, 9, 11, 13, 18, 50, 103, 125, 128, 130, 135, 137, 144, 171, 207, 213, 223, 234, 244, 256, 274
Maldives, 44
Mandarin, 3, 12, 44, 57, 59–63, 66, 69, 70, 72, 73, 170, 263
Masih, 75, 83, 86, 87, 89, 91, 93, 226, 231
Matrix language, 194
Maxim of Agreement, 169
Maxim of Sympathy, 169, 178
Media Permata (MP), 5, 211, 212, 214, 219, 221, 223
Medium of instruction, 5, 100, 256, 259, 262
Medium of the law, 136
Melayu Islam Beraja (MIB), 9, 136, 220, 242, 243, 246, 248, 249, 262, 270, 276
Men's language, 195
Minimal pairs, 65
Ministry of Education, 32, 255, 262, 267, 268, 270, 275
Ministry of Islamic Religious Affairs, 259
Miscommunication, 125
Mission schools, 14, 255

Misunderstandings, 3, 43, 45–48, 50, 51, 53, 54
Mitigating, 170
Models of pronunciation, 100
Mode Seram, 247, 248
Modesty Maxim, 169, 175, 177, 182
Mohd Salleh, 244
Monolinguals, 20, 25, 30, 135, 144, 150, 188, 191, 192
Monophthongs, 41, 50, 58–60, 63–66, 70, 72
Morphology, 83
Mother tongue, 25, 35, 101, 112, 274
Motivation, 108
Multilingualism, 1, 29, 126, 189
Murut, 9, 11–13, 17, 18, 20, 21, 24, 259

N
Nasal codas, 51, 59, 63
National Education Policy, 270
Nation-building, 18
Native speakers, 42, 98, 99, 104, 171
Nativization, 192
Negative face, 168, 171
Nepal, 128
Netspeak, 189, 198
Neutral tone, 57, 64
Newspapers, 5, 12, 203, 211, 213, 214, 220, 222, 248, 273
New York Times, 213
New Zealand, 12, 34, 100, 126
Non-acceptance of praise, 169, 178, 179
Noncount nouns. *See* Uncount nouns, 43, 195
Non-native speaker, 42, 97, 98, 99, 102, 104, 117
Non-verbal communication, 135, 148

O
Official language, 11, 30, 34, 75, 136, 143
Oil and gas, 12, 125, 268, 275
Oman, 44
Omar Ali Saifuddin III, 10
Online texts, 191
Organisation of the Islamic Conference, 10
Overlapping speech, 52, 54
Overlapping vowels, 61, 66

P
Pakistan, 12
Pan-Brunei Malay, 3, 19, 25
Passive knowledge, 21–23
Past tense, 43, 53, 83
Pehin, 206, 207
Penan, 12, 17, 24

Pengiran Shahbandar Pengiran Mohd Salleh, 244
Perfective, 76, 78, 84, 86, 91, 93
Philippines, 9, 12, 125, 126, 128, 130, 256
Phonemes, 59
Phonotactics, 61
PhonR, 65
Photographs, 30, 31, 215, 222
Pinyin, 59, 64
Playful language, 196
Poetry, 242, 243, 245
Politeness, 4, 54, 132, 140, 168, 171, 172, 177, 184
Politeness strategies, 167, 172, 183
Population, 2, 9, 17, 20, 22, 24, 25, 34, 35, 57, 98, 100, 187, 189, 209, 219, 248, 253, 264
Positive face, 168, 171
Post-alveolar sibilants, 57
Postcolonial Literature, 244
Power, 4, 135, 138, 141, 148, 151
Praat, 65, 66
Pragmatics, 168
Praise, 167, 169–171, 174, 175, 181
Prejudice, 98
Prepositions, 203
Pre-school, 5, 260, 262, 264, 272
Press Liaison Office, 217
Press releases, 201, 202, 205, 206, 209
Prestige, 30, 35, 37, 98, 110–112, 116, 193, 195
Primary schools, 256, 260
Private schools, 14
Private sector, 268, 277
Pro-drop, 217
Proficiency, 23, 44, 54, 62, 98, 99, 107, 110, 126, 130, 257
Progressive demise, 18
Promise, 171, 182, 183
Pronouns, 202, 203
Pronunciation, 2, 3, 41–43, 49–51, 53, 54, 57, 102, 115, 195
Proper nouns, 202, 203, 205, 206, 209
Proverbs, 243
Public transport, 269
Publishing, 222, 241, 244, 245, 247, 248
Punctility, 76
Punctuation, 194
Purchasing power parity (PPP), 268

Q
Qi-cheng-zhuan-he, 213
Qidiaku, 35, 37
Qualifications, 14, 53, 112, 116, 170, 177, 181, 277

Questionnaire, 84, 99, 103, 104, 108, 110, 111, 115, 116

R
Radio programmes, 13
Radio Television Brunei (RTB), 33
Raja Isteri Pengiran Anak Damit (RIPAD) Arabic Girls' Secondary School, 259, 260
Rapport, 100, 104, 108, 126, 167, 170, 222
Regularisation, 43
Religion, 10, 136, 190, 202, 209, 253, 270, 272
Rendah diri, 167
Renmin Ribao, 213
Repetition, 135, 139, 140, 196
Request interpretation, 169, 170, 178, 181
Respelling, 36
Retail shops, 127, 130
Retroflex vowel, 60, 64
Rhotacisation, 57
Rhythm, 42, 195
Role models, 98, 106, 111
Roman script (Rumi), 31
Rounded vowels, 59, 66
Russian, 188

S
Sarawak, 9, 11–13, 17
Satellite communication, 269
Scatter plots, 58, 60, 65, 66, 68, 73
Scottish English, 58
SEA Write Award, 242
Secondary schools, 243, 256, 262, 273
Second World War. *See* World War II, 255
Self-censorship, 220
Self-esteem, 99
Semantic network analysis, 201
Semantic reclassification, 17
Sepadu, 260
Seria, 9
Shari'a (Syariah) law, 137
Shopping centres, 35
Shop signs, 2, 3, 29, 32, 36, 208
Sign language, 130, 133
Singapore, 2, 36, 50, 57, 100, 256
Singapore English, 194
Singapore Mandarin, 57
Singlish, 100
Sistem Pendidikan Negara Abad Ke-21 (SPN21), 13, 243
SMS, 4, 196
Social prestige, 101, 103, 105, 110, 116
Sociolinguistic change, 17
Songket Alliance, 247, 248
Southeast Asian Literature, 244

Speaking rate, 42, 46–49, 51, 54
Special Educational Needs Programme, 275
Specialised Education Programme, 275
Spectrograms, 60, 64, 65
Spelling, 77, 195, 196, 273
Spelling pronunciation, 41
Sri Lanka, 256
–s suffix, 41
Stakeholders, 201, 205, 206, 209
Statives, 76, 78–80, 83, 84, 87–92
Status updates, 188, 192–194
Strategic Plan 2012–2017, 275, 271
Sudah, 75, 78–80, 86–88, 91–93
Sukang, 12
Sultan, 9, 10, 14, 207, 221, 222, 260
Sultan Omar Ali Saifuddien Centre for Islamic Studies (SOASCIS), 259
Supreme Court, 136, 142
Swedish, 191
Syllables, 41, 47–49, 51, 54, 59, 60, 63, 64
Symbolic value, 20
Syntax. *see* grammar, 41, 47, 53, 54, 273

T
Taboo, 167, 214
Tact Maxim, 169, 173
Tag, 43, 141, 147
Tagalog, 12, 129
Taiwan, 170
Taiwan Mandarin, 57, 61, 72
Tamil, 12
Tangah, 81
Teachers, 12, 14, 34, 52, 84, 97–101, 117, 254, 256, 259, 273, 274, 276
Teachers' College, 256, 259
Telicity, 76
Telic verbs, 76, 77, 84, 88, 91, 93
Temburong, 9, 11, 12, 14, 20, 217
Temporal marker, 141
Tense marking, 3, 43
Terminal heirs, 18
Tertiary education, 267
Textbooks, 100, 241, 274
Textese, 196
Thai, 12, 126, 127, 130, 191, 213
Thailand, 9, 12, 125, 126, 130, 213
Third formant, 65
TH sounds, 41, 49, 50
Three Circles, 100, 101
Times Square, 31
Titah, 221, 273

Topicalisation, 211, 215, 217
Topic fronting, 42, 43
Trainee teachers, 101, 256
Trajectory length, 65, 66, 70, 72
Translation, 37, 143, 190, 194, 211, 215
Triphthongs, 60
Tun Razak Report, 256
Turn taking, 135, 138
Tutong District, 9, 220
Tutong language, 273
Tweets, 188, 190, 191, 193, 197
Twitter, 4, 188, 190, 192, 193, 196, 197

U
Ugama Schools, 5, 253, 254, 257–262
Uncount nouns, 41
United Kingdom (UK), 256
United Nations, 10
United States (USA), 52, 99, 108
Universiti Brunei Darussalam (UBD), 13, 14, 44, 61, 190, 223, 246, 259
Universiti Islam Sultan Sharif Ali (UNISSA), 14, 259
Urdu, 12

V
Vietnam, 100
Vietnamese, 191
Viewpoint aspect, 76, 85
Violations of Leech's Maxims, 176
Vitality rating, 21
Vocabulary, 13, 23, 100, 101, 104–106, 110, 115, 208
Voiced TH, 50
Voiceless TH, 43, 50
Vowel inventory, 59
Vowel length, 41
Vowel merger, 58, 61, 66, 68, 73
Vowel quadrilateral, 58
Vowel quality, 42, 58, 66
Vowel reduction, 64
Vowels, 3, 36, 42, 49–51, 54, 58–60, 63–65, 73, 195, 196

W
Wawasan 2035 (Vision 2035), 257
Weddings, 22
Welsh, 58, 191
WhatsApp, 4, 188, 189, 193, 194, 197, 220
Whole Foods, 201
Witnesses, 4, 136, 143, 220

Women's language, 195
Word formation, 196
Word order, 53
Writing competitions, 242

X
Xi'an, 170

Y
Yang Mulia, 206, 207
YouTube, 187
Yura Halim, 244

Z
Zikir Nation, 202

Printed by Printforce, the Netherlands